Acknowledgments

As with the other books I've written on antiques and collectibles, this one was made possible only through the collecting community's unselfish willingness to share collections and information, and the understanding and help of my wife, Cindy.

The more than 600 cookie jars of Michigan residents, Stan and Karen Zera, was the first large collection we photographed, which was no easy chore for Stan as most of the jars were stored in the basement. While I was busy shooting them in the kitchen, Stan shuttled them up and down the steps one and two at a time. His leg muscles must have grown as hard as stoneware from the strenuous exercise. A special thanks also goes to the Zera children, Sean, 8, and Brenda, 7, whose patience and nearly perfect behavior during the three days we commandeered their parents exhibited maturity beyond their years.

The Zeras put us in touch with Mercedes DeRenzo, owner of Jazz'e Junque Shop, the first and only cookie jar shop in Chicago. Two days at Jazz'e Junque resulted in another friendship and many more good photos.

Mercedes introduced us to Jay Blumenfeld and Mark Taylor, both of Chicago, who specialize in collecting head jars and fruit and vegetable jars, and who graciously allowed us to photograph their exquisite collections.

Back home in northern Ohio, Floyd and Betty Carson always invited us to photograph jars not only from their personal collection, but also those they often bought for resale.

Betty and Floyd led us to Richard and Susan Oravitz, enthusiastic collectors who supplied the jars for another several hundred photos.

Central Ohioans Jim and Betsy Coughenour, and John and Carol Bosson, contributed greatly to the Brush chapter. They also helped fill in most of the other chapters. Their collections alone would make a respectable cookie jar book.

McCoy collector Georgina Lilly, and Shawnee collector Robert Smith, of different suburbs in the Cleveland area, provided the jars we so badly needed to complete those chapters.

Maureen Saxby, who with her husband, Clifford, edits the *Crazed over Cookie Jars* newsletter, supplied leads and information. And Maureen, aided by Mercedes DiRenzo, even took some pictures for the book.

Others who provided either jars to photograph or information to use were Cloud's Antique Mall, Dorothy Coates, Country Heirs Antique Shop, Elvin R. and Frances (Jerry) Kulp, Joan Eaton, Elyria Public Library, Mary Jane Giacomini, Carol Gifford, Lisa Diane Golden, Grinder's Switch Antique Shop, Herrick Memorial Library, Mary and Bill Hallier, Keith Herklotz, Mary Huffman, Sharon Isaacson, Charles Kidd, Lorain Public Library, Keith Lytle, Carl and Gari McCallum, Irene Mychul, Allan and Michelle Naylor, Vicki Nitecki, Debbie Preussner, Melanie Rollin, Rosa Sberna, Dan Schneider, Homer and Bev Simpson, Claude and Edna Mae Smith, Fred Strunk and Denise Dakoulis, Connie Swaim, Wellington Antiques, and Rick Wisecarver.

I would be remiss if I didn't mention Lucille Bromberek, of Lemont, Illinois. Although I wasn't able to photograph any of Lucille's jars for the book, it was she who first caught the attention of the national and international media through her cookie jar museum. I, as a writer, owe her a debt of gratitude for long ago planting the seed that made this project necessary. Collector's owe her the same debt for creating the interest that made cookie jar collecting a viable hobby.

I would also like to thank those writers who came before me Pamela Coates, Ermagene Westfall, Harold Nichols, and Fred and Joyce Herndon Roerig for the fine job they did photographing and documenting cookie jars for posterity.

But most of all my thanks goes to you, the reader, for considering the book worthy of inclusion in your library.

Three American bisque animals with hands in pockets. The jars on the outside are 11 inches high, while the one in the center, which has a turnabout bank head, is 10-3/4 inches high. The elephant appears to be a married jar considering the two different colors. In addition to the jars shown, the company also made a cat and a cow, and often finished the jars in solid colors. *Bosson Collection.* $100 each

Introduction

A Ludowici Celadon lion, 10-3/4 inches high, marked "Belmont/Patent Applied/USA" on three lines. It appears to be repainted. One of the most troubling aspects of these jars is that some of the white jars definitely attributable to Ludowici Celadon appear to be made of the same clay and glaze as white jars definitely attributable to American Bisque and American Pottery. They also have the same crude workmanship on their bottoms. For a detailed explanation of the crossover between these three companies, see Chapter 8. $75

Because the introduction is the most boring part of any book, I promise to keep this one brief. But there are a couple points that should be covered.

The first concerns measurements. Heights of jars are included in most of the captions, but they must be considered nominal because heights of identical jars can vary by as much as 1/4 inch, and even a little more in extreme cases. If you have a collection with many duplicates, you've probably already noticed that your identical jars aren't always the same size. This occurs because pottery shrinks between 5 percent and 15 percent from the time it's removed from the mold to the time it's removed from the kiln. the rate of shrinkage is determined in large part by the clay mixture. When a pottery changes suppliers for one of its clays, or when human error results in a slip recipe not being followed to the letter, finished pieces will end up being slightly different size due to the modified composition.

Even at that, the measurements stated herein will give you a sound idea of what size object to look for when you wish to acquire a particular jar. They are also accurate enough to indicate the average 10 percent shrinkage that occurs when a cookie jar is used as a mold core in order to produce a fake. (See Chapter 5 for further explanation.)

The other thing is identification of cookie jars. Unless there was compelling evidence to the contrary, I accepted previous cookie jar book authors at their word concerning identity. For instance, If Ermagene Westfall (*An Illustrated Value Guide to Cookie Jars*) said an unmarked jar was American Bisque, then I too considered it American Bisque. But where errors clearly existed, such as Harold Nichols's (*McCoy Cookie Jars—From the First to the Latest,*) accidental insertion of a Regal China Quaker Oats jar in place of a McCoy Quaker Oats jar, I labeled the jars as they are supposed to be, and stated the reason.

When style, glaze, color, or unique markings indicated a previously unidentified cookie jar was in all probability made by a certain company, it was included with the rest of that company's jars. An example of this would be the numerous brown, green, and ochre glazed jars typical of Doranne of California. If there was the slightest indication of Doranne origin, such as a raised or indented design, or a mark showing "CJ" plus a number, or "J" plus a number, all of which Doranne is known for, the jar was placed with the rest of the Doranne jars.

In cases where nothing is sure, such as the quagmire in which American Bisque, American Pottery, and Ludowici Celadon are bogged down, I attempted to use the small amount of information available to draw logical conclusions. While most of these are not labeled as theories per se, inclusion of words such as probably or possibly will telegraph to the reader that such information has not been factually proven.

There's really not much else to say except that I hope you enjoy the book, and Happy Collecting!

The Complete

Cookie Jar Book

Mike Schneider

Revised and Expanded
2nd Edition

Schiffer Publishing Ltd®

4880 Lower Valley Road, Atglen, PA 19310 USA

Dedication

To Betty and Floyd Carson
for their many years of helping writers
inform the public about collectibles

A note from the author about values:

Suggested prices of cookie jars in this book were arrived at through a combination of interviewing collectors and dealers, consulting other price guides, auction and show reports, observations at antique shows, internet sales, and a general feel for the market. They are estimated values only, not rock solid prices.

They are based on what might be paid when a transaction takes place between an informed cookie jar dealer and an informed cookie jar collector. That makes them somewhat higher than what a general antiques dealer could probably charge when looking for a quick turnover. It makes them somewhat lower than what a passionate collector might pay during heated competition at an auction.

Prices will vary according to local area, condition and other factors. The best way to use these estimates is not to base what you pay or charge on them, but to judge one jar's value against another's to arrive at a realistic price.

Two different renditions—and two different glazes—on McCoy's "Happy Face" jar, no. 235. Although the one on the right appears larger, it is only because it is sitting slightly forward in the picture. Each is 11 inches high. They were made from 1972 to 1979. Jar on the left is marked "215/McCoy/LCC/USA" on four lines. Jar on the right is unmarked, while another photographed had the McCoy bull's-eye mark with "USA" below. *Courtesy of Jazz'e Junque Shop, Chicago, Illinois.* $35

Title page photo:
This unmarked Hopalong Cassidy cookie jar is 11-1/2 inches high. *Courtesy of Jazz'e Junque Shop, Chicago, Illinois.* $800.

Revised price guide: 1999
Copyright © 1999 by Mike Schneider.
Library of Congress Catalog Card Number: 98-83295

Typeset in Souvenir Lt BT

ISBN: 0-7643-0826-2
Printed in United States of America
1 2 3 4

Published by Schiffer Publishing Ltd.
4880 Lower Valley Road
Atglen, PA 19310
Phone: (610) 593-1777; Fax: (610) 593-2002
E-mail: Schifferbk@aol.com
Please visit our web site catalog at
www.schifferbooks.com

This book may be purchased from the publisher.
Include $3.95 for shipping. Please try your bookstore first.
We are interested in hearing from authors
with book ideas on related subjects.
You may write for a free printed catalog.

In Europe, Schiffer books are distributed by
Bushwood Books
6 Marksbury Avenue
Kew Gardens
Surrey TW9 4JF England
Phone: 44 (0)181 392-8585; Fax: 44 (0)181 392-9876
E-mail: Bushwd@aol.com

Contents

Acknowledgments...3
Introduction 4

Section I: Cookie Jar Collecting
Chapter 1   A Short History 7
Chapter 2   Types of Ceramic Jars and Decoration 10
Chapter 3   Prices..12
Chapter 4   Condition 14
Chapter 5   Counterfeits, Reproductions and Fakes 17
Chapter 6   Problems of Collecting 21

Section II: The Cookie Jar Giants
Chapter 7   McCoy 23
Chapter 8   American Bisque 59

Section III: Major American Producers
Chapter 9   Abingdon 84
Chapter 10   Brush..87
Chapter 11   California Originals 97
Chapter 12   Doranne of California 105
Chapter 13   Hull...111
Chapter 14   Metlox 114
Chapter 15   Red Wing 119
Chapter 16   Regal China 123
Chpater 17   Robinson-Ransbottom 128
Chapter 18   Shawnee...132
Chapter 19   Treasure Craft 142
Chapter 20   Twin Winton 146

Section IV: Other American Producers
Chapter 21   Potteries...151

Section V: Cookie Jar Handlers
Chapter 22   Decorators, Distributors, Importers and Retailers 175

Section VI: Character Cookie Jars
Chapter 23   Santa Claus..204
Chapter 24   Walt Disney 207
Chapter 25   Other Characters 210

Section VII: Studio Artists

Chapter 26   Glenn Appleman 213
Chapter 27   Carol Gifford 216
Chapter 28   Rick Wisecarver 219
Chapter 29   Others 225

Section VIII: Foreign Cookie Jars

Chapter 30   Pacific-Asian Cookie Jars 227
Chapter 31   Jars From Other Countries 241

Section IX: The Mystery Cookie Jars

Chapter 32   Advertising Jars 245
Chapter 33   Hobby Ceramics Jars 248
Chapter 34   Other Unknown Jars 253

Section X: Non-pottery Cookie Jars

Chapter 35   From Glass to Wood 286

New Additions 296

Appendix 1: Sources 300

Appendix 2: Ceramic Mold Companies 301

Appendix 3: McCoy Cookie Jar Designs by Year 302

Bibliography 303

Index 304

This California Originals mouse is 12-1/2 inches high. It is marked "2630" on the rim of lid, and "2630 USA" on base. *Zera Collection.* $65

Section I: Cookie Jar Collecting

The thing most people told me they like best about collecting cookie jars is the natural high they experience when they find a long sought jar and acquire it. The low, they said, often comes upon returning home with their new trophy. For some it is discovering that the jar isn't nearly as attractive when sitting on a sideboard that's cluttered with two dozen other jars, as it was when it was sitting by itself in a picture in a book. For others it's removing the new jar from the dishwasher and finding half the decoration has disappeared, or realizing their emotions led them to pay more for the jar than it was worth, or more than they could afford at the time.

The purpose of this section, aside from relating a capsule history of cookie jars, is to inform the potential collector of the pitfalls that might be encountered in the quest for jars, and how to avoid them.

Chapter 1
A Short History

Decorative cookie jars appeared on the American scene in the early 1930s. It was the glasshouses of Ohio, Pennsylvania, West Virginia, and New York that first recognized that the stock market crash of 1929, and the Great Depression that followed, had eliminated many folks' daily trip to the bakery, forcing them to bake cookies in their home kitchens. Once baked, cookies had to be stored, preferably in a container that not only kept them handy, but also protected them from atmospheric influences that soften crisp cookies and dry out moist ones. A container that enhanced a kitchen's decor, namely an attractive glass or pottery cookie jar, quickly found favor over cardboard oatmeal boxes, coffee tins, and other make-do receptacles available in most of America's homes.

As early as 1931 the McKee Glass Company, of Jeanette, Pennsylvania, added a lid to its 5-1/2 inch, three-footed jardiniere, and advertised it as a cookie jar. In 1932, circulars of the Hocking Glass Company, Lancaster, Ohio, showed a cookie jar with a screw-on metal lid being sold as an accessory to its popular green glass paneled canister set. And it wasn't long before Hocking's catalogs began referring to the covered pretzel jar that came with its 8-piece beer and pretzel set, as a "pretzel or cookie jar." Several other well-known glass manufacturers also produced cookie jars during the early years of the Depression.

Which pottery served up the first ceramic cookie jar is open to debate, but the Brush Pottery Company, of Roseville, Ohio, seems the likeliest candidate. The green canister cookie jar shown below is from the Brush Kolorkraft line, which was introduced in the 1920s. The cookie jar, No. 344, was added late in 1929. Oddly, Brush didn't start making its beautiful figural cookie jars until the mid-1940s, several years after other potteries had begun pouring them out.

Early pottery jars were generally quite simple, usually either in a cylindrical or bean pot shape. Many were made of stoneware. Painted decoration was usually applied to the outside, either over the glaze or directly to the bisque. Leaves and flowers won the public's nod as the most popular theme.

One of the pioneers of these early stoneware jars was the Harper J. Ransburg Company, a decorating and distributing firm in Indianapolis, Indiana. By the mid-1930s, Ransburg's No. 207 jar was selling to the tune of a quarter-million units per year.

This Brush Kolorkraft jar is 10 inches high, marked with an impressed "344." The Kolorkraft line made its debut in the 1920s. The jar was first available in 1929, making it a good candidate for the honor of being the first pottery cookie jar. *Zera Collection.* $40

Around 1940, potteries began test-marketing figural cookie jars—people, animals, fruits, vegetables and other objects—setting the stage for today's collecting hobby.

The greatest output of American pottery cookie jars occurred from the mid-1940s to the mid-1970s, even though many potteries were forced out of business by foreign competition during the 1950s and 1960s. In the 1980s, American production slowed to a trickle as the inflated cost of materials, labor, energy, and transportation that had wracked the previous decade, spelled bankruptcy for the majority of the few American potteries that remained in business.

Today the flow of new cookie jars is increasing. A good number of jars are currently being made by domestic potteries such as

Treasure Craft, and by studio artists such as Carol Gifford and Rick Wisecarver. But most of today's jars are being imported from overseas. While Pacific-Asian countries lead the pack of foreign manufacturers, cookie jars are also made in Europe, South and Central America, and probably most other places, too.

For a long time collectors turned a blind eye toward foreign jars. Unlike their American counterparts, they were light in weight, shoddily executed, and widely available. This was particularly true of Japanese jars that flooded the market in the wake of World War II. But the picture has changed in recent years. Today's Pacific-Asian jars, and those from other areas, while still lighter in weight, generally meet or closely approach the design and manufacturing standards previously adhered to by American potters. As an example, the Vandor radio, shown below, was made in Korea in 1988. It exhibits every bit as much quality although a different style as the Shawnee Mugsey pictured next to it, which was made in America approximately 40 years earlier.

As for the future, it looks good. More non-collectors are beginning to realize that cookie jars have value, which results in the older rarer jars winding up in collections instead of in landfills. Importers are continuing to hold foreign potteries to high standards. Mold companies that cater to the hobby ceramics market appear to be offering more cookie jar molds with greater detail, while companies that specialize in glaze, paints, and decals have greatly broadened the finishing methods available to crafters. Manufacturers of consumer products apparently have recognized the popularity of cookie jars, and are again using jars for premiums and discount offers. Studio artists are turning out many more cookie jars than they were just a few short years ago. And lately some nice reproductions of older jars—marked as reproductions—have appeared on the scene.

Put all these factors together and tomorrow's skies appear bright and sunny for cookie jar collectors.

For a long time after World War II, Japanese cookie jars offered little but low prices to lure the consumer. Perhaps these two are supposed to imitate Wade Irish Porcelain. The jar on the left is 10-1/4 inches high and has a "Japan" inkstamp. The one on the right stands 13 inches and has a "Japan" paper label. *Oravitz Collection.* Left $20; Right $25

Paper label of Vandor radio.

Today's Pacific-Asian jars are well-designed and expertly crafted. This radio, imported from Korea by Vandor, is 5-1/2 inches high. *Courtesy of Jazz'e Junque Shop, Chicago, Illinois.* $80

Shawnee Mugsey, 11-3/4 inches high. Impressed in the bottom is "Patented/Mugsey/USA" on three lines. *Smith Collection.* $425

8

Here is an early glass cookie jar, dating back to at least 1932. It is 8 inches high and was made by the Hocking Glass Company as an accessory for its green glass paneled canister set. *Zera Collection.* $30

A black glass cookie jar, 8 inches high, made by the L.E. Smith Glass Company, Mt. Pleasant, Pennsylvania. One of three black glass cookie jars illustrated in an early 1930s Smith catalog, it was known as no. 3 and originally included a hand-painted flower decoration. It is unmarked. This jar was also made in clear green glass, as shown in Chapter 35. *Zera Collection.* $90

A real country couple by Roseville, Ohio, studio artist Rick Wisecarver. The jar is 12-1/2 inches high, incised "Wihoa's/Original/Handpainted/Cookie Classic/Roseville/Ohio" on the bottom on six lines, and "Wihoa's/Cookie Classic/By Rick Wisecarver" on the back on three lines. It is hand-signed by the artist. *Oravitz Collection.* $190

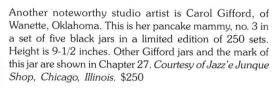

Another noteworthy studio artist is Carol Gifford, of Wanette, Oklahoma. This is her pancake mammy, no. 3 in a set of five black jars in a limited edition of 250 sets. Height is 9-1/2 inches. Other Gifford jars and the mark of this jar are shown in Chapter 27. *Courtesy of Jazz'e Junque Shop, Chicago, Illinois.* $250

There wasn't anything fancy about most early pottery cookie jars. This one, by McCoy, is 7-1/2 inches high, made of yellowware. It is no. 7 in the McCoy line, unmarked, and usually referred to as the round ball shape. It was made from 1939 to 1944. Other colors for this jar were blue and green. It also came in a smaller size. *Zera Collection.* $50

This pilfering cat was made by Treasure Craft, formerly an independent company but now a division of Pfaltzgraff Pottery, of York, Pennsylvania. It is 11-1/2 inches high, with "Treasure Craft/©/USA" impressed on three lines inside the lid. Treasure Craft is one of a handful of American potteries that still makes cookie jars in quantity. *Oravitz Collection.* $75

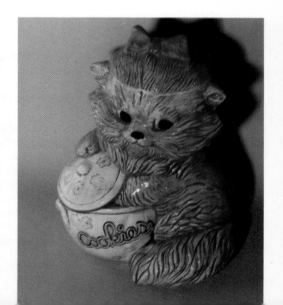

Hocking Glass Company originally called this a pretzel jar and sold it as part of its 8-piece beer and pretzel set. When cookie jars began gaining popularity in the early 1930s, the company switched to calling it a pretzel *or* cookie jar. It is 10-3/4 inches high and unmarked. *Zera Collection.* $35

Cookie jars are made in Europe, too. This one, 10-1/2 inches high, is marked "Made in/Western Germany/3802" on three lines. *Blumenfeld Collection.* $150

Chapter 2
Types of Ceramic Jars and Decoration

While cookie jars are and have been made in several different media such as metal, glass, wood, and plastic, it is ceramic jars that capture the most attention. The large majority of ceramic jars are made of earthenware, usually the white variety. Redware, which has been used on occasion, most often by the Japanese, is also earthenware. Some forms of what is commonly referred to as yellowware is earthenware, but it hasn't been used much for cookie jars. A very few jars are made of porcelain, a more expensive ceramic material that is denser and more durable than earthenware, and which, if poured thin enough, exhibits translucency. Some jars, like those that were produced by the Western Stoneware Company of Monmouth, Illinois, are made of stoneware, the ceramic medium used for crockery.

But the type of ceramic a cookie jar is made of isn't nearly as important as the type of decoration that's been applied to it. Ceramic cookie jars are decorated by five primary methods—glaze, paint, glaze and paint combination, glaze and transfer combination, and a combination of all three materials.

Glaze is the most durable finish. Simply explained, glaze is minute particles of colored or clear glass, suspended in a liquid carrying agent. Glaze is applied by dipping, brushing, or airbrushing. All glazes are fired after they are applied, giving the clay body of a jar what amounts to a glass coating. Glaze can have a gloss or matte finish.

The main problem encountered with glaze is crazing, the tiny cracks you sometimes see that form an unwanted mosaic pattern over all or part of a jar. Crazing in pottery might be compared to latent genetic defects in life forms. Although it may take decades to appear, if a cookie jar is going to craze, its course is set when the jar is made. Crazing is caused by the glaze contracting more than the body of the jar as it cools after firing. This results in the glaze coming under excessive tension. Years later, when the glaze can no longer sustain the tension, it cracks or crazes. Nothing can be done to prevent it, or to slow its progress once it has started. Fortunately, most cookie jars are manufactured correctly, and do not craze.

Some jars appear to have only minor crazing. This is called primary crazing, long cracks in the glaze that run in generally the same direction. In time, shorter cracks will fill in between the long cracks and form squares, triangles and other shapes. This is secondary crazing, and it is inevitable when primary crazing is present.

While crazing will reduce the price of a cookie jar, it should not deter a collector form purchasing a jar that is a rare one at the right price, or one he has been seeking for a long time. Common jars with crazing should be avoided as better examples are readily available.

Paint decoration, often called cold paint, is not fired. It causes the most problems, whether applied directly to bisque, or on top of glaze. The American Bisque pirate is an example of a painted cookie jar, no glaze having been used on it. The unknown gingerbread boy canister is one on which the highlights were painted after the jar was glazed.

Like the paint on the exterior of a house, paint on cookie jars is subject to deterioration from moisture, humidity, temperature extremes, prolonged exposure to direct sunlight, and contact with

This American Bisque round bottom jar is finished entirely with paint, no glaze having been used. It is 13 inches high, with "USA" impressed on the bottom and "Jolly Pirate" impressed on the collar. *Zera Collection.* $175

foreign objects. Most jars that were painted 40 or 50 years ago suffer to a greater or lesser degree from such deterioration. There's little that can be done to halt its progress.

Never immerse a painted jar in water to clean it. Not cleaning it at all is the best bet. But if cleaning does become necessary, use tepid water and a thoroughly squeezed soft sponge or well-rung cloth. Use very gentle strokes or the paint is apt to disappear before your eyes. Cleaning the glazed portion of a jar that's decorated with both glaze and paint presents no problem if the paint is not touched.

Cookie jars that have transfer designs, an example being the McCoy Yosemite Sam cylinder jar, are decorated with a fired-on decal applied over the glaze. While transfers hold up much better than paint, they are more susceptible to damage from foreign objects than glazes. It will usually be the transfer, not the glaze, that will account for the poor condition of a transfer-decorated jar. Immersing a transfer-decorated jar in tepid water will not cause damage as long as the transfer was correctly applied and fired, and is still in good condition.

This is a stoneware jar, 10-3/4 inches high. That's a real cork in the top. On the bottom is the impressed maple leaf mark of Western Stoneware, shown in Chapter 21. *Courtesy of Jazz'e Junque Shop, Chicago, Illinois.* $30

McCoy "Yosemite Sam" cylinder jar, transfer decorated, 10-1/2 inches high. No. 224, it was made in 1972. Its inkstamp mark is shown in Chapter 7. *Zera Collection.* $170

A 9-1/2 inch high, unmarked jar that has been painted over the glaze. *Zera Collection.* $45

The most common problem encountered with glaze is crazing, most noticeable here to the right of the center flower. This unmarked jar is 9-1/2 inches high and was made by American Bisque. *Zera Collection.* $45

Chapter 3
Prices

The most significant event for cookie jar collectors since the Depression occurred in New York on April 23-24, 1988. That's when Sotheby's auctioned the cookie jar collection of deceased pop artist Andy Warhol. Considered an eccentric, Warhol, an ardent collector in many fields, had accumulated 134 cookie jars prior to his death in February 1987, at age 59.

Most of Warhol's jars, which Sotheby's had divided into 35 lots, had book values of $50 or less. This would make his entire collection worth something under $10,000. Yet when the auctioneer's gavel fell for the final time, the collection had sold for an incredible $240,350, an average of $1793 for each jar.

The $2 to $10 bargains collectors had been picking up at flea markets for years disappeared overnight, the same jars resurfacing at antique shows at prices of $25 to $100, or more.

It wasn't the exorbitant amount paid for the Warhol cookie jars that had sent prices skyrocketing. Throughout history collectors have paid outlandish prices for common objects owned by famous people, without having any effect on the general market. Two other factors created the havoc.

First, although Warhol's cookie jars were but a minuscule part of the auction (the entire sale of his belongings took 10 days and raised $25 million), when previewing the auction for a nationwide television audience, network newsmen zeroed in on the cookie jars. This gave millions of people a peek at the hobby. "Entertainment Tonight" and other personality-oriented programs followed suit. A week prior to the sale, *Newsweek* ran a five-page cover story that included a picture of Warhol's kitchen, a McCoy chef head jar and several others prominently displayed on the table. Many people liked what they saw in both the print and video media, and began collecting.

The second, and more subtle, factor was Warhol's silent endorsement of cookie jars. Eccentricities aside, Andy Warhol knew art. The fact that he collected and enjoyed cookie jars told people that he, the top American pop artist of his generation, saw something in the jars he appreciated. If cookie jars were good enough for Andy Warhol, they were certainly good enough for the less schooled masses. In short, Warhol gave cookie jars credibility.

Another auction that set the cookie jar world on its lid was held by Mike Clum in Zanesville, Ohio, on July 18, 1990, a little more than two years after the Warhol sale. Clum sold a lifetime collection of 655 jars. Bidding competition was fierce. A Red Wing king of tarts brought $565, a Brush purple cow $825, and a McCoy mammy with cauliflowers was purchased for $1025. Many others also sold at 50 to 100 percent, or more, above the values shown in then-current price guides.

While prices rose some in the fallout from the Clum auction, they didn't escalate to anywhere near the prices that were paid at the sale, probably for three reasons. First, the auction was made up entirely of cookie jars. Second, the sale was heavily advertised throughout the country. Third, it was held in conjunction with the Pottery Lovers Reunion, and the McCoy Lovers Reunion, both of which were headquartered in Zanesville. These three factors created a seller's dream, a nationwide crowd with a common collecting interest at a onetime event. Zealous bidding was guaranteed.

This is one of the jars readers of *Newsweek* saw sitting on Andy Warhol's kitchen table when the magazine did a cover story on the auction of the artist's estate. The jar was made by Robinson-Ransbottom, is 9-3/4 inches high, and marked "R.R.P. Co./Roseville, Ohio/No-411" on three lines. Some examples of this jar are trimmed in gold (this one is not). *Blumenfeld Collection.* $350

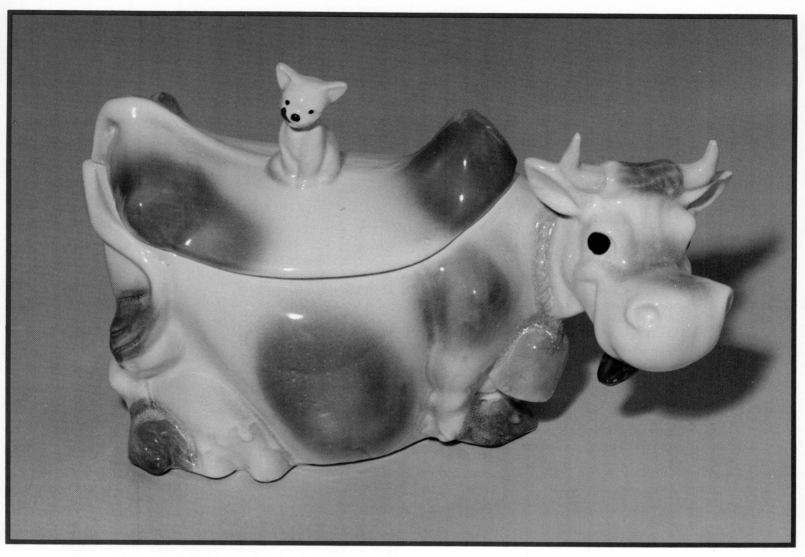

The Brush Purple cow, a jar that sold at the Clum cookie jar auction for $825, a good bit higher than its book value and market value at the time. It is 8-1/2 inches high, and has on its bottom the raised Brush palette mark with a "W10" below it. The jar dates from 1970. *Zera Collection.* $1250

But the results of the Clum sale, and the fact that prices did rise some afterward, show there's a large army of collectors out there whose fever for the hobby will most assuredly keep prices unstable for some time to come.

Due to this instability, it is recommended you do not use the prices in this book to indicate how much you should pay or charge for cookie jars. Six months or more can elapse between the time a manuscript is completed and the time a book is released. By then the prices may no longer be current. But the price guide will give you a good sense of the value of one jar relative to the value of another. By using that information, and by keeping up with the current market, you should be able to make an informed decision when electing to buy or sell.

Chapter 4
Condition

A collector of fine china dinnerware would probably turn up his nose at the two McCoy clown heads pictured below. He would consider one to be in bad condition, the other worse. And no wonder. The typical piece of fine china dinnerware is finished totally with fired-on decoration, spends most of its life behind glass in a protective cabinet, is used only on holidays and special occasions, and normally isn't subject to handling by children.

Cookie jars are not so privileged.

Many cookie jars are decorated with unfired paint applied on top of the glaze or directly to the bisque. Cookie jars are usually forced to endure the hazards of everyday life on a kitchen counter. And they are often used by youngsters who aren't overly careful when handling them.

The clown on the left is in excellent condition considering it was decorated with paint over the glaze 50-odd years ago, sometimes between 1945 and 1947. It's about the best you'll find short of one that's been restored. And the example on the right is pretty good, too, far better than most that are seen today. Consequently,

knowledgeable collectors use a sliding scale when evaluating the condition of painted cookie jars. They often accept jars in worse shape than they would accept them had the jars been decorated entirely with glaze.

Chips on pottery cookie jars reduce value. So do cracks. Knock off 40 percent or more for a chip that shows, 25 percent for one that doesn't show. Jars with tight cracks should be reduced at least 50 percent, open cracks 75 percent. Pay about 35 percent, or less, of the going price for bottoms without lids, or lids without bottoms.

Sometimes jars exhibit factory flaws. Thin spots in the glaze, or small shards that adhered to the bisque and were then covered with glaze, are two examples. When you see these types of flaws on jars that are for sale, throw up a caution flag. Don't give any more credence to an antique dealer who tells you there's nothing wrong with a flawed jar because it came from the factory that way, than you would give to an automobile dealer who feeds you the same line about a brand new car with a dented fender. You

McCoy clown bust, no. 19, 10-1/2 inches high. It was made between 1945 and 1947, and is in excellent condition for a jar painted over the glaze that long ago. Mark is shown in Chapter 7. *Oravitz Collection.* $75

Same clown bust, but decorated differently. It is in better shape than most. *Lilly Collection.* $75

can bet the manufacturer of the flawed cookie jar originally peddled it through a factory outlet store at a reduced price. Full value shouldn't be paid on the secondary market, either, considering that jars in better condition are available at the same price.

Sometimes you'll notice several little holes in the glaze on the underside of a cookie jar. These don't decrease the value because they're not defects. They're caused by stilts, small nail-like objects that pottery sits on during the glaze firing. If they weren't used the glaze would contact the kiln, and the jar and the kiln would become permanently bonded.

One thing that's inevitable is finding tiny spots of wall or ceiling paint on cookie jars. Apparently many people who dutifully cover furniture and appliances when painting their kitchens, are lackadaisical when it comes to protecting cookie jars from the spray of the roller. Paint spots on glazed jars, for example the Holiday Designs pumpkin shown below, seldom cause much problem. If you're not very particular, they may be left as they are. Most people to whom you show your collection won't notice them. If you are the particular type, paint spots can sometimes be removed from glazed jars with household solvents. Be sure to test the solvent first in small area that doesn't show to make sure it won't damage the glaze. Spots of paint may also be scraped from a glazed jar with either a fingernail or a razor blade. If working with a razor blade, use a light touch to avoid scratching the glaze.

Spots on painted jars are best left alone because the razor, fingernail, and solvent will likely take off the spots and the decoration beneath them at the same time.

Restoration of cookie jars is a hotly debated issue. Some collectors prefer to have jars in poor condition restored, others vehemently oppose it.

Restoration most often comes into play in the case of painted jars. Paint is subject to chipping, peeling, and washing off. Restoring painted jars is fairly easy to accomplish when compared to restoring glazed jars, or transfer-decorated jars. But there's more to true restoration than simply brushing on more paint.

The American Bisque fire chief shown below is a sad example of what can happen when a butcher gets hold of a brush. The jar looks nothing like it did when it was new. The colors are wrong, and the paint has been applied to the entire jar. As originally decorated, the fire chief would have been largely unpainted bisque. The jar lacks authenticity, and the repainting has probably reduced its value a significant amount.

But the Donald Duck-Joe Carioca turnabouts are a completely different matter. They show how a competent restorer can benefit a jar that the years have not treated kindly. The

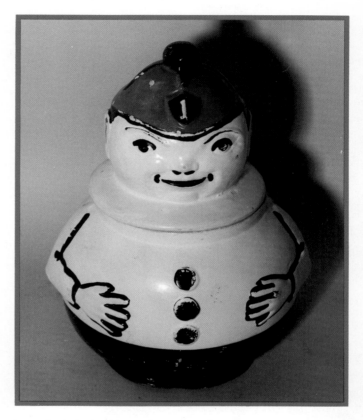

Originally, the body of this American Bisque fireman was largely unpainted. The jar might still be saved by firing off the paint and starting from scratch. The mark is "USA" impressed in the bottom. *Courtesy of Jazz'e Junque Shop, Chicago, Illinois.* $100

This pumpkin looks pretty nice from a distance, but, as the close-up reveals, it is loaded with paint spots from a previous owner's do-it-yourself project. The jar is 8 inches high, has a "6951" inkstamp on the bottom of the base, and a "6483" inkstamp inside the lid. Often called a McCoy jar, it was actually made by Holiday Designs, which, like Nelson McCoy Ceramics, is a subsidiary of Designer Accents. *Zera Collection.* $30

Paint spots on the pumpkin. They are a part of the hobby from which there seems to be no escape.

original colors have been placed where they belong, and the work is a monument to neatness. Regardless, you'll seldom find anyone willing to pay full price for a restored jar, no matter how well it has been done.

As collectors continue to debate the pros and cons of restoring jars, it might be noted that restoration is not looked down on in the art world. Museums routinely pay large sums to restore the works of great masters. It could be that until restoration is no longer looked down on in the cookie jar world, the cookie jar will continue to linger as just another of many collectibles, instead of rising to its deserved place of honor among American art forms.

Here is the result when someone who knows what he's doing restores a cookie jar. This turnabout of Donald Duck and Jose Carioca, from the movie "The Three Caballeros," was sold by the Leeds China Company, a Chicago distributor that worked closely with Ludwici Celadon, American Bisque, and other potteries. (A turnabout is a jar that can be turned about to present a different front. The picture shows different sides of the same jar.) The height is 14 inches, and it is marked "Donald Duck and Joe Carioca from The Three Caballeros Walt Disney USA," although it is unreadable on this particular example. Ludwici Celadon is known to have used this mark when filling contracts for Leeds, but possibly other potteries did, too, and to say which one made this turnabout would be guessing at best. *Bosson Collection.* $200 each

Chapter 5
Counterfeits, Reproductions and Fakes

Back in 1989 and 1990 when I was writing the first edition of this book, reproductions were on everyone's mind, almost to the point of being paranoid about them. This jar is being reproduced, people would say, and that jar is being reproduced. The problem was that no one could show me any of the reproduced jars. Not in collections, not at flea markets, not at antique malls. Not anywhere. Matter of fact, the best I could do on photographs was the four Oscar jars, all of which are probably original. Reproductions just weren't there—yet. But six months after the book was published it was like someone opened a floodgate. Reproductions abounded. Everywhere you looked you saw them. Unfortunately, you still see them, and in ever increasing numbers.

Here's two facts to remember about reproductions. Number one, they are here to stay. Number two, you can deal with them. Let's discuss these facts one at a time.

No matter how much anyone complains about reproductions, or how badly they wish they would go away, they will be with us as long as people continue to collect. Some manufacturers are going to mark them as reproductions, some aren't. Some dealers are going to unwittingly sell them as originals. Other dealers are going to sell them as originals, knowing full well they are not. And even the most knowledgeable collectors will be taken in once in a while. It's what I like to call one of the three inevitables of cookie jar collecting. The other two are discovering damage after the purchase, and occasional breakage. Trying to avoid them and getting upset when they happen is fine. Letting them spoil your enjoyment of the hobby is not, as all three go with the territory.

Now, on to fact number two, you can deal with reproductions.

The big thing here, the only thing here, is for you to know your product, know your collectible. And I can't stress this to you enough. Not me. Not the Roerigs or the Huxfords or the Kovels. You. You are the one laying down the money. You are the one who has to know what you are buying.

That old saw about knowing your dealer and only purchasing from reputable dealers? Worst advice ever written. Forget it. What you really need to know is what you are buying, not whom you are buying it from. Even reputable dealers make mistakes. So do knowledgeable ones.

I know a very knowledgeable dealer who several years ago made a special trip to a huge flea market that I attend regularly. While there his wife happened onto a vendor who was putting out a McCoy Chairman of the Board at a very low price. She bought it from him and a week later, after one thousand dollars had changed hands, the jar was sitting proudly in a collection in another part of the country. And another Chairman of the Board was sitting on that vendor's table, by my conservative estimate it was about the 10th one he had for sale that summer.

Another case. A dealer and collector for whom I have the greatest respect bought a rare Brush Purple Cow at a low price at a long established antiques show in Ohio, only after inspecting it with the utmost care, and being assured by the dealer that it was an original. My friend resold the jar and made a tidy profit. Felt really good about it, too, until he did a show in Michigan the next month and the same dealer told him he had another Purple Cow for sale for the same price. "My stomach knotted up when he told me about the second jar," he said.

Both of these people were knowledgeable and, perhaps more importantly, honest and trustworthy. Both got swindled. Both unwittingly swindled others. So forget about trusting other folks, including those who could normally be trusted, and trust only yourself. You do that by learning as much as possible. View, feel

The Cookie Monster on the right, made by California Originals, is marked "© Muppets Inc. 1970" along the base. The jar on the left is believed to be a counterfeit. It is 11 inches high and unmarked. *Zera Collection.* Left $50; Right $85

This is the reproduction of the Brayton Laguna mammy, commonly called the "Married Mammy" because of her 24 kt gold wedding ring. The jar was sold by Mary Jane Giacomini, of MJ's Collectibles in Sonoma, California, who said she intended to make about 100 of them before destroying the mold. The color of this one is periwinkle blue. *Courtesy of Mary Jane Giacomini.* $175

George Williams' limited edition commemorative of McCoy's Pontiac Indian. The jar is 10-3/4 inches high. Its mark is shown. In 1990 Williams made 300 of these jars and sold them for $79 apiece. *Bosson Collection.* $250

Brayton Laguna mammy reproduction in yellow. These jars are 12-1/4 inches high. Originals are 12-5/8 inches high. Inside the lid of each of the "Married Mammies" is an incised "90" or "91," which is not present on the originals. Neither are the decals on the apron. Other colors for this jar are dusty rose and light green. *Courtesy of Mary Jane Giacomini.* $175

Mark of the Williams Pontiac Indian, showing the jar to be no. 94 of 300.

and pick up every cookie jar you can at malls, shows, shops, and flea markets. Also those in other collections. Read everything you can find on the subject. Talk about cookie jars with other collectors and dealers. Eventually you will become the most knowledgeable person you know and will be able to buy just about any cookie jar with confidence, knowing you are getting an original, not a repro.

To be sure, not all reproductions are bad. Those of J.D.James of Buckeye Lake, Ohio, for example, have filled a niche in that they offer collectors a means of having normally very expensive jars at reasonable prices. A few examples are shown on pages 295 and 299. As you can see, James not only does a very nice job, he also clearly marks his jars as reproductions under the glaze. That's important as it would make it incredibly tough for any shyster to pass one off as an original at 10 or 20 times the price.

Jars of American Bisque's line reproduced by James include Casper, Fred Flintstone, Rubble House, Sitting Horse, Popeye, Olive Oyl, and Swee' Pea. From the Brush Pottery he has done Formal Pig, Hillbilly Frog, Little Angel in both white and black, Little Boy Blue, and Peter Pan. McCoy's Davy Crockett, Leprechaun and Hillbilly Bear, Gonder's Sheriff and Pirate, the Lane Indian, DeForest Halo Boy, and the Regal China Peek-A-Boo are also among James' offerings. Additionally, he has done a Nancy head and Nancy full-bodied jar, Sluggo, Little Lulu, Gleep, Weller dog, and many others.

Roger Jensen, of Rockwood, Tennessee, made reproductions and marked them all McCoy for awhile, according to an article by Stan and Karen Zera in *Antique Week* December 14, 1992. While his McCoy mammy might snag a few unsuspecting collectors, it wouldn't take a long time in the hobby to realize something was awry with Jensen's Mosaic Tile Mammy, Luzianne Mammy, and Hull's Little Red Riding Hood—all with McCoy marks on their bottoms!

Many other companies and individuals have jumped onto the repro bandwagon. Look for the trend to continue as long as prices of rare originals remain high.

A related problem is that of counterfeits. A counterfeit jar is a copy of one that is currently being manufactured, or a copy of a jar that's protected by copyright, trademark, patent or other legal means. The Cookie Monster on page 17 is believed to be a counterfeit as there is no copyright notice on it.

Oscar is 10 inches high, and was made by Robinson-Ransbottom. There seems little doubt this jar is an original. *Zera Collection.* $175

Oscar still looks old, but is in better shape than the one with the blue hat. In all liklihood this is also an original. *Zera Collection.* $175

19

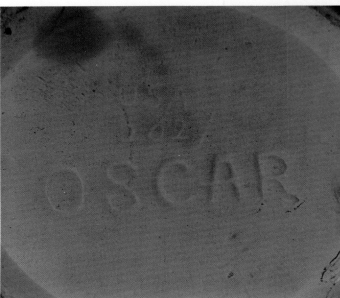

Two more Oscars, the one on the left looks like it came off the shelf yesterday. Did it? Probably not, but it pays to be careful. *Blumenfeld Collection.* $175 each.

Mark of the single Oscar with the red hat. Somewhat hard to read, it says "USA/202/OSCAR" on three lines.

Jars that are often confused with reproductions and fakes are those made from molds produced for the hobby ceramics market. The mammy and granny below are an example. While it appears one might have been copied from the other, both were made from the same mold, sold by Alberta's Molds, Inc., of Atascadero, California. Making and selling jars from these types of molds is a legal and very common practice.

Mark of the Carol Gifford mammy.

Studio artist Carol Gifford, who made the mammy on the left, is sometimes criticized for copying the design from the older jar on the right, thereby producing a fake. Nothing could be further from the truth. Both jars were rendered from identical Alberta's molds, a fact Gifford doesn't attempt to hide. These jars, 9-3/4 inches high, have been made and sold at craft shows by hundreds of home ceramists across the country. The jar on the right is unmarked, and the mark of the Carol Gifford jar is shown. *Courtesy of Jazz'e Junque Shop, Chicago, Illinois.* Left $200; Right $75

Chapter 6
Problems of Collecting

Until a few years ago cookie jar collectors faced three major problems in pursuing their hobby—a lack of information about jars and their makers, financial resources to purchase jars, and the large amount of space jars require for display and storage.

Problem number one, a lack of information, has been eased considerably by the publication of several excellent books. In addition to this book, all cookie jar collectors should consider familiarizing themselves with the following volumes:

1. *An Illustrated Value Guide to Cookie Jars, books 1 and 2,* by Ermagene Westfall.
2. *McCoy Cookie Jars—From the First to the Latest,* by Harold Nichols.
3. *The Collectors Encyclopedia of Cookie Jars, books 1, 2 and 3,* by Fred and Joyce Herndon Roerig.
4. *Dictionary Guide to United States Pottery and Porcelain (19th and 20th Century),* by Jenny B. Derwich and Dr. Mary Latos.
5. *Lehner's Encyclopedia of U.S. Marks on Pottery, Porcelain & Clay,* by Lois Lehner.

The information contained in the above books, along with the information in this book, will not tell you everything there is to know about cookie jars, but it will enable you to enjoy the hobby to a much greater degree. At the same time it will drastically reduce your chances of being taken advantage of by unscrupulous or misinformed dealers.

Sources of the above publications are listed in Appendix 1.

Problem number two, financial resources to purchase jars, relates directly to the amount of disposable income at hand, the amount of time available to search for jars and, let's face it, a collector's skill at what might be called creative budgeting. There are few true collectors, myself included, who haven't used part of the house payment, the vacation savings, or money designated for some other specific purpose, to take advantage of an unexpected good deal.

The cookie jar collector's money crunch has become more severe the past few years as jar prices have shot up at a rate many times that of the average growth in personal income. But good buys still exist for those willing to ferret them out.

Flea markets are the best hunting grounds for the person limited on both time and cash. Get there early before everything has been picked over.

If you have more time than money on your hands, a common syndrome among parents of college-aged children, garage sales are a good route. Many families have a cookie jar or two, a lot don't realize what they're worth. At garage sales where no cookie jars are displayed, ask the people if they have any. The results might surprise you.

Don't overlook antique shops and shows, either. While shooting cookie jar pictures at antique malls, I spotted a tan Brush squirrel on log jar for less than one-third of its average book value, a McCoy asparagus jar for $10, a Shawnee Smiley pig for $16, and many other good buys. Make the round of shops often because good deals don't remain on the shelves very long.

At antique shows you'll have the greatest success by arriving two to three hours before the show opens, while the dealers are still setting up. Some shows charge a premium for early admission, others don't.

Auctions can be good, too. At auctions where many jars have been advertised, the bidding is nearly always very competitive. You might find the jars you want, but be prepared to pay book price or more for them. At estate auctions you'll find less quantity but usually better prices, especially when the jars haven't been advertised.

By displaying cookie jars on modular aluminum shelving units, you focus attention on the jars themselves, not the piece that is holding them. (Note American Bisque Olive Oyl on middle shelf, not shown elsewhere in the book.)

Close-up of aluminum shelving.

Bookcases and similar storage units can easily be used for displaying cookie jars.

Bookcases can serve double duty by holding books and displaying cookie jars at the same time.

You don't need anything fancy to exhibit your cookie jar collection. Here, construction grade pine lumber, stained but not varnished, has been used to create basement shelving.

The third problem cookie jar collectors face is an eternal one: space. There's no way around it, cookie jars take up a lot of room. Start a collection and before long your house will be taken over by it. But houses can be taken over by many things, such as pets, so its no big deal, providing you love your jars.

Space problems are greater in the early stages of collecting when a person has gone beyond the point of being able to pass up a great jar, but has not yet committed to a long term, if not a lifetime, endeavor. Once that commitment is made, most people devise attractive display units and adequate storage facilities.

The built-in and modular displays shown here will give the neophyte some ideas to copy or enhance. While work by skilled tradesmen can be quite expensive, the cost of a professionally built display unit will pale when set against the value of the jars it holds. The competent do-it-yourselfer can get by for much less.

Storage of undisplayed jars can be easily accomplished by building rough shelves of inexpensive grade lumber in a basement or garage, or even a dry unheated shed if you live in the proper climate. Doors made of 1 x 3 furring strips with clear plastic stretched across them will protect your cookie jars from dust, smoke and other undesirable elements while they're being stored.

Section II: The Cookie Jar Giants

Numerous American potteries in business between the 1930s and the present have made cookie jars, but two—McCoy and American Bisque—stand above the others as giants of the industry, both in the number of different jars they produced and in the standard of quality they maintained. It's probable other potteries noted the success of these two companies and decided to grab their own share of the market, thereby making McCoy and American Bisque the driving force that gave today's cookie jar collectors their hobby.

They've been placed at the beginning as a tribute to their contribution.

Chapter 7
McCoy

No other pottery has made more different cookie jars—well over 300—than McCoy. While an entire book could be written on the history of this company, suffice to say its roots go back to 1848 when W. Nelson McCoy went into the pottery business in Putnam, Ohio, to produce stoneware crocks and other utilitarian pieces for local consumers. W. Nelson McCoy's uncle, W.F. McCoy, assisted in the venture. Putnam, incidentally, no longer exists as it was later annexed to Zanesville. As time went on the quality of the pottery's wares improved to the point they were eventually transported by flatboat down the Ohio and Mississippi rivers to eager wholesale buyers as far away as New Orleans.

W. Nelson McCoy taught the business to his son, J.W. McCoy, who founded the J.W. McCoy Pottery in Roseville, Ohio, on September 5, 1899. Like its predecessor, the new company dealt mainly in domestic use stoneware, but also dabbled in glazed spittoons, jardinieres, pedestals, and other large pieces popular at the time. These met with considerable success, encouraging the firm to experiment with artware of the type produced by trend setters such as Weller and Rookwood.

J.W. McCoy continued the family tradition of handing down the craft, and in 1910 formed a separate corporation with his son, Nelson McCoy. It was called the Nelson McCoy Sanitary Stoneware Company. This is the company that eventually made McCoy cookie jars. Meanwhile, the J. W. McCoy Pottery became the Brush-McCoy Pottery Company in 1911 when General Manager George Brush bought into it. The affiliation lasted until 1925 when the McCoys sold their interest and redirected the capital to the Nelson McCoy Sanitary Stoneware Company, which at some point along the way changed its name to the Nelson McCoy Pottery Company.

In 1967 Chase Enterprises bought the firm, sold it in 1974 to Lancaster Colony Corporation. In 1991 it was owned by Designer Accents, of Sebring, Ohio, and goes by the name Nelson McCoy Ceramics. It is now out of business.

The first McCoy cookie jars are believed to have been made in the late 1930s, but the exact date is unknown. These were very plain bean pot type jars. The first figural jar to come from McCoy was the mammy with cauliflowers, which emerged from the kiln in 1939, and is highly prized by collectors today.

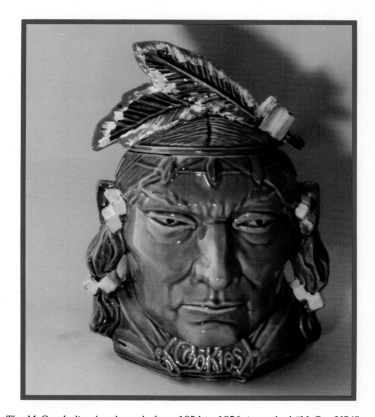

The McCoy Indian head, made from 1954 to 1956, is marked "McCoy/USA" on two lines. No. 50, it is 11-1/2 inches high. Long said to be finished in both a light and dark glaze, the glazes are actually one in the same. The shade depended upon how thickly the glaze was applied. The proof is inside each jar. Compare the inside of a light Indian head jar to the inside of a dark Indian head jar and you will find they are both the same color. To paraphrase our forefathers, all McCoy Indian head jars were created equal, but only on the inside, not on the outside. The insides of the cookie jars are finished by pouring glaze in, then dumping it out, giving each interior an even coating. Exteriors are finished by brushing or airbrushing, both of which result in varying thicknesses of glaze. As a further test, lightly rub your finger over the part in the Indian's hair. On a darker jar, (which has a thicker glaze) you will notice less of a depression than on a lighter jar (which has a thinner glaze). *Blumenfeld Collection.* $400

While the 1950s are often thought of as the golden age of McCoy cookie jars, the company actually hit its stride in jar manufacturing during the 1960s, and peaked in the 1970s, both in terms of the number of different jars offered during any particular year, and number of new designs offered. Peaks and lulls of McCoy cookie jar production are shown in the two graphs in Appendix III.

Most McCoy cookie jars exhibit very detailed mold features, yet rather plain decoration, a combination that obviously pleased consumers. Airbrushing was used sparingly, hand-painting of details on top of the glaze was used extensively. So were decals. McCoy made more fruit and vegetable cookie jars than any other company. More canisters, too.

McCoy marked most of its jars. The many different marks it used are shown at the end of the chapter. Jars that aren't marked can often be identified by the three bars they have across the bottom, which are shown along with the marks. The names and numbers in the accompanying captions are those used by Nichols.

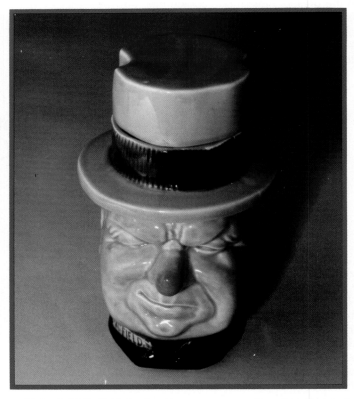

This 9-1/2 inch high sad clown is McCoy no. 255, made in 1970 and 1971. It has the McCoy bull's-eye mark. *Zera Collection.* $140

McCoy's W.C. Fields jar has become very popular with collectors in recent years. No. 153 in the McCoy line, it is 11 inches high, and was made from 1972 to 1974. Its mark is shown below. *Zera Collection.* $250

It seems all Davy Crockett cookie jars command a premium, and McCoy's jar is no exception. The jar, no. 140, is 10 inches high, and was made in 1957. It is marked "USA." *Zera Collection.* $600

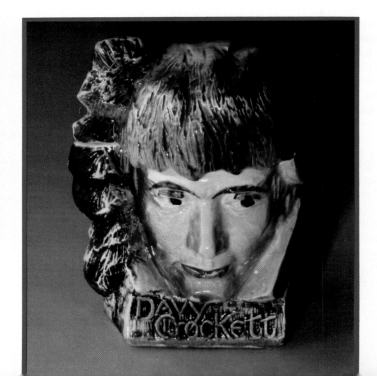

A much earlier clown bust, 1945 to 1947, 10-1/2 inches high. It is no. 19, and marked "McCoy." *Zera Collection.* $75

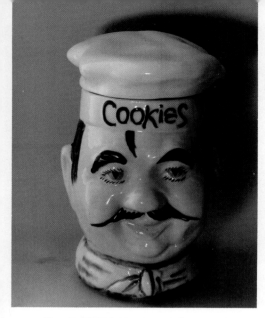

This hand-decorated chef (bust) is 11 inches high, marked "McCoy/USA" on two lines on the hat band, which is an unusual place for a McCoy mark. Made from 1962 to 1964, it is McCoy no. 206. *Blumenfeld Collection.* $160

The unmarked McCoy leprechaun is an exceptionally rare jar. Besides green, it was made in brown, red, and multi-color. Seeing very limited production, the 12-1/2 inch high jar never appeared in McCoy catalogs. Nichols assigned it no. 169. Exact date of the jar has not been ascertained. While a debate rages among collectors as to how many were made, most estimates range from a few hundred to a few thousand. *Bosson Collection.* $1500

This late addition to the McCoy line stands 11 inches high, and has "McCoy Limits" impressed in the bottom on one line. *Blumenfeld Collection.* $250

The McCoy Christmas tree is 11-1/2 inches high. It is no. 174, made in 1959, and marked "McCoy/USA" on two lines. *Bosson Collection.* $1000

Here is McCoy's giant economy size Santa. Standing 21-1/2 inches high, it is really a lawn ornament but is often called a cookie jar because it was made in two pieces, split at the belt. It is unmarked. A close-up of the accompanying Keebler jar appears elsewhere. *Bosson Collection.*

"Cookie Boy," no. 16, manufactured in 1944 and 1945. This 11-1/4 inch high jar was also finished in aqua. The incised mark of the yellow jar is shown below. *Zera Collection.*

The "Boy on Football" was made in 1983, and stands 11-/12 inches high. The jar is McCoy no. 222, according to Nichols, but it is marked "127/McCoy/LCC/USA" on four lines. *Lilly Collection.* $250

Not surprisingly, "Betsy Baker" is no. 184. Apparently not as popular as Bobby, it was made in 1974 only. The jar is 10-3/4 inches high. The example shown is unmarked, while others are marked "184/McCoy/USA/LCC" on four lines, and still others have a similar mark without the LCC logo. Finding different marks on identical McCoy jars is not unusual. Several different hats, or lids, were made for this jar. *Zera Collection.* $300

In addition to the three colors shown, the "Clown (in barrel)" was also finished in blue. *Bosson Collection.* $135 each

This clown is 8-1/2 inches high. It is no. 27, made in 1945. Like most older jars that were painted over the glaze, it is difficult, if not impossible, to find it in perfect condition. The mark, shown below, is "McCoy" in raised letters. *Courtesy of Jazz'e Junque Shop, Chicago, Illinois.* $110

"Boy on Baseball" is 13-1/2 inches high. Offered in 1978, it is no. 221, and marked "221/McCoy/LCC/USA" on four lines. *Bosson Collection.* $350

"Bobby the Baker" is the name the McCoy Company gave to no. 183, the 10-3/4 inch chef, manufactured between 1974 and 1979, and again beginning in 1983. Impressed into the bottom of this particular jar is "183/McCoy" on two lines, while other examples are marked "USA." *Oravitz Collection.* $45

This is called "Animal Crackers," made in 1960. Some examples have raised dots on them; this one does not. It is no. 175, and is marked "McCoy"/U.S.A." on two lines. *Oravitz Collection.* $120

The "Clown (in barrel)" was sold from 1953 to 1955. Standing 11-1/2 inches high, it is McCoy no. 40., and is marked "McCoy/U.S.A." impressed on two lines. *Coughenour Collection.* $135

The mammy on the left has been repainted, the mammy on the right has not. This 11 inch high jar, no. 17, has a bit of intrigue connected to it. According to Nichols, it originated in 1944 with the words "Dem cookies shor am good" on it; it was made like this until 1946 when the degrading phrase was dropped in favor of "Cookies." However, no collectors who were interviewed, including many aficionados of black collectibles, reported ever seeing the jar, and most indicated they believe it was never made. Either way, production on this model ended in 1957. Both of these examples are marked "McCoy." *Zera Collection.* $200 each

Not all McCoy mammies wore white dresses. Size and mark are the same as above. *Bosson Collection.* $800

The example on the left was made in 1972 and 1973, while the one on the right was made the following two years. Both are "Granny," no. 159, and are 11 inches high. The mark is "159/USA" on two lines, though it is often unreadable. The plainer version is generally considered to be more desirable, which is reflected in the price guide. *Oravitz Collection.* Left $130; Right $150

"Mammy with Cauliflowers," no. 8 (assigned by Nichols), is 11-3/4 inches high. Made in 1939, this is one of the most sought after—and expensive—McCoy jars, even in this condition, which is typical for old jars that were painted over the glaze. This jar is said to be McCoy's first figural cookie jar. *Zera Collection.* $1200

One of the things to be aware of when collecting cookie jars is the potential of running into repainted jars. This "Mammy with Cauliflowers" has indeed been repainted, but so long ago it now looks like the original. As far as is known, however, all scarfs were originally painted yellow by the company. *Coughenour Collection.* $1200

"Rag Doll" (Raggedy Ann) is 11 inches high. Its mark, "U.S.A./741" on two lines, includes its model number. The jar was made from 1972 to 1975. *Courtesy of Jazz'e Junque Shop, Chicago, Illinois.* $100

The unmarked McCoy monk is 12-1/2 inches high. It is no. 846, made from 1968 to 1973. Many others companies made monk jars. *Zera Collection.* $50

Monk in solid color, 12-1/2 inches high, and unmarked. *Lilly Collection.* $50

One of two kangaroos the company made, this model was first produced in 1965. Standing 11-1/2 inches high, it is no. 234, marked "McCoy/USA" on two lines. *Coughenour Collection.* $500

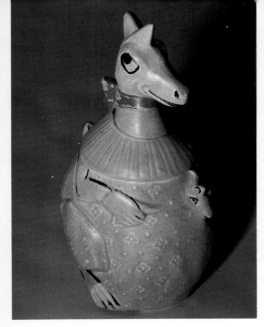

McCoy's second kangaroo, 13 inches high, no. 234, identified by its three-bar bottom, an example of which is shown below. While it is known that the other model was taken out of production in favor of this one, the exact dates of manufacture for each have not been determined. *Lilly Collection*. $400

"Teddy Bear and Friend," no. 154, is 11-1/2 inches high, marked "154/USA." Made in 1986 and 1987, it also came in dark brown. *Lilly Collection*. $70

Occasionally you find a cookie jar that has been customized to suit a previous owner's specific purpose. While this generally devalues a jar (perhaps if it said something like, To Lady Bird from Lyndon, it might increase the value), it certainly makes it a more interesting piece of Americana. *Zera Collection*. $300

McCoy's "Chairman of the Board," a jar whose price has skyrocketed since 1985, the only year it was made. It is 10-1/2 inches high, no. 162, and marked "162/USA" on two lines. *Coughenour Collection*. $900

"Hamm's Bear," McCoy no. 148, made in 1972. It is 13 inches high, marked "148/USA." *Lilly Collection*. $300

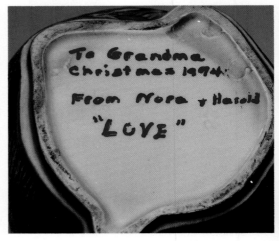

Bottom of customized "Hamm's Bear." Note faint mark to the right of "Love," an impressed "148," but no USA as on above jar.

"Chairman of the Board" with brown pants instead of burgundy as above. The difference is much more apparent than conveyed in the pictures. The size and mark are the same as above. Because the tops of both these jars are tinted differently than the bottoms, the first impulse is to consider them to be married. They're probably not, as the example Nichols shows is the same way. Slight color variations between tops and bottoms is a common occurrence with McCoy cookie jars, far more prevalent than with any other company. *Bosson Collection*. $900

This jar, "Bear (cookies in vest)," no. 22, is seen in two different styles. The original, shown here, was made in 1945, and does not have "Cookies" in raised letters between the feet, as the next example does. The jar is 10-3/4 inches high, with "McCoy" impressed in the bottom. *Zera Collection*. $75

28

Brother to the jar in the previous picture, this model was manufactured in 1953, and has the lettering between the feet. The mold appears to have been altered a bit, too, specifically in the area below the bow tie. This version is the rarer of the two. *Zera Collection.* $125

Panda, 11 inches high, no. 141. Made in 1978, its mark is "141/USA." *Bosson Collection.* $300

"Honey Bear" is 9 inches high, and was made from 1953 to 1955. McCoy no. 37, it has a "McCoy/USA" mark on two lines. *Zera Collection.* $130

This is "Brown Bear," also no. 22, but according to Nichols, not shown in any McCoy catalog. The height is 10-3/4 inches, and the mark is "McCoy" impressed. *Coughenour Collection.* $1000

Everything the same as the previous bear, except for the bright yellow clothes. *Bosson Collection.* $1000

The koala bear is 11-1/4 inches high, no. 216. The jar was made in 1983. Its mark is shown below. *Oravitz Collection.* $100

What's happening here is hard to grasp. Apparently the bear is supposed to be wrapped around the bee-hive, but it looks very unnatural. No. 143, the jar stands 9 inches high, and is marked "143/U.S.A." impressed on two lines. It has been made since 1983, and could still be bought at discount stores in 1990. *Oravitz Collection.* $50

"Honey Bear" with a different color lid, plus one other difference. This one is marked "McCoy" in raised letters. *Zera Collection.* $130

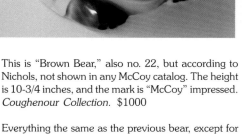

Labeled "Snow Bear" by the company, this 1965 jar, no. 235, is 11 inches high. It is marked with an impressed "USA," but examples are also seen marked "McCoy/U.S.A." in raised letters on two lines. *Lilly Collection.* $90

"Upside Down Bear" is 11-1/2 inches high, marked "McCoy/U.S.A." on two lines with LCC logo impressed quite far below. McCoy no. 210, it was made in 1978 and 1979. *Lilly Collection.* $100

Now it is 1953 and the elephant emerges with a new designation, no. 41, and a trunk that is no longer split between top and bottom. This version is occasionally seen in red. Height is 11 inches. The jar is unmarked. *Zera Collection.* $150

The "Rocking Chair (Dalmatians)" cookie jar is highly prized by collectors. It is 10 inches high, and marked "McCoy/U.S.A." in raised letters on two lines. No. 189, it was made in 1961. *Courtesy of Betty and Floyd Carson.* $450

"Upside Down Bear" with clear glaze. *Courtesy of Jazz'e Junque Shop, Chicago, Illinois.* $100

"Dog House," no. 206, 13 inches high, made in 1983. The one on the left is the eyes-closed version, the one on the right the eyes-open version. The left jar is marked "206/McCoy/LCC/USA" on four lines. The right jar is unmarked. *Coughenour Collection.* $400 each

These two jars are McCoy's "Elephant with Split Trunk," manufactured prior to the "Elephant without a Split Trunk," shown below. Note that one has round eyes, the other pointed eyes. It is believed the round-eye version was manufactured around 1940, and the pointed-eye version, in 1945. McCoy no. 20, some of these jars are impressed "McCoy." They are 11 inches high. Both of these have been restored. *Bosson Collection.* Left $225; Right $200

Some dogs are deep thinkers, others are deep sleepers. "Snoopy," no. 247, is 11-1/4 inches high, and was made in 1970. Its mark is "USA" impressed, plus gold stamp, "© 1970 United/Feature Syndicate, Inc./World Right Reserved/Made in USA" on four lines. This is a fairly expensive McCoy jar, which is strange because, according to Nichols, it was made for Sears meaning they must have made kennels full of them. *Courtesy of Jazz'e Junque Shop, Chicago, Illinois.* $275

This is "Mac Dog," no. 208, 11-1/2 inches high. It was made in 1967 and 1968, and is marked "208/ USA" on two lines. *Zera Collection.* $100

"Clyde (dog)," McCoy's no. 182. It is 12 inches high. The mark is "McCoy/182" on two lines, and the year of production was 1974. *Saxby Collection.* $425

"Puppy with Sign," no. 185, is a 1961-1962 offering, 10 inches high. It is marked "McCoy/USA" on two lines. Although the paint on the sign wears off rather easily, the jar is believed to have been made with the sign both painted and unpainted. While the jar on the right appears taller than the one on the left, look closely and you will see the lid is not seated properly. *Oravitz Collection.* $100 each

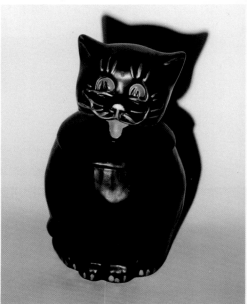

"Coalby Cat," no. 207, 11-1/4 inches high. Manufactured in 1967 and 1968, it is marked "USA/207" on two lines. *Bosson Collection.* $500

"Thinking Puppy," 11 inches high, is McCoy's no. 272. It was offered between 1977 and 1979. The mark, shown below, includes the Lancaster Colony Corporation logo. *Courtesy of Mary and Bill Hallier.* $20

Another rendition of no. 272, this jar's mark, also shown below, is different than the mark on the darker model. *Zera Collection.* $20

31

"The Kittens on Ball of Yarn," 9 inches high, dating from 1954 and 1955. The jar is no. 24, and marked "McCoy/USA" on two lines. *Zera Collection.* $130 each

While the "Rocking Horse" was made in these basic colors, this is a repainted jar. As they came from the factory, the flowers were not painted. Size and mark as above. *Coughenour Collection.* $190

The "Chipmunk" was made in 1960 and 1961. It stands 10-3/4 inches high, and is marked "McCoy/USA" on two lines. Its McCoy number is 172. *Zera Collection.* $150

The same jar in green, with size and mark identical to above jars. *Oravitz Collection.* $130

"Circus Horse," no. 193, is from 1961. It stands 9-1/2 inches high, and is marked "McCoy/USA" on two lines in raised letters. *Zera Collection.* $250

Besides the colors shown, this jar was also made in blue and possibly other colors. Called "Hocus Rabbit," it is quite tall measuring 14 inches. The number is included in the mark, "211/McCoy/LCC/U.S.A." on four lines. "Hocus Rabbit" was made in 1978 and 1979. *Zera Collection.* $50

"The Kitten on Coal Bucket" jar, no. 218, was made in 1983. It is 10 inches high, marked "218/McCoy/LCC/USA" on four lines. *Bosson Collection.* $400 each

No. 36, "Rocking Horse," is 10-1/4 inches high and was sold between 1948 and 1953. The mark is "McCoy" in raised letters. *Zera Collection.* $190

Two more colors of "Hocus Rabbit." Size and marks are the same as above. *Oravitz Collection.* $50 each

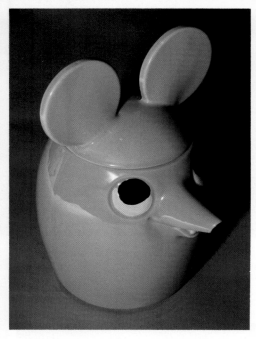

"Yellow Mouse," no. 208, 11-1/2 inches high. The mark is "208/McCoy/LCC/USA" on four lines. This jar is also seen without painted eyes. *Lilly Collection.* $75

From wren on house to hen on nest, sounds like Dr. Seuss no less. Made in 1958 and 1959, this jar is 10-1/2 inches high, marked "USA." No. 139, it also comes with a yellow bottom. *Zera Collection.* $100

"White Rooster," 1970 to 1974. It is no. 258, stands 13-1/4 inches high, and carries the McCoy bull's-eye mark. *Lilly Collection.* $100

The McCoy "Wren House," no. 153. Check out the two different lids. Jar on the left is 9-1/2 inches high, jar on the right is 10 inches high. Both are marked "McCoy/USA" on two lines in raised letters. The standard version, on the left, was made from 1958 through 1960. The one on the right, believed to be extremely rare, undoubtedly dates from the same era. *Coughenour Collection.* Left $200; Right Value Undetermined

"The Rooster," no. 55, was made between 1956 and 1958. It is 10-3/4 inches high, marked "McCoy/U.S.A." on two lines. *Oravitz Collection.* $125

McCoy made two turkey cookie jars, one in 1945, another in 1960. This one, finished in brown and green, is the 1945 model. No. 23, it is 11-1/2 inches high. The mark is "McCoy" impressed. *Coughenour Collection.* $300
Another turkey, vintage 1945, in a different color scheme. *Zera Collection.* $300

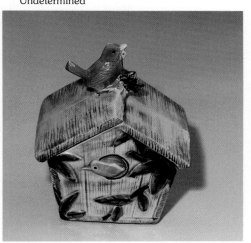

Variation of "Wren House," 9-1/2 inches high, with the same mark as above. *Zera Collection.* $200

Gray version of above, but made only in 1957 and 1958. Same size but different mark, "McCoy" impressed. *Bosson Collection.* $125

The 1945 turkey was also made in white. *Coughenour Collection.* $300

"Woodsy Owl," no. 201, 12 1/2 inches high. The jar is marked "USA." It was made in 1973 and 1974. *Zera Collection.* $400

"Mother Goose," made between 1948 and 1952, and shown in two different glazes. It is 10-3/4 inches high, no. 34, and has a "McCoy/USA" mark on two lines in raised letters. *Bosson Collection.* $150 each

The 1960 model, no. 176. Standing only 9-1/2 inches high, it is considerably shorter than its predecessor. Note that the feet are different, and, although it doesn't show in the pictures, the tail feathers flare more on this one. The mark is different, too, "McCoy/USA" on two lines. *Coughenour Collection.* $300

"Mr. and Mrs. Owl," 1952 to 1955, no. 38. Written on the back of this 10 3/4 inch high jar is, "When shadows fall." It is marked "McCoy/USA" on two lines. *Oravitz Collection.* $150

While McCoy cookie jars are notorious for poor lid fits, this might well be a married jar because it appears the leaf edges and veins won't line up no matter how the lid is adjusted. It is called "The Duck," and was made in 1964. Unmarked, the 11-1/2 inch high jar has the McCoy three-bar bottom. *Zera Collection.* $85

While this jar is simply called "Owl," the owners of this trio like to refer to them as "patriotic owls" because they envision the birds standing to say the pledge of allegiance. The owls were made in 1978 and 1979. They are all McCoy no. 204, but aren't marked the same. The left and right owls sport "204/McCoy/LCC/U.S.A.," impressed on four lines, while the one in the middle has "204/U.S.A." impressed on two lines. *Oravitz Collection.* $45 each

Modern chick, offered in 1976 and 1977. It is 9-1/2 inches high marked "McCoy/LCC/U.S.A." on three lines. *Oravitz Collection.* $300

"Goodie Goose," 12-1/2 inches high. McCoy's no. 166, this jar is unmarked. Production began in 1986. Goodie has also been made with pink and yellow ribbons. *Lilly Collection.* $35

This penguin is "Chilly Willy," no. 155, which began production in 1986. It is 12 inches high. The mark is "155/U.S.A." impressed on two lines. *Oravitz Collection.* $110

The glaze on this "Stump with Frog Finial" could almost be mistaken for a Frankoma glaze (Chapter 21) if seen from a distance. The jar, no. 216, is 12 inches high, and was made in 1971. It has a McCoy bull's-eye mark. *Zera Collection.* $65

"The Love Birds (kissing penguins)," 8-3/4 inches high, no. 29, was also finished in a black glaze which is much more valuable. This jar, made in 1946, is marked "McCoy." *Zera Collection.* $85

"Timmy Tortoise," no. 271, sold from 1977 to 1980. Timmy is 10-1/2 inches high, and marked "271/McCoy/LCC/U.S.A." impressed on four lines. *Oravitz Collection.* $45

A close cousin to the "Stump with Frog Finial" is the "Cookie Log with Squirrel Finial." The 11-1/4 inch high jar was made from 1965 to 1969, and has the McCoy three-bar bottom. The designation is no. 240. *Oravitz Collection.* $35

McCoy labeled this big-billed bird a penguin. Westfall coined it a "pelguin," which seems more appropriate. It is McCoy's no. 18, stands 11-1/4 inches high, and was made from 1940 to 1943. In addition to solid yellow, it was also glazed in solid white and solid green. On the painted versions the head is sometimes black. *Oravitz Collection.* $140

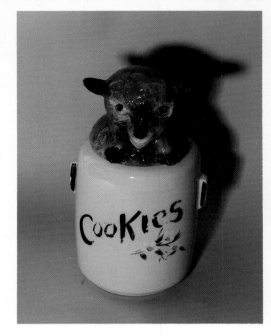

Another relative, the "Monkey on Stump," no. 253, is 11-1/2 inches high, and marked "253/(bull's-eye) ©/ USA" on three lines. It was made in 1970. *Lilly Collection.* $45

"Winking Pig," no. 150, 13-1/2 inches high. The mark is "150/USA" on two lines. The jar was made in 1972. *Coughenour Collection.* $500

Nichols doesn't show animals on cylinder jars, but the Roerigs show two, a pair of puppies and a kitten. Said by some to be a McCoy impostor, this "Lamb on cylinder" is 11-1/2 inches high, and is stamped "McCoy" on the bottom. *Courtesy of Jazz'e Junque Shop, Chicago, Illinois.* $200

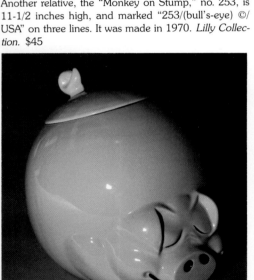

The "Pig," no. 201, is 8 inches high. It was made in 1978 and 1979, is marked "McCoy/USA/201" on three lines. The lid of this jar has an L-shaped catch that prevents it from sliding off. On this example, the catch is on the same side as the tail. On others, it is placed opposite the tail, which puts the tail too high up on the back of the pig. *Zera Collection.* $65

This McCoy jar is 8 inches high, and marked "8166/ USA" on two lines. *Lilly Collection.* $100

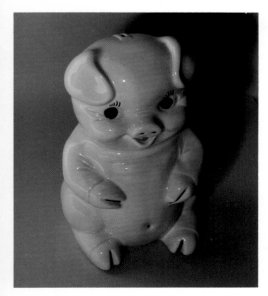

Look closely at the head of this pig and you'll see a slot that allows it to serve double duty as a bank. It is 10-1/2 inches high, and was made in 1985. McCoy number is included in the mark "224/U.S.A." impressed on two lines. *Oravitz Collection.* $225

McCoy made several different tops for its basketweave bottom. They're referred to as "Lamb on Basketweave," "Dog on Basketweave," etc. Their average height is 10-1/4 inches. No. 127 is on the left, no. 128 on the right. Both of these were made in 1956 and 1957. The marks are "McCoy/USA" in raised letters on two lines. *Zera Collection.* $60 each

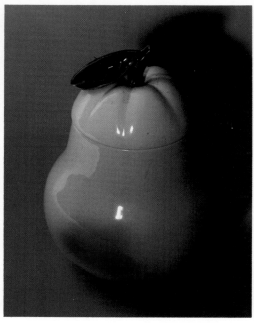

The "Duck on Basketweave" has two heads, one in the front, one in the rear. It was made in 1956. McCoy's no. 129, its mark is "McCoy/USA" in raised letters on two lines. *Oravitz Collection.* $80

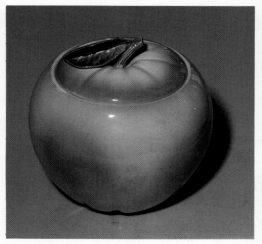

Yet another color. *Zera Collection.* $50

The McCoy "Pear" is 10 inches high, marked "McCoy USA" in a circle in raised letters. It is no. 18, made from 1952 to 1957. *Coughenour Collection.* $85

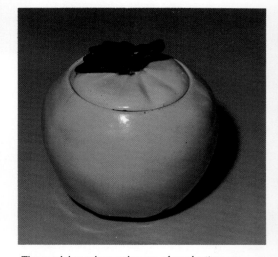

The model number and years of production are not known for this 7-1/2 inch McCoy apple, but it is obviously older than those above. Note the saw-tooth edge on the leaf. *Zera Collection.* $85

"Pinecones on Basketweave," no. 133, 1957, and "Kitten on Basketweave," no. 126, 1956 to 1959. Both are marked "McCoy/USA" in raised letters on two lines. *Zera Collection.* Left $50; Right $85

"Pears on Basketweave," no. 135, made in 1957. A similar top, made the same year, has apples on it. The mark is "McCoy/USA" in raised letters on two lines. *Zera Collection.* $75

One of several colors for the McCoy "Apple," no. 20. It's 7-1/2 inches high, and is marked "McCoy USA" in a small circle around the blossom end. Long popular, this apple was made from 1950 to 1964. *Zera Collection.* $35

Basically the same apple, but it has a "M" impressed in the lid. *Zera Collection.* $50

Here is another style of apple, no. 261, 9-1/2 inches high, made from 1972 to 1979. McCoy mark on bottom. *Zera Collection.* $60

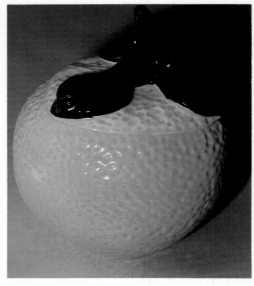

This is called the "New Strawberry," no. 263, as opposed to the "Old Strawberry," no. 54. This one was made from 1972 to 1979, is 9-1/2 inches high. It was glazed in these two colors plus white, shown below. The mark is "263/USA" on two lines. *Taylor Collection.* $40 each

This orange isn't exceptionally tall, 12 inches to the top of the stem, but its girth makes it a really large cookie jar. No. 257, it carries the McCoy bull's-eye mark, and was made during 1970 and 1971. *Zera Collection.* $50

Same as above but marked differently, "263/McCoy/LCC/U.S.A." on four lines. The McCoy bull's-eye mark, with the number "263," was also used on this jar. *Taylor Collection.* $60

Same strawberry but minus the white drip glaze. It has a different mark, too, "McCoy" in raised letters. *Lilly Collection.* $75

A 7-1/2 inch high tomato, made in 1964. No. 210, it is marked "McCoy/USA" in raised letters on two lines. *Zera Collection.* $50

Strawberry with white drip glaze, made from 1955 to 1957. Note the different top than in above examples. Mark is "McCoy/U.S.A." in raised letters on two lines. This jar is McCoy's no. 54, measuring 9 inches high. *Taylor Collection.* $95

The lemon is 9 inches high, was made in 1972, and has McCoy bull's-eye mark. It is no. 262. As seen here, McCoy used the same lid for several different fruit jars. *Zera Collection.* $90

This pineapple with gold tint, no. 52, goes for more money than the pineapple in natural colors shown below. It is 10-1/2 inches high, was made from 1955 to 1957, and is marked "McCoy/USA" on two lines. *Zera Collection.* $140

"The Bananas," no. 33, was made from 1948 through 1952. The jar is 11 inches high, and marked "McCoy" in raised letters. Most examples have tops that vary slightly in color from their bottoms. While such a mismatch often indicates a married jar, in this case it is probably the result of being glazed by different people at the factory, or perhaps the tops being done at different times than the bottoms. *Courtesy of Jazz'e Junque Shop, Chicago, Illinois.* $160

McCoy crock jar, no. 3, from 1939 to 1944. It is 9-3/4 inches high. *Oravitz Collection.* $30

Same jar as above in tan. *Courtesy of Jazz'e Junque Shop, Chicago, Illinois.* $30

Natural color version of above pineapple. Same size and mark. *Zera Collection.* $90

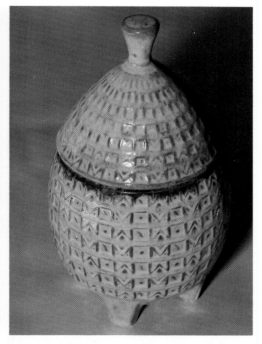

This is McCoy's "Modern Pineapple," no. 823, 13-1/4 inches high, "USA" impressed. *Lilly Collection.* $100

Modern pineapple in a different color. Everything else same as above. *Bosson Collection.* $100

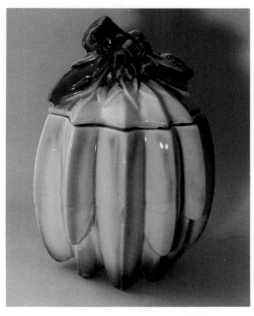

Just like at the supermarket, cookie jar bananas come in different stages of ripeness. *Taylor Collection.* $160

Nearly white bananas. *Lilly Collection.* $160

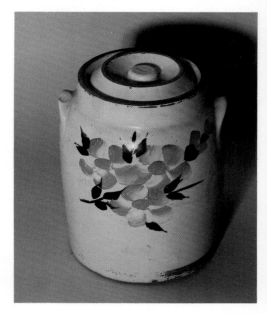

The McCoy "Asparagus" cookie jar was a 1977 to 1979 offering. It is 10-1/2 inches high, no. 267. It is unmarked but has the familiar McCoy three-bar bottom, an example of which is shown below. *Zera Collection.* $75

The "Ear of Corn" jar is 12-1/2 inches high, and was made in 1958 and 1959. It is no. 156. Mark is "McCoy/USA" in raised letters on two lines. The white is rarer and more valuable than the yellow. *Zera Collection.* Yellow $250; white $500.

McCoy "Pumpkin (jack-o-lantern)," 9 inches high. It is no. 53, marked "McCoy/USA" on two lines, and was manufactured in 1955. The green lid is harder to find than the matching orange lid (not shown). *Bosson Collection.* $550

"Fruit in Basket (bushel basket)," McCoy's no. 157 is 12 inches high and dates from 1961. It is marked "McCoy/USA" on two lines. *Zera Collection.* $80

Another McCoy corn jar, no. 275, from 1977. It is 8-3/4 inches high, and marked "272/McCoy/LCC/USA" on four lines. Also appears in white. What a shame McCoy didn't finish it in the same manner as the "Ear of Corn." $125

Called "Forbidden Fruit," this 9-1/2 inch high jar was available in 1967 and 1968. The mark is "McCoy/USA.," no. 205. The jar was also made with a red apple. *Zera Collection.* $75

"Picnic Basket," no. 191, 7-3/8 inches high, made between 1961 and 1963. The word "cookies," painted diagonally on the side, has worn off. The jar is identified by its McCoy three-bar bottom. *Zera Collection.* $80

The "Peppers" were made from 1972 to 1980. They stand 10 inches high. The McCoy number is 157. The mark of the green pepper is shown below. Mark on the yellow example is the same but with smaller lettering. *Taylor Collection.* Left $60; Right $50

Besides the way it is shown here, the "Strawberry Basket" was also made with the entire top red with the exception of the finial, which was green. It is no. 223, 8-1/2 inches high, and dates from 1978. This example is unmarked. Nichols shows it being marked "McCoy/USA/LCC" on three lines. *Zera Collection.* $70

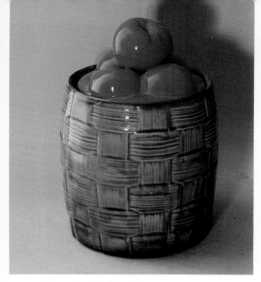

Unmarked basket of tomatoes, late vintage, 9-1/4 inches high. *Taylor Collection.* $80

The basket of eggs is 9-1/2 inches high, marked as above "0274/McCoy/LCC/USA" on four lines. It was manufactured from 1977 to 1979. Pear, apple, and lemon tops were also made for this bottom. *Lilly Collection.* $70

The "Touring Car" was sold from 1962 to 1964. It is no. 201, and is marked "McCoy/USA" in raised letters on two lines. Height is 6-1/2 inches. *Oravitz Collection.* $140

Same bottom as above, unmarked, 10-1/2 inches high. The apples look nearly real enough to eat. *Taylor Collection.* $45

Baskets of strawberries and potatoes, both 9 inches high. Each is marked "0274/McCoy/LCC/USA" on four lines. The potato jar is no. 203, made in 1978 and 1979. The strawberry jar was made about the same time. Note that the bases are different colors. *Lilly Collection.* Left $70; Right $60

More good eating, the "Ice Cream Cone" stands 11 inches high. No. 159, the start of its production run was in 1978. Mark is "159/USA" on two lines. *Lilly Collection.* $45

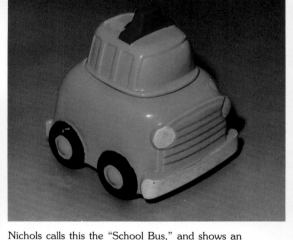

Nichols calls this the "School Bus," and shows an example with a white windshield and a yellow roof sign with the word "Bus" on it. Perhaps this one was made to be a taxi cab. It is an incredibly poor likeness of a school bus, if indeed that is what it is supposed to be. It doesn't fair much better as a cab. Regardless, it is 8-1/4 inches high, marked "352/ USA" on two lines. *Zera Collection.* $65

The "Traffic Light" is 10-1/2 inches high, no. 351, first offered in 1978. This one is marked "U.S.A./McCoy/LCC" on three lines, while another that was photographed was marked "351/USA on two lines. *Courtesy of Jazz'e Junque Shop, Chicago, Illinois.* $60

The "Engine" is no. 207, offered between 1962 and 1964. It stands 8-1/2 inches high. The mark is "McCoy/USA" on two lines. *Zera Collection.* $200

"Engine" in light yellow. It looks like the lid was originally red. *Zera Collection.* $225

The same "Engine" with a black lid. *Bosson Collection.* $225

The "Tugboat," a 1985 creation. The name on side is "SS Cookie." It is no. 354, marked "354/USA," and stands 7-1/2 inches high. *Lilly Collection.* $50

Fairly recent, the "Hot Air Balloon," no. 353, was made in 1985 and 1986. It is 9 inches high, marked "353/USA" on two lines. This jar was also sold with the horizontal bands on the balloon painted, sometimes brown, like the gondola, other times red or green. *Zera Collection.* $45

"Cookie Wagon," sometimes seen in gold, is no. 148, 7-1/4 inches high. Made in 1961 and 1962, the mark is "McCoy/USA" on two lines. *Zera Collection.* $110

The "Caboose," no. 182, is 7-1/2 inches high. Usually white with a red roof and yellow trim, the 1961 offering is rarely found in red. The mark is "McCoy/USA." *Zera Collection.* $200

"Barnum's Animals." The top of this jar is hand decorated while the front is a transfer. It is 11-1/2 inches high. The number is included in the mark, "152/USA" on two lines. The jar was made in 1972 and 1973. *Zera Collection.* $300

The same jar as "Barnum's Animals" but undecorated, which detracts from its value. *Courtesy of Jazz'e Junque Shop, Chicago, Illinois.* $90

McCoy "Globe," 1960 vintage. Height is 10 inches, mark is "McCoy/USA" on two lines. It is no. 173 in the McCoy line. *Zera Collection.* $400

"Spaceship (Friendship 7)" from 1962 and 1963. McCoy's no. 204, it is 11-1/2 inches high and can be identified by its three-bar bottom, which is shown below. *Zera Collection.* $225

"Astronauts," 11 inches high, marked "USA" in raised letters. Made in 1963, Nichols assigned it no. 226. *Bosson Collection.* $1000

The "Cookie House," no. 151, marked "McCoy/USA" on two lines. The height is 8 inches. It was marketed between 1958 and 1960. *Zera Collection.* $100

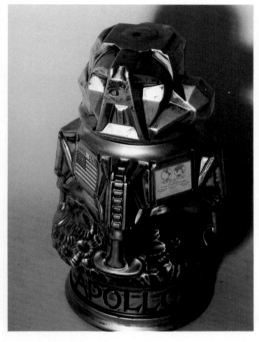

"Apollo" was made in 1970 and 1971. It is 13 inches high. McCoy number is 260, and the mark is "260/(bull's-eye)©/USA" on three lines. Carefully note the two stickers on the front. It is often sold without them. To those not familiar, it appears complete without them. *Bosson Collection.* W/Stickers $1150; W/O Stickers $900

"Frontier Family," no. 213, made between 1964 and 1971. Also came with an eagle finial. The jar is 9-1/2 inches high, and has the McCoy three-bar bottom. *Zera Collection.* $55

"Cookie Cabin," made from 1956 through 1960. This is the plain version. Others, as shown below, say "Cookie Cabin," while still others have only the word "Cookies." The jar is 7 inches high, and its number is included in its mark, "McCoy/USA/136" on three lines. *Zera Collection.* $100

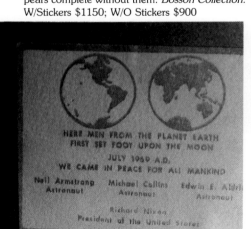

Close-up of sticker on "Apollo."

Reverse of "Frontier Family."

This jar varies from the previous one, not in one way, but in two—the inclusion of the words "Cookie Cabin" and the mark "McCoy/U.S.A./100" on three lines. *Oravitz Collection.* $100

"Cookie Bank," dating from 1961, really is a bank in addition to being a cookie jar. Standing 6-1/2 inches high, no. 192 is marked "McCoy/USA" on two lines. *Zera Collection.* $175

Reverse of "Cookie Bank" showing the coin slot in roof.

The lid of this "Red Barn" has small lugs at all four corners to prevent it from falling off. It is no. 218, made in 1963. The height is 10-1/2 inches, and the mark is "McCoy/USA." *Lilly Collection.* $350

McCoy "House," 11-1/2 inches high, no. 161. Also made with a blue roof. Some are marked "161/McCoy" on two lines, while others are unmarked. Made in late 1980s. *Bosson Collection.* $200 each

The unmarked "Dutch Treat" barn is McCoy's no. 847. It was made between 1968 and 1973, and is 13 inches high. Some examples were made with a much heavier coating of the black antiquing. *Zera Collection.* $60

The "Windmill" looks like a married piece, but it is not. Nearly all of them were decorated with non-matching blues, for an unknown reason. This jar stands 11 inches high, is no. 187, and was made in 1961. It is marked "McCoy/USA" on two lines. *Zera Collection.* $90

The "Teepee," a very popular McCoy jar, comes in two different styles. This one has a straight lid. The other example shown has a slanted lid, meaning it is cut diagonally. The slanted lid model sells for a little more. The teepee was made from 1956 to 1959, is 11-1/4 inches high, and has its number incorporated into its mark, "McCoy/USA/137" on three lines. *Zera Collection.* $400

"Slant Top Teepee" with the same mark as above. *Bosson Collection.* $500

The "Wishing Well," 9-1/2 inches high, was made between 1961 and 1970. It is no. 180, and marked "McCoy/U.S.A." on two lines. *Oravitz Collection.* $40

Another rendition of the black "Pot Belly Stove" featuring additional gold trim and a fire. This one is marked "McCoy/USA" on two lines. *Zera Collection.* $45

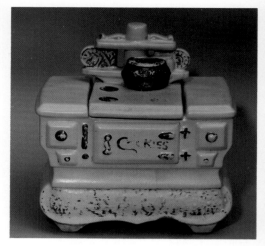

White version of the "Cookstove." *Courtesy of Claude and Edna Mae Smith.* $40

The more you look at the "Colonial Fireplace," no. 209, the more detail you see. The 9-1/2 inch jar was made in 1967 and 1968. The mark is "USA" in raised letters. *Zera Collection.* $110

The "Cookstove" is 10 inches high, marked "McCoy/USA" on two lines. Produced between 1961 and 1969, it is no. 190. *Courtesy of Claude and Edna Mae Smith.* $40

The "Cookie Churn," first made in 1977, is 10 inches high. It is no. 266, and has the McCoy three-bar bottom. *Zera Collection.* $30

This jar, no. 236, the "Pot Belly Stove," was originally manufactured from 1963 to 1972, again in 1978, and a third time in 1983. The height is 10 inches. The example on the left is marked "USA," the one on the right "McCoy/USA" on two lines. *Zera Collection.* $45 each

McCoy "Old Churn," 11-1/2 inches high. Made in 1961, it also has the McCoy three-bar bottom. Nichols assigned it no. 164. Though very similar to the previous jar, this jar's short production run and to a lesser degree its age give it a value several times that of the later model. *Bosson Collection.* $250

45

The "Coffee grinder," 1961 to 1968. Standing 10 inches high, it is marked "McCoy/USA" on two lines. The jar is no. 179. *Courtesy of Vicki Nitecki and Irene Mychul.* $40

McCoy "Kettle," no. 188, 9-1/2 inches high. Marked "McCoy/USA" on two lines, this jar was made from 1961 to 1967. Nichols shows one with flowers on it. *Lilly Collection.* $30

"Kookie Kettle," no. 171. This was made from 1960 to 1977. It stands 12-1/2 inches to the top of the handle and the mark is "McCoy/USA" on two lines. It has also been seen in white. *Courtesy of Claude and Edna Mae Smith.* $30

According to Nichols, McCoy called this jar "Aladdin." It is 9-3/4 inches high, no. 244, and was made in 1965. The mark is "McCoy/U.S.A." *Zera Collection.* $50

The "Cookie Pot" is 12 inches high, no. 220 in the McCoy line. It is also seen in light blue and with various decals. The jar was made from 1964 to 1974. The mark is "McCoy/U.S.A." in raised letters on two lines. *Courtesy of Jazz'e Junque Shop, Chicago, Illinois.* $50

The "Tea Kettle" is 7 inches high. No. 185, it was made in 1974, and is marked "McCoy/USA" on two lines. *Zera Collection.* $40

The company titled this cookie jar "Chuck Wagon," apparently because it is the type of coffee pot found on chuck wagons. The height of the pottery is 10-3/4 inches. McCoy's no. 206, these jars were not marked. They were made in 1974 and 1975. *Bosson Collection.* $110 each

The "Coffee Mug" is 9-1/4 inches high with a three-bar bottom. It is McCoy's no. 232, made from 1963 to 1966. *Lilly Collection.* $60

This is the "Cookie Kettle," no. 243. Made from 1965 to 1968, it is unmarked but has the McCoy three-bar bottom. Most of the gold lettering has worn off on this one. *Lilly Collection.* $50

Called the "Nibble Kettle," and often shown with title in gold lettering on the front, this jar is marked "McCoy/USA" on two lines. It is 8 inches high not including the handle. Nichols assigned it no. 167, date is unknown. *Zera Collection.* $40

"Gay Time Pitcher," made in 1974. McCoy no. 184, it is 9-1/2 inches high. The mark is "McCoy/USA" on two lines. *Bosson Collection.* $65 each

The "Jewel Box (cookie box)," no. 215, is 9-1/4 inches high, marked "USA," and was made in 1963. *Zera Collection.* $130

McCoy's "Little Red Bean Pot" is 8 inches high, not including the wire handle. No. 259, the jar is marked "McCoy/USA" impressed on two lines. It was made in 1971. This example is incomplete, it should have a coil grip. *Lilly Collection.* $40

Here is McCoy's "Gypsy Pot," which was also finished in white. The jar is 7 inches high not including the handle, and dates from 1975. Although not marked, it is McCoy's no. 7056. *Zera Collection.* $35

The "Early American Chest (chiffonier)" was made from 1965 to 1968. The mark is shown below. No. 245, the jar is 11-1/2 inches high. *Zera Collection.* $100

McCoy "Grandfather Clock," 12-1/4 inches high, no. 203. It was made between 1962 and 1964. In addition to having a McCoy three-bar bottom, "U.S.A." is impressed on the back. *Courtesy of Jazz'e Junque Shop, Chicago, Illinois.* $95

This is called "Time for Cookies" because "Time for" is written directly above the word cookies, although you probably can't make it out on either of these two examples. It is easy to read on other models that have gold lettering, gold hands, and gold numerals. No. 848, it is 13-1/2 inches high, and was made from 1968 to 1973. It has no mark but it does have the McCoy three-bar bottom. *Oravitz Collection.* $50

Here's a jar that creates a certain amount of confusion due to Regal China having also made a Quaker Oats jar. This one, measuring 10 inches high, is McCoy's no. 208. It was made in 1970, and is marked "USA." (For a side-by-side comparison of this jar and its Regal counterpart, see Chapter 16). *Bosson Collection.* $900

Similar to "Time for Cookies," but antiqued, and numerals in gold, much of this has worn off. *Zera Collection.* $50

"Pirate's Chest," no. 252, 1970. This jar is 9 inches high, has the McCoy bull's-eye mark with "252" above, "USA" below. *Zera Collection.* $250

On the left is the "Coke Can," no. 1003, on the right the "Coke Jug," no. 1004. Can is 10-3/4 inches high, jug 9-3/4 inches high. Both have "McCoy" impressed in their bottoms. Year of production was 1986. *Oravitz Collection.* Left $150; Right $125

"Keebler Cookie Jar," no. 350, made by McCoy in 1986, 1987, and possibly later. It stands 9-1/2 inches high. Also made by Haeger Potteries. Although the sizes are different, the best way to tell the difference is that the Haeger jar displays a molded, hand-painted elf, while McCoy's elf is a decal applied to a flat surface. There is a side-by-side comparison in Chapter 21. *Lilly Collection.* $65

"Cookie Jug," no. 144, made from 1958 through 1970. The first of several McCoy cookie jar jugs, it is unmarked but has the three-bar bottom. That is an actual cork in the top. This example is 9-1/2 inches high, was also made in another size. Sometimes these jars have brown lettering. *Lilly Collection.* $40

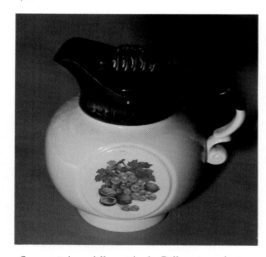

The "Pitcher (blue willow)" was available from 1973 to 1975. The jar has a McCoy bull's-eye mark, and is 9-1/8 inches high. It is no. 202. *Zera Collection.* $70

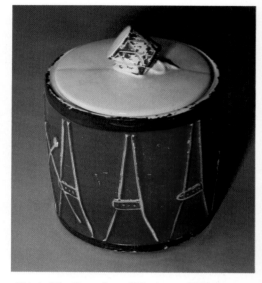

"Tilt Pitcher" in blue. *Oravitz Collection.* $35

This "Cookie Jug" made its debut in 1971, and lasted through 1978. It is no. 145, and stands 11-1/4 inches high. It has a McCoy three-bar bottom, and was also made in brown and white. *Zera Collection.* $30

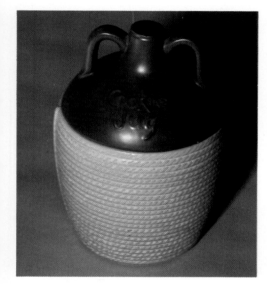

Same pitcher, different look. Different mark, too: "202/McCoy/LCC/USA" on four lines. *Lilly Collection.* $20

This is "The Drum," no. 170, vintage 1960. It is 9-1/2 inches high, has "McCoy/USA" in raised letters. *Zera Collection.* $90

"Cookie Jug" with two handles and rope bottom. The McCoy number is 240. It was made from 1965 to 1968, is 9-3/4 inches high, marked "McCoy/USA" on two lines in raised letters. *Lilly Collection.* $55

McCoy "Tilt Pitcher," an unmarked offering from 1939. No. 6, it is 8-1/4 inches high. This jar was finished in an assortment of colors such as yellow, green, black, and the blue shown below. *Oravitz Collection.* $35

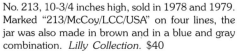

No. 213, 10-3/4 inches high, sold in 1978 and 1979. Marked "213/McCoy/LCC/USA" on four lines, the jar was also made in brown and in a blue and gray combination. *Lilly Collection.* $40

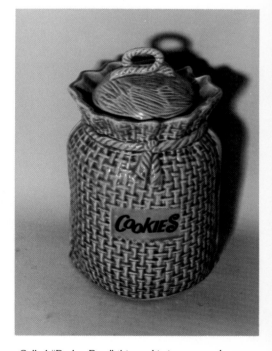

Called "Burlap Bag," this cookie jar was made from 1973 to 1977. In 1972, it was produced with a bird finial. This one is 11-1/2 inches high, and the top with a bird finial is slightly higher. The number is part of mark, "158/U.S.A." impressed on two lines. *Courtesy of Jazz'e Junque Shop, Chicago, Illinois.* $50

The "Barrel" cookie jar on the left is 10 inches high, the one on the right 8-3/4 inches high. Both have three-bar bottoms. No. 147, it was produced from 1958 to 1968. *Lilly Collection.* $30 each

"Lunch Bucket," no. 357, first made in 1978, continued into 1980s. It is 7 inches high. The jar on the left is unmarked, and the jar on the right is marked "357/U.S.A." on two lines. *Lilly Collection.* $75 each

This "Barrel" replaced the one pictured above in 1969, was made through 1972. No. 146, it stands 12 inches high. It is marked with the McCoy bull's-eye mark with "©" next to it, "146" above, and "USA" below. *Lilly Collection.* $35

"Liberty Bell," from 1975. The height is 7-3/4 inches, and the mark is "McCoy/LCC/USA" on three lines. Nichols assigned it no. 264. *Lilly Collection.* $65

"Fortune Cookie (Chinese lantern)" is 9-1/2 inches high, and was made from 1965 to 1968. McCoy no. 242, it is marked "McCoy/USA" in raised letters on two lines. It also came in other colors. *Zera Collection.* $65

"Cookie Bell," 9-1/2 inches high, McCoy three-bar bottom. No. 231, its years of manufacture were 1963 through 1966. *Courtesy of Jazz'e Junque Shop, Chicago, Illinois.* $45

The "Garbage Can" came out in 1978, and sold until 1987. It is no. 356, 9 inches high, marked "USA/356" on two lines. *Zera Collection.* $55

This plain Jane is McCoy's no. 1, called the "Ball Shape," and made sometime prior to 1940. The unmarked jar is 7-3/4 inches high, was glazed in different colors including a darker brown, light blue, maroon, and green. *Courtesy of Charles Kidd.* $30

The "Hobnail Pattern" jar, no. 15, is 8 inches high. Circa 1940, this model was also made in several different colors. Many examples sport an angled finial instead of the rectangular finial that this one has. The jar is not marked. *Zera Collection.* $25

Made from 1969 to 1979, the "Round Canister" is no. 7024, 8-1/2 inches high. The mark is "U.S.A." impressed. Besides the brown drip glaze, it was made with a yellow glaze, and also with a cream bottom and very dark top. *Zera Collection.* $25

Marked "1420L/McCoy/LCC/U.S.A." on four lines, this jar is 8 inches high. It was probably made around 1979. *Courtesy of Jazz'e Junque Shop, Chicago, Illinois.* $35

"Round Ball Shape," no. 7. Both jars are 7-1/2 inches high. These jars, with the angled finials, date from 1939 to 1944. The "Round Ball Shape" was offered again in 1948, 1950, and 1952 in similar colors but with rectangular finials. *Bosson Collection.* $50 each

Called simply "Canister," this jar is McCoy's no. 131, 9 inches high. The example on the left is marked "USA," while the example on the right shows "McCoy/LCC/USA" on three lines. Both jars have rubber gaskets similar to canning jar seals in their lids. This same basic shape was finished with a wide variety of decals. On some lids the company replaced the knob finial with a disc about 3 inches wide by 1-1/2 inches high. *Lilly Collection.* $25 each

"Round Ball Shape" in green. *Oravitz Collection.* $50

"Canister Jar" with brown drip glaze. The height is 10 inches, and the mark is "133/USA" on two lines. Nichols shows it as no. 7083, marked "7083/LCC USA/McCoy" on three lines enclosed in a circle. It was made in 1976 and 1977. *Lilly Collection.* $25

Actually a bean pot but collected as a cookie jar, this piece is 6-1/2 inches high. It is marked by an impressed "McCoy." The length of time the jar was made is unknown, but it was offered in McCoy's 1947 catalog. *Lilly Collection.* $35

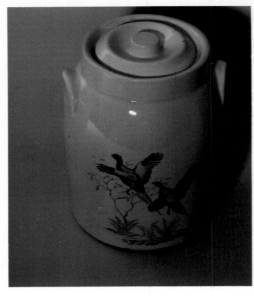

This old crock jar (1939 to 1944) doesn't have a name. It is made of yellowware, is 9-3/4 inches high, and is unmarked. It is McCoy's no. 3. Chances are good this one was repainted. It comes in several colors. *Zera Collection.* $35

Here is a bit of nostalgia put out by McCoy. The height is 8-1/2 inches, the year is unknown, and the mark is shown. *Courtesy of Betty Carson.* $45

Same jar and mark, but with attractive pheasant decal. *Coughenour Collection.* $50

Old milk can shape in green, 9-3/4 inches high. *Oravitz Collection.* $35

Mark of tan glazed reproduction crock.

More of the same, everything as above. *Bosson Collection.* $50

Same jar as above in gray. *Courtesy of Jazz'e Junque Shop, Chicago, Illinois.* $35

On the left is "Dutch Girl (round shape)," 7-1/2 inches high, on the right is "Dutch Boy," 9-1/2 inches high. The boy, no. 24, was made in 1946. The girl, no. 25, was made one year later. Both are marked "McCoy" in raised letters. *Zera Collection.* Left $50; Right $70

McCoy made cylinder jars like these from 1946 to 1954, and again beginning in 1961. The one on the left is 9-1/2 inches high, and is marked "McCoy/USA" impressed on two lines. The jar on the right is slightly more than 1/4 of an inch taller, and obviously bigger around. It is marked "McCoy" in raised letters. *Oravitz Collection.* $35 each

Two more cylinders, 9-1/2 inches high, both marked "McCoy/USA." *Zera Collection.* $35 each

This jar is 9-3/4 inches high, marked "McCoy" in raised letters. *Zera Collection.* $45

Cylinder with peach cobbler recipe decal, made 1983 or later. The jar is 9-1/2 inches high, and marked "McCoy/USA." *Lilly Collection.* $40

Yellow glaze with flower decal, 9-1/2 inches high, marked "McCoy/USA" on two lines in raised letters. *Lilly Collection.* $35

"Cylinder with Poinsettia," 9-3/4 inches high, marked "McCoy" in raised letters on bottom. *Courtesy of Allan and Michelle Naylor.* $35

Close-up of peach cobbler cylinder jar showing 1983 date at bottom.

This jar is 9-1/2 inches high. Its impressed mark is "USA" with the curved tail at the right bottom of the "U," typical of many McCoy "USA" marks. It also has the McCoy cylinder lid. *Zera Collection.* $45

"Gingerbread Boy" is 10-1/4 inches high, marked "USA" in raised letters. The jar, no. 158, was made in 1961. *Zera Collection.* $50

The "Bugs Bunny" cylinder jar is one of three jars made in the early 1970s with cartoon character transfers. This one was offered in 1971 and 1972. It is 10-1/2 inches high, no. 223. In addition to the McCoy three-bar bottom, all the jars are marked with a "McCoy/USA" inkstamp shown below. *Zera Collection.* $150

A cylinder shape referred to as "Modern," this jar was made in different color glazes. No. 254, it sold from 1970 through 1974. The height is 11 inches. Its mark, the McCoy bull's-eye, is shown below. The design is contact paper, which often falls off. *Bosson Collection.* $60

"Mary, Mary Quite Contrary" is the theme of this nursery characters cylinder jar, no. 225, 8-3/4 inches high. The finial is metal. It has no mark but it does have the McCoy three-bar bottom. *Lilly Collection.* $75

"Popeye," no. 222, 1971 and 1972. The third jar, "Yosemite Sam," appears in Chapter 2. *Zera Collection.* $150

"Modern" cylinder with darker glaze. This is how they are usually seen—minus the contact paper. The size and mark are the same as above. *Zera Collection.* $50

Three more as above: "Humpty Dumpty," "Baa Baa Black Sheep," and "Little Miss Muffet." Also in the set but not shown are "Little Boy Blue" and "Little Bo Peep." *Oravitz Collection.* $75 each

McCoy "Milk Can (Antique Dutchland)" is 9-3/4 inches high, marked "USA." Dating from 1974, it is no. 190. *Zera Collection.* $50

"Milk Can with Brown Drip Glaze," no. 7019, was made from 1972 to 1977. It is 10 inches high, has '76 emblem on its reverse as shown below. Its mark, shown at the end of the chapter, includes the Lancaster Colony Corporation logo. Note the thinner lid and narrower handle than in the following example, the "Early American Milk Can," no. 154. *Zera Collection.* $40

Reverse of milk can with brown drip glaze. The riveted seam is a nice detail.

"Early American Milk Can," no. 154, made from 1972 to 1974, is marked "USA/154" on two lines. It is 10-5/8 inches high. It was also made with the can silver, the Liberty bell gold, and the flags red, white, and blue. *Zera Collection.* $45

"Spirit of '76 Milk Can," no. 333. It is 9-3/4 inches high, and was sold from 1973 to 1975. The mark is "9/U.S.A." impressed on two lines, plus printed information about the eagle, which is shown below. In 1973, Avon bought a large quantity of these jars, along with bean pots and pitchers of the same design, packed them in Avon boxes and gave them as prizes during sales campaigns. *Zera Collection.* $50

Inkstamp on bottom of "Early American Milk Can."

Another style of milk can, this one without handles, was made in 1978, and again from 1980 through 1985. It is McCoy's no. 253, and is 12 inches high. Mark is "254/McCoy/LCC/USA" on four lines. *Lilly Collection.* $50

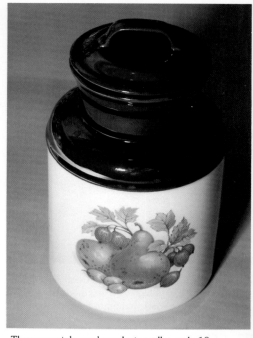

The same style as above but smaller, only 10-1/4 inches high. This one was made in 1975 and 1976. Mark is "253/USA." Both these jars have rubber seals in their lids. *Lilly Collection.* $50

Another descriptive name, "Square Jar." No. 30, it was made in 1947, stands 8 inches high, and is not marked. *Zera Collection.* $50

This hexagon jar was made from 1947 to 1949. It is 9 inches high, and is marked "McCoy." The company referred to it as both no. 31 and no. 32. *Oravitz Collection.* $50

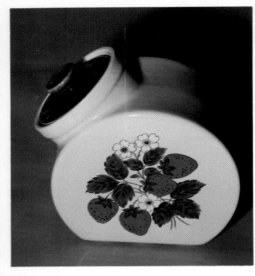

McCoy called this a "Tilt Cookie/Candy Jar." No. 268, it is 8-1/2 inches high, and was made from 1977 to 1980. It has no mark, but has a three-bar bottom. *Lilly Collection.* $40

Called "Panel," this jar is no. 1123, 8 inches high, and was made in 1985. It also comes with a white top sporting a small finial. Mark is "1123/USA" on two lines. *Bosson Collection.* $35

Probably part of a canister set instead of a cookie jar, this was made in 1978 and 1979. It stands 7-1/2 inches high. The mark is "214/McCoy/LCC/USA" on four lines. *Lilly Collection.* $25

Same as above but with a different decal. *Lilly Collection.* $40

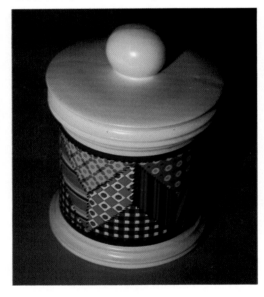

"Gingham Patchwork Cylinder," 9-1/2 inches high, made in 1975. Its interesting mark is shown at the end of the chapter. *Lilly Collection.* $35

"Lollipops" is 9-1/2 inches high and marked "McCoy/USA" on two lines, although Nichols records it as having the model number included in the mark. Perhaps the one pictured here is the result of being poured in a well-used mold on which the numerals had worn down. Or maybe the company just used a different mark, a very common occurrence not only with McCoy, but with most potteries. The jar is no. 143, produced between 1958 and 1960. *Zera Collection.* $60

Same size and mark as "Lollipops" above, but with different colors. *Lilly Collection.* $60

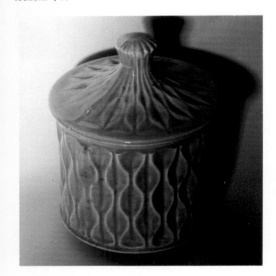

"Honeycomb Cylinder," 9-3/4 inches high, no. 250, made in 1968. The mark is unusual, "MCP/250/19©68 USA" on three lines. *Bosson Collection.* $60

"Basketweave (wide weave)," 9 inches high, no. 1109. Dates of manufacture are 1978 through 1987. It is marked "1109/USA" on two lines. It was also made in solid ivory. $30

56

The "Wedding Jar" is 10-1/2 inches high, and has 22K gold trim. The mark is "McCoy/USA" on two lines, and the vintage is 1961. *Zera Collection.* $100

The "Nabisco" jar is 9-1/4 inches high, and was made in the 1970s. Its mark is shown below. *Lilly Collection.* $100

The "Oaken Bucket" was made from 1961 to 1971. It is 9-1/2 inches high, no. 178, and has the three-bar bottom. *Zera Collection.* $30

A second jar with gold trim, this is called "Round Plain." It is a 1964 offering. The height is 8 inches. It has no mark, but it does have a three-bar bottom. *Zera Collection.* $60

Called the "American Eagle," this jar is 9-1/2 inches high, and was made in 1968 and 1969. No. 221, it is unmarked. Also glazed in a darker brown and in gray and white. *Lilly Collection.* $65

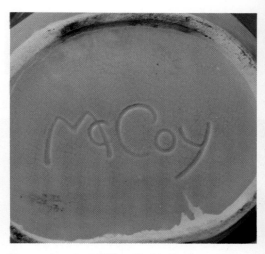

Impressed mark of "Yellow Cookie Boy."

Raised mark of "Bear with Cookies in Vest."

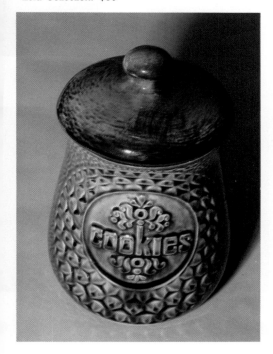

"Peanut," no. 260, 10-1/2 inches high. This jar is marked "260/McCoy/LCC/USA" on four lines. It was made in 1976 and 1977, and also comes in yellow. *Lilly Collection.* $40

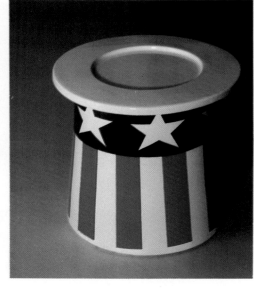

"Uncle Sam's Hat," 7 inches high, and marked appropriately "USA." This 1973 offering is McCoy's no. 200. *Zera Collection.* $1000

Mark of "Cat on Basketweave."

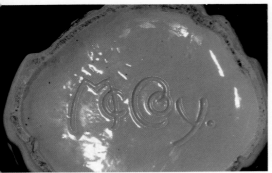
Mark of "Clown (bust)." Note period.

Mark of "W.C. Fields Head" jar.

Bull's-eye mark variation on "Happy Face (Have a Happy Day)."

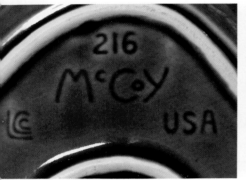
Raised mark of "Decorated Clown (Little Clown)."

Mark of McCoy "Old Apple." Note detail of dead blossom.

Mark of "Bicentennial Milk Can." Note squared letters in LCC logo.

Mark of "Koala Bear."

Mark of "Early American Chest (chiffonier)."

Three-bar bottom of "Spaceship (Friendship 7)," the telltale clue that often identifies unmarked McCoy cookie jars.

Mark of "Brown Thinking Puppy," showing Lancaster Colony Corporation logo.

Inkstamp mark of "Yosemite Sam Cylinder" jar, showing three-bar bottom.

Mark of "Gingham Patchwork Cylinder."

Mark of "Rattan Thinking Puppy," with LCC logo absent.

McCoy bull's-eye mark on "Brown Cylinder (Modern)" jar.

Mark of "Nabisco" jar.

Chapter 8
American Bisque

American Bisque appears to be second only to McCoy in the number of different cookie jars it produced, although it could actually be ahead because the total number is not known. As a general rule, American Bisque jars are more detailed than those of McCoy, both in the amount of relief design and in the way they were decorated. American Bisque made very few solid color jars. It also shied away from fruit and vegetable motifs. With few exceptions, American Bisque glazed its jars by airbrushing.

Located in Williamstown, West Virginia, the company got its start in 1919 as a maker of Kewpie Doll heads, World War I having cut the European supply line. B.E. Allen purchased the company in 1922. It remained in the Allen family until being sold in 1982. The plant closed in 1983.

When the Ohio River overflowed its banks in 1937, depositing more than 10 feet of water in the pottery, all stock, molds, and materials were lost. This may have been when American Bisque began making cookie jars, the total loss providing a perfect opportunity to abandon some of the old line and experiment with some new ones. The plant was struck by fire eight years after the flood, and had to be entirely rebuilt.

Identifying American Bisque cookie jars can be a frustrating experience. In most cases the company did not mark its jars with anything other than a simple "U.S.A.," and sometimes a number. Most of the paper labels it used have long since disappeared.

One of the easiest ways to recognize American Bisque cookie jars is by the pattern on their bottoms, as shown below. Heavy lugs, often called wedges, were generally incorporated into the bottoms of its jars. The unglazed wedges gave the jars a firm footing when being fired, and later when resting on a homemaker's kitchen counter. The same feature is also prevalent on jars American Bisque made for the Cardinal China Company, a New Jersey distributor.

Several of American Bisque's incised marks show the abbreviation, "A.B. Co." Note that several of the jars in this chapter previously credited to American Bisque were actually made by Ungemach Pottery, which operated in Roseville, Ohio from 1937 to 1984. These are "Pinky Lee," square cat jar with tail handle, fawn jar, and the puppet jars. Captions reflect the changes.

American Pottery Company
Ludowici Celadon, and Terrace Ceramics

It is impossible to adequately cover American Bisque without discussing American Pottery, Ludowici Celadon, and Terrace Ceramics at the same time. Because of interaction between the four companies, it often can't be determined which company made which jars.

The American Pottery Company stemmed from the Stoin-Lee Pottery company, of Byesville, Ohio. Byesville is a small town 70 miles east of Columbus, just south of Cambridge. Stoin-Lee incorporated in 1942. Two years later it came under the control of J. B. Lenhart, who changed the name to American Pottery Company. Lenhart then moved at least part of the operation to Marietta, Ohio, directly across the Ohio River from Williamstown, West Vir-

ginia, home of American Bisque. That's not surprising because at the same time he was running American Pottery, Lenhart was sales manager of American Bisque. To complicate matters further, Lenhart sold half his interest in American Pottery to American Bisque owner, A.N. Allen. Consequently, there is a crossover between the two companies' products. Jars normally attributed to American Bisque sometimes bear the mark of American Pottery, and vice-versa.

The jars and marks shown below seem to indicate American Pottery functioned, to a certain extent, as an arm of American Bisque. In all likelihood, American Pottery and American Bisque caught each other's overflow, one filling the orders of the other when it proved expedient. Barring cookie jars learning to talk, there will probably always be questions as to which company made which jars. (Text continued on page 75).

For a more thorough explanation you may want to consult *American Bisque-Collector's Guide With Prices,* by Mary Jane Giocomini (Schiffer 1994).

American Bisque's people cookie jars reflect some of the company's best work. This granny is 12-3/4 inches high. The jar has the letters "USA" impressed in the back. *Zera Collection.* $150

The same granny but with gold trim, a feature that generally increases the value of a jar. *Coughenour Collection.* $225

A Pennsylvania Dutch girl 11-1/4 inches high with an American Bisque bottom. The jar was also made with a yellow hat, and possibly other colors. Additionally, American Bisque made a Pennsylvania Dutch boy with a broad brim hat. *Bosson Collection.* $400

To avoid confusion, compare this American Bisque churn boy to Regal China's version in Chapter 16, which currently sells for nearly twice the price. Height is 11-3/4 inches. *Bosson Collection.* $300

Mark from the bottom of the gold trimmed granny. It's from the G.C. Shafer Pottery Company, of Zanesville, Ohio. Between 1939 and 1980, Shafer provided a gold decorating service for many potteries, American Bisque, McCoy, and Hull to name three.

Dutch boy, 13 inches high, sometimes seen in white. *Zera Collection.* $500; White $200

The umbrella kids stand 11-1/2 inches high with "USA-834" impressed in bottom. *Zera Collection.* $375

One of several clowns American Bisque produced, this jar is 11 inches high. "USA" is impressed in back at base. *Zera Collection.* $125

Same as above but with colors reversed. Probable repaint on hat, nose, and mouth. *Bosson Collection.* $125

This chef stands 11-1/4 inches high, and looks like he enjoys his work. The jar is unmarked. *Oravitz Collection.* $135

Another funny fellow, 12 inches high, unmarked. Some references say this jar is not American Bisque; however, its American Bisque bottom strongly suggests that it is. $275

A third American Bisque clown, also 12 inches high. *Bosson Collection.* $100

Compare this Davy Crockett with the one in the previous picture, and you'll know why it's best to never use generic price guides to evaluate cookie jars. In this case, a non-specific listing such as "American Bisque Davy Crockett cookie jar" could lead to a mistake costing hundreds of dollars. The jar is 11 inches high. It is not marked. *Zera Collection.* $1000

Sometimes you can date cookie jars by the characters they portray—like this 12-1/4 inch unmarked Davy Crockett,. Walt Disney and Fess Parker unveiled Davy Crockett to the American public in 1955, creating a marketing phenomenon of a caliber that hadn't been seen since the days of Shirley Temple movies. Potteries, including American Bisque, were quick to get in on the action. *Zera Collection.* $600

Obviously the same jar as above, but with one subtle difference—it was poured in a much newer mold. Look closely and you'll see much more detail on this example: the ribbing going up the left side of the hat, the indentations on the bottom of the hat, and many more. Even the ruffle is crisper. While both jars have basically the same value, this one is more desirable. *Bosson Collection.* $275

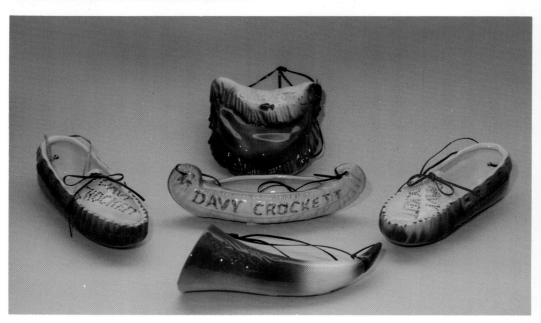

American Bisque accessories for its Davy Crockett cookie jars. All have raised areas similar to wedges on their bottoms. *Coughenour Collection.* $75-100 each

The yarn dolls are 12 inches high. Neither is marked. *Zera Collection.* $130 each

Same doll in green. *Courtesy of Jazz'e Junque Shop, Chicago, Illinois.* $130

Blue yarn doll with gold trim. *Bossom Collection* $180

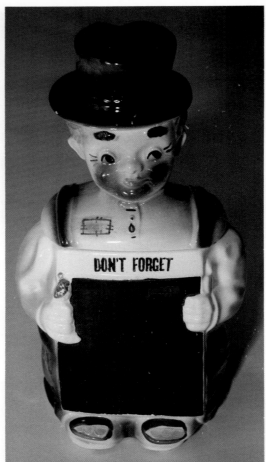

Blackboard hobo, reminiscent of the sandwich board days of the Depression but made much later. It's 14 inches high and has "U.S.A." in raised letters at base on reverse side. The blackboard the hobo is carrying can be used as a chalkboard for leaving message or reminders. *Zera Collection.* $300

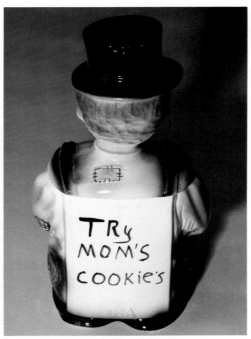

Reverse of hobo with sandwich board showing white surface and mark at bottom.

The blackboard clown is 13-3/4 inches high, marked with "Patent Pending U.S.A." ink-stamp. *Oravitz Collection.* $325

This girl with sandwich board is marked with an inkstamped "Patent Pending U.S.A." and also has "USA" at base on the reverse side. The first mark is shown. American Bisque also made a boy companion. *Courtesy of Jazz'e Junque Shop, Chicago, Illinois.* $350

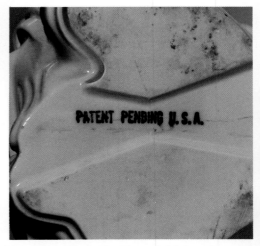

Inkstamp mark of girl with sandwich board. Note the telltale wedges.

American Bisque paper label from the blackboard clown. It was designed to represent a child's toy block. Paper labels aren't seen very often on American Bisque cookie jars.

"The Cheerleaders" is distinguished for two reasons. It is one of American Bisque's flasher face jars, and also a corner jar, triangular in shape. The corner jar idea seems like a good one, but it apparently never caught on with the public as there wasn't a lot of them made. The flasher faces themselves are made of plastic and glued in place. They show the eyes open or closed depending upon the angle from which the jar is viewed. Marked "802-USA," "The Cheerleaders" is 11 inches high. *Blumenfeld Collection.* $450

"The Cow Jumped Over the Moon" flasher stands 11 inches high, is marked "806 USA" on back at base. *Blumenfeld Collection.* $1050

This somewhat rare jar is commonly called Pinky Lee. In case you're not old enough to remember the former vaudevillian's one-half hour comedy series, which ran on NBC from 1950 to 1955, imagine Pee Wee Herman in black-and-white with a checkered sports coat and derby hat, and you'll pretty much have the picture. This jar was made by Ungemach Pottery, of Roseville, Ohio. *Bosson Collection.* $650

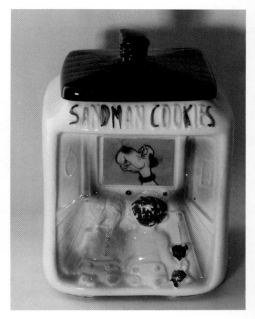

This flasher, 9-3/4 inches high, is not marked. Most, however, are marked "801/USA." *Blumenfeld Collection.* $450

Reverse of "The Cheerleaders" corner jar. These must have appealed to the company as only one surface had to be decorated.

The American Bisque majorette is a popular jar, and like the churn boy above, very similar to the one made by Regal China (Chapter 16). This jar is 11-1/4 inches high. It is not marked but has the American Bisque bottom. *Blumenfeld Collection.* $400

Another corner flasher face, this one is 10 inches high, "804/USA" impressed on two lines. In addition to the corner jars shown here, there was also one made with oak leaves on the front and a lid in the shape of an acorn cap, a corner chiffonier, and possibly others. *Oravitz Collection.* $650

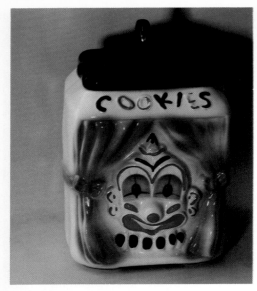

"The clown on Stage" flasher face is 10-1/4 inches high. Impressed at the base of the reverse side is a mark that appears to read "905 USA" on one line. Considering that the other flashers carry 800 series marks, in all probability that's what the mark actually is, the 8 not printed fully due to a problem with the mold. *Blumenfeld Collection.* $400

"Tortoise and the Hare" flasher face but with the face missing, which decreases the value a considerable amount. It's 9-3/4 inches high. *Bosson Collection.* $900 w/ flasher; 400 w/o

Yogi Bear with a dark sign. This variation is similar to the Brush Davy Crockett jars in Chapter 10 that have light and dark gun stocks, but it doesn't draw the same interest. *Zera Collection.* $500

With character jars such as this "Yogi Bear," it is often difficult to identify the pottery that made them because the only mark they generally carry is the name of the copyright holder, in this case, "© Hanna Barbera-1961 Productions USA" incised on one line. But identification is a snap here because of the jar's American Bisque bottom. *Courtesy of Betty and Floyd Carson.* $500

"Fred Flintstone" is 12-1/2 inches high and unmarked except for its American Bisque bottom. *Oravitz Collection.* $1000

Dino carrying Fred's golf clubs. The jar is 13-1/2 inches high, has American Bisque bottom. Other jars in the company's Flintstone series are Barney and Betty Rubble's house and Wilma sitting in a chair while talking on the telephone. All American Bisque Flintstones jars are expensive and highly prized. *Courtesy of Betty and Floyd Carson.* $1200

Popeye, 10-1/2 inches high, unmarked. The pipe is not original. *Blumenfeld Collection.* $900

Popeye's little buddy, Swee'Pea. The jar is 9-1/2 inches high. American Bisque also made a head jar of Olive Oyl, shown at a distance in Chapter 6. *Bosson Collection.* $3500

Casper, 13-1/2 inches high, unmarked.

A different rooster, this one is 12-1/2 inches high. It isn't marked. *Courtesy of Jazz'e Junque Shop, Chicago, Illinois.* $80

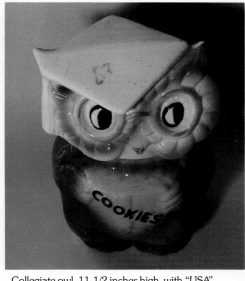

Collegiate owl, 11-1/2 inches high, with "USA" in raised letters at base. *Oravitz Collection.* $100

The "Kitten on Beehive" is 11-3/4 inches high, unmarked. It was shown in American Bisque's 1959 catalog. *Zera Collection.* $85

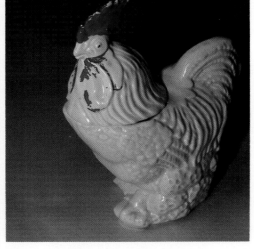

This American Bisque rooster was made in several different colors, including multi-color. Yellow is somewhat rare for the 11-1/4 inch high jar. It is unmarked except for its American Bisque bottom. *Zera Collection.* $100

Hen with chick, 9-1/4 inches high. American Bisque bottom and "USA" impressed. *Bosson Collection.* $65

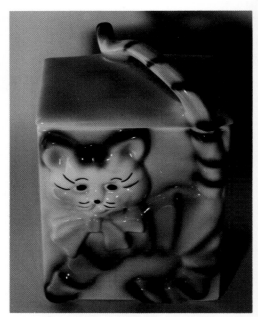

Mystery time. This rooster lacks wedges but is taller, 12 inches. Impressed in the bottom is "Marston of California" on one line. Although shot facing the opposite direction of the yellow rooster, if you compare to Westfall's and the Roerigs' pictures, you'll see this is the same jar. Marston may have been a distributor or a retailer for which American Bisque made pottery in the same manner that it did for Cardinal. Or it may have been a company that bought an American Bisque cookie jar patent, waited for a patent to expire to make the jar, or just plain ripped it off. *Courtesy of Betty and Floyd Carson.* $100

This cat jar was produced by Ungemach Pottery. The piece is 10-1/2 inches high and unmarked. *Oravitz Collection.* $200

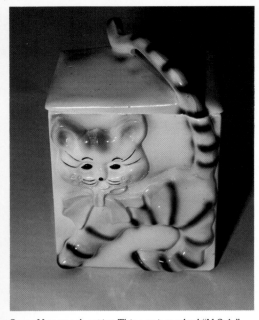

Same Ungemach cat jar. This one is marked "U.S.A." on the base. *Zera Collection.* $200

This kitty is 12 inches high. *Bosson Collection.* $90

What an appropriate place to keep snacks for the family dog. The poodle jar is 10-1/2 inches high with a "USA" mark. *Zera Collection.* $140

The "Kittens with the Ball of Yarn" jar in two sizes. The one on the left is 9-1/2 inches high, and the other is 10-1/2 inches high. While both have American Bisque bottoms, only the one on the left carries a mark, "USA" in raised letters on the back. *Oravitz Collection.* $110 each

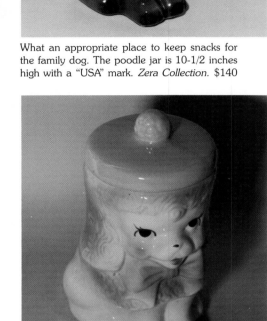

Blue poodle. It is the same size as the previous poodle with no mark. *Courtesy of Jazz'e Junque Shop, Chicago, Illinois.* $140

The larger jar in blackish green. *Bosson Collection.* $200

A puppy and a kitten on quilted bases, perhaps pillows. Each jar is 13 inches high. *Bosson Collection.* $200 each.

Another color scheme. *Courtesy of Jazz'e Junque Shop, Chicago, Illinois.* $140

This "Bear with Cookie" was made in at least two different versions: with the shirt pocket (*above*) and with the bib (*below*). It is 11-1/4 inches high and marked "USA." *Zera Collection.* $110

Bibbed version of the "Bear with Cookie." Same size as above, but unmarked. *Courtesy of Betty and Floyd Carson.* $110

This 9-inch high jar was made by Ungemach. As with Pinky Lee above, and a few other Ungemach jars, it has the U-shaped dry foot shown below. *Zera Collection.* $160

The U-shaped foot on the bottom of the deer jar. Note "USA" mark near top of picture.

The lamb with paws in pockets is just one of several similar jars. It is 11 inches high, unmarked. *Zera Collection.* $150

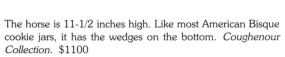

The horse is 11-1/2 inches high. Like most American Bisque cookie jars, it has the wedges on the bottom. *Coughenour Collection.* $1100

Some of the "paws in pockets" jars were made with turnabout heads, such as this pig. It's a boy on this side, a girl on the other. Note that the head is also a bank. The jar is 10-1/2 inches high, marked "USA" on the base. *Zera Collection.* $180

Reverse of the turnabout pig.

Not only does this jar have a brown ruffle, as opposed to the green ruffle above, it is also much shorter, only 8-3/4 inches. *Zera Collection.* $150

American Bisque's boy pig, 11-1/2 inches high, is a splendid example of how airbrushing can be combined with hand painting to make attractive, yet reasonably priced ceramic art. *Zera Collection.* $125

Here's a lady pig. She is 11-1/2 inches high. *Oravitz Collection.* $175

The lamb is 13 inches high with an American Bisque bottom. *Coughenour Collection.* $150

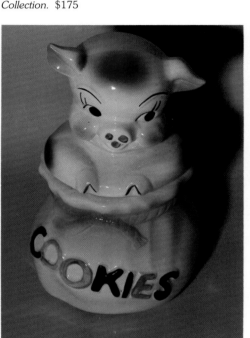

Another boy pig, but 12 inches high instead of 11-1/2 inches. Like the previous example, it has the American Bisque bottom. The difference in size is probably due to the jar being redesigned. Among the slight changes, note that there are no coverall straps on this version. *Oravitz Collection.* $175

This jar is referred to as "Pig-in-Poke" in American Bisque's 1959 advertising. It is 12-1/2 inches high, has "USA" in raised letters at rear of base. *Oravitz Collection.* $110

Rabbit, 11-3/4 inches high, with an American Bisque bottom. *Courtesy of Betty and Floyd Carson.* $250

The rabbit in hat, or "Magic Bunny" as the company called it, is 12-1/4 inches high, unmarked. *Courtesy of Jazz'e Junque Shop, Chicago, Illinois.* $110

Meet farmer pig, 13-1/2 inches high. The foreign copy that's sometimes seen lacks the American Bisque bottom and "USA" marking that this one has. *Bosson Collection.* $175

Lid to the "Magic Bunny" jar. The pieces of cork will help prevent accidental damage.

Nothing like a baseball player with a built-in bat. The elephant is marked with a "USA" impressed in its base. *Coughenour Collection.* $150

Canister-shaped cookie jars didn't hold a very high priority with American Bisque, ranking just above fruits and vegetables on the company's design ladder. This animal cookies jar is in pretty good shape for being painted over the glaze. The jar is 8-1/2 inches high. In addition to the paper label, it is marked "USA" on the back. *Zera Collection.* $40

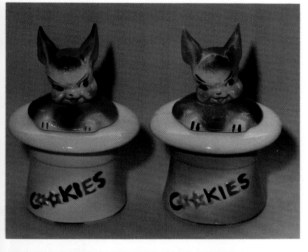

Brown rabbits in hats. Hats also show up in blue. *Oravitz Collection.* $110 each

The "Puppy in Pot" jar, showing both front and back of bottom. Puppy on the left has a star on his head. Each jar is 11-1/2 inches high. These bottoms were also made in blue and possibly other colors. *Oravitz Collection.* $85 each

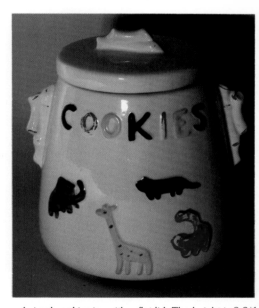

Animal cookies jar with a flat lid. The height is 8-3/4 inches, and it has "USA" impressed at the base. *Oravitz Collection.* $40

Baby elephant in two different sizes. *Left:* 11-1/2 with American Bisque, bottom. *Right:* 13-1/4 inches with a flat bottom and marked "Cookies/ USA/Jar" on three lines. These jars are sometimes found with gold trim. *Bosson Collection.* $225 each

Ring cookie jar, 8-1/2 inches high. *Oravitz Collection.* $40

This is the apple jar. It is 9 inches high. *Zera Collection.* $35

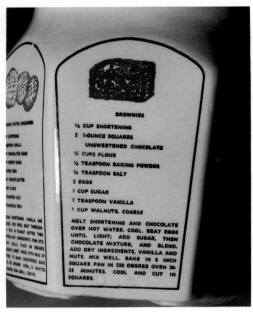

Close-up of recipe jar panel.

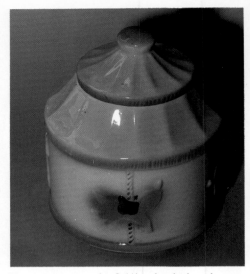

The merry-go-round is 9-1/4 inches high and is marked "USA" on its side. *Courtesy of Jazz'e Junque Shop, Chicago, Illinois.* $125

This attractive jar with its gold "Cookies" is 9-1/4 inches high. It is unmarked, but has an American Bisque bottom. A very similar jar, but with sides tapered toward the bottom, was made by Abingdon. *Oravitz Collection.* $90

Cookie barrel, 9-1/2 inches high, marked "USA." *Courtesy of Jazz'e Junque Shop, Chicago, Illinois.* $50

Jack-in-the-box, 12 inches high, with "USA" impressed in back. *Oravitz Collection.* $190

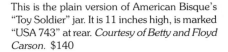

Like characters, animals, and people, objects were also a favorite at American Bisque. The train jar is 7-1/4 x 11-3/4 inches and has "USA 200" impressed. This is one of the few American Bisque jars that was completely hand decorated on top of a clear glaze. It also has gold trim. *Zera Collection.* $150

American Bisque hexagonal recipe jar. It stands 9-1/2 inches high and is marked "USA." *Zera Collection.* $100

This is the plain version of American Bisque's "Toy Soldier" jar. It is 11 inches high, is marked "USA 743" at rear. *Courtesy of Betty and Floyd Carson.* $140

The "Treasure Chest," 8-3/4 inches high. *Oravitz Collection.* $200

Fancy version of "Toy Soldier" jar. The Roerigs show another version stamped "Walt Disney Productions, copyright 1961." *Blumenfeld Collection.* $140

"Sad Iron," 11-1/2 inches high, no mark. *Courtesy of Grinder's Switch, Avon, Ohio.* $150

Bottom of the "Treasure Chest" showing diagonal variation of American Bisque wedges.

These are Ungemach Puppet jars. *Bosson Collection.* $275 each.

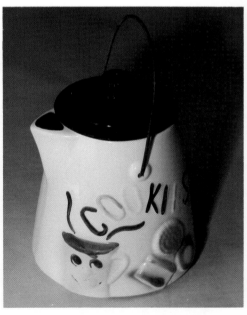

This jar is called a "Sea Bag." It is 10-1/4 inches high and has "USA" in raised letters on base. *Oravitz Collection.* $300

The "Thread Spool" is 10-3/4 inches high. *Bosson Collection.* $300

This coffee pot is 9-1/2 inches high measuring the jar only, not the handle. It's marked "USA." *Zera Collection.* $50

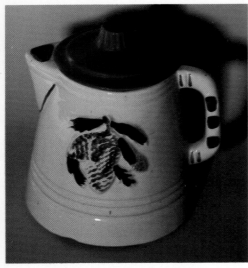

A second coffee pot, also 9-1/2 inches high. Note that the lids are of identical design. *Bosson Collection.* $50

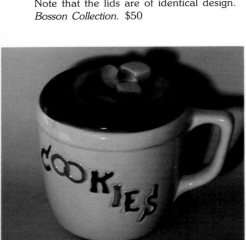

Hot chocolate mug, 9 inches high, American Bisque bottom. *Bosson Collection.* $65

The churn on the left is 10-1/2 inches high and unmarked. The one on the right is 10-3/4 inches high and is marked with an impressed "USA." Both jars have American Bisque bottoms. *Oravitz Collection.* $40 each

A water bucket, 9-3/4 inches high, with the American Bisque bottom and "USA" impressed in back. *Lilly Collection.* $200

Same design as above (check knot and other details) but larger, 11 inches high, and with a finish not on a par with American Bisque. Possibly not American Bisque. *Bosson Collection.* $200

"Pot Belly Stove," 11-1/4 inches high, no mark. *Zera Collection.* $40

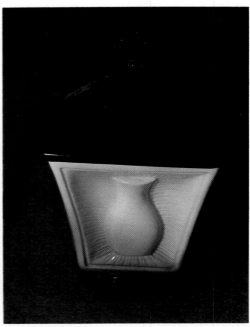

This lantern is 13 inches high, not marked. *Courtesy of Grinder's Switch, Avon, Ohio.* $225

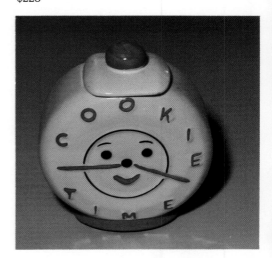

The clock is not marked. It stands 9 inches high. This is another American Bisque cookie jar that was completely hand decorated aside from the initial clear glaze. Sometimes seen with gold trim, including hands. *Zera Collection.* $100

The "Milk Wagon" is 9 inches high, unmarked. *Zera Collection.* $200

Yellow version of the "Milk wagon," pulled by a palomino. *Bosson Collection.* $200

Another four-wheeled vehicle, the "Cookie Truck" in two different sizes. *Left:* 13-1/4 inches high, marked "USA/744" on two lines on the opposite side above the running board. *Right:* 11-1/2 inches high. *Bosson Collection.* $95 each

Close-up of "Cookie Truck" mark.

Not only is the locomotive similar in shape to the cookie truck, it also has the same top. The jar is 12 inches high. *Bosson Collection.* $150

"Stern-wheeler," 8-3/4 inches high, has a "USA" mark. This jar's lid contains a bell. *Bosson Collection.* $270

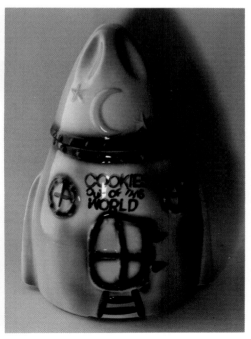

"Spaceship," 12-1/4 inches high, no mark. *Blumenfeld Collection.* $350

Here is an example of how American Bisque made jars for Cardinal. The one on the *left*, 10 inches high is impressed "USA, Cardinal" on two lines. The one on the *right*, 8 inches high, is not marked. Note that the bases of the jars are the same size. Both have American Bisque bottoms. *Oravitz Collection.* $50 each

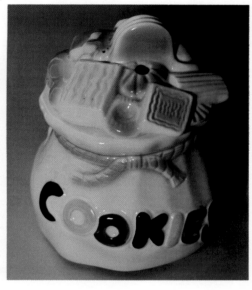

"Cookie Bag" with different bottom colors, and showing reverse view of lid. Like the one above, it is 10 inches high but is unmarked. *Courtesy of Betty and Floyd Carson.* $50

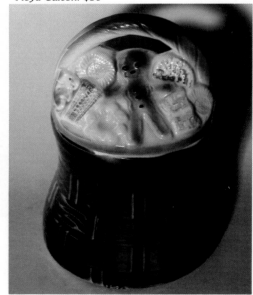

A "Cookie Basket," 11-1/4 inches high, marked "USA." The Roerigs show it with a chartreuse bottom and blue top, probably made complete in both those colors and possibly others. *Bosson Collection.* $120

The cookie feed sack is 9-1/2 inches high. *Bosson Collection.* $190

The "After School Cookies" jar was made with a bell on the lid, too. It is 10-1/2 inches high, unmarked. It is also seen with gray sides and brown roof. *Zera Collection.* $100

This saddle not only displays reversed lid colors, but also does not have a blackboard on either side. It is 12 inches high. *Coughenour Collection.* $275

Although hard to see in black, the top says "COOKIE TRAY" in raised letters. The jar is 6-3/4 inches high, marked "USA-602," and has the American Bisque bottom. *Bosson Collection.* $75

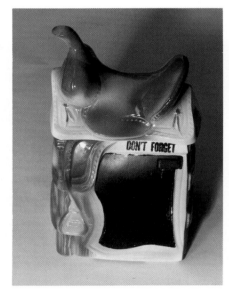

As with the sandwich board jars above, this is another message center waiting to be used. This "Saddle Blackboard" is marked "USA" on one line and "Pat Pend/USA" on two lines. The jar is 12-1/4 inches high. *Zera Collection.* $225

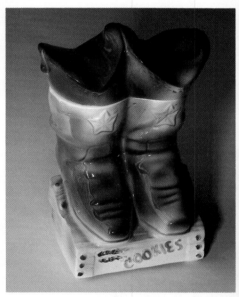

There is no mark on this cowboy boots jar. The height is 12-1/2 inches. *Zera Collection.* $200

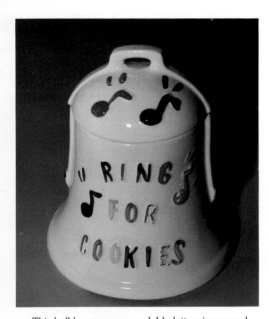

This bell has some unreadable letters impressed in its lid. The lid also contains a real bell, just the thing to foil the plans of a potential cookie thief. The jar is 10 inches high, marked "USA" on back. *Zera Collection.* $60

Reverse of "Saddle Blackboard." Note "USA" at bottom.

On the left are the modified wedges of a "Paws in Pockets" animal jar, on the right are those of the after school cookies jar.

The "Lamb with Red Suspenders," 11-1/2 inches high. Mark is "Design/ Pat. Pen. 117120/ABCO" on three lines. *Zera Collection*. $80

The only good news in this incestuous maze of free enterprise is that the American Pottery Company went out of business in 1965. The plant has since been torn down, never to befuddle cookie jar collectors again.

But there is more. some time after World War II, the Ludowici Celadon Company, of New Lexington, Ohio, peddled some, or perhaps all, of its cookie jar molds to American Bisque. This means there are certain jars that might have been made by any one of the four companies, American Bisque, American Pottery, Terrace Ceramics, or Ludowici Celadon. In case you've ever wondered why the Belmont lion smacks of American Bisque and American Pottery, it's because "Belmont" was a mark used by Ludowici Celadon. So was "Fluffy," as on the cat jar referred to above.

Ludowici Celadon began in 1902 when Celadon Terra Cotta purchased the former Imperial Brick Company, to convert it to a roofing tile operation. Four years later it was bought by a person or a company named Ludowici, and the name changed to Ludowici Celadon. (Celadon is a gray-green stoneware of Chinese origin.) When World War II shut down the construction industry the demand for roofing tile plummeted. Ludowici Celadon then explored other avenues, including cookie jars, to survive the conflict. It made Walt Disney jars including turnabouts, and other jars. The end of the war in 1945, and the construction boom that followed, allowed Ludowici Celadon to get out of the cookie jar business and back into the roofing tile business.

Looking over the jars below, it appears that after American Bisque bought Ludowici Celadon's cookie jar patents, it restyled the jars to its own liking, then produced them with a greater degree of sophistication than the original maker had.

Now let's bring Ludowici Celadon into this crossover mess. This 13-1/4 inch high jar has "Fluffy" incised in script on the bottom, a mark known to have been used by Ludowici Celadon. *Courtesy of Jazz'e Junque Shop, Chicago, Illinois*. $50

Scale "Fluffy" down to 12 inches and it turns into a cat with indented spots, a jar commonly credited to American Bisque and American Pottery. Some, in fact, are known to carry the American Pottery mark. This jar, probably a repaint, is marked "USA/ 131A" on two lines. *Bosson Collection*. $70

75

The "Animals with Red Suspenders" series is an example of the crossover between the American Bisque and American Pottery Company. This "Pig with Red Suspenders" is 11-1/4 inches high. Its mark, shown below, clearly indicates it was made by American Bisque. *Zera Collection.* $80

Here is a series mate, the "Cow" (or bull if you prefer) "with Red Suspenders." Standing 11-1/4 inches high, its mark shows it was made by American Pottery Company. Included in the series but not shown is the "Lamb with Red Suspenders." *Zera Collection.* $80

Mark of "Pig with Red Suspenders." A bit dark, it reads "Design/Patent/132170/ABCO" on four lines.

Mark of the "Cow with Red Suspenders." It reads "Design/Patent/Applied/APCO" on four lines.

The bear with eyes closed on the left is American Bisque all the way—style fits and the jar has wedges. The one on the right has indented spots, no wedges, and is marked similar to the cat with indented spots, "USA/130" on two lines. The left jar is 10-3/4 inches high, and the right jar is 12 inches high, probably repainted. Considering that "Fluffy" was scaled down to make the cat with indented spots, it is possible that this could be a mold American Bisque bought from Ludowici Celadon, immediately made some jars with it, then trimmed it to a smaller size and finished it in much the same manner as most of American Bisque's other jars. *Bosson Collection*. $75 each

Here is the "Bear with Eyes Open." It is unmarked, 11-3/4 inches high, and appears to have the same bottom as the two jars above. *Oravitz Collection*. $75

Teddy bear with indented spots, 12-1/4 inches high. The mark is "USA/123A" on two lines. *Bosson Collection*. $90

Pigs with indented spots, each 11-1/2 inches high, no marks. Matching bank is 5 inches high. All three have probably been repainted. American Bisque or American Pottery? *Bosson Collection*. Cookie jars $140 each; Bank $80

Pig with indented clover, 11-1/2 inches high and unmarked. Matching salt and pepper shakers are 4-1/4 inches high. While this is basically the same jar as the pig with indented spots, the airbrushing is characteristic of American Bisque. *Bosson Collection*. Cookie jar $150; Salt & Pepper Shakers $50

"Bear with Eyes Open," glazed but not painted. The same size, with no mark. *Zera Collection*. $75

77

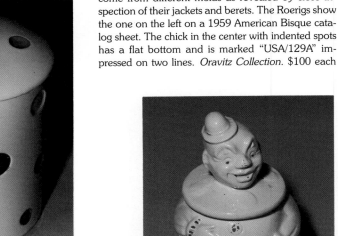

Another pig with indented clover, and a jar with a similar top but having a different bottom. Pig with indented clover is 11-1/2 inches high. Neither of these jars is marked. *Oravitz Collection.* Left $125; right $125

Here is an interesting trio, all 12-1/4 inches high. The chicks on the right and left both have wedges, but come from different molds as revealed by close inspection of their jackets and berets. The Roerigs show the one on the left on a 1959 American Bisque catalog sheet. The chick in the center with indented spots has a flat bottom and is marked "USA/129A" impressed on two lines. *Oravitz Collection.* $100 each

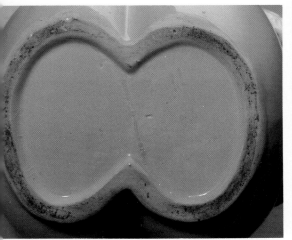

The bottom of pig on the right in above photo. The bottom of pig on the left matches it.

Canister with indented spots. It is 9 inches high, marked "Pat Applied For/USA" impressed on two lines. $50

This clown is 8-1/2 inches high, marked "Design/Patent/Applied/APCO" impressed on four lines. *Zera Collection.* $60

The angle of the picture belies the difference in size between these two jars. The one on the left is 11-1/2 inches high, the one on the right 13 inches high. The brown jar looks like it might have been finished by an amateur. Both jars have wedges, as shown. This is another design that American Bisque apparently reduced in size, which makes it likely that there may be some white jars floating around in the larger size. *Oravitz Collection.* $75 each.

There is no doubt about this 8-3/4 inch high bear. Its mark, shown below, identifies it as a product of American Pottery Company. *Zera Collection.* $85

APCO mark of above bear.

The glazed wedges on the brown jar support the theory that it was finished by an amateur. There is no advantage to glazing them. It seems unlikely a profit-minded company would do so considering the added time and material it would have required.

"Horseshoes" and "Spots." The bases are the same, but the lids are different. The clown with indented spots appears earlier in the chapter with a ruffle added and American Bisque airbrushing. *Left*: 11-1/4 inches high with an unreadable mark. *Right*: 11-1/2 inches high, "USA" impressed. *Oravitz Collection.* $80 each

Mickey-Minnie turnabout with original paint. It is 13-1/2 inches high, marked "Patented/Turnabout/4 in 1/Mickey and Minnie/Walt Disney" on five lines. Both Ludowici Celadon and American Pottery use marks that include the word "turnabout." *Zera Collection.* $180

Same turnabout but repainted. *Zera Collection.* $180

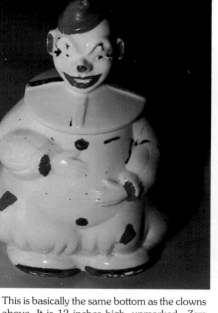

This is basically the same bottom as the clowns above. It is 12 inches high, unmarked. *Zera Collection.* $60

Reverse of Mickey-Minnie turnabout.

Reverse of repainted turnabout.

This repainted Dumbo turnabout jar is 14 inches high. Here again, it might have been made by Ludowici Celadon or American Bisque since Ludowici Celadon sold its turnabout molds to American Bisque. Or it might have been made by American Pottery Company because of its ties to American Bisque. In any event, it was probably marketed through the Leeds China Company, a Chicago-based distributor. *Oravitz Collection.* $150

Both sides of a turnabout bear. Parts appear to be repainted. It is 12-1/2 inches high, marked "Turnabout/the four in one" on two lines. An identical jar that was photographed had a mark that read "Patent Applied/Turnabout/The 4 in 1/USA" on four lines. Ludowici Celadon, American Pottery, or American Bisque? *Zera Collection.* $75 each

This Piece of Pottery is **decorated with lacquers** by hand. These lacquers with ordinary usage will last for a considerable period of time. When washing is necessary, **tepid water and a mild soap should be used.** Boiling water, strong alkalies and scouring abrasives should not be used.

Original instructions packed in Mickey-Minnie turnabout jars.

Reverse of the turnabout Dumbo. The jar is 14 inches high.

This 13-inch high Dutch girl is marked "Pat Des/ 138597/USA" on three lines. *Zera Collection.* $75

The mate to the Dutch girl, 13-1/4 inches high. *Courtesy of Jazz'e Junque Shop, Chicago, Illinois.* $75

On the right is the same Dumbo as above with what's left of the original paint. It is marked "Patented/Turnabout 4 in 1/Dumbo/ ©Walt Disney" on four lines. On the left is a Dumbo-Pluto turnabout, 13-1/2 inches high. It is marked "Dumbo Pluto/USA/5231/ ©Walt Disney" on four lines. It is the same story as above—American Bisque, American Pottery, or Ludowici Celadon? *Courtesy of Jazz'e Junque Shop, Chicago, Illinois.* $150 each

The same Dutch girl in different colors. *Courtesy of Jazz'e Junque Shop, Chicago, Illinois.* $75

The jar on the left is 12 inches high. "Royal Ware" is impressed in the bottom. The jar on the right is 10-1/2 inches high with no mark. Both appear to be repainted. This is the same bear shown with American Bisque airbrushing earlier in the chapter. At some point the design was changed to eliminate the bib and add a shirt pocket, which is how it appears in the company's 1959 catalog. *Oravitz Collection.* $60 each

Reverse of the above turnabout jars.

This one is 11-1/4 inches high, also appears to be repainted, and has a gold cookie. The mark is "Royal Ware." *Zera Collection.* $60

80

Charcoal Royal Ware bear with cookie, 12-1/2 inches high. *Bosson Collection.* $60

This unmarked basket jar is 11-3/4 inches high. *Oravitz Collection.* $75

According to the Roerigs, these unmarked basket jars have been identified as early American Bisque. They are undoubtedly early something, as they are very heavy and much more crudely made than the photos show. They are, in fact, about what you would expect from a roofing tile company that decided to take a stab at making cookie jars. The puppy is 13 inches high, the kitty 12 inches. Both are marked "Pat./Pen." on two lines. *Oravitz Collection.* $75

81

The American Bisque-Robinson Ransbottom Controversy

Probably the greatest revelation for cookie jar collectors since cookie jar collecting began came in 1990 with the publication of *The Collector's Encyclopedia of Cookie Jars,* by Fred and Joyce Herndon Roerig. In it, the authors presented a compelling argument that the round bottom jars shown below were made by American Bisque. Previously, the nearly universal belief had been that the jars were products of Robinson-Ransbottom, mainly because they resembled Robinson-Ransbottom's Oscar cookie jar. But according to Fred Roerig, a letter from former American Bisque owner A.N. Allen, now deceased, states that American Bisque did indeed manufacture the jars. Also according to the Roerigs, a confirmation from J.C. Woodward, who was president of Robinson-Ransbottom in 1982, states that Robinson-Ransbottom did not make them.

Opponents of American Bisque attribution, a group not small in number, point out that Robinson-Ransbottom has always been known for its yellowware—more accurately stoneware of yellow color—while American Bisque specialized in whiteware. They also question how reliable people's memories are in recalling rather insignificant events that took place 50 or more years ago.

Since the best evidence to date indicates these jars were made by American Bisque, they've been included in this chapter. Also included are a few similar jars previously attributed to Robinson-Ransbottom.

No doubt this debate will continue until a catalog or sales sheet verifying the origin of the jars surfaces.

Mark on the collar of the brownie.

This is the "Captain," 12-1/2 inches high. "Captain" is inscribed on the collar. *Zera Collection.* $175

All of the controversial round bottom jars have basically the same bottoms, but different tops. Each jar's collar is marked with the name of the jar, as shown. On the left is the "Brownie," 12-1/2 inches high, on the right the "Preacher," 12-3/4 inches high. *Zera Collection* $175 each.

This repainted jar, 13 inches high, is marked "Jolly Pirate" on its collar. It was obviously worked on by someone who either didn't know how it was originally decorated, or who simply wanted to change it. A "Jolly Pirate" with original paint appears in Chapter 2. *Oravitz Collection.* $175

This jar and the two that follow are similar to the above jars except that only their hats, instead of the entire heads, form the lids. They might or might not have been made by American Bisque, but according to Joyce Roerig, officials at Robinson-Ransbottom deny ever having offered them. Some collectors call this jar a "pilgrim," others call it an "Amish man," while still others refer to it as a "waiter." It is 9-3/4 inches high and unmarked. *Courtesy of Jazz'e Junque Shop, Chicago, Illinois.* $175

The "Cop" is the largest jar in the series, 13-3/4 inches high. "Cop" is marked on the collar. *Zera Collection.* $175

The same jar but with an orange hat and red pants, commonly called a "waiter." No mark. *Oravitz Collection.* $175

"Fire Chief," 12-3/4 inches high. "Fire Chief" is marked on the collar. *Zera Collection.* $175

Here is the "World War I Soldier." Note the "U.S." on the helmet. Unmarked, the jar is 8-1/2 inches high. *Zera Collection.* $200

American Bisque? Robinson-Ransbottom? Teddy Roosevelt? Someone else? Correct lid? All that is known for sure about this jar is that it is 8-1/4 inches high, unmarked. *Bosson Collection.* $250

83

Section III: Major American Producers

The firms included in this section weren't determined by company inventory lists, annual reports, or other supposedly reliable data historians often get balled up in . They were chosen by collectors themselves, through their appreciation of the companies' cookie jars, a much more accurate indicator when evaluating the size of any organization's contribution to a collecting hobby.

The criterion was simp . After photographing the more than 1800 cookie jars that appear in the book, manufacturers that were represented by at least 15 different jars, including variations, were admitted to this section, No doubt this method of selection belies actual production figures. On the other hand, it is likely the firms that made the most cookie jars deemed worthy of saving by today's collectors, are the same ones whose quality wares commanded the most respect on the primary market, too.

Chapter 9
Abingdon

Unlike some companies that allowed cuteness to win the race against usefulness, the Abingdon Potteries, Inc., of Abingdon, Illinois, made cookie jars that were generally designed with utility in mind. There are few Abingdon jars that you can't get your whole hand into when your sweet tooth suddenly demands attention.

Abingdon started out about as far from cookie jars as a pottery can get. From its 1908 inception as the Abingdon Sanitary Manufacturing Company, until 1934, it specialized in commodes and other toilet fixtures. Many of them were built specifically for the penal system, Abingdon at one time being the country's leading manufacturer of prison lavatories. By 1934, the Depression had shut down the building trades and forced the pottery to turn to artware. It kept the name, Abingdon Sanitary Manufacturing Company until 1945 when it switched to Abingdon Potteries, Inc., which was used until the firm was sold in 1951.

An Abingdon cookie jar is somewhat of a lesson in geography as the company used clays from several different places to make its slip. Slip is clay that has been thoroughly mixed with water to make a homogenized, pourable liquid. Abingdon's slip formula consisted of ball clays from Tennessee and England, China clays from England and Georgia, feldspar from Abingdon's mines in the Black Hills of South Dakota, and ground silica sand from Illinois.

Abingdon's artware department was formed in 1934, but when it began making cookie jars isn't clear. Derwich and Latos give a lengthy and interesting accounting of Abingdon, in which they state handpainting of the company's pottery didn't begin until 1942. That would indicate Abingdon's handpainted cookie jars were made between 1942 and 1950, the year the artware department shut down.

In 1951, Briggs Manufacturing Company bought the plant and reconverted it back to a sanitary ware operation. Molds, however, were sold to the Pigeon Pottery, Barnhart, Missouri, later ending up with the Western Stoneware Company in Monmouth, Illinois. Some of the molds apparently made one more move, to the Regal China Company, of Antioch, Illinois, as several of Regal's cookie jars are near duplicates of Abingdon's.

The most common mark on Abingdon cookie jars is shown below. All other marks and paper labels the company used include the word Abingdon except two. One is an "A" inside a diamond. the other resembles a capital "H" with a curved horizontal bar, a "J" above the bar, and "R" below. "Made in U.S.A." is also included in this mark. To date, no cookie jars have surfaced with either of these marks.

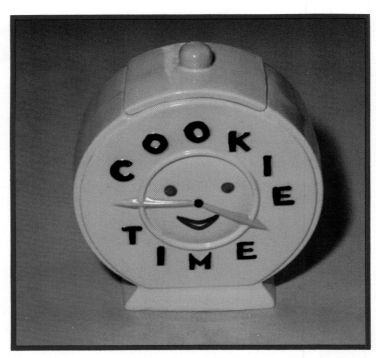

It was always time for cookies at Abingdon. The jar is 9 inches high, marked with "Abingdon U.S.A." inkstamp on two lines and boxed as shown below, and "653" impressed. *Zera Collection.* $150

The same mold and same mark, but different color. Note that the entire lid is colored on this one whereas only the finial is colored on the other one. *Zera Collection.* $150

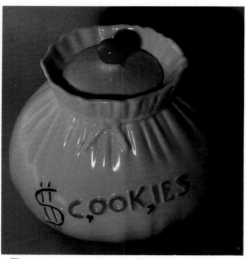

The two commas in "cookies" cleverly suggest a number instead of a word. The jar is 7-3/4 inches high, "Abingdon/USA" inkstamp. *Oravitz Collection.* $140

Nursery rhymes were a favorite theme with Abingdon designers. Is this Mother Goose? The jar, which also comes with light blue trim, is 12-1/4 inches high. "Abingdon/USA" inkstamp, "695" impressed. *Zera Collection.* $400

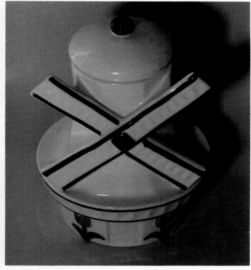

This windmill is 10-3/4 inches high, carries the Abingdon inkstamp, and has "678" impressed. *Oravitz Collection.* $275

Abingdon hippo, 8-1/4 high, "U.S.A./547" impressed on two lines. *Zera Collection.* $275

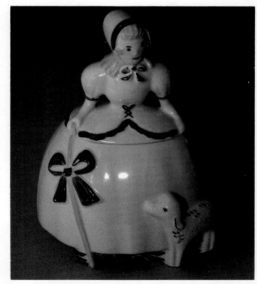

"Bo Peep" jar, 12 inches high, with "694" impressed. *Zera Collection.* $400

The locomotive is 7-1/2 inches high. Abingdon inkstamp, plus "651" impressed. *Courtesy of Jazz'e Junque Shop, Chicago, Illinois.* $200

The "Three Bears" cookie jar is marked with an impressed "969." Its height is 8-3/4 inches. *Courtesy of Jazz'e Junque Shop, Chicago, Illinois.* $175

The Abingdon "Fat Boy" is 8 inches high. It is not marked. *Zera Collection.* $450

Bases of the "Granny" jars. Note the recessed rim on the one on the right.

"Humpty Dumpty" is 11-1/2 inches high, with "663" impressed. Regal China made a nearly identical jar decorated in red. *Zera Collection.* $300

Marked with an "Abingdon/USA" inkstamp and "561" impressed, this jar is 11 inches high. *Zera Collection.* $300

"Granny" jar with hand decoration, 9-1/2 inches high. Mark is shown below. *Courtesy of Betty and Floyd Carson.* $300

This is an Abingdon "Granny" repainted to look like a mammy. The jar is 10 inches high, with an "Abingdon/USA" inkstamp and "401" impressed in base and lid. *Coughenour Collection.*

Inkstamp and impressed mark of above hand-decorated Granny jar. $550

This Abingdon "Little Miss Muffet" jar is not marked. It is 11-1/4 inches high. *Courtesy of Betty and Floyd Carson.* $275

The Abingdon "Granny." The jar on the left is 9-1/2 inches high, and the jar on the right is 10 inches high. The bottoms are different, as shown in the next picture. Impressed in each lid is "471." Abingdon inkstamp mark on each bottom. This jar was also made with a green glaze. *Zera Collection.* $250 each

Chapter 10
Brush

In business until 1982, this Roseville, Ohio, pottery made some of today's most desirable cookie jars.

The Brush Pottery Company came into being in 1925 when the McCoy family withdrew from the Brush-McCoy Pottery, which had existed since 1911, the year George Brush became a partner in the former J.W. McCoy Pottery. Brush had been general manager of the McCoy firm since 1909, following a 1908 fire that had wiped out his own fledgling ceramic operation.

Ross and Don Winton, twins who formed Twin Winton Ceramics, designed many cookie jars for Brush, most of which are marked with a "W" and a number, as shown below.

Most Brush cookie jars were airbrushed. Many have hand decorated details such as eyes. Most of the company's jars are multi-colored, a few are glazed with but one color.

A picture of Brush's first cookie jar, No. 344, which is the first mass-produced ceramic cookie jar known, appears in Chapter 1.

Several Brush Pottery marks are shown below, including those that incorporate the famous palette and brushes logo. Most difficult to recognize are Brush cookie jars that weren't marked, and those marked only "U.S.A."

The Collector's Encyclopedia of Brush-McCoy Pottery, by Sharon and Bob Huxford, is an excellent reference for Brush cookie jar collectors and Brush collectors in general.

The Brush clown, 12-1/2 inches high, which comes in several different color combinations, is marked "W22/Brush/U.S.A." on three lines. According to the Huxfords, the yellow pants indicate this jar was first made in 1964. *Zera Collection.* $350

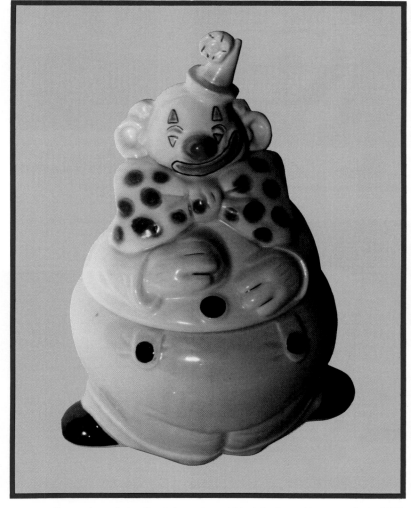

Same clown but with pink pants and black buttons. It was made in 1965. *Bosson Collection.* $350

No spots on this guy's bow tie. Note that the hat colors are reversed on this one. The oldest of the three, it was first made in 1959. *Courtesy of Jazz'e Junque Shop, Chicago, Illinois.* $300

This clown head, from 1970, is one of the most sought after of the Brush jars. It stands 11 inches high and is unmarked. *Blumenfeld Collection.* $350

The bottom of the clown bust is similar to the bottoms of some American Bisque jars.

The Brush Davy Crockett is 10-1/4 inches high. Its mark is simply "USA." Some were trimmed in gold. The jar was made in 1956. Brush's Davy Crockett is the youngest looking of all of them. *Zera Collection.* $350

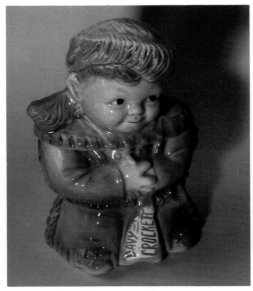

Davy Crockett with a white gun stock, which is more common than the brown gun stock. Same size, same mark. *Courtesy of Jazz'e Junque Shop, Chicago, Illinois.* $350

The little girl stands 11-3/4 inches high and is marked "0-17/USA/Brush" on three lines. It is from 1957. *Bosson Collection.* $650

Like the clown above, this Brush "Granny" is also seen in different colors, as are many other jars not just by Brush but by lots of companies. It is 11 inches high, marked "W19/Brush/USA" on three lines, and was made in 1956. *Zera Collection.* $375

This "Granny" with polka dots added to the skirt was a 1957 variation. It is the same size and mark as the "Granny" above. *Bosson Collection.* $375

Brush made mugs to accompany some of its cookie jars. This unmarked piece is 4-3/4 inches high. Note the heavy crazing. *Private Collection.* $65

Put wings on a little girl and put her in an apron and you have an angel. The apron says "For good little/angels only" on two lines, but is doesn't show up well in the picture. The jar is 12 inches high, marked "W17/USA/Brush" on three lines, and was made in 1956. *Bosson Collection.* $800

The Brush Raggedy Ann was made in two different styles. One is featured above, the other has an apron. This model is 11-1/2 inches high, marked "W-16/USA" on two lines, and is believed to have been made in 1956. *Coughenour Collection.* $450

"Peter Pan" completes the trio of jars that Brush turned out in two sizes. This one with gold trim is 10-3/4 inches high. The larger one is 12-3/4 inches high. The mark is "USA," and the date is 1956. Matching mugs were also marketed. *Bosson Collection.* Small $600, large $800.

The "Balloon Boy" is one of the Brush Pottery Company's last jars, made in 1971. It is 11 inches high, unmarked except for a paper label on the bottom. *Coughenour Collection.* $1250

"Little Boy Blue" in two sizes, 12-1/4 inches, and 10-1/4 inches. Both are marked "K24/USA" on two lines. A matching mug was also made. The first year of manufacture was 1956. *Bosson Collection.* $750 each

"Little Red Riding Hood," another 1956 offering, is 11-1/2 inches high and marked "Brush/K24/USA" on three lines. It also comes in a 9-1/2 inch size, and was made by Brush with an accompanying mug. *Bosson Collection.* $550 large or small

From 1959, "Peter Pumpkin Eater" is 11-1/4 inches high. The mark W24/USA is shown. *Zera Collection.* $425

Paper label of Brush "Balloon Boy."

Mark of Brush "Peter Pumpkin Eater."

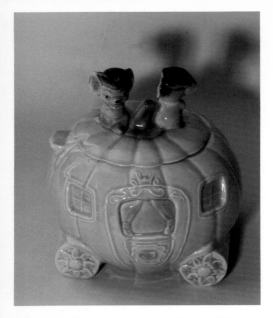

Another pumpkin, this time Cinderella's, is 9-3/4 inches high and was made in 1962. The mark is shown below. *Courtesy of Betty and Floyd Carson.* $350

The covered wagon stands 11-3/4 inches high and is marked "W30/Brush/ USA" on three lines. It was first made in 1962. *Coughenour Collection.* $400

Like most Brush jars, Cinderella's pumpkin comes in a variety of color combinations. *Zera Collection.* $350

Brush touring car, 6-3/4 inches high, with no mark. It was made in 1971. *Bosson Collection.* $1250

The Brush "Humpty Dumpty with Beanie" is 10 inches high. It is marked "Brush/W18/USA" on three lines. It was initially made in 1956. *Blumenfeld Collection.* $250

Mark of Cinderella's pumpkin.

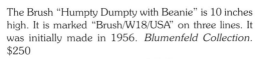

Similar to the previous jar, this one is called "Humpty Dumpty with Cowboy Hat." It is somewhat taller at 11-1/4 inches and also newer, emerging from the kiln in 1962. Mark is "W29/Brush" on two lines. *Zera Collection.* $175

The "Old Shoe," circa 1959, stands 10-1/4 inches high, is marked "W23/USA" on two lines. *Oravitz Collection*. $95

This "Squirrel on a Brown Log" was first made in 1961. It is 10-3/4 inches high. The mark is "USA." *Zera Collection*. $100

The Roerigs attribute this jar to Doranne of California. The main difference is that this jar sits flat while the jar below rests on a dry foot. The height is the same. The ear on this one appears to stick out farther from the hat only because of the angle from which the photo was shot. Everything else appears to be identical, right down to the creases in the pants. The fact that neither jar is marked adds intrigue. Obviously, a mold had to pass from one company to the other. Perhaps a reader knows the direction it traveled. *Oravitz Collection*. $100

The same as above, but red. *Bosson Collection*. $200

The "Dog with Basket" is 12 inches high and unmarked. It was made in 1971. *Coughenour Collection*. $350

This one is called "The Laughing Hippo." It is 9 inches high, marked "W27/Brush/USA" on three lines. Its first appearance was 1961. *Coughenour Collection*. $750

The "Squirrel on the Gray Log" came out in 1965. Size and mark are the same. *Oravitz Collection*. $100

The Brush "Sitting Hippo" was made in 1969. Standing 11 inches high, it is unmarked. *Zera Collection*. $300

Another unmarked Brush jar, the "Hobby Horse" is 10 inches high. It was first produced in 1971. *Zera Collection.* $1000

The "Happy Bunny" in gray was made in 1960, then the color was changed to white in 1965. It is 12-3/4 inches high, marked "W26/Brush/USA" on three lines. *Bosson Collection.* $200

Referred to as the Brush "Squirrel with Top Hat," this jar is 12 inches high. It was made in the early 1950s. The mark is "W15/USA" on two lines. *Oravitz Collection.* $350

While the brown cow with cat finial is much older (early 1950s) than the purple one (see Chapter 3), its value is quite a bit less. The height is 8-1/2 inches. The mark is shown. *Zera Collection.* $100

"Happy Bunny" in white. *Zera Collection.* $200

Mark of the brown cow.

The same jar as above, but in a different color. *Bosson Collection.* $350

Repainted Brush cow with cat finial. The size is the same, but the mark is different, "W10/USA" on two lines. *Courtesy of Jazz'e Junque Shop, Chicago, Illinois.* $90

The exact year of the "Circus Horse" is not known, but it is believed to be somewhere between 1950 and 1955. The unmarked jar is 9-1/2 inches high. It was made in different color schemes. *Bosson Collection.* $1050

"Puppy Police," 9-1/4 inches high, marked "W39/Brush/USA" on three lines. First made in 1966. *Bosson Collection.* $550

The panda made its debut in 1959. Its height is 10-3/4 inches, and its mark is "W21/Brush/USA" on three lines. *Oravitz Collection.* $275

Teddy bear, feet together version, from 1957. Like the previous example, it is 10-1/2 inches high. The mark, which is shown below, is somewhat different than the version with the feet apart. *Zera Collection.* $200

The "Formal Pig" in green, 11-1/4 inches high, is marked "W7/USA" on two lines. Production is believed to have started sometime in the early 1950s. *Courtesy of Jazz'e Junque Shop, Chicago, Illinois.* $250

This panda has subtle differences (whiter white, grayer black), but is considered a bona fide variation by some collectors. The size and mark are the same as above. *Coughenour Collection.* $275

Mark of Brush teddy bear, feet together version. It is one of the few Brush jars on which the mark is raised instead of incised.

Same color as the "Formal Pig" above, but gold lined. *Bosson Collection.* $400

Another rendition of the "Formal Pig." *Oravitz Collection.* $250

The teddy bear with feet apart stands 10-1/2 inches, is marked "W14/USA" on two lines, and was made in the early 1950s. *Zera Collection.* $275

"Smiling Bear," 11 inches high, has no mark but has a dry foot similar to the clown bust. It was first sold in 1969. Also made in yellow, brown, and possibly other colors. *Bosson Collection.* $300

Yellow is a rare color for Brush's "Formal Pig." *Bosson Collection.* $300

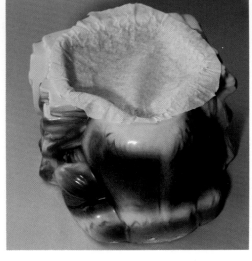

A simple and inexpensive way to give cookie jars an added measure of protection is to put a coffee filter over the opening, put on the lid, and cut to shape with shears. The filter was removed when the above picture was taken.

The "Elephant with Ice Cream Cone" is a good size jar, standing 13 inches high. On this example the ice cream cone has been broken off and glued back on, a common fate for this jar. It was made during the early 1950s and is marked "W8/USA" on two lines. *Zera Collection.* $400 if not broken

On the left is the sitting pig cookie jar, on the right the sitting pig bank. The heights are 11-1/4 inches and 11 inches, respectively. The jar is marked "W37/Brush/USA" on three lines, and the bank is marked "837/USA/Brush" also on three lines. The jars date from 1966. *Bosson Collection.* Left $450; Right $300

While the film didn't capture the difference in these two "nite" owls as well as it might have, the one on the left is finished in a gloss glaze, the one on the right a matte glaze. Both are 10-3/4 inches high, and neither is marked. According to the Huxfords, the gray nite owl is from 1967. *Oravitz Collection.* Gray $130; Yellow $190

The "Donkey with Cart" was made in the 1960s, and appears in different color combinations. It is 10-1/2 inches high, marked "W33/Brush/USA" on three lines. *Coughenour Collection.* $350

This stylized owl, 9 inches high, has no mark, but does have a U-shaped dry foot on the bottom. Also from 1967. *Coughenour Collection.* $400

The "Chick and Nest" is 11-3/4 inches high, marked "W38/Brush/USA" on three lines. Its first year was 1966. *Bosson Collection.* $325

The "White Hen on Basket" hails from 1969, stands 10-1/4 inches high, and is marked with a paper label on the bottom. *Bosson Collection.* $130

"Cloverleaf" cookie jar, 9-1/2 inches high, with matching salt and pepper shakers. A sugar and creamer were included in the same set, which was made in 1955. The jar is not marked. *Bosson Collection.* Jar $75; Salt & Pepper Shakers $35

The lighter version of the "Cookie House" appeared in the Brush line in 1965. The size and mark are the same as above. The line between the top and bottom is protective paper, as shown with the picture of the donkey and cart. *Coughenour Collection.* $110

These Brush crocks are marked "K26/USA" on two lines. The one on the left is 10-3/4 inches high, the one on the right 10-1/4 inches high. Besides the little girl praying and the duck, there is also one with a kitten finial. Believed to have been made in 1956, they were also finished in pink and possibly other colors. *Oravitz Collection.* $75 each

The "Three Bears" cookie jar is marked "K-2/Brush/USA/" on three lines. The jar is 9-3/4 inches high, and dates from the 1960s. *Bosson Collection.* $125

The "Old Clock," 10 inches high, marked "W-20/Brush/USA" on three lines, is from 1956. Verse on the back is shown below. *Oravitz Collection.* $275

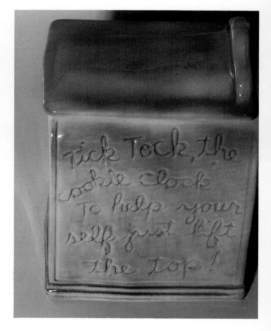

The chocolate dollop is 9-1/2 inches high, has the Brush palette mark plus a "P30." The date is unknown. *Bosson Collection.* Value undetermined

The "Cookie House," marked "W31/Brush/USA" on three lines, stands 10-3/4 inches high. This dark version was first offered in 1962. *Zera Collection.* $110

Verse on back of "Old Clock."

Lantern, 9-1/2 inches high. The mark is "K1/Brush/USA," and the date is unknown. *Oravitz Collection*. $100

Although this cherries jar is rather mundane for Brush, it still shows quality styling. The height is 9-1/2 inches, the date is unknown, and the mark is shown below. *Zera Collection*. $75

Mark of Brush cherries cookie jar.

The treasure chest was made in 1962. It is not marked. *Bosson Collection*. $180

The date of this obscure Santa and matching mug is not known. The jar is 9-1/2 inches high. While unmarked, it has been identified as Brush by a leading Brush scholar. Placed here until proven otherwise. *Bosson Collection*. Value Undetermined

Chapter 11
California Originals

Like Abingdon, California Originals is another firm that switched to kitchen artware after starting out in a completely different direction. William D. Bailey began the company in 1945 in Manhattan Beach, California, as Heirlooms of Tomorrow. True to the name he chose, Bailey, at the time, made porcelain lace figurines that are said to be on a par with those manufactured by old line European potteries.

Sometime during the late 1940s or early 1950s, Bailey changed the name to California Originals, moved the operation to Torrence, California, and switched over to pottery artware. He produced ceramic pieces in quantity for retail stores such as Sears, Penneys, and Montgomery Ward, as well as for trading stamp firms such as Top Value and S & H. Avon was another customer.

In 1979 Bailey sold the firm to Harold Roman, of Roman Ceramics, Mayfield, Kentucky, maker of Cumberland Ware. California Originals closed three years later.

The majority of California Originals cookie jars depict animals. Other prolific themes are copyrighted characters, like Superman and Big Bird, and to a lesser extent, people. The predominant color in any representative collection of California Originals jars is brown, which is evident below. Most jars have a matte finish; the company seldom used high gloss glazes.

California Originals jars are fairly easy to recognize because of the way they're marked. In most cases the firm used a three-or four-digit number, plus the letters "USA," impressed on one line. In many instances bases and lids are marked, a circumstance not found with most other cookie jar manufacturers. Lids are generally marked on the outside of the neck, that part of the lid that extends down into the base of the jar. Bases might be marked anywhere, on the back near the top, on the back near the bottom, underneath, etc. Sometimes the three- or four-digit number was used without the accompanying "USA," and in many cases the jars weren't marked at all.

A few of the cookie jars below are not marked, but are *assumed* to be California Originals. They have been included here because they've either been identified as such by previous writers, or because they exhibit the seemingly unmistakable style, color, and finish for which California Originals is known.

Some of the brown cookie jars in Chapter 34, "Other Unknown Jars," are probably California Originals. Also, some California Originals jars were marketed by Gilner.

A much meaner looking canine sits atop this jar that measures 13-1/4 inches high. Not marked but one of a least three cookie safes by California Originals. The other ones sport a sitting cat and a standing cat. *Zera Collection.* $50

This puppy is 11 inches high and has "958" impressed in both top and bottom. *Oravitz Collection.* $50

Some folks think this bear looks cute, while others find it unnerving, saying it looks evil. It is 12 inches high and has "405 USA" impressed on one line on the rim of the lid. The Roerigs show it having a mark "G-405," while another example is without marks. Different marks or a lack of marks on identical jars is common not only with California Originals but other companies as well. *Oravitz Collection.* $50

"The Tortoise and the Hare," a cookie jar theme used by several companies. It is 13 inches high, marked with an impressed "728 USA" on one line on the base. *Courtesy of Betty and Floyd Carson.* $65

A different style of "The Tortoise and the Hare," it is unmarked but the base matches the one above. This jar is 10-1/2 inches high. *Oravitz Collection.* $65

Another slow creature, the snail stands 12 inches high, with "878/USA" impressed on two lines on side of base. *Courtesy of Jazz'e Junque Shop, Chicago, Illinois.* $45

The clown on this jar makes it rather tall at 14-1/2 inches. It is marked with an impressed "896" on the neck of the lid. *Courtesy of Jazz'e Junque Shop, Chicago, Illinois.* $160

Back to turtles again, this one is 13 inches high with "2035" impressed in both top and bottom. *Courtesy of Jazz'e Junque Shop, Chicago, Illinois.* $30

A little smaller here, the turtle measures 11-1/2 inches high. Impressed in both the base and the lid is "842/USA©." *Oravitz Collection.* $30

The frog stands 10-1/2 inches high and is marked "2645b" on base at back. *Zera Collection.* $50

This frog is marked "906" on the neck and "906/USA" on the base. *Oravitz Collection.* $50

A bit more leisurely, this frog is 10-1/4 inches high and marked "877-USA" in lid. *Oravitz Collection.* $60

The jar on the left is 16 inches high, and the one on the right is 15-1/4 inches. Both jars are unmarked. *Bosson Collection.* Left $40; Right $40

Unmarked, but same mold and same size as the frog above. *Courtesy of Betty and Floyd Carson.* $60

Both jars are 15 inches high and unmarked. *Bosson Collection.* Left $25; Right $30

This frog, also unmarked, was shown in California Originals advertising. It is 8-1/2 inches high. *Zera Collection.* $70

This unmarked wise owl is 15 inches high. *Bosson Collection.* $25

Another owl and fairly colorful for a California Originals brown jar. It is 12-3/4 inches high. Impressed mark top and bottom is "856 USA" on one line. *Oravitz Collection.* $50

A nice looking dog, 13 inches high. "905/ USA" is impressed in the bottom on two lines, "905" impressed on the lid. *Bosson Collection.* $190

Given as a team leader gift by Avon in 1979, this unmarked bear has been identified as a California Originals. It stands 11-1/2 inches high. *Courtesy of Jazz'e Junque Shop, Chicago, Illinois.* $50

This Winnie is 11-1/2 inches high, and is marked "©Walt Disney Production." *Zera Collection.* $175

Unmarked rabbit, 13-1/2 inches high. *Oravitz Collection.* $90

Ears like a bear and nose like a pig, this jar is 11 inches high and has "2648" impressed. *Courtesy of Jazz'e Junque Shop, Chicago, Illinois.* $60

Tigger is 12 inches high and has two marks. "©Walt/Disney/Prod./902" is on each side of the tail, while "902" is impressed in the lid. *Oravitz Collection.* $250

Baby tiger, 8 inches high. While not marked, it was shown in the company's advertising. *Zera Collection.* $75

This jar has "907" impressed in the lid. One in another collection had "907/USA" impressed in the lid. It is 10-1/4 inches high. *Oravitz Collection.* $175 *Left*: Nearly the same but not quite. The surface detail is absent, and the unmarked jar is only 12-1/2 inches high. *Oravitz Collection.* $90

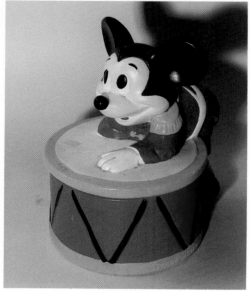

Donald's buddy, Mickey Mouse. The jar is 11-3/4 inches high and marked "©Walt Disney Productions" around the base. Part of the mark shows in the picture. *Courtesy of Jazz'e Junque Shop, Chicago, Illinois.* $400

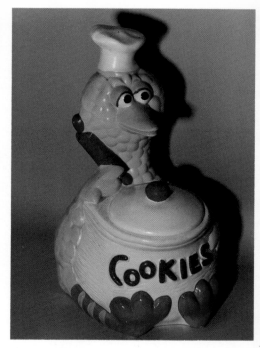

A second Big Bird, this one 14 inches high, has two marks "976/USA" impressed on two lines and "© Muppets Inc./971/1977" impressed on three lines. *Bosson Collection.* $150

Superman is one of California Originals' more popular jars. More expensive, too. It stands 13-1/2 inches high, is marked "California Originals USA 846" on one side, "© DC Comics Inc. 1978" on the other. A similarly shaped jar, not shown, depicts Wonder Woman tying a burglar to a vault. Both jars were also made in an aluminum color. *Courtesy of Jazz'e Junque Shop, Chicago, Illinois.* $550

Probably the most appropriate subject you could ever find for a cookie jar. Cookie Monster is 12 inches high and marked "©Muppets Inc. 970." In addition to the Muppets jars shown here, California Originals also made one of Bert, Ernie, and Cookie Monster all behind a counter with a platter of cookies sitting on the counter. *Zera Collection.* $75

Oscar is 11-3/4 inches high and marked "©Muppets Inc. 972." *Oravitz Collection.* $100

Ernie, 12-1/2 inches high. "©Muppets Inc. 973" is impressed on the back at bottom and also in the lid. *Zera Collection.* $75

Donald Duck is 12-1/4 inches high. It is marked "©Walt Disney Productions 865" around the base. *Courtesy of Betty and Floyd Carson.* $300

Big Bird, 13 inches high, with "©Muppets Inc. 971" impressed in base. *Zera Collection.* $75

The Count is 12 inches high with "975" impressed. *Bosson Collection.* $800

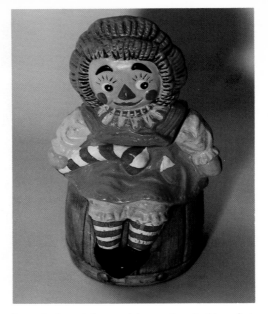

Raggedy Ann. A few scratches on her stockings, but isn't her face nice and crisp. She is 13-1/2 inches high and has "859" impressed in the lid and base. *Courtesy of Betty and Floyd Carson.* $120

Here's the sheriff before the gunfight. An inch shorter than the above jar and unmarked, there is some controversy as to whether or not this one was actually made by California Originals. Still, this seems like the best place to put it. *Oravitz Collection.* $75

Poor Eyore is a bit worse for wear. The jar is 9-3/4 inches high and marked "901/©Walt Disney Prod." on two lines. Two of these were photographed. It was a close race to determine the one in the best condition, which suggests they may have been manufactured with a defective finish. *Zera Collection.* $550

Humpty Dumpty California Originals style. The jar is 13 inches high with "884-USA" impressed in both bottom and top. *Oravitz Collection.* $140

This lucky fellow is 13 inches high and has "726 USA" impressed in back. *Courtesy of Jazz'e Junque Shop, Chicago, Illinois.* $75

Little Red Riding Hood is 13-1/2 inches high and has "320" impressed in bottom. *Oravitz Collection.* $250

A young baseball player, 12-1/2 inches high. "875 USA" is impressed in lid. *Oravitz Collection.* $75

This juggler is 13 inches high. It is marked "876 USA." *Bosson Collection.* $100

The scarecrow with pumpkins is marked "871 USA." *Bosson Collection.* $150

This jar is 12-1/4 inches high and unmarked except for the rare California Originals paper label on the roof. *Oravitz Collection.* $75

Close-up of paper label on above jar.

Same elf school house jar as above but with a blue roof. *Bosson Collection.* $75

Another building, the "Cookie Bakery," is 9 inches high and has "863" impressed in base and lid. *Courtesy of Jazz'e Junque Shop, Chicago, Illinois.* $60

This is the same size as the bakery with the green roof, but is marked "863 USA." *Bosson Collection.* $60

The school house is 12-1/2 inches high and is marked "869 USA." *Bosson Collection.* $100

Except for the absence of the elves, this mold is the same as the two other school house jars. It is also the same size, 12-1/4 inches, and like the others is unmarked. The glaze and the gold trim seem inconsistent with California Originals' style. Another one of the many mysteries of cookie jar collecting. *Oravitz Collection.* $60

103

This school house is shorter than the green and red one, measuring 11-1/2 inches. The reason? The lid is made differently. Impressed in the lid is "869." *Oravitz Collection.* $100

The mark in this locomotive's lid, "2628," is somewhat of an exception for California Originals because it is composed of raised letters. The mark on the wheel is "2628 USA" impressed. The jar is 7-1/2 inches high. *Courtesy of Jazz'e Junque Shop, Chicago, Illinois.* $50

"Cookie Time Clock," 12-1/2 inches high. Impressed in both the top and bottom is "860." *Oravitz Collection.* $50

Circus wagon, 10-3/4 inches high. The top is marked "2631," the bottom "2631 USA." *Oravitz Collection.* $90

An ark, 12 inches high, is marked "881 USA." *Bosson Collection.* $75

This windup phonograph is 12 inches high. The mark is "891 USA." *Bosson Collection.* $200

The unmarked gumball machine is 12-1/2 inches high. *Courtesy of Jazz'e Junque Shop, Chicago, Illinois.* $85

Doranne's cookie jars can often be recognized by the company' distinctive mark, even though the mark doesn't state its name. Most marks on Doranne of California jars include the letters "CJ," plus a one-, two-, or three-digit number, and sometimes the letters "USA." For instance, "CJ 46 © USA" as on Pinocchio below. This won't identify all Doranne jars because sometimes the "C" was dropped, just the "J" remaining. Other times the jars were marked with "USA" in conjunction with a number.

Other telltale indicators of Doranne jars are the ochre, green, and brown glazes the firm favored, and Doranne's propensity toward using raised or incised designs on its solid color jars. Examples would be the raised palm trees on its camel, and the incised flowers on its elephant.

Doranne of California was started in 1951. The company was based in Los Angeles. It went out of business in 1991.

This clown is 13-3/4 inches high with the "Doranne of California" mark incised. *Zera Collection.* $95

An 11-inch high Doranne of California Pinocchio, marked "CJ46/©USA" on two lines. *Oravitz Collection.* $450

This clown is the same size as the previous one, but the impressed mark is simply "Doranne." *Courtesy of Betty and Floyd Carson.* $95

The "J-1 USA" marking on the bottom of this puppy identifies it as Doranne. It is 12-1/4 inches high. *Courtesy of Jazz'e Junque Shop, Chicago, Illinois.* $70

This bandit stands 11-1/2 high. No mark, but everything about it screams Doranne. *Bosson Collection.* $200

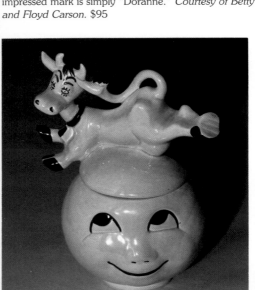

"Cow Jumped Over the Moon," 13-1/2 inches high. The mark is "USA" impressed on back of base. *Zera Collection.* $250

The same jar as above, but in a different color. The mark is also different, "J2," but impressed in the same place. *Courtesy of Jazz'e Junque Shop, Chicago, Illinois.* $250

Same pooch, same mark, different glaze. *Oravitz Collection.* $70

The dapper cat was also made in green, and in a yellow, white, and blue combination. It is 13-1/2 inches high, marked "J5 USA." *Bosson Collection.* $50

Another puppy, 13 inches high. It is marked "California USA/MM600" on two lines and shown in company advertising. *Oravitz Collection.* $85

Note the palm trees decorating this camel, another clue to identifying Doranne jars. Quite often the company used this style of design on animal cookie jars. The camel is 9-1/4 inches high, marked "©USA J-8." *Zera Collection.* $125

This monkey is 12 inches high, unmarked. Often they are marked "CJ-21." *Courtesy of Jazz'e Junque Shop, Chicago, Illinois.* $75

This jar is very tall at 16 inches. It is marked "CJ44/USA" on two lines. *Oravitz Collection.* $60

Here is another example of Doranne decorating the body of an animal jar. The elephant is 12-1/2 inches high and has "USA" impressed in back. *Courtesy of Jazz'e Junque Shop, Chicago, Illinois.* $90

Pink and blue elephant, of the same size and mark as above. This jar is also seen in the palomino glaze. *Zera Collection.* $125

Another unmarked monkey of the same size as the brown one. *Oravitz Collection.* $75

This baby bear is 12-1/2 inches high. While unmarked, the bees and the glaze color are dead giveaways of Doranne origin. *Oravitz Collection.* $75

This rabbit is 9-1/2 inches high. Its only marks are a written "P" and an impressed "4." *Zera Collection.* $60

Same rabbit, different glaze, and bigger—13-1/2 inches high. Unmarked. *Oravitz Collection.* $60

During the 1980s, Doranne of California marketed a series of kitchen accessories called "Bear Essentials," which included canisters, napkin holders, cups, spoonrests, etc. Originally, this jar included a cloth bib. The bear is 11-1/2 inches high and not marked. *Oravitz Collection.* $40

Doranne of California standing elephant, 9-1/2 inches high. The mark is "©/Calif USA/CJ 15" on three lines. *Oravitz Collection.* $80

Frog, 10-1/2 inches high. The jar is unmarked but shown in Doranne advertising. *Zera Collection.* $100

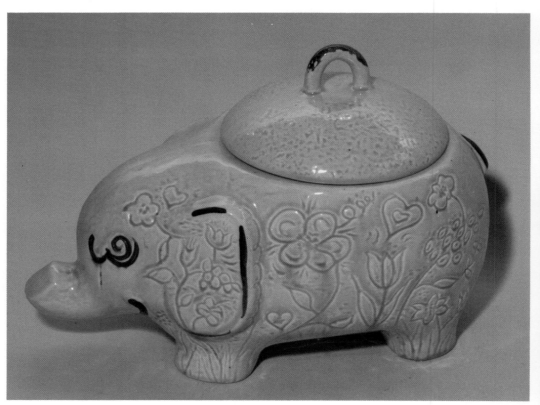

An 11-1/2 inch high hen, marked "CJ 103©USA." This jar is part of Doranne's Farmyard Follies series from 1984. Others in the series included a rooster crowing, usually done in colors, a pumpkin, plus a duck, rabbit, bull, pig, and donkey, all sitting holding something similar to the basket of eggs this hen is holding. Like the hen, the other sitting jars were finished in clear (white) glaze with colored highlights. *Oravitz Collection.* $80

Standing elephant with the same size and mark. *Bosson Collection.* $80

Don't those flowers and that lid look familiar. The turtle is 7 inches high and marked "Calif USA-CJ." *Zera Collection.* $50

This unmarked lion is 10-1/4 inches high. Note the ladybug on its nose. *Zera Collection.* $60

The fish is 10-1/2 inches high and marked "J9/USA" on two lines on each side of the tail. *Bosson Collection.* $80

The mark on this mouse is "J53 Calif. USA." The jar is 12-1/2 inches high. *Bosson Collection.* $60

The sundae is 13-1/2 inches high, unmarked but shown in Doranne advertising. *Courtesy of Jazz'e Junque Shop, Chicago, Illinois.* $60

A cookie for cookies. It is 10-1/2 inches in diameter. While unmarked, it appears on company advertising sheets. *Courtesy of Betty and Floyd Carson.* $50

A very realistic looking three-lobe bell pepper, 10-3/4 inches high, with "U.S.A./CJ30" impressed on two lines. *Zera Collection.* $60

At 13 inches high, this is one very large cookie jar because of the way it flares toward the top. It is marked "USA" and is shown in Doranne advertising. With a small bag of ice set in the bottom, wouldn't this be a wonderful accessory from which to serve homemade ice cream. *Courtesy of Jazz'e Junque Shop, Chicago, Illinois.* $50

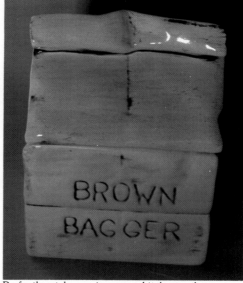

Perfectly at home in many kitchens, the Doranne brown bag is 10-3/4 inches high, unmarked. *Oravitz Collection.* $40

The fire hydrant stands 11-1/2 inches high. The jar is unmarked. *Bosson Collection.* $75

Ten inches high and marked "USA," original advertising shows this cupcake with a top similar to the sundae. Perhaps this is a married jar, the base of the cupcake and the top of the ice cream cone. *Courtesy of Jazz'e Junque Shop, Chicago, Illinois.* $40

Canning jar, 11-1/2 inches high and unmarked. Both this and the brown bag appear on Doranne advertising sheets. *Oravitz Collection.* $75

Although it doesn't show up well in the photo, "1971/ Chianti" is impressed on the neck of this jar. The bottom is marked "USA/J73" impressed on two lines. *Courtesy of Betty and Floyd Carson.* $70

"Bean Pot," 11-1/2 inches high. Believed to be Doranne because of the glaze, its mark is shown below. *Courtesy of Jazz'e Junque Shop, Chicago, Illinois.* $40

This mailbox is 10-1/2 inches high. The mark is "CJ-52/©USA" on two lines. *Zera Collection.* $95

Mark of "Bean Pot."

Chapter 13
Hull

The oldest cookie jar in many collections is the Hull yellow and brown stoneware jar shown below. It was originally designated a pretzel jar. First made during the 1920s, by 1934 the wholesale price of this jar was $0.31 when purchased in lots of one dozen. Wouldn't it be wonderful to have a time machine.

Anchored in Crooksville, Ohio, the firm was organized by Addis E. Hull Sr. in July 1905, as the A.E. Hull Pottery Company. The date is sometimes given as 1903, the confusion existing because Hull later bought out the Acme Pottery Company, which did begin operations in 1903.

Although Hull made several styles of cookie jars, its Little Red Riding Hood jar attracts the most attention. The design patent for Little Red Riding Hood jar was issued to Louise E. Bauer, of Zanesville, Ohio, on June 29, 1943, with Hull Pottery listed as the assignor.

No doubt many collectors have noticed the uncanny similarity between the red glaze on Hull's Little Red Riding Hood, and the red glaze on Regal China's Van Tellingen peek-a-boo baby and other Regal jars. That's because they're one in the same. According to Brenda Roberts in *The Collectors Encyclopedia of Hull Pottery,* Hull manufactured the Little Red Riding Hood blanks, then shipped them to Regal, in Antioch, Illinois, to be decorated. Strictly a marriage of convenience between the two companies, it made for an excellent product because the jars are still popular nearly 50 years after they were first offered, and most of them that have survived are in very good condition.

Cookie jar collectors look at Little Red Riding Hood jars in much the same manner that philatelists look at postage stamps. While stamp collectors consider identical stamps that have different perforations, different printing methods, and other fairly insignificant variations to be entirely different stamps, so do cookie jar collectors consider Hull Little Red Riding Hoods to be different jars if they display only slight variations of decoration.

The only other company with whose jars this occurs to as great a degree is Shawnee Pottery, of Zanesville, Ohio, about 15 miles north of Hull's Crooksville location. A.E. Hull Jr., then president of the A.E. Hull Pottery Company, jumped ship to accept the presidency of Shawnee when that company was formed in 1937. Many of A.E. Hull's relatives remained at the Hull Pottery when he left, so perhaps constantly changing the decoration in little ways was a family inspired technique aimed at keeping otherwise tired designs fresh.

In 1950, 20 years after the death of Addis E. Hull Sr., a fire and flood destroyed the Hull plant. It was rebuilt from the ground up, reopened in 1952 as the Hull Pottery Company. Hull closed in 1986.

Most Hull cookie jars are marked by impression, inkstamp, or a gold stamp. Examples of several marks are shown below.

These are the two basic forms of Hull's "Little Red Riding Hood," one with a closed basket, the other with an open basket. Each is 13-1/4 inches high. The mark of the jar on the right is shown, mark of the jar on the left is similar. *Zera Collection.* Left - $350, Right - $300

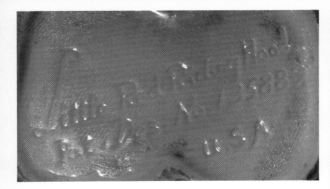

Impressed mark of "Little Red Riding Hood" on the right in the picture above.

At first glance these might appear identical to the two jars above. A closer look reveals larger flower decals, plus the absence of the extra flower on the closed-basket jar and a completely different flower pattern on the open-basket jar. Both jars are 13-1/4 inches high. The mark of one is shown below. *Oravitz Collection.* $350 ea.

Same jar, same size, but only one flower transfer. Mark is similar to the one above. *Oravitz Collection.* $300

Here is something really different: an entirely hand-decorated jar, believed to be a one-of-a-kind done by someone who worked at either Hull or Regal China. Marked "967/Hull Ware/Little/Red Riding Hood/Pat. App'd For/USA" on 6 lines. *Courtesy of Jazz'e Junque Shop, Chicago, Illinois.* $350

The mark of the jar above, different than other mark shown.

More subtle differences. *Coughenour Collection.* $350

Another strange one, correct size and mark, but probably home decorated. *Courtesy of Betty and Floyd Carson.* $225

This Hull Little Red Riding Hood has only a coating of clear glaze. *Oravitz Collection.* $225

Two more jars with subtle differences. Note the decal on the apron of the jar on the right. Same size as above, similar marks. *Zera Collection.* $350 ea.

Yet another flower pattern, plus gold design on apron. Standard size and mark. *Courtesy of Hillary DiRenzo.* $400

Stoneware pretzel jar, first made by Hull in the 1920s. It is 9-1/2 inches high and marked with an impressed "H" within a circle. *Courtesy of Dan Schneider.* $225

Mark of gray-blue gingerbread boy.

Tan gingerbread boy, 12-1/4 inches high, with the same mark as above. *Courtesy of Jazz'e Junque Shop, Chicago, Illinois.* $160

Reverse of Hull pretzel jar.

Brown gingerbread boy, 12-1/4 inches high, with the same mark as shown above. *Zera Collection.* $160

According to the Roerigs, this barefoot boy was made for Hull by Gem Refractories. It is 13 inches high. On the left side of the base is "Blessings on Thee" and on the right side, "Barefoot Boy." *Oravitz Collection.* $525

This is probably the second most popular Hull cookie jar. It stands 12-1/4 inches high. The mark is shown. *Zera Collection.* $220

The duck on the left is 11-3/4 inches high, the one on the right 11-1/4 inches high. Their marks are "Hull/966/USA" impressed. *Oravitz Collection.* $60 ea.

113

Chapter 14
Metlox

Looking over the Metlox cookie jars shown below—as benign as they are beautiful—it's hard to believe this pottery spent World War II making parts for B-25 bombers. Apparently it is not only politics, but also war that creates strange bedfellows.

The pottery was located in Manhattan Beach, California, where it was started by T.C. Prouty in 1927 as the Metlox Manufacturing Company. The original purpose was to make ceramic parts for neon signs. The name Metlox is an acronym derived from the words metal oxide, an ingredient used in neon sign production.

By 1934 Prouty had taken over the Malinite Corporation to produce dinnerware for department stores. Prouty sold Metlox to Evan K. Shaw in 1947. Eleven years later Shaw acquired the fixtures and design patents of Vernon Kilns. Over the years Metlox did some contract work, most notably for National Silver Company during the mid-1940s. Metlox went out of business in 1989.

According to Lehner, the pottery fired its bisque for 40 hours at 2100 degrees F., which is longer and somewhat hotter than most pottery is fired. The result is a fine quality ceramic product.

Unfortunately, not all Metlox cookie jars are marked, the Pinocchio jar below being one example. There are several jars in Chapter 34 whose look and feel strongly suggest Metlox made them, but because there was no definite proof, they haven't been placed here.

Metlox used a variety of marks and paper labels, some of which are illustrated below.

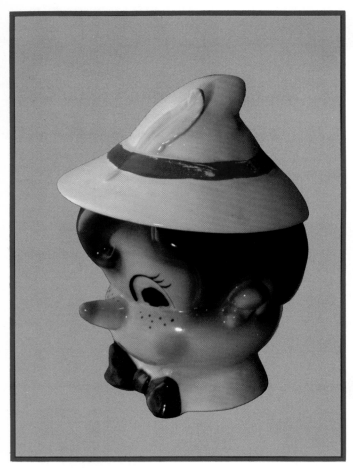

"Pinocchio" is an unmarked Metlox cookie jar, 11 inches high. *Blumenfeld Collection.* $450

This toy soldier is an exceptionally heavy jar. It is 10-3/4 inches high and is not marked. Metlox called it "Drummer Boy." *Blumenfeld Collection.* $1000

The owl on the left is 10-1/2 inches high, and the one on the right is 9 inches high. The jar was also made in white. Each owl carries the Poppytrail mark shown below. *Oravitz Collection.* Blue - $110, Yellow - $80

Koala, 12-1/2 inches high, marked, "Metlox/Calif/USA" on three lines. *Oravitz Collection.* $150

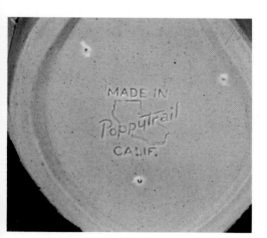

The mark of the owls above.

Rabbit on cabbage, 11-1/2 inches high, no mark. Note the lifelike veins in the cabbage and the hand finished detail on the rabbit's face, both typical of Metlox quality. *Zera Collection.* $250

This bear on roller skates is marked "Metlox/USA" and stands 12-1/2 inches high. *Courtesy of Jazz'e Junque Shop, Chicago, Illinois.* $150

Another Metlox bear. This one is 11-1/2 inches high and marked as the owls above. *Oravitz Collection.* $100

An unmarked Metlox mouse, 12 inches high. *Courtesy of Jazz'e Junque Shop, Chicago, Illinois.* $100

This unmarked Metlox cow head jar is 11 inches high. *Courtesy of Jazz'e Junque Shop, Chicago, Illinois.* $400

115

The cow is 10-1/4 inches high, marked "Metlox/Calif./USA" on three lines. The jar was also made in purple, which is more popular. *Courtesy of Jazz'e Junque Shop, Chicago, Illinois.* Yellow - $300, Purple - $600

Squirrel on pine cone, 12 inches high and marked "Made/in/U.S.A." on three lines. *Courtesy of Mark Taylor.* $125

A 9-1/4 inch high lamb's head jar. It has the Metlox Poppytrail mark shown below. Turn the lid upside down and it bleats like a sheep. *Oravitz Collection.* $150

116

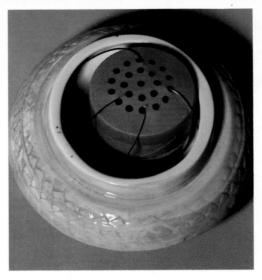

The noisemaker inside the lid of the lamb jar. Most aren't in nearly this good of a condition if they are present at all.

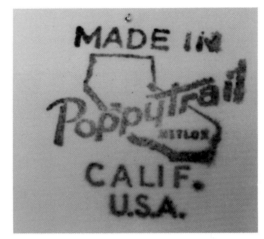

Poppytrail inkstamp mark of the lamb.

Remnant of the lamb's paper label.

Another cookie jar with sound, this kitten meows when its hat is tipped. The height is 9-1/2 inches, and the piece is unmarked. *Zera Collection.* $175

This dinosaur is 13 inches high, has two marks. One is "Metlox/California/USA" on three lines. The other is "©87/by Vincent" with Vincent in script. *Zera Collection.* $150

Penguin, 12 inches high. This jar is marked "Metlox/Calif./USA" on three lines. $125

Here's "Granny Goose," not to be confused with "Mother Goose," which Metlox also made. This jar is 14-1/4 inches high and marked with an impressed "Metlox/Calif/USA." *Oravitz Collection.* $150

"Puddles the Duck," 11-1/4 inches high. *Oravitz Collection.* $75

This pelican is marked "Metlox/Calif/USA" impressed on three lines. It stands 10-1/2 inches high. *Coughenour Collection.* $300

The Metlox rose is an all time favorite. It is 7-1/2 inches high and has "Made/in/USA" impressed on three lines. *Courtesy of Betty and Floyd Carson.* $600

Metlox grapes, 8-1/4 inches high. Note the paper label below the leaves. A close-up is shown below. *Taylor Collection.* $250

Paper label of the Metlox grapes. Wording above Poppytrail is "Made in/California" on two lines.

Second paper label and pottery mark of the Metlox grapes.

The orange blossom adds a nice touch to this 8-3/4 inch high jar. The bottom is marked "Made/in USA" on two lines. *Taylor Collection.* $125

Strawberry, 9 inches high, with "Made in USA" impressed. *Courtesy of Jazz'e Junque Shop, Chicago, Illinois.* $100

Unusual in that the hoops are made of copper, this barrel of apples is 10-3/4 inches high. It is not marked. *Taylor Collection.* $85

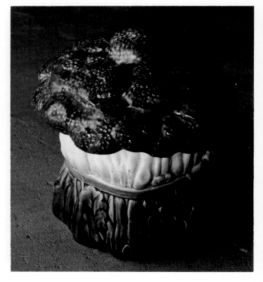

This Metlox broccoli cookie jar carries the Poppytrail mark with the outline of California. *Oravitz Collection.* $200

This tomato is 7 inches high. Its mark and paper label are shown below. *Courtesy of Jazz'e Junque Shop, Chicago, Illinois.* $80

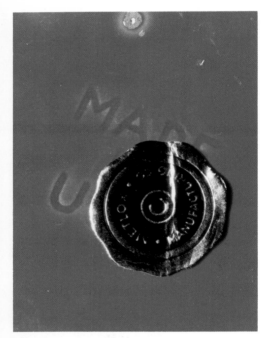

Paper label and partially obscured mark of the tomato. The mark reads "Made/in/USA" on three lines.

This jar, 9-1/2 inches high, is part of a canister set. It is marked "Poppytrail by Metlox Made In USA" in a circle. *Courtesy of Dorothy Coates.* $50

This clown also appears in yellow. It is 13-1/2 inches high and has the Metlox Poppytrail mark. *Oravitz Collection.* As shown - $200, Yellow - $150, Blue & White - $350

Raggedy Ann in yellow, with her size and mark same as above. *Oravitz Collection.* $200

A 13-1/4 inch high Metlox Dutch girl. The jar is marked "Metlox/Calif./USA" on three lines. *Bosson Collection.* Girl - $350, Boy - $300

Raggedy Andy and Raggedy Ann, each 11 inches high. Andy has the Poppytrail mark, and Ann is unmarked. Metlox referred to the jars as "Rag Doll Girl" and "Rag Doll Boy." *Coughenour Collection.* Left - $250, Right - $200

Chapter 15
Red Wing

The name of this pottery comes from its location, Red Wing, Minnesota, a Mississippi River town about 25 miles southeast of Minneapolis-St. Paul, and near which there are excellent clay deposits of the kind used in making stoneware.

The first successful commercial pottery in Red Wing was formed by a group of investors in 1878, who took their lead from several small independent potters who operated in the area during the 1860s and 1870s. But to give credit where credit is due, archeological digs in the area reveal that hundreds of years before the white man ever laid eyes on Minnesota, Native Americans had discovered the quality of the clay and took advantage of it by fashioning containers for both cooking and storage.

The firm formed in 1878 was called the Red Wing Stoneware Company. Through a series of mergers and acquisitions, it became known as Red Wing Potteries, Inc., in 1936. A strike drove the company out of business in 1967.

During the early years only stoneware crockery was manufactured. In the 1920s Red Wing began to include artware in its offerings, moving into dinnerware a few years later. By 1947 all stoneware production had ceased.

Besides the jars shown here, Red Wing also made a carousel, a flattened pumpkin with an elf on it that people call Jack Frost, and a crock jar in its familiar bob white dinnerware pattern. The Brush Art crock jar shown in Chapter 22 is a Red Wing blank.

Red Wing cookie jar marks are shown below, but not all of the company's jars are marked. Some were marked with paper labels.

Dutch girl in tan and brown, a rarer color combination that is more expensive on today's market. It is the same size and mark as above, but also has an inkstamp, "Red Wing/Pottery/Hand Painted" on three lines. *Zera Collection.* $125

These Dutch girls are typical of Red Wing—simple color schemes accompanying a texture that hints strongly of the firm's expertise in crockery. Height of the jars is 10-1/2 inches. Each is marked "Red Wing/USA" on two lines. Additionally, the yellow jar has a Red Wing inkstamp with a series of patent numbers: D-130-328, D-130-329, and D-130-330. These are sometimes present on other jars and are shown below with the yellow chef. *Zera Collection.* $100 ea.

This green and brown Dutch girl, like the tan and brown, commands a premium. Same size as the others, with an impressed mark and inkstamp like the tan jar. *Zera Collection.* $150

This is commonly called the "Peasant Design." The unmarked jars are 10 inches high and date from the early 1940s. *Zera Collection.* $75 ea.

Most attractive of these more colorful jars, the white glaze and unpainted rings make for a cleaner appearance. Same size, no mark. Red Wing also made a wider, flatter jar of the same design. The flatter piece was probably sold as a casserole, but it is often collected as a cookie jar. *Zera Collection.* $75

Another chef, same size as the previous one, but marked differently as shown below. This jar was also made in at least two other colors, blue and green. *Courtesy of Rosa Sberna.* $90

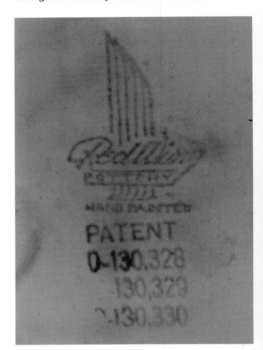

Inkstamp of the yellow chef. The color is different due to shooting the picture at an incorrect exposure.

Darker than the jar above, it is the same size and unmarked. *Zera Collection.* $75

Red Wing chef, 11-1/2 inches high. "Red Wing" impressed. *Zera Collection.* $125

Monk, 10-3/4 inches high. The jar carries Red Wing inkstamp on bottom. *Zera Collection.* $100

Same jar in beige, with the same height and mark. *Courtesy of Mary Huffman.* $100

This is called a fish, but it looks more like a composite aquatic creature, part snail, part fish. Maybe "snish" would be a better name. It is 6 inches high and marked "248/Red Wing/USA" on three lines. *Saxby Collection.* $75

Yellow bananas, with the same size and mark as above. *Bosson Collection.* $100

Perplexing. The jar on the left is definitely Red Wing, has "Red Wing/USA" impressed on two lines. The mark on the one on the right was apparently sponged off when it was cleaned, or it never received a mark. The decoration on the jar on the right isn't consistent with Red Wing, and the jar is somewhat smaller, too, but only by 3/8 of an inch. Possible solutions to this puzzle include it being a remolded jar, a jar made with a different clay mixture than the other, or a jar decorated at home by a factory worker or a decorating firm to which Red Wing sold bisque. *Zera Collection.* Blue - $100, Black - $150

This is the coveted Red Wing "King of Tarts" cookie jar. It is 10 inches high, has "Red Wing/ USA" incised on two lines. This jar was also made in pink with a dark crown. The Roerigs show a splendid multi-color example. *Zera Collection.* As shown - $500, Multicolor - $800

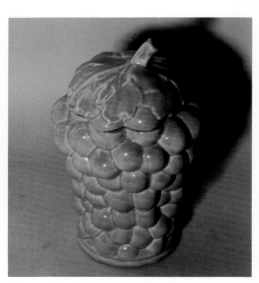

Fruit is a major theme of Red Wing cookie jars. This hand of bananas is 9 inches high and marked "Red Wing/USA" on two lines. *Zera Collection.* $125

Grapes, 10 inches high, with "USA" impressed. *Courtesy of Jazz'e Junque Shop, Chicago, Illinois.* $200

Another unmarked Regal jar that is typical of the fine design and workmanship for which this company is known. *Blumenfeld Collection.* $1000

Like the majorette, the Regal China churn boy imitates an American Bisque cookie jar shown in Chapter 8. The boy faces to his right on both jars. There is also a third model circulating, possibly Japanese, on which the boy faces to his left. The Regal jar is 12 inches high and unmarked. *Coughenour Collection.* $300

Same as the previous one, but with a much lighter colored bottom. Possibly a married jar. *Courtesy of Jazz'e Junque Shop, Chicago, Illinois.* $450

This "Peek-A-Boo" was designed by Ruth Van Telligen, creator of the well-known "Snuggle-Hug" salt and pepper shakers, and is said to be the only cookie jar Van Telligen ever designed. A very rare jar, various sources state production numbers between 1000 and 1400. It is 11-3/4 inches high. Its mark is shown below. *Courtesy of Jazz'e Junque Shop, Chicago, Illinois.* $1100

Davy Crockett, 11-3/4 inches high. The mark is "Translucent/Vitrified China/©C.Miller/55-140." *Blumenfeld Collection.* $550

The Regal China baby pig is 12 inches high, with "404" impressed. *Oravitz Collection.* $450

Regal Dutch girl, 12 inches high and unmarked. *Courtesy of Betty and Floyd Carson.* $700

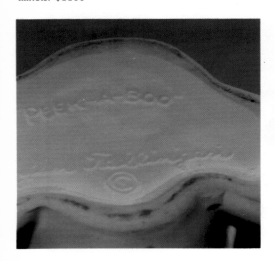

Mark of Regal China Van Telligen Peek-A-Boo jar.

Like the Shawnee "Puss'n Boots," this cat is 10-1/4 inches high. Subtle differences in addition to the bird on the hat being replaced by a fish, include the beaded area below the head, the texture of the fur, and a different ribbon. As far as is known, all Regal "Puss'n Boots" jars are unmarked. *Oravitz Collection.* $450

Goldilocks is 12-1/2 inches high. The bottom of the jar is marked "405" above and "Pat. Pend." below. *Courtesy of Betty and Floyd Carson.* $350

Jar on the left is McCoy, jar on the right is Regal. The height of the McCoy jar is 10 inches, but Regal jar wasn't measured. McCoy jar is marked "USA" on bottom, and the Regal mark is shown. *Bosson Collection.* Left - $900, Right - $100

In the first edition I made quite a deal out of this "mystery" Goldilocks jar, so different from the others appearing here. Imagine my embarrassment when I received a note from cookie jar collector and future author, M.J. Giacomini (American Bisque, Schiffer 1994), informing me I had the base turned backwards. Make no mistake, it's marked the same, is the same. $350

This Goldilocks, with blue hat and cape, is the same size as the one above but marked differently, "H405/ 'Goldilocks'/Pat. Pending" on three lines. *Oravitz Collection.* $350

This chef is 12 inches high with "54-192" impressed in the bottom. *Courtesy of Jazz'e Junque Shop, Chicago, Illinois.* $300

Back of the Regal China Quaker Oats cookie jar.

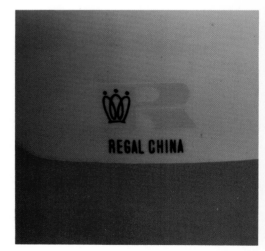

The same mold, but did Regal pour it and decorate it? Probably not since it is not only unmarked, but also decorated entirely by hand, something that can't be said for any of the other jars in this chapter. Perhaps a factory worker took home a piece of bisque to finish. *Oravitz Collection.* $150

Close-up of Regal mark on back of Quaker Oats jar.

Kraft Marshmallows advertising cookie jar from 1982. It is 15 inches high and marked as shown. *Zera Collection.* $125

Regal barn cookie jar made for the same series as the canisters or to compliment it. The mark is "381/Pat. Pending" impressed on two lines; height is 9 inches. *Bosson Collection.* $325

The same barn with a clear glaze. *Courtesy of Betty and Floyd Carson.* $200

Mark of Kraft Marshmallows advertising jar.

On the left is the Regal China version of Humpty Dumpty, with "Humpty Dumpty/707" impressed on two lines. On the right is the Abingdon version, with an "Abingdon/USA" inkstamp and "663" impressed. Both jars are 11-1/2 inches high. *Oravitz Collection.*
Left - $375, Right - $300

Two pieces of an entire line of barrel canisters, spice jars, and other accessories made by Regal. Although only one was made with a "Cookies" sign, when the others are turned so the sign faces the rear, they make acceptable cookie jars and are often collected as such. The jar on the left is 11 inches high, marked with an impressed "387/Pat. Pending" on two lines. The right jar is 10-1/2 inches high and marked "389/Pat. Pending." *Courtesy of Betty and Floyd Carson.* $250 ea.

Marks of the Humpty Dumpty.

One of the rarest and most expensive of Regal's cookie jars is "Alice in Wonderland," which I didn't run across. This is the sugar and creamer that were made as accessories for it. The green matches the grass that's behind Alice's feet on the cookie jar. The blue matches her dress, over which she is wearing a white apron. *Courtesy of Betty and Floyd Carson.* Creamer & Sugar - $400, Cookie Jar (not shown) - $3500

According to the Roerigs, this is not a Regal China cookie jar, but Regal made one almost exactly like it except the Regal jar was glazed instead of painted as this one is. Also, this jar is unmarked whereas the Regal jar is marked "Uncle Mistletoe Cookie Jar, Pat. Copyright 50028." Height of the above jar is 12 inches, height of the Regal jar may be different. If you see this jar with a Regal red glaze, be sure to pick it up because it is moderately rare. *Zera Collection.* Jar shown - $90, Uncle Mistletoe - $700

Mark of the creamer. The Alice in Wonderland cookie jar is marked in a similar fashion.

Sailor with white hair. If you ever see this jar at a show or in someone else's collection, be extra careful when you handle it because the lid is extremely top heavy toward the rear. *Zera Collection.* $350

The Robinson-Ransbottom Pottery Company, which is still in business today in Roseville, Ohio, was the result of a 1920 merger of Robinson Clay Products, of Akron, Ohio, and the Ransbottom Brothers Pottery, of Roseville. At that time the former was a brick producing operation. The latter was mainly devoted to stoneware jugs, reportedly outdistancing Red Wing in volume if not in reputation.

Because many of its products are marked in part with the word "Roseville," a lot of collectors, dealers, and auctioneers confuse Robinson-Ransbottom with the Roseville Pottery Company of Zanesville, Ohio. The two were not affiliated. It is an unfortunate situation because the average Roseville piece is worth several times more than the average Robinson-Ransbottom piece. The difference in value is not as great with cookie jars as it is with other lines of pottery. But to avoid any possible confusion, you might want to compare the jars below to the Roseville examples shown in Chapter 21.

Robinson-Ransbottom cookie jars are on a par with those of American Bisque, Brush, and other quality potteries, but for some reason their prices are often lower, making them a good area of exploration for beginning collectors, or collectors with limited finances.

According to a company spokeswoman, today Robinson-Ransbottom's focus is on stoneware crocks, garden ware, and very large flower pots.

Robinson-Ransbottom marks accompany the pictures. The round-bottom yellow bisque jars such as the cop and the brownie, long attributed to Robinson-Ransbottom, will be found at the end of Chapter 8, with an accompanying explanation. Robinson-Ransbottom Oscar jars are shown in Chapter 5.

Although unmarked, these jars are attributed to Robinson-Ransbottom through a 1943 catalog. The jar on the left is 11 inches high, and the jar on the right is 11-1/4 inches high. *Blumenfeld Collection.* Left - $350, Right - $300

Some collectors call this cookie jar a "toy soldier," others say it resembles a Dutch boy. Whatever it is, its height is 12-1/2 inches. The mark is "R.R.P Co./Roseville Ohio/No.423" impressed on three lines. *Blumenfeld Collection*. $300

View of mark on young lady cookie jar—"R.R.P. Co./Roseville, Ohio/No" on three lines.

This wise bird is 12 inches high and marked "R.R.P. Co./Roseville, Ohio/No. 359" on three lines. *Oravitz Collection*. $125

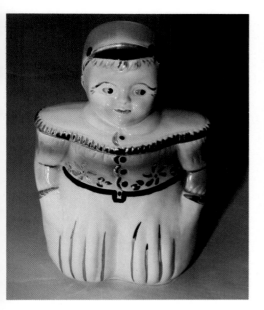

Same jar with gold trim. Same size and mark as above. *Zera Collection*. $400

This young lady is 12 inches high. The mark is shown. *Zera Collection*. $250

This snowman is 14 inches high. It is marked "Roseville Ohio/U.S.A./R.R.P.Co." on three lines. *Courtesy of Betty and Floyd Carson*. $750

The chef is 11 inches high. It is marked "R.R.P. Co./Roseville, Ohio/No. 411" on three lines. *Courtesy of Lisa Diane Golden*. $175

Here's "Jocko," Robinson-Ransbottom's banana-eating monkey. He is 11-1/2 inches high and marked "Roseville, O./USA/R.R.P. Co." on three lines. *Zera Collection*. $300

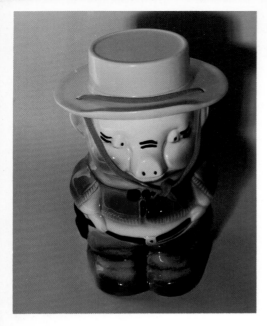

Sheriff Pig stands 12-1/2 inches high, is marked "R.R.P. Co./Roseville/Ohio/No. 363" on four lines. It is also seen with a gray hat. The hat strap is real leather. Also note the fringe on the jacket. Apparently a favorite with Robinson-Ransbottom, it's similar to that on the previous boy and girl. *Oravitz Collection.* $150

No lack of nursery rhyme characters at Robinson-Ransbottom says Old King Cole, that merry old soul. The jar is 10-1/4 inches high, its mark is shown. *Zera Collection.* $450

Old King Cole with blue legs and a yellow coat. It is the same size as the other but has a slightly different mark, "Roseville/Ohio/R.R.P. Co." on three lines. *Coughenour Collection.* $450

Sheriff Pig with gold trim. Same size and mark as above. *Bosson Collection.* $200

Mark of Old King Cole, different than most Robinson-Ransbottom marks, it reads "Roseville, 0/U.S.A./R.R.P. Co." on three lines.

"Cow Jumped Over the Moon," gold trim. The height is 9-3/4 inches, and the mark is "R.R.P.Co./Roseville, Ohio/No-411" on three lines. *Zera Collection.* $600 with gold, $350 without.

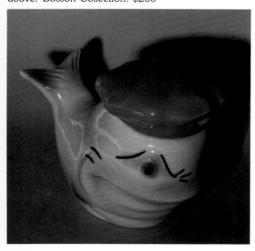

The Robinson-Ransbottom whale isn't easy to find, and it generally necessitates a fatter wallet to acquire it than most other R.R.P. cookie jars. It is 7-3/4 inches high, marked "RRP Roseville, Ohio." *Bosson Collection.* $650

Peter, Peter, Pumpkin Eater, had a wife and put her in a Robinson-Ransbottom cookie jar. This jar is 8-3/4 inches high; its mark is shown. *Oravitz Collection.* $300

130

This round jar is 8-1/2 inches high and marked "R.R.P.Co./Roseville, Ohio/No-350." Westfall shows the same jar with aqua stripes. *Bosson Collection.* $40

Mark of Peter Pumpkin Eater. Note that the lettering is both raised and impressed.

A pair of similar jars, but one made of whiteware, the other yellowware. They are 8-1/2 inches high. The impressed mark is "R.R.P.Co./Roseville, Ohio/312" on three lines. *Zera Collection.* $75 ea.

A pair of tiger kittens, 10 inches high. Mark is shown. *Courtesy of Jazz'e Junque Shop, Chicago, Illinois.* $60

Likely one of the earliest Robinson-Ransbottom cookie jars, this 8-1/4 inch high crock is marked "R.R.P/Roseville Oh/1500/USA" on four lines. *Bosson Collection.* $40

Mark of tiger kittens.

Chapter 18
Shawnee

This company operated in Zanesville, Ohio, from 1937 to 1961. According to Shawnee advertising, the plant was capable of turning out 100,000 ceramic items per day. Shawnee was housed in the former plant of American Encaustic Tiling Company.

As with Hull's Little Red Riding Hood, Shawnee cookie jars poured in identical molds will often exhibit major to minor variations in the way they are decorated. Most Shawnee cookie jar collectors pursue these variations. It's not uncommon to find several examples of the same jar in one collection, each decorated a bit differently. This is particularly true of Smiley pigs, Winnie pigs, Mugsey dogs, Puss'n Boots cats, and Dutch boys and girls.

The Smiley pig, designed by Rudy Gantz, was one of Shawnee's most successful products. The company was good at merchandising and made many spin-offs of its cookie jars, including Puss'n Boots creamers, and salt and pepper shakers to compliment Smiley, Cooky, Mugsey and other jars.

Many Shawnee pieces are marked with a simple and non-identifying, "USA," but this causes more of a problem for collectors of other Shawnee items than for collectors of cookie jars, as most Shawnee cookie jars are pretty well known. A few Shawnee cookie jars carry the marks, "Great Northern," and "Kenwood."

Shawnee Puss'n Boots jars bear a copyright notice. Puss'n Boots was a registered trademark of the Coast Fishing Company, of California, from 1934 until 1950 when Coast was purchased by the Quaker Oats Company. Quaker Oats is known to have favored cookie jar premiums (F & F mammy, F & F Ken L Ration pup) at that point in time, but thus far no connection has been found between Shawnee and Quaker, other than permission apparently had to be granted to use the Puss'n Boots name on the jar.

Terrace Ceramics Inc., which often used Shawnee cookie jar molds after Shawnee's demise, is discussed below.

Terrace Ceramics, Inc.

When Shawnee closed its doors in 1961 then-general manager, John F. Boinstall, bought Shawnee's molds for Terrace Ceramics, Inc., a marketing firm he had started one year earlier. Bonistall then contracted with other companies to produce cookie jars for Terrace by using the Shawnee molds. Terrace Ceramics jars are easily distinguished from Shawnee jars, not only because they're usually marked, but also because the decoration is much different than that used by Shawnee.

Most Terrace cookie jars were made by the McNicol China Company, Clarksburg, West Virginia, a pottery that was mainly into hotel ware. A few were apparently made by either American Bisque or American Pottery Company, as covered in Chapter 8.

The mark of Terrace Ceramics, which is often unreadable due to glaze filling in the space between the letters, is shown below. Pictures of Terrace Ceramics cookie jars begin at the bottom of page 140.

Probably the most familiar of all the Shawnee cookie jars are the "Smiley" and "Winnie" pigs, which, like most Shawnee jars, was adorned with a variety of decoration. Smiley, on the left, is 11-1/4 inches high. Winnie, on the right, is 11-1/2 inches high. Both are marked with an impressed "USA". *Oravitz Collection.* Left - $350, Right - $325

Here's Winnie and Smiley in their bank forms, a slot having been cut in each of their heads. There are no bottom holes in the heads to get the money out. Winnie is 11-1/2 inches high, Smiley is 11-1/4 inches high. The mark of Smiley is shown. Winnie is marked "Patented/Winnie/Shawnee/USA/61" on 5 lines. *Oravitz Collection.* $500 ea.

Smiley and Winnie bank forms, but darker duds on both, plus gold trim on Smiley. Everything else same as previous ones. *Courtesy of Jazz'e Junque Shop, Chicago, Illinois.* $500 ea.

Mark of Smiley cookie jar/bank.

Same size as the other Smileys, but different flowers. The mark is "USA" impressed. *Smith Collection.* $350

Red clover, gold trim, 11-1/4 inches high. The mark is "Pat'd/Smiley/USA" in script on three lines. *Courtesy of Jazze's Junque Shop, Chicago, Illinois.* $450 w/gold trim.

Basically the same Smiley as in the first picture, but this one has gold trim, plus additional color on ears, cheeks, nose, and arms. Note "Smiley" written in gold below neckerchief. Some folks differentiate, calling those without the name written on them "Farmer Pig." *Zera Collection.* $450

Smiley with tulips, "USA" impressed mark, 11-1/4 inches high. Incidentally, Shawnee also made creamers and salt and peper shakers of many of its cookie jar patterns including this one. *Courtesy of Jazz'e Junque Shop, Chicago, Illinois.* $450

Red clover but no gold. Height and mark same as above. *Boson Collection.* $350

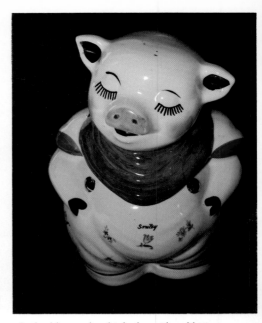

Smiley with green neckerchief, shamrocks, and gold trim, 11-1/4 inches high, "USA" impressed. *Courtesy of Jazz'e Junque Shop, Chicago, Illinois.* $500

Gold-trimmed Smiley with different transfer flowers. "USA" impressed, 11-1/4 inches high. *Courtesy of Jazz'e Junque Shop, Chicago, Illinois.* $500

And a blue neckerchief, also with gold trim. "USA" impressed, 11-1/4 inches. *Courtesy of Allan and Michelle Naylor.* $500

Same green neckerchief and shamrocks minus the gold trim. "USA" impressed, 11-1/4 inches high. *Zera Collection.* $400

Small transfer flowers and gold trim decorate this Smiley. It is 11-1/4 inches high with "USA" impressed. *Courtesy of Betty and Floyd Carson.* $500

Something really different, a yellow neckerchief. Note gold trim. Height is 11-1/4 inches, mark is an impressed "USA." *Smith Collection.* $400

Plain Smiley, 11-1/4 inches high, "USA" impressed. *Zera Collection.* $150

All paint, no flowers—unusual to say the least. Possibly Terrace Ceramics but not verified. *Bosson Collection.* $200 ea.

134

Winnie with both red and gold decoration. She is 11-1/2 inches high and "USA" impressed. *Zera Collection.* $500

Winnie with a beige collar, and blue and pink flowers. The height is 11-1/2 inches, and the mark is "Pat'd/Winnie/USA." *Zera Collection.* $350

Several differences here including the decals and the maroon bow. The jar is 10-1/2 inches high, and marked "Patented/'Puss N Boots'/USA" on three lines. *Smith Collection.* $550

Blue collar, gold trim, 11-1/2 inches high, "USA" impressed. *Smith Collection.* $350

A much simpler "Puss 'N Boots," 10-1/4 inches high, same mark as above. *Zera Collection.* $200

The only difference here is the decoration surrounding the top button. "USA" impressed, 11-1/2 inches high. *Smith Collection.* $500

Winnie in green with shamrocks. The height is 11-1/2 inches, and the mark is "USA" impressed. *Zera Collection.* $350

So much for pigs—on to cats, dogs, and elephants. Here is an exquisitely decorated example of "Puss'n Boots"—hand painting, transfers, and gold trim. It is 10-1/4 inches high, and marked "Patented/'Puss N Boots'/USA" on three lines. *Zera Collection.* $550

A Mugsey dog with floral transfers and gold trim. The jar is 11-3/4 inches high and marked "Patented/Mugsey/USA" on three lines. *Bosson Collection.* $900

135

A pair of "Lucky" elephants with gold trim. Note "Lucky" on chest. The height is 12 inches, and the mark is "USA" impressed. *Zera Collection.* $550 ea.

Mark of pink elephant with white collar.

Close-up of paper label on right "Lucky."

A completely different mold here, and possibly a married jar judging by the two different colors. It is 10-1/2 inches high, has "60" incised, "Shawnee/USA" in raised letters. *Oravitz Collection.* $200

Lid of pink elephant jar showing original black gasket.

Not as fancy as the above pair, this elephant has paint applied over clear glaze. "USA" impressed, 12 inches high. *Zera Collection.* $150

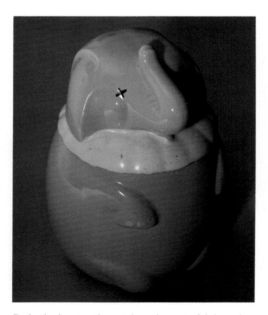

Pink elephant with matching base and lid, and a white collar. Height is 10-1/2 inches. Kenwood mark is shown. *Smith Collection.* $200

What a beautiful job of decorating. The owl jar is 11-1/2 inches high with "USA" impressed. *Zera Collection.* $350

136

Plainer winking owl, but still a pretty jar. Same size and mark as previous one. *Zera Collection.* $150

Dutch girl with tulip, 12 inches high, "USA" impressed. *Smith Collection.* $200

Much more cheerfully decorated Cooky but nevertheless the same jar. Height is 12-1/4 inches. Mark is impressed "USA." *Oravitz Collection.* $300

This is "Cooky" (note name on right shoulder), Shawnee's Dutch girl, sporting gold trim. The jar is 12-1/4 inches high, "USA" impressed. *Zera Collection.* $350

No gold, different transfer, and hand-painted tulip. Same size and mark as above. *Zera Collection.* $250

Decals plus hand decorating and gold trim. Height is 12 inches, "USA" impressed. *Smith Collection.* $400

Plain and simple, 12 inches high, "USA" impressed. *Smith Collection.* $150

Blue instead of green on the hat and pigtail bows, different gold trim on skirt, no red trim on skirt hem. No "Cooky" on shoulder, either. Same size and mark as above. *Zera Collection.* $400

Cooky with a white skirt. "USA" mark impressed, 12-1/4 inches high. *Zera Collection.* $300

Similar to previous one but red flowers and highlights. Same size and mark as above. *Zera Collection.* $300

Different hat trim and different flowers, but size and mark the same as previous one. *Zera Collection.* $350

Red scarf, gold trim, and transfer flowers. Mark is "USA" impressed, and the height is 12-1/4 inches. $350

This jar is not as tall as the others—only 10-3/4 inches—because of the different bottom. Mark is "Great/Northern/USA" in raised letters on three lines, plus "1026" incised. All Shawnee cookie jars with this same base and top shown by the Roerigs and Westfall and by Mark E. Supnick in his book *Collecting Shawnee Pottery* have identical facial expressions, the girl's eyes cast to her right. Supnick pictures one finished in green both top and bottom. *Zera Collection.* $300

"Happy" with blue pants and patches, and gold trim. Height is 12 inches, "USA" impressed. *Smith Collection.* $350

Yellow pants, blue trim, no gold, 12-1/2 inches high and "USA" impressed. *Smith Collection.* $250

Plain Dutch boy, painted over the glaze with much of the paint chipped away. Same size and mark as above. *Zera Collection.* $150

Sailor, 11-3/4 inches high, "USA" impressed. Look closely and you'll see a star on the side of the cap. The hands behind the back on Shawnee's sailor jars hold a cookie. *Oravitz Collection.* $175

Where you find Dutch girls you usually find Dutch boys, the Shawnee Pottery Company is no exception. "Happy" (on pants) is 11-1/2 inches high, has "USA" impressed. *Zera Collection.* $350

Overall better condition and blond hair. The height is 12 inches, with "USA" impressed. *Smith Collection.* $175

Sailor with gold trim, note "GOB" on left. The jar is 11-3/4 inches high, with "USA" impressed. *Smith Collection.* $800

This "Clown with Seal" is 9-1/2 inches high, and its mark is shown. The jar is also seen with gold trim. *Courtesy of Jazz'e Junque Shop, Chicago, Illinois.* $650

Mark of "Clown with Seal." This is exceedingly crisp for a Shawnee mark, many of which are barely readable.

Drummer boy, 10 inches high, with "USA" impressed. *Blumenfeld Collection.* $400

Here we're back to, "If it looks like a duck....." This jar is attributed to Regal China by some collectors, but the prima facie evidence pointing to Shawnee origin is overwhelming. The green and yellow match one of the "Cooky" Dutch girl jars above, while the transfer flowers can be found on the Smiley pigs. There is also the gold "Cooky" on the right shoulder, which is a carbon copy of the "Cooky" Shawnee used. Maybe Shawnee didn't make the jar, but clearly the company, or someone within it, had a hand in its decoration. The unmarked jar is 12 inches high. A mate that says "Cinderella" on it is shown in Chapter 34. *Courtesy of Jazz'e Junque Shop, Chicago, Illinois.* $300

This jar, 10 1/2 inches high and marked "Shawnee/USA" in raised letters, is but one of many accessories for the company's famous corn pattern dinnerware. *Zera Collection.* $250

More produce from Shawnee, 8 inches high, and marked "Shawnee/USA" on two lines in raised letters with "84" impressed below. *Zera Collection.* $150

Shawnee house cookie jar. It is 6 3/4 inches high, marked "USA/6" on two lines. This jar is quite rare. *Courtesy of Jazz'e Junque Shop, Chicago, Illinois.* $550

Jug with hand-painted tulips, and a well-preserved example of a Shawnee red paper label. The jar is 8-1/4 inches high, with "USA/75" impressed. *Oravitz Collection.* $200

Two plain jugs, same height and mark as the tulip jug. *Smith Collection.* $100 ea.

Close-up of paper label on jug cookie jar.

This is Shawnee's little chef cookie jar, hexagon-shaped and 8-1/2 inches high. Mark is an impressed. "USA." *Zera Collection.* $375

This octagon jar is 8-3/4 inches high, "USA" impressed. *Smith Collection.* $85

Same height and mark as the tulip jug but with a different design. *Smith Collection.* $100

Little chef in green without added decoration. The height is 8-1/2 inches, with "USA" impressed. The jar was also made in solid yellow and possibly other colors. *Smith Collection.* $250

The jar on the left is 12-1/4 inches high, the jar on the right, 11-3/4 inches high. Both are marked "Terrace/Ceramics" on two lines. *Oravitz Collection.* $100 each.

The mark of Mugsey. The two lines at the top are raised; the two at the bottom are impressed.

Terrace Winnie pig, 12 inches high, believed to have been repainted. The mark is "Terrace/Ceramics" on two lines. *Courtesy of Jazz'e Junque Shop, Chicago, Illinois.* $150

This jar, 12-1/2 inches high, is marked "Terrace/Ceramics/USA 4253" on three lines. Another one photographed had only the first two lines. This same jar appears twice in Chapter 8: as "Fluffy," assumed to have been made by Ludowici Celadon, and as the cat with indented spots. *Courtesy of Jazz'e Junque Shop, Chicago, Illinois.* $70

White Mugsey, with the same size and mark as the brown model. *Oravitz Collection.* $125

This corn jar is quite nice compared to many other Terrace Ceramics jars. It stands 11-1/2 inches high. The mark is "Terrace Ceramics/USA" on two lines, with a "290" on the left and a similar unreadable mark to the right. *Courtesy of Jazz'e Junque Shop, Chicago, Illinois.* $100

Very much like Abingdon's cookie bag except the Abingdon product has a flat lid that is recessed down to the drawstring. This jar is 8-3/4 inches high and marked "Terrace/Ceramics" on two lines in raised letters. *Zera Collection.* $50

Often called "Thumper" but never having a Disney copyright notice, these jars are 11-1/2 inches high. The one on the right is marked "Terrace/Ceramics" in raised script on two lines. The mark of the one on the left is "Reg. U.S. Pat. Off./Celebrate/Made in USA" on three lines. The Celebrate mark is that of the George Borgfeldt Company, a New York selling agency discussed in Chapter 22. $65 ea.

Like the ear of corn and the money bag cookie jars, the quality of this teddy bear cookie jar is far above that of most Terrace jars. The high gloss glaze is said to be rare on this jar. The height is 12 inches, and the mark is "USA/42514X52" impressed on two lines and "Terrace/Ceramics" in raised letters on two lines. *Oravitz Collection.* $85

A Terrace Ceramics Mugsey, in aesthetic terms a mere shadow of those made by Shawnee. The jar is 12 inches high, and the mark is shown. *Courtesy of Betty and Floyd Carson.* $125

141

Chapter 19
Treasure Craft

Treasure Craft was founded in Gardena, California, in 1945 by Alfred A. Levin, and is one of the few American potteries that still produces cookie jars on a fairly large scale. Levin started the pottery in a single-car garage, using a 15 cubic foot kiln. The company is now located in Compton, California, in a 250,000 square foot complex, and employs between 500 and 600 people. It was sold to Pfaltzgraff Pottery, of York, Pennsylvania, in 1988. Pfaltzgraff retained Treasure Craft management.

If potteries had cheers as football teams do, Treasure Craft's would probably go something like, "Dark brown, light brown, ivory and white; our favorite glazes, fight, fight, fight!" Those colors dominate the company's output. The muted earth tones probably account for the failure of Treasure Craft cookie jars to capture the fancy of many collectors. It seems probable they will gain respect at some point inthe future, because Treasure Craft's molds are quite often more detailed than those of many other companies.

When Twin Winton Ceramics was sold in 1977, Treasure Craft purchased its molds. According to Alfred Levin, Treasure Craft has used some of the molds, making "technical changes the average person wouldn't recognize."

Most Treasure Craft jars are marked inside the lid, as shown below. Paper labels, also shown below, have been used, too.

This cookie chef and several jars following it are from the predominantly ivory colored line spoken of above. This one is 12-1/2 inches high, "Treasure Craft/©Made in USA" impressed in lid on two lines. *Courtesy of Lisa Diane Golden.* $80

Marked "Treasure Craft/©Made in USA" on two lines in lid, this jar stands 12 inches high. *Oravitz Collection.* $100

The mouse is 11-1/2 inches high, and is marked "Treasure Craft/©USA" on two lines inside lid. *Oravitz Collection.* $80

Also made in brown, this rocking horse is 13-1/4 inches high. The mark "Treasure Craft/©Made in USA," is shown in the lid. *Courtesy of Jazz'e Junque Shop, Chicago, Illinois.* $90

As his sign says, this puppy is actually part of a canister set. But the same jar was made as a cookie jar, too. The cookie jar model has a top hat about the same size as the hat on this jar. Possibly the heads were interchangeable. The jar is 10 inches high and carries the Treasure Craft paper label shown below. *Oravitz Collection.* $65

A cookie trolley, 9-1/2 inches high. The mark is "Treasure Craft/©/Made in USA" impressed under lid on three lines. *Courtesy of Betty and Floyd Carson.* $90

Mark of Treasure Craft rocking horse.

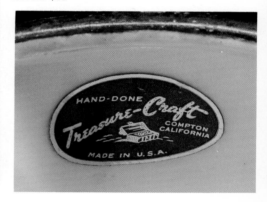

Paper label from puppy coffee canister.

Different mode of transportation, 8 inches high. This jar is unmarked. If it isn't Treasure Craft, someone certainly did a fine job of imitating it. *Oravitz Collection.* $75

This monk also appears in light tan. He is 12 inches high and marked "Treasure Craft/© Made in USA" on two lines inside the lid. *Oravitz Collection.* $60

The lamb is 11-1/2 inches high and marked Treasure Craft/19©68/Comptom, Calif." on three lines on side of base. *Oravitz Collection.* $45

Marked the same as the brown lamb, the monkey is 12-1/2 inches high. *Courtesy of Betty and Floyd Carson.* $90

This Victorian house is 11-3/4 inches high and marked "Treasure Craft/©Made in USA" on two lines inside lid. Cookie jar or part of a canister set? *Courtesy of Floyd and Betty Carson.* $75

Sleeping sheep dog, 7-1/2 inches high. "Treasure Craft/©Made in USA," inside lid on two lines. *Courtesy of Jazz'e Junque Shop, Chicago, Illinois.* $85

Big Al from Disneyland's "Bear Country, U.S.A." Made by Treasure Craft, the jar stands 12-1/2 inches high and is marked "Walt Disney Productions" around the base. *Coughenour Collection.* $150

Similar to the Victorian house above, yet different, most notably for the additions of curtains on second floor windows and clapboards on third floor porch. What appear to be different shingles on the spire may simply result from the vertical divisions between the shingles filling in with glaze. *Courtesy of Jazz'e Junque Shop, Chicago, Illinois.* $75

The owl is 11-1/4 inches high, with "Treasure Craft/©USA impressed across back of base. *Oravitz Collection.* $65

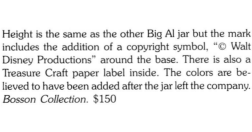

Height is the same as the other Big Al jar but the mark includes the addition of a copyright symbol, "© Walt Disney Productions" around the base. There is also a Treasure Craft paper label inside. The colors are believed to have been added after the jar left the company. *Bosson Collection.* $150

This is the football house from Rose Petal Place, made by Treasure Craft but unmarked. This is the Football House from Rose Petal Place. The jar is 8 inches high. *Courtesy of Jazz'e Junque Shop, Chicago, Illinois.* $250

"Gingerbread House," 10-1/2 inches high. It has an incised mark and paper label, both shown. *Courtesy of Jazz'e Junque Shop, Chicago, Illinois.* $110

The barn is 12 inches high and marked "Treasure Craft/©" on two lines inside lid. *Oravitz Collection.* $55

The balloon is 12 inches high with "Treasure Craft/©/Made in USA" impressed in lid. *Oravitz Collection.* $80

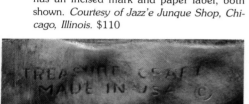

Incised mark of "Gingerbread House."

Paper label of gingerbread house. Basically same as the paper label illustrated, but it does not include the phrase "Hand done."

This jar, 15-1/2 inches high, has a white counterpart clothed in a blue dress. Unmarked but shown in Treasure Craft literature. *Courtesy of Jazz'e Junque Shop, Chicago, Illinois.* $65

One of the few Treasure Craft jars that doesn't give much of a visual hint as to who made it. It is 12-1/2 inches high, with "Treasure Craft©USA" incised around the back. *Zera Collection.* $45

The saguaro is 12 inches high, not marked. This jar was available in stores in 1991. *Blumenfeld Collection.* $75

Juke box, 11-1/2 inches high and marked "Treasure Craft/©Made in USA" inside lid. *Courtesy of Jazz'e Junque Shop, Chicago, Illinois.* $100

Chapter 20
Twin Winton

Here is a typical Twin Winton cookie jar—cute, wood tone, matte glaze, and hand-painted details. The jar is 12-1/4 inches high, was offered in Twin Winton's 1975 catalog. It was also made for the Collectors' Series, some examples of which are shown elsewhere in this chapter. The inkstamp mark is shown. *Zera Collection*. $75

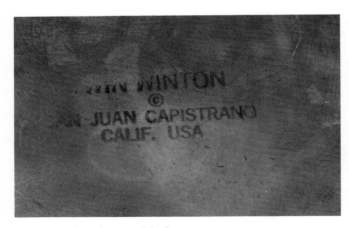

Inkstamp mark on bottom of the bear.

Twin brothers Don and Ross Winton began producing ceramics while attending high school in Pasadena, California, during the 1930s. Following hiatus of several years for World War II, the brothers formed Twin Winton Ceramics upon returning to Pasadena in 1946. Another brother, Bruce Winton, participated by overseeing the business end of the enterprise. The first cookie jars were made in 1951.

Operations were moved to San Juan Capistrano, and El Monte, California, sometime in the early 1950s. The El Monte plant closed in 1964, but the San Juan Capistrano plant remained open until 1977 when it was sold to William F. Bowmaster. Molds were sold to Treasure Craft.

Twin Winton specialized in kitchen artware, making things such as cookie jars, salt and pepper shakers, napkin rings and other fancies. For its cookie jars, the company favored a wood tone matte glaze the majority of the time. Wood tone type finishes were applied in three different shades, light, medium and dark, all illustrated below. The Collectors' Series, which encompassed 18 jars, was initiated in 1974. All Collectors' Series jars are marked as such.

Despite the commercial success of Twin Winton Ceramics, collectors tend to hold in higher esteem the cookie jars the Wintons designed for the Brush Pottery Company, of Roseville, Ohio, from the mid-1940s through 1971.

Similar in style to the above jar, but a police chief is 11 inches, and the mark is "Twin Winton/©/Calif.USA" on three lines. *Oravitz Collection*. $90

This Twin Winton swashbuckler is 12 inches high and has two marks. Impressed is "Twin Winton made in California/©(two unreadable numerals)." The accompanying inkstamp proclaims "Twin Winton/©/California, USA" on three lines. This design was included in the Collector's Series. *Oravitz Collection.* $100

The Wintons made this fellow a lot more ambitious than the squirrel on a log they designed for Brush, which is shown in Chapter 10. The jar is 11-1/2 inches high and marked "Twin Winton/Calif. USA" on two lines. It was offered in the company's 1965 catalog. *Oravitz Collection.* $65

Twin Winton jars that are basically one color appear plain at first glance, but a closer look reveals nice detailing such as the collar and ear on this horse. The jar is 14-1/4 inches high and has an inkstamp mark "Twin Winton/San Juan Capistrano/Calif. USA" on three lines. Some examples also include the year 1962. *Courtesy of Betty and Floyd Carson.* $100

Squirrel, 10-3/4 inches high, appeared in 1965 catalog. The mark is the inkstamp "Twin Winton ©/San Juan Capistrano/ Calif." on three lines. Apparently the same work was carried on at both Twin Winton plants as the Roerigs show this jar with a similar mark, except that it reads "El Monte, Calif." *Oravitz Collection.* $65

This pretty lady is 13-1/2 inches high and marked "Twin Winton ©/Calif. USA" on two lines. *Oravitz Collection.* $90

The cow is 8-1/2 inches high and is marked with a simple "Twin Winton" on one line. *Courtesy of Betty and Floyd Carson.* $70

Some might say the biggest difference between this jar and the McCoy "Mouse on Clock" in Chapter 7 is the time, 11:50 as opposed to 9:34. This one came first, at least in the production phase, as it is shown in Twin Winton's 1965 catalog. McCoy's didn't appear until 1968. The jar is 14-1/2 inches high and the mark is shown. *Oravitz Collection.* $50

Impressed mark of above jar showing the design was copyrighted in 1960.

147

Both rabbits are 13-1/2 inches high. The mark of the one on the left is shown. The mark of the one on the right is "Twin Winton ©/Calif. USA" on two lines. *Oravitz Collection.* Left - $200, Right - $100

This lion is 13-1/2 inches high and is also seen in wood tone and in reddish brown. Impressed mark reads "Twin Winton©/ Calif. USA" on two lines. *Oravitz Collection.* $75

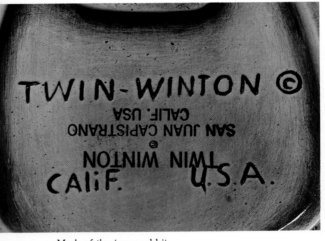

Mark of the ivory rabbit.

The lamb on the left is not marked. The lamb on the right carries the Twin Winton inkstamp. Both jars are 12-1/4 inches high. A very similar jar is sometimes seen with a mark that takes up nearly the whole bottom and says "Lamb, World Wide, P.O. Drawer L, Lafayette, Louisiana." One of the main differences between that jar and these two is that the lettering on the front of the jar with the "Lamb" mark does not appear wavy as it does on both of these. *Oravitz Collection.* Left - $80, Right - $60

Owl, 11-3/4 inches high. The mark is shown. The jar was also made in wood tones. *Zera Collection.* $60

Mark of the gray owl.

Each is 11-1/2 inches high, marked Twin Winton. *Oravitz Collection.* $60 ea.

Collectors' Series jar, 13 inches high. The impressed mark reads "Twin Winton©/California USA" on two lines, and the inkstamp states "Twin Winton Collectors' Series/©/California USA" on three lines. *Courtesy of Betty and Floyd Carson.* $125

Standing 13 inches high, the elf on the right is 1/4 of an inch taller than the one on the left. Both are stamped "Twin Winton." The brown elf was in 1965 catalog. *Oravitz Collection.* $60 ea.

This little guy showed up in the company's 1975 catalog. The jar is 11-1/4 inches high. A mark is present but unreadable. *Oravitz Collection.* $90

This jar is virtually identical to the brown jar but 1/4 of an inch taller at 11-1/2 inches. It has strange marks: an "EA" carved in the lid and a "W" inkstamp on both the lid and base. *Oravitz Collection.* $130

This lovely Dutch girl is 13 inches high and has two marks. "Twin Winton" is impressed on one line while an accompanying inkstamp reads "Twin Winton/©California USA" on two lines. The jar was included in the company's 1965 catalog. *Courtesy of Betty and Floyd Carson.* $85

Mother Goose, 13-3/4 inches high. The mark is shown. *Bosson Collection.* $125

Mark of Mother Goose.

149

Appearing in Twin Winton's 1965 catalog, this jar is 10-1/2 inches high, and is marked "Twin Winton©/Calif. USA." *Courtesy of Jazz'e Junque Shop, Chicago, Illinois.* $65

The ark is 11 inches high and has a Twin Winton mark. The Roerigs show it in white with greenish-yellow antiquing. *Bosson Collection.* $75

This jar stands 12-1/4 inches high, has a Twin Winton inkstamp. It was shown in a 1965 company catalog. *Oravitz Collection.* $90

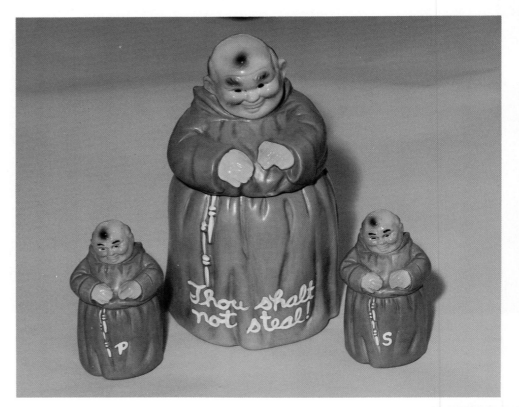

The bird in the chimney adds a nice touch to this 12-inch high jar. The mark is "Twin Winton©/Calif. USA" impressed on two lines. *Courtesy of Jazz'e Junque Shop, Chicago, Illinois.* $85

The cookie jar is 12 inches high, and the accompanying salt and pepper shakers are 6-1/4 inches high. The jar is marked "Twin Winton Calif. USA©60." *Courtesy of Joyce Hollen.* Cookie Jar - $80, Salt & Pepper - $75

This is a small jar, only 7-1/2 inches high. While most Twin Winton cookie jars are marked on the bottom, this one's mark is on one of the hoops in the back. It reads "Twin Winton©59." *Oravitz Collection.* $60

This elephant found a place in Twin Winton's 1965 catalog. It is 11-1/2 inches high and unmarked. *Oravitz Collection.* $60

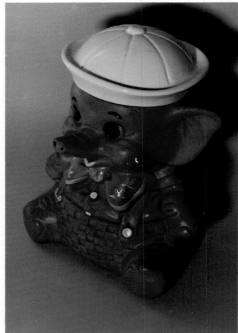

Section IV: Other American Producers

This section covers pottery cookie jars that were made in the United States by companies other than those listed in Sections II and III. If you can't find a particular company in this section, it will probably show up in Section V "Cookie Jar Handlers," which encompasses decorators, distributors, importers and retailers. For instance, Ransburg, familiar to many for its crock jars, was a decorating and distributing firm that did not manufacture pottery. And Pottery Guild, also familiar to many collectors as a company that made quality cookie jars, was in reality a sales organization that marketed ceramic products made by the Cronin China Company, of Minerva, Ohio.

Chapter 21
Potteries

Bauer Pottery

The Bauer Pottery, of Los Angeles, California, was started shortly after the turn of the century by J.A. Bauer as a family run organization. It lasted until the late 1950s or early 1960s.

It is believed Bauer used California clays nearly exclusively. Cheerfully colored mix-and-match dinnerware, made famous by Homer Laughlin's Fiesta Ware, is said to have been a Bauer innovation of the 1930s.

Apparently more into table service than cookie jars, Bauer, along with Gladding McBean, Pacific Clay Products, Vernon Kilns, and Metlox was rated by Jo Cunningham (*The Collector's Encyclopedia of American Dinnerware*) as one of California's "big five" of dinnerware.

California Cleminsons

Called California Clay during its first two years, 1941 to 1943, this El Monte, California, pottery was run by George and Betty Cleminson. She handled the creative side of the venture, he took care of the commercial end. Like many successful potteries of that year, the Cleminsons began as an in-home business, soon outgrew their garage facilities, and eventually employed 165 people. The pottery lasted until 1963.

California Cleminsons cookie jars are unusual in that they were slip-decorated, a process by which colored liquefied clay is used to adorn pottery. The difference between slip decoration and glaze decoration, although slight, can be determined by running your fingers over it. Glaze decoration will be smooth, slip decora-

BAUER POTTERY

CALIFORNIA CLEMINSONS

This Bauer Pottery swirled jar, perhaps a poke, is 9 inches high. The mark is "Bauer/Made in Calif./823" on three lines. *Courtesy of Betty and Floyd Carson.* $150

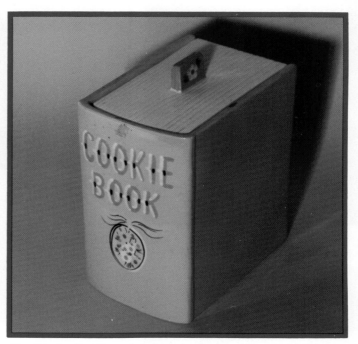

This "Cookie Book" stands 9-3/4 inches high and is marked "Cleminsons/ Hand Painted" on two lines. *Oravitz Collection.* $120

tion will be raised slightly. Slip-decorated pottery is more costly to produce as the decoration must be applied when the greenware is at the leather stage, shortly after being removed from the mold. The leather stage is the point when the greenware is dry enough to handle without altering its shape, yet wet enough that slip will still adhere to it. The increased cost is partially due to the pottery's fragility in the leather stage, which means much more breakage occurs than when fire hardened bisque is decorated.

Other jars produced by the California Cleminsons include a canister jar with straight sides, which is part of a set decorated with a single fruit such as a pear, apple or pineapple. A plain, somewhat bulbous canister that says "Cookies" on the front was made, too.

Most pottery was labeled with an inkstamp. All known marks include the word "Cleminsons."

Coors Ceramics

Cookies and beer instead of cookies and milk? Maybe. This firm, located in Golden, Colorado, is owned by the Adolph Coors Company, the parent corporation of Coors Brewery.

The pottery was founded in 1910 as the Herold China and Pottery Company, its name being changed to the Coors Porcelain Company 11 years later. It is still operating today, but is now known as Coors Ceramics. Heavily into industrial ceramics throughout its history, a foray into the artware and dinnerware markets during the 1930s helped Coors Porcelain limp through the Great Depression. According to Lehner, all artware and dinnerware production ceased in 1939.

Although it made a few giftware items for Coors Brewery in the 1950s, today the company is devoted solely to industrial ceramics that have applications in fields such as chemistry, rocketry and electronics.

Do not confuse Coors Ceramics, or its predecessors, with the H.F. Coors Company, Inc. of Inglewood, California. The California pottery was started by Adolph Coors' brother, Herman F. Coors,

and his wife, in 1925. As far as is known, the H.F. Coors Company never made cookie jars.

DeForest of California

A family-owned, family-operated pottery in Duarte, California, DeForest bucked the trend and proved that the right product, coupled with efficient business practices, can stand up in the face of intense foreign competition.

Margaret DeForest turned her ceramics hobby into a thriving business in 1950, during the same era that many established American potteries were closing down due to Japanese undercutting. At times DeForest of California employed as many as 80 people. Margaret DeForest's husband, Jack, and sons John and Roger, were also involved in the enterprise.

Besides the cookie jar shown below, DeForest of California made jars depicting bears, clowns, elephants, monkeys and owls, and also a cookie barrel. Most, but not all, DeForest jars are finished in the same earth-tone brown shown below. Earth tones were favorites with many California potteries during the 1960s and 1970s.

DeForest cookie jars may have been marketed regionally, as they appear to be much more common in California and the West than in the Midwest.

DeForest of California ceased operations in 1970.

Monks are fairly common in cookie jars, nuns are much rarer. This one is 12-1/2 inches high and its mark is shown. *Courtesy of Jazz'e Junque Shop, Chicago, Illinois.* $300

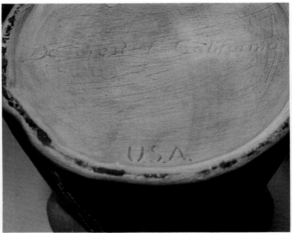

Mark of the nun. Somewhat light, it reads "Deforest of California/U.S.A." on two lines.

The Coors crock is 10 inches high and its mark is shown. *Zera Collection.* $50

Mark of Coors jar.

Frankoma Pottery, Inc.

The work of John Frank, founder of Frankoma, is somewhat drab when compared to the brightly colored, upbeat cookie jars put out by most other potteries. But any representative jar collection should probably include at least one example, as it seems virtually certain that Frankoma will be remembered as one of the important smaller potteries of mid-20th Century America.

Frank, who had been educated at the Chicago Art Institute, started a studio pottery in Norman, Oklahoma, in 1933 while

152

working in the ceramics department of the University of Oklahoma. He went full-time beginning in 1936, and moved his business to Sapulpa, Oklahoma in 1938. Frank died in 1973. His daughter, Joniece, ran the pottery until February 1991 when it was sold to Richard Bernstein. It's still operating today.

Frankoma jars can be roughly dated by the color of the bisque. Prior to 1954, Frank used a yellowish tan clay from the Arbuckle Mountains near Ada, Oklahoma. Since then Frankoma has been made with a red clay taken form Sugar Loaf Hill, near Sapulpa.

Most Frankoma cookie jars are marked with the name of the company, either impressed or in raised letters. But decoration, and to a lesser degree style, often makes Frankoma instantly recognizable. Glaze is most often two-tone, with the darker color being that of the body of the jar. Designs generally reflect a country flavor, or the simple lines of Art deco influence.

FRANKOMA POTTERY

This barrel jar is 7-1/2 inches high. It is a red clay, indicating it was made later than 1953. Mark is "Frankoma." Westfall shows a similar jar finished with a coal black glaze. *Zera Collection.* $50

Looks the same, but looks can be deceiving. This jar is larger than the brown one, 9 inches high, and marked "97V/Frankoma" impressed on two lines. *Courtesy of Grinder's Switch, Avon, Ohio.* $75

Some say it is a dove, others say it is a duck. The height is 7-1/2 inches. It is marked "U.S.A./F.A.P.co." impressed on two lines. *Zera Collection.* $75

Fredericksburg Art Pottery Company (FAPCO)

Birds and bartenders comprise the cookie jars for which this company is best known, but other themes also exist.

John McClane and George Hisler opened Fredericksburg Art Pottery in 1939 in a vacant building in Fredericksburg, Ohio. By then the plant had seen a good bit of ceramics history. At one time or another since 1911, it was owned and operated by the Wooster China Company, National Sanitary Company, Mansfield Sanitary Company, and the American Beleek Company. McClane had made some collectibles history by then, too, being co-founder and president of the Sun Rubber Company of Barberton, maker of children's toys. Fredericksburg closed in 1948. In 1949, the Pilgrim Pottery took over the plant with George Standford Jr. (Stanford Pottery) as president, and McClane as vice president. The new company made artware until going broke in 1952, but it hasn't been determined if it made cookie jars. The general belief is that Pilgrim didn't mark its pottery, so the answer may never be known. The plant was occupied by two other pottery companies prior to fire claiming it on May 26, 1965.

One of Fredericksburg's most popular cookie jars is said to have been the brown hen with the chick on her back, shown below.

FAPCO is often credited with making the National Silver Company's mammy and chef. While this may be true, many potteries made products for National Silver, which was a New York distributor. Attempting to attribute individual National Silver mammies or chefs to FAPCO would be extremely difficult at best, probably impossible.

Most Fredericksburg cookie jars are marked. A variation of the most common mark is shown below.

FREDERICKSBURG ART POTTERY (FAPCO)

This hen with a chick on her back is said to have been one of FAPCO's best-sellers. Each jar is 7-1/4 inches high. The impressed mark reads "U.S.A./F.A.P.co." on two lines. *Taylor Collection.* $50 ea.

Two more of the same birds with the same size and mark. *Oravitz Collection.* $75 ea.

153

Brown bear, 12-1/4 inches high. The mark is the same as the polar bear, which is shown. *Bosson Collection.* $110

The "Bartender" in blue and green. The jars are 10-1/2 inches high and marked "USA." Long credited to Fredericksburg, the bartender was recently found with a Pan-American art paper label, according to Joyce Roerig. Perhaps this explains why the mark on the "Bartender" doesn't include the words "FAPCO," or "FAP," as other FAPCO jars do. Other Pan-American Art cookie jars appear on page 170 under the heading "San Jose Potteries." *Bosson Collection.* $350 ea.

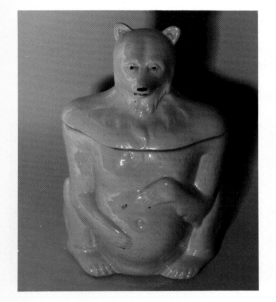

FAPCO polar bear, 12-1/4 inches high, with mark shown. *Oravitz Collection.* $110

Dutch windmill, 10 inches high, marked "F.A.P.co." *Zera Collection.* $75

Windmill with red trim, the same size as the previous example, but marked a bit differently: "F.A.P." Besides the colors shown, the windmill was also made with blue, yellow, and gray blades. *Zera Collection.* $75

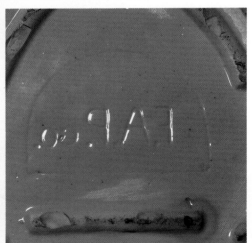

Reversed mark of FAPCO polar bear. You see the same thing with other potteries occasionally, particularly with Niloak of Benton, Arkansas.

Gilner

Very little is known about Gilner, including exactly what it was. It might have been a pottery, distributor, importer, or line. It might even have been a department store.

Here's what is known: Gilner was located somewhere in California, and was active in 1951. The information comes from Fred Strunk and Denise Dakoulis, well known cookie jar collectors who have a Gilner spoon holder marked "Gilner Calif./©1951" on two lines.

Gilner was somehow connected to Triangle Studios, of Los Angeles and El Monte, California, which made cookie jars marked "Vallona Starr." The Peter Pumpkin Eater cookie jar below is often seen with a Vallona Star mark.

In addition to the jars shown below, Gilner is known to have made or marketed a crowing rooster, sitting bear, and a goose commonly referred to as Mother goose. While it appears all Gilner cookie jars were of very high quality, it is the mammy head jar that excites collectors the most.

Although this 11-inch high jar is unmarked, the spoonrest that was mentioned previously holds a companion shaker. *Blumenfeld Collection.* $2000

Gladding, McBean & Company (Franciscan)

This California firm was started in 1875 by transplanted Chicagoans Charles Gladding, Peter McGill McBean, and George Chambers. Original product was sewer tile from clay deposits near its Lincoln plant in Placer County, about 20 miles north of Sacramento. Terra-cotta ceramics for the construction industry followed about 10 years later. After a series of acquisitions—including, most notably, the Tropico Pottery in 1923 and the west coast facilities of American Encaustic Tiling Company in 1933—Gladding, McBean began producing dinnerware and art pottery in 1934. Frederick J. Grant served as the first art director. He was the former Weller Pottery president who had left that position one year earlier upon his divorce from Ethel Weller, daughter of the founder. Artware and dinnerware were made at plants in Los Angeles, and Glendale, California.

In 1962 Gladdening, McBean merged with Lock Joint Pipe Company, the name being changed to Interpace Corporation in 1963. Concentrating primarily on construction products, Interpace proved to be more than a casual dabbler in ceramics by acquiring the Shenango China Company, of New Castle, Pennsylvania, in 1964, and Alfred Meakin, of Tunstall, England, in 1974. In April 1979, Josiah Wedgewood and son, Ltd., of Barlston, Stoke-on-Trent, England, bought Interpace's Franciscan Division. Wedgewood closed the plant five years later.

With a heritage so rich in pottery royalty, you would expect Gladdening, McBean cookie jars to be truly spectacular. Unfortunately, it appears the company restricted production to rather mundane canister type jars as additions to canister sets, and to complement lines of dinnerware.

As far as is known, all marked Gladdening, McBean cookie jars include the word, "Franciscan," as shown below. Jars that evaded marking can often be identified by comparing them to Franciscan dinnerware patterns.

This Peter Pumpkin Eater, 8-1/4 inches high, is marked "Gilner/Potteries/Design Pat./©" impressed on four lines. Interestingly, the Roerigs photographed an identical jar that was marked "Vallona Starr Design Pat. copyright 49 California." *Courtesy of Betty and Floyd Carson.* $300

This canister jar is 11 inches high. Its mark is shown. *Courtesy of Homer and Bev Simpson.* $250

Mark of the canister jar.

This Franciscan cookie jar, or canister as the case may be, is 10-1/2 inches high. *Zera Collection.* $100

Haeger Potteries, Inc.

The Haeger Potteries began as a brickyard in Dundee, Illinois, in 1871, the same year of the Chicago Fire. It's still in operation today.

Always stronger in artware than kitchenware or dinnerware, Haeger has made few cookie jars. Besides those shown below, it also made a 12-1/2 inch high cookie barrel with the words "Cooky Barrel" on the front, and possibly other jars.

Two of Haeger's many marks are shown below.

The jar on the left was made by Haeger, the jar on the right by McCoy. The heights are 10-1/2 and 9-3/4 inches. The Haeger jar is unmarked, while the McCoy version is generally marked "USA/350" on two lines. The easiest way to tell them apart is by the elf, which is molded (three-dimensionally) on the Haeger jar, but is a flat decal on the McCoy jar. In *Collecting Royal Haeger*, co-author Lee Garmon cites a letter received from Haeger Potteries indicating the Haeger jar was made sometime prior to the McCoy jar, which was introduced in 1986. *Bosson Collection.* Left - $90, Right - $65

Hall China Company

The Hall China Company, of East Liverpool, Ohio, was set up in August, 1903 by Robert Hall, who died the next year. The business was than carried on by his son, Robert Taggart Hall.

Hall China Company took an unsuccessful stab at dinnerware from 1908 to 1911, long before the concept of the cookie jar was ever thought of. Hall reentered the dinnerware market in 1936, and this time latched on to the brass ring, making lines for major retailers such as Montgomery Ward and Sears, and also providing restaurant-type ware, not only for restaurants but also for railroads and, later, airlines.

During World War I, Hall became the largest maker of teapots in the world, thanks in part to a well run advertising campaign aimed at educating the public about tea and the proper method of brewing it. Had the company pursued the same course when cookie jars were beginning to gain popularity 15 years later, there's no telling what might have been possible.

HALL CHINA COMPANY

This owl is 12-1/2 inches high and can easily be identified by its Hall backstamp. *Zera Collection.* $250

Inkstamp mark of Hall owl.

A canister jar, 9-1/2 inches high. The mark is shown. *Courtesy of Jazz'e Junque Shop, Chicago, Illinois.* $30

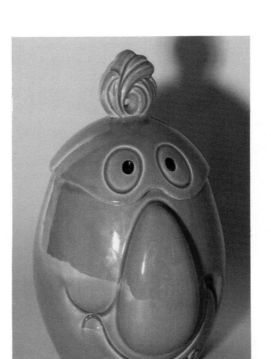

This jar is 11-1/2 inches high. Its mark is shown. *Oravitz Collection.* $300

Mark of the Haeger canister jar.

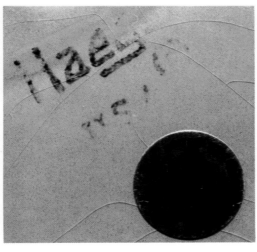

Inkstamp mark of above jar.

On the right is the autumn leaf pattern made for Jewel Tea. Both jars are 9-1/2 inches high, with marks showing. *Zera Collection.* Left - $85, Right - $150

Instead, it followed a path similar to Gladdening, McBean and Company (Franciscan), for the most part limiting cookie jar production to canister-type jars to be sold as accessories to its dinnerware and kitchen utility lines. Every so often a surprise will pop up, such as owl shown below, which Hall apparently made for itself and Carbone, Inc. a Boston distributor listed in Chapter 22. Best known of the Hall jars is the Autumn Leaf pattern, made exclusively for the Jewel Tea Company from 1933 until 1976.

Hall is still in business today.

Hall used many, many back stamps to mark its pottery. Several are shown below.

Mark of Hall autumn leaf cookie jar that was also used on other pieces in the Jewel Tea line.

Hall Flare Ware jar, 9 inches high. The mark is shown. *Zera Collection.* $85

This jar, and the other three of the same shape, are 8-1/2 inches high. The mark is shown. *Courtesy of Jazz'e Junque Shop, Chicago, Illinois.* $60

Unmarked Hall jar with geranium transfer. Probably part of a canister set, the jar stands 8-1/2 inches high. *Zera Collection.* $50

Mark of Hall Flare Ware jar.

Hall jar with poppy transfer. The height is 6-3/4 inches. The Hall backstamp is shown. *Zera Collection.* $200

Mark of the green Hall jar.

Same as the geranium jar but a solid color. This jar is also unmarked. *Zera Collection.* $50

Mark of the Hall jar with poppy transfer.

This jar is also 8-1/2 inches. The mark is very similar to that of the green jar, but is done in gold. *Courtesy of Jazz'e Junque Shop, Chicago, Illinois.* $85

157

Another jar like that above. *Courtesy of Charles Kidd.* $50

A slightly different story here. The jar is 9-1/2 inches high, poured very heavy, and is marked by a gold "Hall" stamp with a circle around it. The mark is found inside the lid. *Courtesy of Betty and Floyd Carson.* $50

William H. Hirsch Manufacturing Company

Although manufacturing is in this company's name it was actually a sales organization, not a pottery. Aside from that little is known other than that it was active by 1946, and trade journals from that time place it in Hollywood, California. The mark shown below, however, very clearly states Los Angeles. It also shows that the company lasted until at least 1958. Hirsch is said to have made florist ware, figurines, miniatures, and other ceramic products.

While most collectors are aware of the monk cookie jar, those interviewed did not know of any other jars the company might have made.

This monk is 12-1/4 inches high. It is a fairly common jar in the midwest, having shown up in several of the collections photographed. *Courtesy of Betty and Floyd Carson.* $60

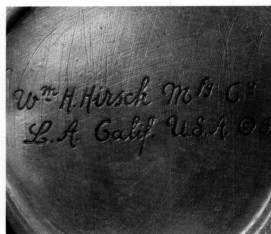

Mark of the Hirsch monk. Some of these jars were marked by an inkstamp.

Hoening of California

All that was found on Hoenig is what you see below—that it made a nice pumpkin jar, somewhat in the Art Deco style, and that the firm was apparently located in California. While the possibility exists that Hoenig might have been an importer, the inclusion of California in its name suggest a domestic pottery. Hoenig of California console sets that are seen have a definite late-1950s or early-1960s flavor.

HOENIG OF CALIFORNIA

A Hoenig pumpkin, 7-1/2 inches high. The mark is "Hoenig/of/California/660" on four lines. *Taylor Collection.* $40

Holiday Designs, Inc.

Holiday Designs, located in Sebring, Ohio, was established in 1964, but today functions as an arm of Designer Accents, the same parent company that bought Nelson McCoy Ceramics. Kitchen artware is its main output. Many of its products have been marketed through Sears, and other major retailers. The pottery is made in the same plant that was used by Spaulding China Company, the maker of Royal Copley, which is now just beginning to be fully appreciated by collectors.

Some Holiday Designs cookie jars are marked with its name, but many are not. However, a lot of the company's jars can be identified by an inkstamped, "22222."

The owls are 12-1/4 inches high. Their marks indicate Holiday Designs. *Oravitz Collection.* $65 ea.

HOLIDAY DESIGNS, INC.

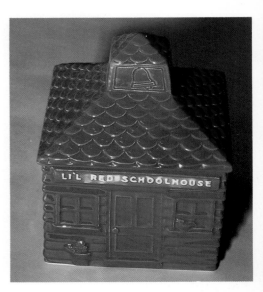

Due to its glaze and design, if this cat cookie jar wasn't marked one would probably tend to think it was Doranne of California. It is 12 inches high, and its mark is shown. *Courtesy of Jazz'e Junque Shop, Chicago, Illinois.* $70

A 12-inch high panda is marked "Holiday Designs/USA" on two lines on the bottom. Another example photographed was marked "Holiday Designs" on one line inside the neck of the lid. *Oravitz Collection.* $75

The little red schoolhouse is 9-1/2 inches high, with a "22222" inkstamp. *Lilly Collection.* $45

Mark of the Holiday Designs cat. The change in color resulted from a combination of the critical nature of lighting in close-up photography, and the writer's noncritical approach to it.

These instructions were packaged inside the little red schoolhouse jar.

This jar is called a "Dawg," according to Holiday Designs. It is 12 inches high. The mark is a simple "USA" impressed in the head. However, the advertising on the original box is "4193 Dawg, Almond, ©Holiday Designs, USA, Sebring, OH, Ph 216-938-2194." *Oravitz Collection.* $65

Obviously the king of beasts, this jar is 12 inches high, with "©Holiday Designs/USA" impressed on two lines and a "22222" inkstamp. *Bosson Collection.* $75

Snoopy is 12-1/4 inches high and has "22222" stamped on bottom along with "USA©Holiday Designs." *Courtesy of Betty and Floyd Carson.* $75

159

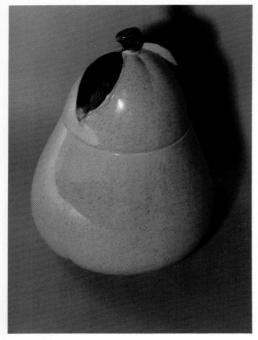

A 12-1/2 inch high pear, with a "22222" inkstamp. *Oravitz Collection.* $45

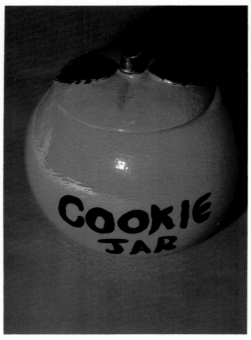

This orange is 8-1/2 inches high and has a "22222" inkstamp. *Lilly Collection.* $45

Canister, 13 inches high. The bottom of the jar is inkstamped "22222." *Lilly Collection.* $35

House of Webster Ceramics

House of Webster cookie jars are not marketed as such, but are used as containers for gifts of honey, jam, jelly, etc. The jars are made by Eastland Ceramics, Eastland, Texas, but are filled at, and shipped from, Rogers, Arkansas. In the past, House of Webster is said to have shipped as many as 200,000 pieces of pottery per year.

One House of Webster mark is illustrated below. Another shows a similar cabin with a fence in front, a tall pine tree at each end, and a mountain in the rear, but no wording.

HOUSE OF WEBSTER

The telephone is 8-3/4 inches high, the coffee grinder 8 inches high. Both have House of Webster inkstamps. *Courtesy of Jazz'e Junque Shop, Chicago, Illinois.* Left - $40, Right - $30

There's a real bell in the bell tower of this 8-1/2 inch high House of Webster jar. The mark is shown opposite. *Zera Collection.* $50

House of Webster mark.

An unmarked House of Webster raspberry, 6-1/2 inches high. *Zera Collection.* $30

Shock of wheat, 7-1/4 inches high, with the House of Webster inkstamp. This design is very similar to a jar made by Metlox. *Oravitz Collection.* $30

160

The basket of strawberries is 7-1/4 inches high and has the House of Webster backstamp. *Taylor Collection*. $20

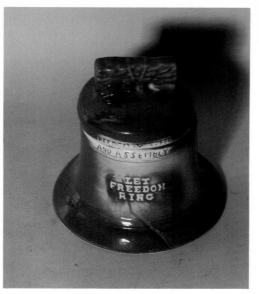

Liberty Bell, 6 inches high, with House of Webster inkstamp. *Courtesy of Jazz'e Junque Shop, Chicago, Illinois*. $35

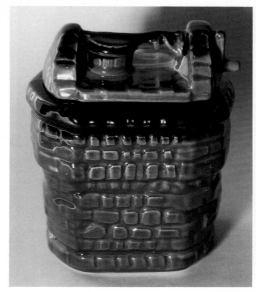

Unmarked House of Webster wishing well, 7 inches high. *Oravitz Collection*. $35

Imperial Porcelain Corporation

This company was located in Zanesville, Ohio. It was established by three doctors in 1946, remained in business until 1960 when it was sold to Denzil Harding, who changed the name to Imperial Pottery. A fire claimed the plant in 1967, by which time a change in Zanesville's zoning code is said to have prevented rebuilding.

Imperial Porcelain is best known for its Paul Webb figures. These included the Al Capp "Dogpatch" series, Americana Folklore Miniatures, and the Paul Webb Mountain Boys series. They were the joint effort of artist Paul Webb, who developed Li'l Abner for Al Capp, and Imperial ceramic designer, Paul Genter. The Paul Webb characters are said to have made and broke the pottery. They were the firm's most popular pieces, but the high cost of royalties paid to Capp and Webb made them unprofitable.

The two jars shown below do not contain a recognizable Imperial mark. But one does have a Daisy Mae copyright, and both jars reek of the various Paul Webb lines. They were photographed in Zanesville at a shop whose owner is somewhat of a historian on Zanesville potteries, and for those reasons they are *assumed* to be Imperial Porcelain. It is hoped that in they future concrete evidence will surface to prove their origin one way or another.

Judy of California

No information was found on this company. All of the jars below were copyrighted in the 1970s. Obviously from canister sets, they are often collected as cookie jars.

JUDY OF CALIFORNIA

This jar, commonly referred to as "The Bum," is 13 inches high. It is marked "USA." *Courtesy of Elvin R. and Frances (Jerry) Culp.* $900

"©Daisy Mae" is marked inside the lid of this jar. It stands 13 inches high. A collector from New Jersey sent me a picture of this same base with a plain flat lid. However, the color of the glaze on the lid did not exactly match that of the base, so I hesitate to say Imperial made a third jar until other examples surface. *Courtesy of Elvin R. and Frances (Jerry) Culp.* $1000

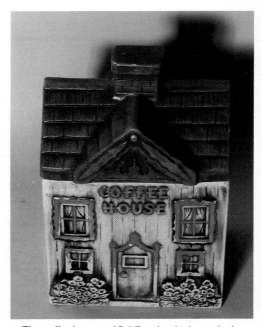

This coffee house is 10-1/2 inches high, marked "Judy/of California/©1977 USA C841" on three lines. *Courtesy of Jazz'e Junque Shop, Chicago, Illinois*. $65

161

The bake shop is marked "Judy/of California/©1977 USA BS-4" on three lines. *Courtesy of Jazz'e Junque Shop, Chicago, Illinois.* $65

The mill is 12-1/2 inches high. The mark is the same as the bake shop. *Courtesy of Jazz'e Junque Shop, Chicago, Illinois.* $65

Los Angeles Potteries

Started in 1940 by the owners of a company that made brass plumbing fixtures, the original intent of this Lynwood, California, firm was to make sanitary ware. Equipment limitations kept it from doing so, and forced the pottery down the path of artware and figurines.

The N.S. Gustin Company, of Los Angeles, distributed its products. According to Derwich and Latos, at least one cookie jar became a staple of Sperry & Hutchinson (S & H green stamps). As far as is known, all of Los Angeles Potteries' cookie jars were hand decorated.

In 1970 Los Angeles Potteries liquidated and sold its molds to N.S. Gustin which used them at Designcraft, a pottery it owned in West Los Angeles, California. Designcraft is still operating in West Los Angeles, but its name has been changed to Los Angeles pottery. It is now owned by David Gustin, grandson of Nelson Sage Gustin, founder of the Gustin company. The pottery makes ceramic products, including cookie jars, for the N.S. Gustin Company, of which David Gustin is vice president.

LOS ANGELES POTTERIES

This jar is called the wedding pineapple. It is 11-1/2 inches high and marked "L.A. Potteries ©'65/89 Calif. USA" on two lines. *Courtesy of Jazz'e Junque Shop, Chicago, Illinois.* $100

The height of this little porker is 10 inches. It is marked "Los Angeles/84/Potteries/hand Decorated/Calif. USA" impressed on five lines. *Oravitz Collection.* $50

Maddux of California

The company was established by William Maddux in Los Angeles in 1938. Louis and Dave Warsaw purchased it in 1948. Morris Bogdanow bought Dave Warsaw's share in 1956 and later bought out Louis Warsaw, too. A new plant was built in 1958, pottery was no longer made after 1974, and Maddux of California went out of business in 1980, four years after Morris Bogdanow's son, Norman, had taken over the business. Add that Maddux acquired two other potteries over the years, Hollywood Ceramics and Valley Vista Pottery, and you have its 42-year story in a nutshell.

Perhaps best known for the many flamingo figurines it made during the earlier years, Maddux isn't believed to have begun making cookie jars until the late 1950s or early 1960s. Besides the jars shown below, Maddux also did a series that included a rabbit, cat, and bear, each carrying a basket and an umbrella. The bottoms of three jars are identical, only the tops being different.

As far as is known, all Maddux cookie jars are marked.

MADDUX OF CALIFORNIA

Tall at 15-1/4 inches, this particular Raggedy Andy is marked "USA©2108" but other examples include the Maddux name. *Zera Collection.* $225

162

Marcia Ceramics of California

According to Derwich and Latos, this Los Angeles firm started about 1940, and was run as a family business. In the early 1980s it was being operated by Gerald and Michael Siegal, and their father, George Siegal.

MARCIA CERAMICS OF CALIFORNIA

An 8-legged reindeer, 11-1/2 inches high. The mark is "DCJ-19©1985©/NAC" on two lines. *Zera Collection*. $35

Squirrel or chipmunk, 13 inches high, marked "Maddux of /Calif.©/Romanelli 2110" on three lines. The Romanelli is possibly for Carl Romanelli, a Los Angeles sculptor known to have worked for Metlox and, apparently, other potteries. *Oravitz Collection*. $225

This bear is very much like one made by Metlox. It is 12-1/4 inches high and marked "Marcia Ceramics©84" around the base in back. *Oravitz Collection*. $45

The same size and mark as the above jar, but without the lavender trim. *Courtesy of Jazz'e Junque Shop, Chicago, Illinois*. $35

Humpty Dumpty, 11 inches high. The mark is "2113/Maddux of California/©USA" on three lines. The jar is also seen with a white collar and, sometimes, a white vest. *Oravitz Collection*. $225

Goat, 12-1/2 inches high. The mark is "GKJ8©1987/NAC/USA" on three lines. *Zera Collection*. $35

The black cat is 6-1/2 inches high. It is marked "DCJ 18©1985/NAC" on two lines. *Zera Collection*. $65

The dinosaur is 8 inches high, marked "CJ-50©1986/NAC USA" on two lines. *Coughenour Collection*. $65

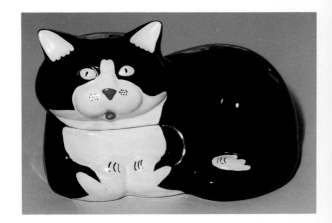

163

Maurice Ceramics of California

This company is located in Los Angeles, and is run by Maurice Peckman. It was in business by 1967, perhaps earlier.

In addition to the jars shown below, Maurice is also known to have made a large rooster, a brown sitting bear with a drum, brown sitting monkey, a brown, sitting puppy with a pink "Love me" sign, a chef head, an elephant, an Indian with a bow and arrow, and a locomotive.

One Maurice mark is shown below. A second mark is similar but incised in script.

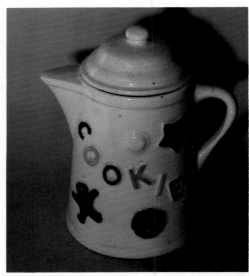

The clown is 13-1/2 inches high. Its mark is "JD 19-Maurice©California USA" on one line. Sometimes it is seen unmarked. *Oravitz Collection.* $300

MAURICE CERAMICS OF CALIFORNIA

Pair of cats, 10-1/2 inches high. Westfall shows this jar in yellow. The mark is pictured below. *Courtesy of Mercedes DiRenzo.* $85

Mark of the Maurice cats.

The frog is 11 inches high and marked "Maurice Ceramics/MP21" on two lines. *Bosson Collection.* $190

MORTON POTTERIES

Morton coffee pot, 11-3/4 inches high, marked "USA-3721." *Bosson Collection.* $75

Morton Pottery Company

The Morton Pottery Company has a long and involved history that is far too complicated to cover in a book on cookie jars.

In a paragraph, what collector's generally refer to as the Morton Pottery was incorporated in Morton, Illinois, near Peoria, on December 8, 1922. The first kiln of pottery was fired seven months later on July 7, 1923. Incorporators of the company were William Rapp, Dan W. Rapp, and J.E. Gerber. The Rapps were sons of Andrew Rapp, the oldest of six brothers who founded the Rapp Brothers Brick and Tile Company in Morton in 1877. Several other sons of Andrew Rapp were also involved in the new pottery.

The company was sold to William York and Ronald Cowan in 1969, after which it underwent several changes in name and ownership before the kilns cooled permanently in 1976. The building was razed in 1979.

Morton made utility ware, and later expanded to giftware and figurines. According to the Roerigs, it was one of the earliest players in the cookie jar game, making the hen jar with chick finial in 1930. It also made a similarly designed turkey. All known Morton jars are either unmarked, or have a non-attributing mark such as that on the coffee pot below.

Unmarked Morton hen, 8-3/4 inches high. *Zera Collection.* $80

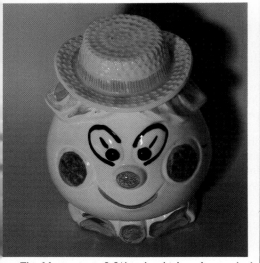

This Morton jar is 9-3/4 inches high and unmarked. It is very heavy. *Oravitz Collection.* $125

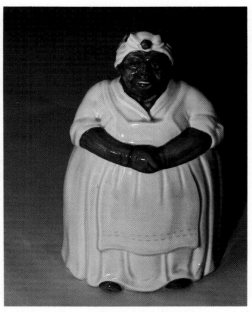

Mosaic Tile mammy, 13-1/4 inches high, unmarked. *Zera Collection.* $500

Yellow mammy, the other most common color for Mosaic's only cookie jar. *Coughenour Collection.* $500

Mosaic Tile Company

Mosaic Tile Company was organized in 1894 in Zanesville, Ohio, by American Encaustic Tiling Company renegades, Herman Mueller and Karl Langenbeck, and several other partners. Throughout the years it bought out several other tile companies. These acquisitions included Atlantic Tile and Manufacturing Company (Matawan, New Jersey) 1920, Carlyle Tile Company (El Segundo, California) 1937. Mosaic Tile Company was a large operation that had branch offices, sales agencies, and warehouses scattered across the country. By 1925 it employed 1250 people. The company was dissolved in 1967.

The mammy shown here is the only cookie jar Mosaic Tile is known to have made. The design of the jar was patented by Kenneth Gale in 1943 or 1944. Gale was Mosaic's director of design. He was 16 years old in 1923 when he began working in Mosaic's design department during summer vacation. He started full-time with the company upon graduating from high school. Mosaic sent him to Chicago to study art for a year, and to Europe to study for another year. Gale retired when the company closed in 1967. He died in December 1990 at age 83.

According to Roy Greene, a designer who spent 31 years with the company, and who was Gale's assistant, the mammies were made and decorated at the Mosaic plant. But they were not made as a sales item. Greene said they were given as gifts, primarily to architects. This was during World War II when the demand for tile was low and the competition among building material manufacturers was stiff, if not cutthroat. At the end of the war, production was halted, he said. How many mammies were made is not known.

It is known, however, that prototypes or limited production examples were made in at least six additional colors.

Pacific Stoneware, Inc.

Pacific Clay Products Company, of Los Angeles, California, used a mark that included the words "Pacific Stoneware, Inc.," so it is likely that Pacific Clay made the jars illustrated below.

The company was established in Los Angeles in 1881 as a brick and tile manufacturer. It made products of red clay, another point toward attribution. In 1932 Pacific Clay switched to dinnerware and made quite a name for itself in the field. During World War II it dropped dinnerware to make radio insulators. What happened after that is uncertain, but it apparently remained in business for some years later.

Attempts to reach Pacific Stoneware and Pacific Clay Products were unsuccessful.

PACIFIC STONEWARE

Mark on the side of the orange pig. If you look closely at the picture of the jar, you'll see the lavender also appears between the pig's feet.

Bottom of orange pig.

This pig is 14-1/2 inches high. The Roerigs picture it with the colors reversed, green with orange trim, but the orange is very muted. Its marks are shown. *Oravitz Collection.* $75

Pacific Stoneware cat, 13-3/4 inches high. The mark is shown. *Zera Collection.* $95

Mark of the cat, somewhat different from that of the pig.

Pearl China Company

Pearl China was owned by George Singer, possibly in partnership with his brother, Dennis Singer. It was located in East Liverpool, Ohio, in a plant leased from the Hall China Company. George Singer was a jobber who is said to have opened the pottery as a means of acquiring additional inventory. The company employed about 165 people during the mid-1940s, was bought by Craft Master Corporation, Toledo, Ohio, in 1958.

The only cookie jars thus far associated with Pearl China are the Cooky and Mammy shown below, a watermelon mammy in the same color, and a sitting bear. The bear appears in the light yellow glaze of the Cooky and Mammy, and also in a light blue glaze.

All known Pearl China jars are trimmed with gold.

PEARL CHINA COMPANY

"Cooky" and "Mammy." *Left*: 10-3/4 inches high. *Right*: 10-1/2 inches. The mark of Cooky is shown below. Salt and peppers in range size and table size were made to accompany these jars. *Courtesy of Jazz'e Junque Shop, Chicago, Illinois.* Left - $500, Right - $800

Mark of Pearl China Cooky. There is also "639" impressed in another area of the bottom.

PENNSBURY POTTERY

Red barn Pennsbury cookie jar, 8-1/2 inches high. The mark is shown. *Courtesy of Jazz'e Junque Shop, Chicago, Illinois.* $100

Reverse of Pennsbury jar.

Pennsbury Pottery

The Pennsbury Pottery was started in Morrisville, Pennsylvania, in 1950, by husband and wife team Henry and Lee Below who were natives of Germany. Both had worked for the Stangl Pottery, of Trenton, New Jersey, directly across the Delaware River from Morrisville. Pennsbury Pottery was named for the nearby Bucks County estate of Pennsylvania founder William Penn.

The company filed for bankruptcy in 1970, two years after the death of Lee Below, and 11 years after Henry Below had passed away. An April, 1971 fire claimed the building that had housed the pottery.

In her book, *Pennsbury Pottery*, Lucille Henzke presents a Pennsbury catalog that refers to the jar shown below as the red barn cookie jar. Four others of the same shape are illustrated on the same page—"Red Rooster," "Black Rooster," "Harvest" depicting an Amish man and woman carrying a litter of vegetables, and "Hex" showing a Pennsylvania Dutch hex sign. The same designs were used on pitchers, plates, and other Pennsbury pieces.

As far as is known, all Pennsbury cookies jars are marked. In the event some did slip through unmarked, the pottery is distinctive enough that identifying them should not pose a problem.

Mark of Pennsbury jar.

The Pfaltzfraff Company

Those whose collections include a Pfaltzgraff cookie jar have the pleasure of owning a jar made by the oldest pottery in the United States to make cookie jars. The company was founded in 1811 by German immigrant George Pfaltzgraff, whose initial efforts encompassed utilitarian redware and stoneware. Pfaltzgraff is still in business, a subsidiary of Susquehanna Pfaltzgraff Company, which is owned by the descendants of George Pfaltzgraff. Treasure Craft and Syracuse China Corporation are also subsidiaries of Susquehanna Pfaltzgraff.

The Derby Dan Muggsy jar below is an accessory for a line of mugs with names such as Sleepy Sam and Pickled Pete. Lehner dates the mugs (and presumably the cookie jar) in the 1940s, while Derwich and Latos place them in the 1950s. They probably overlapped both decades. Dates of the other jars are unknown.

PFALTZGRAFF POTTERY COMPANY

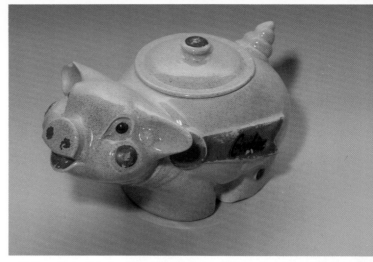

Pfaltzgraff pig, 7 inches high. The mark is a "P" in a keystone. *Oravitz Collection.* $75

Here's old "Derby Dan," 8-1/2 inches high. The mark is "Derby Dan/Muggsie/the Pfaltzgraff Pottery Co./York, Penn/Designed by Jessop" on five lines. *Zera Collection.* $200

This locomotive is 9 inches high and marked "USA." The Roerigs show it unmarked with a white body, the Derby Dan colors for trim, and a face painted on the front. *Oravitz Collection.* $150

The clock is unmarked, 10 inches high. *Zera Collection.* $150

Purinton Pottery Company

On the same day that the Japanese air force destroyed our navy at Pearl Harbor—December 7, 1941—the Purinton Pottery Company, of Shippenville, Pennsylvania, fired its first kiln load of ceramics.

The company was named for its president and principal investor, Bernard S. Purinton, of Wellsville, Ohio. It remained in business until 1960. Most of the company's products, including cookie jars, were slip decorated. Dark red, close to but not quite burgundy, was a predominate color at Purinton Pottery. Many Purinton pieces are unmarked.

For those who would like a more detailed view of the Purinton Pottery Company and its products, *Purinton Pottery,* by Jamie Bero-Johnson and Jamie Johnson (Schiffer) is an excellent source.

Unmarked Purinton Humpty Dumpty, 11 inches high. This is a heavy jar. *Coughenour Collection.* $450

Purinton Howdy Doody, 9-3/4 inches high and unmarked. *Courtesy of Jazz'e Junque Shop, Chicago, Illinois.* $650

Canister type cookie jar, 10 inches high, unmarked. *Zera Collection.* $100

PURINTON POTTERY COMPANY

Same as the jar previously but 9-3/4 inches high. *Oravitz Collection.* $110

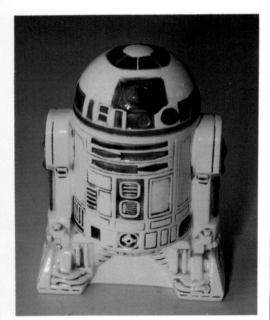

Unmarked apple, 9 inches high. It is believed to be Purinton because of the color and the brush strokes in the apple. *Zera Collection.* $125

Roman Ceramics

Roman Ceramics was located in Mayfield, Kentucky, a city about 25 miles south of Paducah in the western part of the state. It was owned by Harold Roman, who also owned California Originals beginning in 1979. Production at Roman Ceramics is said to have started prior to World War II. It ended in 1982.

Roman Ceramics referred to its line as Cumberland Ware, which accounts for its mark, a "C" through a "W," as shown below. In addition to the two jars illustrated, the company is known to have made a mouse sailor jar, monk, koala, and head jars of W.C. Fields, Stan Laurel, and Oliver Hardy.

ROMAN CERAMICS

Mark of Smokey the Bear.

Smokey the Bear, 13-3/4 inches high. The mark is shown. *Oravitz Collection.* $100

R2-D2 from the Star Wars movie series. When photographed this jar had a white plastic liner. It fit perfectly, and prevented cookies from falling down into R2-D2's feet where they would have been accessible only by turning the jar upside down and letting them fall out. The height is 12-1/2 inches and the mark is shown. *Zera Collection.* $350

Smokey with blue bow tie and red buttons. *Bosson Collection.* $100

Mark of R2-D2. Marks such as this show only the year of the copyright, which is often different than the year the jar was manufactured.

Roseville Pottery, Inc.

For 56 of its 64 years in business, Roseville Pottery's name was a misnomer. The company made a permanent move to Zanesville, Ohio, in 1898, eight years after being founded in Roseville, about 15 miles to the south. The original name was Roseville Pottery Company, which was changed to Roseville Pottery, Inc. in the early 1930s.

Breaking the stereotypical image many have of 1890s businessmen and business practices—gray hair and mustache, wire-rimmed glasses, scowl, stogie, and a conservative approach—the company hired George Frank Young in 1891, at the tender age of 27, to serve as secretary and general manager. Young guided Roseville on a path that eventually led to it being recognized as one of the foremost art potteries in the United States. Along the way, he bought up shares of stock until he owned the company outright.

The flowered cookie jars shown below were made in the 1940s. Note that the jars comprise four different shapes, the handles being the most variable feature. Sharon and Bob Huxford, in *The Collector's Encyclopedia of Roseville Pottery*, show another shape, known as No. 5. It's a slightly more rounded form, with handles to match; the line is Zephyr Lilly.

Most Roseville cookie jars are marked. A couple examples of Roseville's many marks are shown below.

ROSEVILLE

Two more "Clematis" colors. Same size and similar mark to others on page. *Zera Collection.* $300 ea.

Two Magnolia jars. Both are 10-1/2 inches high. The blue jar has same mark as the rust Water Lily; the green jar's mark is the same as the Freesia cookie jar but with the numbers "2.8." *Zera Collection.* $300 ea.

Roseville "Clematis" cookie jar, 10-1/2 inches high. Mark is shown. *Zera Collection.* $300

Roseville "Freesia" cookie jar, 10-1/2 inches high. Same mark as above but the number is "4.8." *Zera Collection.* $300

Rust with "Water Lily," same mark but the number is "1.8." *Zera Collection.* $350

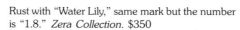

This is from Roseville's "Glossy Utility" line from the 1950s. It is 10 inches high, and the mark is shown. Jar was also made in green and possibly other colors. *Zera Collection.* $75

Mark of blue "Glossy Utility" cookie jar.

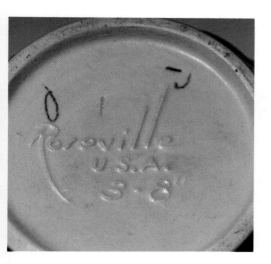

Mark of Roseville "Clematis" jar.

San Jose Potteries

This pottery was located in San Antonio, Texas. It is known to have been in business by 1945, perhaps earlier. San Jose Potteries was owned by James M.A. Cassel, who was manager of a New York firm called Michaelian and Kohlberg, Inc., which was listed in trade journals as operator of the pottery. In all probability, Michaelian and Kohlberg was a distributor that decided to open a pottery, or buy an already existing one, in order to have more control over its product lines. San Jose made dinnerware, art pottery, and decorative accessories.

The two cookie jars shown below are the only ones known to date that were made by San Jose. Both are marked, "Pan American Art." San Jose is known to have used a paper label with its name on it, possibly an incised mark with its name on it, too, so it wouldn't be surprising if a jar marked San Jose showed up in the future.

Another jar by San Jose is shown on page 154.

Clown, 11-1/4 inches high. Marked "Pan-American/Art" impressed on two lines. *Zera Collection.* $75

SAN JOSE POTTERIES

Often called "Southern Belle," this jar is 11-1/2 inches high. The mark is shown. *Courtesy of Jazz'e Junque Shop, Chicago, Illinois.* $75

Mark of "Southern Belle." Somewhat light, the mark "©Pan-American/Art" appears on two lines.

"Southern Belle" in lighter bisque, 11-1/2 inches high. "Pan-American/Art" incised on two lines. *Zera Collection.* $75

Sierra Vista Ceramics

By most accounts, Sierra Vista Ceramics was founded in Sierra Vista, California, in 1942 by the father and son team of Reinhold and Leonard R. Lenaburg. Also, by most accounts, the elder partner retired in 1951, where upon the younger partner moved the company to Phoenix, Arizona, where it is assumed to have died a natural death some years later.

Generally left unexplained is the many Sierra Vista cookie jars marked "*Pasadena*, California," that show copyright dates as late as 1958. A recent article in *Crazed Over Cookie Jars*, however, stated Walter Starnes bought some of Sierra Vista's molds in 1952 and used them through at least part of 1954. Lending credibility to this statement is that Sierra Vista jars are often found carrying Starnes paper labels. But it still doesn't account for the later dates.

Sierra Vista is said to have relied on California clays to produce the cookie jars, lazy Susans, and other utility pieces and giftware for which it was known. The company made its own glazes but not always its own molds. Because it sometimes purchased molds from established mold companies, the possibility remains open that you may occasionally encounter homemade jars that are normally credited to Sierra Vista.

The cookie jar is 11 inches high, the bank 5-1/2 inches. The jar is marked "Sierra Vista/California" impressed on two lines. Westfall shows this jar with an earth-tone brown finish similar to Twin Winton or DeForest of California. *Blumenfeld Collection.* Left - $100, Right - $75

SIERRA VISTA POTTERY

The locomotive is 9-3/4 inches high. The smoke is the handle of the lid. The mark is "Sierra Vista/California" impressed on two lines. *Oravitz Collection.* $125

The locomotive is only 9-1/2 inches high here and a has different mark, too, "California/SC" impressed on two lines. *Bosson Collection.* Value not determined.

Sierra Vista owl with Starnes paper label. The height is 10-1/2 inches and the mark is shown. *Oravitz Collection.* $80

Humpty Dumpty, 11-3/4 inches high. Impressed mark is "Sierra Vista/Ceramics/Pasadena Calif." on three lines. *Bosson Collection.* $325

The rooster is 12 inches high and marked with an impressed "Sierra Vista/California" on two lines, plus a Starnes paper label. Was also made in earth-tone brown. *Taylor Collection.* $90

Mark of Sierra Vista owl.

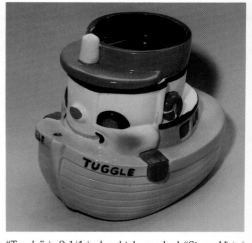

"Tuggle" is 9-1/4 inches high, marked "Sierra Vista/California" impressed on two lines, and also carries the remnant of a Starnes paper label. *Oravitz Collection.* $120

Close-up of Starnes paper label on Sierra Vista rooster.

The 10-1/2 inch high squirrel is marked "Sierra Vista/Ceramics/Pasadena Calif." on three lines. *Bosson Collection.* $140

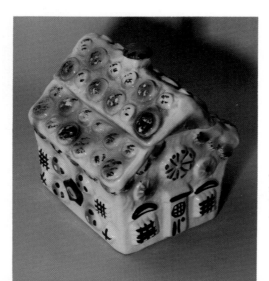

Same jar, same size, but no mark or paper label. The smokestack and mouth may have been remodeled. *Bosson Collection.* $120

Great cookie house, 8-1/2 inches high. Impressed mark is "Sierra Vista/Ceramics/Pasadena Calif./©1958 USA" on four lines. *Courtesy of Betty and Floyd Carson.* $110

171

House, 9 inches high, with "Sierra Vista/©53/California" impressed on three lines. *Bosson Collection*. $80

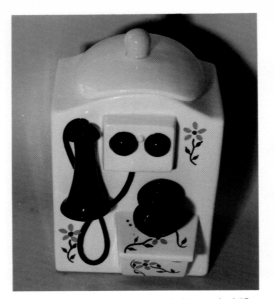

The telephone is 11-1/2 inches high. It is marked "Sierra Vista/Ceramics/Pasadena, Calif." impressed on three lines. *Courtesy of Jazz'e Junque Shop, Chicago, Illinois*. $90

This telephone cookie jar is 11-1/2 inches high, just as the other one, but has different decoration and is also unmarked. The bank is 5-3/4 inches high. Note the three bars under the cookie jar. These are often a sign of a jar being made by Sierra Vista and also appear on the unmarked "Tuggle" boat on the previous page. *Bosson Collection*. Left - $90, Right - $60

Southeast Minnesota Pottery

In the fall of 1986, Kellogg, Minnesota, residents Peter and Debbie Preussner decided they needed a change. After 20 years on the job, Peter had had enough of tool and die making, and Debbie wanted something more challenging than sending the kids off to school each morning and waiting for them to return in the afternoon. So, with no background, experience or training, the couple bought a ceramics business and set about making flower containers to wholesale within the Minneapolis-St. Paul metropolitan area, about 100 miles north of Kellogg.

The Indian head shown below is the only cookie jar they've made. It is from an old mold Peter Preussner purchased after discovering it in the basement of a ceramics shop that was going out of business. The mold is not marked, so at this time it is not known which mold company made it. The Preussners did not used the Inidan mold, or any of several thousand they acquired with their business, until they opened a storefront for retail sales in 1989. At that time only four of the jars were poured, after which they were decorated by Patricia Wiech, an artistically inclined former employee. Debbie Preussner said none of the Indian heads are identical due to being hand decorated.

After the publication of this book in 1991 the Preussners made more jars for collectors who requested them.

Stanford Pottery, Inc.

Located in Sebring, Ohio, this pottery was founded by George Stanford, Sr., George Stanford, Jr., and two other partners in 1945. The Stanfords were also involved in the founding of the Spaulding China Company, in Sebring, in 1939, and the Pilgrim Pottery Company, of Fredericksburg, Ohio, in 1949.

Stanford Pottery is said to have employed about 150 people. It was another of many companies that made products for National Silver Company. The plant was destroyed in a fire in January 1961, but the company remained in business for several years as a selling agency.

As far as is known, the corn cookie jar shown below is the only one Stanford made that can be identified. It may have made others under the names of distributors.

STANFORD POTTERY

Standford Pottery ear of corn cookie jar, 10 inches high. The mark is shown. Note the leaf closely resembles the letter C. Cookies? *Zera Collection*. $95

Mark of Stanford corn jar.

SOUTHEAST MINNESOTA POTTERY

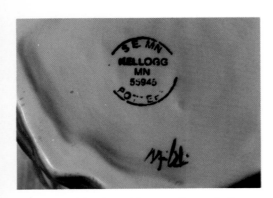

Mark of Southeast Minnesota Pottery Indian.

The Indian head is 10 1/4 inches high. The mark is shown. *Blumenfeld Collection*. $150

172

Starnes

Starnes was listed in trade journals as a pottery in the early 1950s. It was located in Los Angeles. Not much more is known about it, except that it bought some molds from Sierra Vista. Jars marked Sierra Vista often have Starnes paper labels.

Starnes paper label on ABC bear.

STARNES

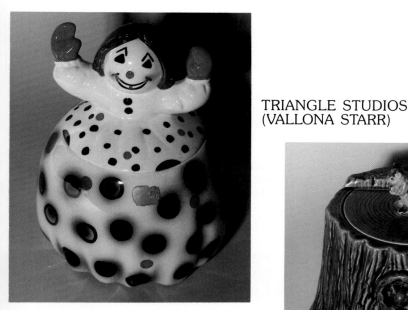

Rag doll, 11 inches high. There is no mark, but it has the Starnes paper label on front. *Oravitz Collection.* $225

TRIANGLE STUDIOS (VALLONA STARR)

Triangle Studios (Vallona Starr)

Trade journals show Triangle located in Los Angeles in 1945 and 1948, El Monte, California, in 1949, a name change to Vallona Starr Ceramics in 1951, and no listing after 1953. Owners of the company in 1945 were Valeria de Marsa and Everett S. Frost. Besides cookie jars, they are said to have made salt and pepper shakers, sugars and creamers, bowls, boxes and vases.

For more extensive information, *Vallona Starr Ceramics,* by Bernice Stamper (Schiffer 1995) is recommended.

Mark of Vallona Starr squirrel on stump.

Vallona Starr squirrel on stump. The mark is shown. *Courtesy of Jazz'e Junque Shop, Chicago, Illinois.* $65

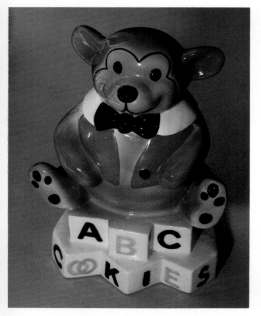

This 11-3/4 inch high bear raises some questions. The only mark is the Starnes paper label shown on this page. The Roerigs show the same jar as Marsh (a Los Angeles pottery) and give a catalog number and a date, 1967. The brown glaze is exactly the same as that on Sierra Vista's owl. What could have been the link between the three companies? *Courtesy of Betty and Floyd Carson.* $275

Weller Pottery

Samuel A. Weller began throwing pots in a one-room log cabin in Fultonham, Ohio, in 1872, graduated to a small pottery in Zanesville in 1882. By the early 1900s he had one of the largest ceramics operations in the country. The Essex Wire Company of Detroit, Michigan, purchased the pottery in 1947, shut it down one year later.

While Weller was one of the most important 20th Century potteries in the United States, it's forte was art pottery for rooms other than the kitchen. Consequently, its impact on cookie jar collecting is minimal, other than it's mammy with watermelon jar, which is highly prized and commands a premium price.

WELLER

Mark of Weller Pierre cookie jar.

This basketweave cookie jar is from the Weller Pierre line, a product of the mid-1930s. It is 10 inches high, was also made in blue green. The mark is shown. *Zera Collection.* $110

"Watermelon Mammy" from Weller's Decorated Novelty Utility line. The jar is 11 inches high. The line included a teapot and syrup, each with the mammy on top, a batter bowl, and creamer and sugar. The bowl, creamer, and sugar have black children for handles: two on the sugar and one each on the bowl and creamer. The pieces were introduced in 1935. The mark is shown. *Bosson Collection.* $3800

Western Stoneware Company

Many collectors refer to this company as the Monmouth Pottery because in many cases its familiar maple leaf mark says "Monmouth," the city in Illinois were the pottery was located. There was a Monmouth Pottery Company in Monmouth at one time, but in 1906 it merged with six other potteries to form the Western Stoneware Company. Western Stoneware went out of business in 1985.

The company is probably best remembered as the last producer of the now popular and expensive Old Sleepy Eye pottery. Primarily blue and white, Old Sleepy Eye depicted a Sioux Indian chief, and was made as premiums for the Sleepy Eye Milling Company, of Sleepy Eye, Minnesota.

As you can see below, "Stoneware" belonged in the firm's name, that being the type of ceramic in which it specialized. The clay the pottery used was mined near Colchester, Illinois, a small town about 30 miles south of Monmouth, which in turn is an equal distance south of the Davenport-Moline area. Western Stoneware made stoneware for Marshall Burns, a Chicago distributor. These pieces were marked Mar-Crest. While Western Stoneware used many different marks, all that are known, aside from Marcrest, incorporate the word "Monmouth," or the name of the company.

Mark of Weller "Watermelon Mammy."

Stoneware crock by Western Stoneware. The jar is 8-1/2 inches high. The mark is shown. *Courtesy of Homer and Bev Simpson.* $40

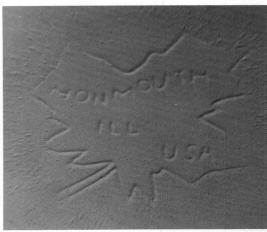

Monmouth mark of Western Stoneware crock cookie jar.

Lenell advertising jar, 9-1/4 inches high, with Monmouth mark. *Courtesy of Jazz'e Junque Shop, Chicago, Illinois.* $55

Bean pot, 8 inches high. The mark is shown. *Courtesy of Jazz'e Junque Shop, Chicago, Illinois.* $25

Mark of the bean pot. Note that the wording is different.

Section V: Cookie Jar Handlers

This section presents American and foreign cookie jars that have been identified not by the companies that made them, but by the American firms that handled them at one point or another along the road from manufacturer to consumer. These firms include decorators, distributors, importers, and consumer outlets.

Foreign cookie jars that have been identified only by country of origin appear in Section VIII. American jars that have not been traced to a specific company, along with foreign jars that have not been positively identified by country, are shown in Section IX.

Chapter 22
Decorators, Distributors, Importers and Retailers

Decorating companies buy bisque cookie jars from potteries, then apply either glaze, paint or transfer decorations, or a combination of those techniques, before passing the jars on to distributors, or selling them through their own marketing departments. An example of a decorating firm would be the Harper J. Ransburg Company, of Indianapolis, Indiana, which was well known for its crock cookie jars. Ransburg acted as its own distributor.

Distributors sell cookie jars produced by other companies, sometimes obtaining their items from potteries, sometimes from decorators. While it was common for many potteries to market their jars through distributors, the jars shown here are only those that don't include the name of the manufacturer. Cardinal China Company, which bought cookie jars made by American Bisque but had them marked with the Cardinal name, is an example of a distributor.

Until the late 1940s, most pottery distributors specialized in American wares. Since the end of World War II, however, nearly all distributing firms have become mainly importers due to the large amount of ceramics generated form overseas.

Importers obtain their cookie jars in three ways, by contracting with overseas potteries, by contracting with foreign exporters (often owned by the same parent company as the importing firm), or by setting up their own potteries in foreign countries where labor costs are usually more attractive than at home. Some importing companies—Fitz & Floyd and Lefton to name two—offer only the highest quality wares, while others settle for merchandise that would be hard to categorize as anything but second class.

Sometimes retail chains contract with potteries to buy cookie jars, eliminating the markup charged by a distributor. The cookie jars may be marked with the name of the retailer, as in the case of the Sears strawberry, or with the name of a line the retailer has registered, such as Grantcrest, which was sold exclusively by the W.T. Grant Company.

Accents Unlimited
If you have a jar marked Accents Unlimited, you have something rather unusual—a cookie jar made of plaster. The company makes molded plaster objects, sells them in kit form for people to decorate at home. Accents Unlimited is based in Milwaukee, Wisconsin. It was founded in 1970. According to a company spokeswoman, in recent years the firm has shown a preference toward working with items that are quite a bit smaller than cookie jars.

Owl cookie jar, 11-1/2 inches high. The marks are "Accents/Unlimited, Inc./ 1976" impressed on three lines inside the jar, "2131" impressed at base, and "L. Cross" incised on side. *Oravitz Collection.* $40

Arcadia Export-Import Corporation

Very little is known about Arcadia and it probably wouldn't even deserve a mention except for one thing. The Shenango China Company, of New Castle, Pennsylvania, and Jackson China, Inc. of Falls Creek, Pennsylvania, made products for it, presumably for export. But since import companies act as their own distributors, it's possible some of the American-made items may have been sold here.

Arcadia is known to have been in business during the 1950s. The only known mark that implies its location includes the words "Newark" and "New York," in that order. There is a Newark, New York, just north of the finger lakes about halfway between Rochester and Syracuse. Whether the mark stands for this city, or whether it means the company had offices in Newark, New Jersey and New York City, has not been determined.

ARCADIA EXPORT-IMPORT CORPORATION

German garden scene, 8-1/2 inches high. The mark is "Arcadia/C-6672" on two lines. *Zera Collection.* $45

George Borgfeldt Corporation

Borgfeldt was a long time New York importer and distributor that, according to Lehner, was in business prior to 1891. The date makes sense because Borgfeldt is well known among collectors of Limoges porcelain for marketing decorative Limoges plates under the name Coronet, during the American china painting fad of the late Victorian era. The company remained in business into the 1950s, possibly longer.

The mark of "Thumper" was lightly impressed on a light colored surface, so it will be explained in addition to being shown. It basically looks like a spoked wheel complete with a tire. A seven-point crown emerges from the top of the tire. Around the bottom of the tire is the word "Celebrate." Over the crown is "Reg. U.S. Pat. Off.," Below the tire is "Made in U.S.A." All of the words in the mark are written in block letters.

GEORGE BORGFELDT CORPORATION

Mark of Thumper.

Often called "Thumper" but never displaying a Disney copyright, this jar is 11-3/4 inches high. Mark is shown. *Zera Collection.* $100

Avon Products, Inc.

Avon Products, originally called the California Perfume Company, was founded in New York by David Hall McConnell about 1886. The name was changed to Avon Products, Inc. on October 6, 1939.

On occasion the company has used cookie jars as sales awards for its representatives.

AVON PRODUCTS, INC.

Mark of Avon bear.

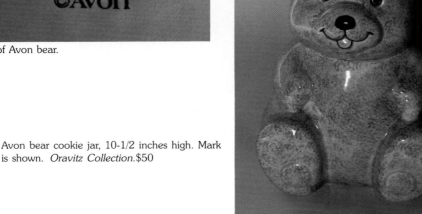

Avon bear cookie jar, 10-1/2 inches high. Mark is shown. *Oravitz Collection.* $50

Avon house canisters. *Left:* 6-1/2 inches high. *Right:* 9-3/4 inches high. Mark is shown. *Bosson Collection.* Left - $100, Right - $130

HAND PAINTED IN BRAZIL EXCLUSIVELY FOR AVON REPRESENTATIVES

Mark of Avon canisters.

Brush Art

Apparently a decorating company, nothing was found on Brush Art. The crock jar shown below is Red Wing bisque, identified by Delores Simon in *Red Wing Pottery with Rumrill*.

BRUSH ART

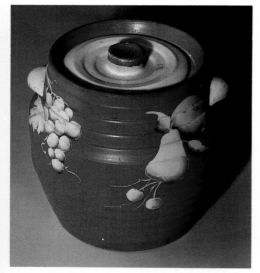

Brush Art crock cookie jar, 8-1/2 inches high. The Brush Art signature appears above the grape vine on the right side above the handle. *Zera Collection.* $85

Brush Art signature.

Cardinal China Company

The Cardinal China Company was formed in 1946 in Carteret, New Jersey, a suburb of Newark. Early on it manufactured its own pottery but somewhere along the line, presumably quite early, switched to being a distributor.

During the late 1950s Cardinal marketed cookie jars made and decorated by American Bisque, which explains why the bottoms of Cardinal jars have the wedges that are usually found on American Bisque jars.

Still in business, the firm's name has been changed to Cardinal, Inc. During the late 1980s its offices were moved a few miles away to Port Reading, New Jersey. Today Cardinal functions as an importer and distributor.

CARDINAL CHINA COMPANY

Cardinal soldier, 12-3/4 inches high. Most are marked, but this one isn't. *Bosson Collection.* $275

This jar is 9-1/2 inches high. The mark on back is "©Cardinal/USA" impressed on two lines. In the shadow at the left of the cap is "For Smart Cookies." *Zera Collection.* $100

Carbone, Inc.

Look in Chapter 21 under Hall China Company, and you'll find a white owl identical to the one shown below. That's because Hall was one of several American potteries that made products for this Boston, Massachusetts, distributor. Two others were Taylor, Smith, and Taylor, and Zanesville Stoneware Company.

Exact dates for Carbone aren't known, but suffice it to say it was around a long time. It registered a trademark (Castelli) in 1926, claiming use since 1920. At that time the company is believed to have been strictly a distributor of American pottery. By 1967 it was calling itself an importer in the trade journals. It was listed in *Trade Names Directory* as late as 1982, showing a Norwood, Massachusetts, address, but attempts to contact it there in 1991 were not successful.

CARBONE, INC.

Each of the owls is 12-1/2 inches high. Mark is shown. *Oravitz Collection.* $250 ea.

Mark of Carbone owls.

This Cardinal cookie bag is 10 inches high. It is marked "USA/#4200" on two lines. *Zera Collection.* $80

The cookie jar is 8 inches high, but the height of the jam jar was not recorded. The mark of the cookie jar is shown below. *Blumenfeld Collection.* Left - $125, Right - $50

Mark of the smiling boy cookie jar. Note the American Bisque wedges.

Cookie safe, 10-1/2 inches high, marked "Cardinal 309©USA" on one line. *Oravitz Collection.* $100

Sad clown, 9-1/2 inches high, marked "©Cardinal/USA" on two lines. *Zera Collection.* $100

Cookie garage, 6-1/2 inches high, unmarked. *Bosson Collection.* $150

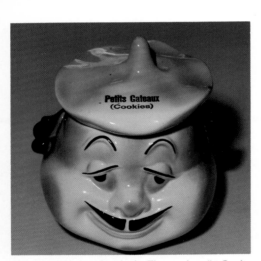

French chef, 9 inches high. The mark is "©Cardinal/USA" on two lines. *Zera Collection.* $130

Telephone, 11-1/2 inches high. The mark is "Cardinal©/311/USA" on three lines. *Zera Collection.* $90

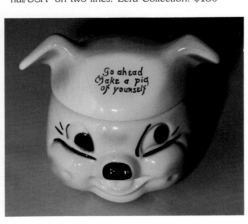

The pig is 7-1/2 inches high. It is not marked. *Zera Collection.* $100

Cardinal cookie castle, 11-1/2 inches high. The mark is "Cardinal/301©USA" on two lines. Cardinal's numbering system was apparently inconsistent. On this jar the number is 301. The Roerigs show it as 307, Westfall 3100. *Oravitz Collection.* $190

China and Glass Distributors

This is the New York distributor that sold cookie jars marked "Pantry Parade," the example shown below being the only shape currently known. The Stanford Pottery, of Sebring, Ohio, did some contract work for China and Glass Distributors around 1949, but it has not been established whether or not it made cookie jars for them. Another well known line of China and Glass Distributors was Charm House.

CHINA AND GLASS DISTRIBUTORS

Pantry Parade tomatoes, 8-1/4 inches high. The mark is shown below. *Zera Collection.* $50 ea.

Same tomato but unmarked. *Bosson Collection.* $50

Another unmarked tomato, 8-1/2 inches high. *Zera Collection.* $50

Mark of red Pantry Parade tomato.

Dayton Hudson Corporation

This corporation resulted from the 1969 merger of the J.L. Hudson Company, a Michigan retail chain, and The Dayton Corporation, a similar chain based in Minnesota. The company is headquartered in Minneapolis. In June, 1990 it acquired Marshall Field's the Chicago-based retailer. With that acquisition, Dayton Hudson now has 61 stores in 11 states. (Marshall Field's is treated separately later in this chapter.)

The Hudson stores were started by Joseph Lowthian Hudson in Detroit in 1881. George D. Dayton opened his first store in Minneapolis in 1902.

Although the cookie jars below have marks showing "Dayton Hudson," the stores have retained their own names. People in Michigan, Indiana and Ohio shop at Hudson's, while folks in Minnesota, North Dakota, South Dakota and Wisconsin patronize Dayton's.

Due to these stores having a limited geographical area, there may be a tendency on the part of collectors outside the upper midwest to consider Dayton Hudson cookie jars rare finds, but that's not the case.

DAYTON HUDSON CORPORATION

Mark of B.W. Bear. A tad light, it reads "B.W.Bear/ ©1986/Dayton Hudson" on three lines. Paper label indicates the jar was made in Taiwan.

The dog is 10-1/4 inches high. Mark is "©1986 Dayton Hudson" on one line. *Oravitz Collection.* $50

B.W.Bear is 11-1/2 inches high. Its mark is shown. *Zera Collection.* $60

Demand Marketing

Though this is obviously a marketing firm based in Henderson, Kentucky, attempts to reach the company have not been successful. It is believed to have been in business during the 1970s. As the pictures show, it sold very nice Sesame Street jars.

DEMAND MARKETING

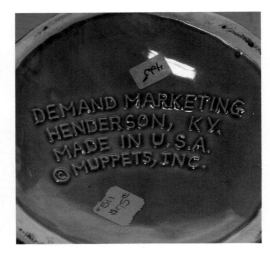

Mark of Oscar.

Oscar the Grouch, 12-3/4 inches high. The mark is shown. *Courtesy of Jazz'e Junque Shop, Chicago, Illinois.* $60

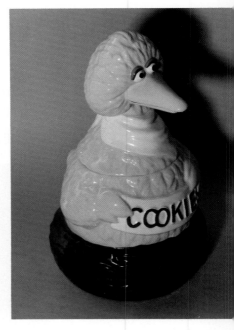

Big Bird is 13-1/2 inches high. This one is not marked, but the Roerigs found it with the same mark as the one to the left. *Courtesy of Jazz'e Junque Shop, Chicago, Illinois.* $60

Dept. 56

Dept. 56 is an importer and distributor located in Eden Prairie, Minnesota, in the Minneapolis-St. Paul metropolitan area. The firm has been in business since the mid-1970s. It handles giftware in all price ranges, and imports from many different countries. The majority of its merchandise relates to Christmas. According to a company spokesman, Dept. 56 acquired its unusual name, "Because it was the next number in the computer."

Dept. 56 has handled many cookie jars over the years, but never as single items. The company deals strictly in groupings of coordinated accessories. The chef head jar below is from a line called "Le Chef," which included a garlic jar, potholders, and other coordinated kitchen items. The other jar, "Peasant People," was accompanied by things such as matching vases and serving bowls.

Most of Dept. 56's giftware is designed by an in-house staff of artists, but it also works with freelancers.

DEPT. 56

Dept. 56 peasant woman cookie jar, 12 inches high. The mark is shown. *Oravitz Collection.* $100

Paper labels on Le Chef cookie jar.

"Le Chef" head jar, 10 inches high. Impressed mark is "Le Chef Cuisine/©Dept. 56" on two lines. Paper labels are shown. *Blumenfeld Collection.* $110

Mark of the peasant woman.

180

ENESCO

ENESCO is an import company headquartered in Elk Grove, Illinois, a Chicago suburb. To say it handles a lot of giftware would be an understatement, the Elk Grove complex consisting of 455,000 square feet of warehouse space, and another 33,000 square feet of office space. Additionally, it has showrooms in 12 major cities. ENESCO designs the products it markets.

The company was formed in 1959 as an import division of the N. Shure Company, the acronym being derived from that name (N.S. Co.). As with many import companies of that era, its early merchandise did not draw rave reviews. In recent years its lines have been upgraded, and now it markets much higher quality pieces, often unique such as the Mickey Mouse jar with leatherette ears and the penguin with textile cap and scarf.

All known ENESCO paper labels bear the company name.

ENESCO

Garfield, 8-3/4 inches high. Paper and cellophane labels are shown. *Zera Collection.* $175

Garfield labels.

The house is 7-3/4 inches high. Its marks are shown. *Courtesy of Jazz'e Junque Shop, Chicago, Illinois.* $45

Mark of ENESCO house.

The cat jar is 11-3/4 inches high. Its cellophane label is shown. *Courtesy of Jazz'e Junque Shop, Chicago, Illinois.* $45

Label of the cat jar.

This jar, unmarked and 9-3/4 inches high, has been repainted. Originally the main body of the jar was red, feet and bells were gold. The Roerigs show it with an ENESCO paper label. Unusual jar in that it has a glass bezel. *Zera Collection.* $350

Back of repainted Mickey Mouse clock.

Mickey Mouse with leatherette ears. The mark is "©Walt Disney Productions." The jar has an ENESCO paper label. *Blumenfeld Collection.* $400

These jars are commonly called "Prunella the Pig" and "Pomeroy the Pig." Prunella is 11-1/4 inches high, while Pomeroy is 10-1/2 inches high. Both have the "Styled by/Lorraine Elam" mark shown below, and Pomeroy has an ENESCO paper label. *Oravitz Collection.* $75 ea.

Designer's mark on Prunella and Pomeroy.

Betsy Ross, 9 inches high, unmarked, but shown by the Roerigs with ENESCO label. *Courtesy of Jazz'e Junque Shop, Chicago, Illinois.* $225

Penguin with textile scarf and cap believed to be original. The jar is 11 inches high, ENESCO paper label. *Bosson Collection.* $60

Ethan Allen, Inc.

Ethan Allen is a furniture company headquartered in Danbury, Connecticut. Besides producing what is generally acknowledged as the finest furniture made in America today, it also sells decorative accessories. Several calls to the corporate offices resulted in very little information, other than that the company was founded in 1936 by Ted B. Ancell.

It was apparently named for the Revolutionary War figure, Ethan Allen, who with his Green Mountain Boys captured Fort Ticonderoga on May 10, 1775, shortly after the start of the war. Allen is featured on the company's logo.

The age of the cookie jar shown below is not known, other than that it was purchased several years prior to Ethan Allen's 1991 television advertising campaign that spotlighted accessories.

ETHAN ALLEN, INC.

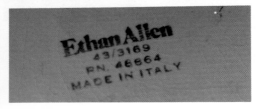

Marks of Ethan Allen beehive jar.

Somewhat unsettling perhaps, but nicely modeled with excellent mold detail. The jar is 11 inches high, with marks showing. *Zera Collection.* $65

Fitz and Floyd

Fitz and Floyd is a ceramics importing company in Dallas, Texas. It was started by Pat Fitzpatrick and Bob Floyd in the late 1950s. Although its cookie jars are made by Pacific-Asian potteries, Fitz and Floyd supplies its own designs. On the quality scale, Fitz and Floyd cookie jars ride far above the vast majority of imports.

Marks of the company are shown below.

FITZ AND FLOYD

Fitz and Floyd's "Rio Rita," 10-3/4 inches high. The mark is shown. *Courtesy of Jazz'e Junque Shop, Chicago, Illinois.* $100

Bottom of Rio Rita, with a warning about cleaning.

Nicely painted granny, but the bonnet makes her head look too small. The jar is 11-1/2 inches high. The mark is shown. *Courtesy of Jazz'e Junque Shop, Chicago, Illinois.* $90

Raccoon, 9-3/4 inches high. The mark is shown. *Oravitz Collection.* $115

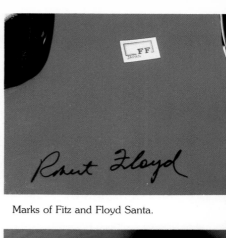

Marks of Fitz and Floyd Santa.

The mark of the Fitz and Floyd granny.

Inkstamp mark of the raccoon.

This jar is 10 inches high. Its mark is "©FF" impressed, with a Fitz and Floyd paper label. *Courtesy of Jazz'e Junque Shop, Chicago, Illinois.* $125

This jar is 9-1/2 x 16 inches. Santa and his deer are removable, so if you see one on which they're missing, it is not necessarily a different jar. It isn't, however, worth as much. The marks are shown. *Courtesy of Jazz'e Junque Shop, Chicago, Illinois.* $500

The elephant is 10-1/2 inches high. Its mark is "Fitz & Floyd Inc./©MCMLXXVI/FF" on three lines. *Oravitz Collection.* $160

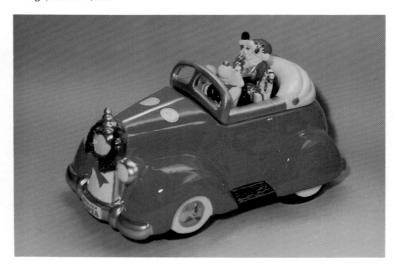

Grantcrest

Grantcrest is a mark that was used by the W.T. Grant Company prior to its sale to Ames Department Stores in 1985. The mark was stamped on china produced for Grant by domestic potteries such as the Salem China Company, of Salem, Ohio, and, as shown below, by foreign potteries also.

William Thomas Grant was born in 1876, opened his first "25-cent store" in 1906 at a Y.M.C.A. in Lynn, Massachusetts. The premise was to adhere to a 25-cent cap on all merchandise,

which cut about halfway between the 5-and-10 cent stores of F.W. Woolworth, and the nominal 50-cent minimum common to department stores of that era. The ceiling was raised to $1 following World War I, and was discontinued in 1940. By the time Grant died in 1972 at the age of 96, his chain had multiplied to 1190 outlets covering 43 states, and generating annual sales of $1.5-billion.

Mark of the cat jar.

Both of these biscuit jars are assumed to be Grantcrest, but only one, the cat, is so marked. The dog has a Japan inkstamp. Perhaps it was originally marked with a paper label. The height of the dog is 8 inches, and the height of the cat is 7-1/2 inches. Neither measurement includes the handle. The mark of the cat is shown. *Oravitz Collection.* $35 ea.

Great American Housewares

The only currently known information about this company is that shown on its mark, that it was located in New York. Directory Assistance could not find it listed. The jar shown is fairly recent; perhaps the company merged with another, or is operating under a different name.

Green Products

No information was found about Green Products, but several aspects of the two jars below may be more than coincidental.

Before it was broken up and sold in pieces during the 1980s, Durkee Famous Foods, Inc. was located in Cleveland, the same city where Green Products was located. According to old trade journals, at one point Durkee sold a margarine called Kook-E-Special Margarine. While there is no explanation for the difference in spelling, both jars could easily be related to using margarine, so maybe there's a connection.

GREAT AMERICAN HOUSEWARES

GREEN PRODUCTS

Mark of Kooky-Kook.

Kooky-Kook, 13 inches high. The mark is shown. *Zera Collection.* $110

Transformers jar, 8-1/2 inches high. The mark is shown. *Courtesy of Betty and Floyd Carson.* $100

Mark of Transformers jar.

"Kooky-K-Egg" is 11 inches high. Its mark is shown. *Zera Collection.* $110

Mark of Kooky-K-Egg—"Kooky-K-Egg©/ by Newhauser/Pat Pending/Green Products/Cleveland O." on five lines.

N.S. Gustin

Nelson Sage Gustin founded the N.S. Gustin Company in Los Angeles, California, in 1941. According to David Gustin, grandson of the founder and current vice president, the company has the distinction of being one of the few pottery distributors that still deals mainly in domestic wares. Only two of its lines are imported.

Gustin distributed the products of Los Angeles Potteries until that firm was liquidated in 1970, at which time its molds were acquired by Gustin for use at Designer-Craft, a West Los Angeles pottery the distributor owned. Today Designer-Craft is owned by David Gustin, but the name has been changed to Los Angeles Pottery. It is still located in West Los Angeles, and still produces cookie jars. Some of them are marked Los Angeles Pottery; others are marked N.S. Gustin.

Currently, the main thrust of N.S. Gustin's business is supplying ceramic giftware to mom-and-pop franchise operations such as Hallmark Card stores, and other quality gift shops.

N.S. GUSTIN

Paper label and mark of the N.S. Gustin sitting cat.

This cat is 13 3/4 inches high. Its mark is shown. *Oravitz Collection.* $40

HIMARK Enterprises

HIMARK is a giftware importer located in Hauppauge, New York, a city on Long Island about 40 miles from Manhattan. A company spokesperson declined to give any further information.

HIMARK ENTERPRISES

HIMARK cat, 8 inches high. Its paper label is shown. *Courtesy of Mercedes DiRenzo.* $50

Toucan, 9-1/2 inches high, has same paper label as the cat. *Oravitz Collection.* $140

Paper label of HIMARK cat.

Hoan, Ltd.

Apparently an importer that has dealt in Walt Disney products in the recent past.

HOAN LTD.

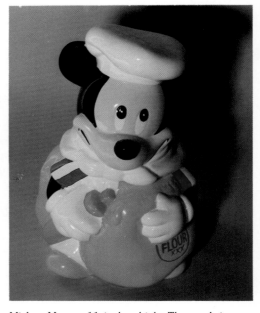

Mickey Mouse, 11 inches high. The mark is "©The Walt Disney Co./By/Hoan Ltd" on three lines plus a "Made in Taiwan" paper label. *Oravitz Collection.* $80

185

Donald Duck is 12-1/2 inches high and has the same mark as Mickey Mouse. *Oravitz Collection.* $80

Holt Howard

Holt-Howard was founded in 1949 in New York City by A. Grant Holt and John Robert Howard. At first the company's focus was strictly on Christmas items.

After a few years it expanded to kitchenware such as cookie jars, salt and pepper shakers, creamers and sugars, etc. Favorite among today's collectors is Pixieware but to my knowledge no Pixieware cookie jar was produced. It did make cookie jars for lines such as Cozy Kitten and the popular Red Rooster dinnerware.

In 1968 Holt-Howard was sold to General Housewares Corporation, of Hyannis, Massachusetts. Holt and the two Howards stayed on for a while but all of them left after a few years. In 1990 Charles Donnell and Richard Rakauskas, former vice presidents of General Housewares, formed Kay Dee Designs in Hope Valley, Rhode Island, and bought the company.

HOLT HOWARD

Holt Howard Santa jar broken down.

Three-piece Holt Howard Santa Claus candy and cookie jar, 8-1/2 inches high. Holt Howard paper label. *Oravitz Collection.* $150

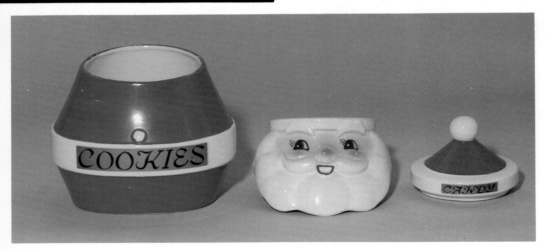

International Artware Corporation (INARCO)

The history of INARCO is sketchy at best. It was apparently in business as early as 1961, because in 1965 it filed a trademark registration claiming use since May 1961. All known INARCO paper labels show Cleveland, Ohio. But officials at National Potteries Corporation (NAPCO) say the company was operating out of Twinsburg, Ohio, about halfway between Cleveland and Akron, when NAPCO purchased it in 1985. Perhaps its main offices were located in one city, its warehouses in the other. One year after NAPCO took over INARCO, it moved the company to Jacksonville, Florida.

In the field of ceramics, INARCO is best known for knickknacks, and probably didn't handle a lot of cookie jars. While there's nothing particularly outstanding about the jar shown below, the workmanship is adequate, and nuts are an unusual theme for a cookie jar.

INTERNATIONAL ARTWARE CORPORATION (INARCO)

INARCO nut cookie jar, 9 inches high. The mark is "E-2981/INARCO" on two lines. *Bosson Collection.* $50

M. Kamenstein, Inc.

Although the two cookie jars shown below are quite recent (1984), this firm dates all the way back to 1893 when a man named M. Kamenstein started it as a housewares company. It has always been based in the state of New York, moving to its present location in White Plains during the early 1970s. The company is both an importer and manufacturer, making some plastic and wooden products.

M. KAMENSTEIN, INC.

M. Kamenstein paper label on pencil and light bulb.

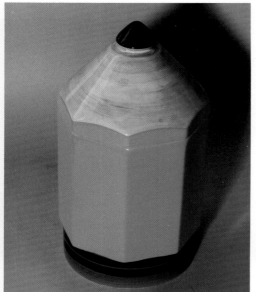

One big pencil, 12-1/2 inches high. Its paper label is shown. *Courtesy of Jazz'e Junque Shop, Chicago, Illinois.* $45

Like the pencil, the light bulb is 12-1/2 inches high and has the same paper label. *Courtesy of Jazz'e Junque Shop, Chicago, Illinois.* $45

Laurel Sales

While no information was found on Laurel Sales, it must have been in business during the early 1950s. The Romper Room was a one-hour children's television program that was syndicated in 1953.

LAUREL SALES

Romper Room jar, 7-1/2 inches high. The mark and paper label are shown. *Zera Collection.* $275

Mark and paper label of Romper Room cookie jar.

Leeds China Company

The Leeds China Company was a Chicago distributor. All references consulted agreed that Leeds was licensed to produce Walt Disney products from 1944 to 1954. According to Lehner, Leeds contracted with Ludowici Celadon, of New Lexington, Ohio, to produce Disney turnabout cookie jars between 1941 and 1945. But Heide and Gilman (*Cartoon Collectibles - 50 Years of Dime-Store Memorabilia*), state these jars were made only from 1947 to 1949. Either could be right as all of the characters depicted on turnabout jars - Jose Carioca, Donald Duck, Dumbo, Mickey and Minnie Mouse, and Pluto - made their debut prior to 1945.

Beginning and ending dates for Leeds are not known.

Other jars in the Leeds turnabout series appear in Chapter 8.

LEEDS CHINA COMPANY

Turnabout Dumbo, 13-3/4 inches high, believed to have been marketed by Leeds China. It is marked "Patented/ Turnabout/4 in 1/Walt Disney" on four lines. *Zera Collection.* $150

Reverse of Dumbo.

187

George Zolton Lefton China Company

In recent years some import companies, ENESCO for example, have considerably upgraded the quality of their ceramics to the point that there is little doubt they will become the collectibles of tomorrow. Lefton has not because there was no need to. Ever since this Chicago-based importer began operations in 1940, its wares have been superior to those of most other importers, and now both early and later pieces appear to be rising significantly in price. Many of Lefton's ceramic products that appear to be poured thin are made out of porcelain.

Still in business, Lefton has showrooms in several cities across the nation. Lefton marks often display a crown. All known Lefton marks include the word "Lefton" except one that has only a crown with a cursive "L" above. Some early pieces that would be impossible to attribute without old catalogs were simply marked "Made in Occupied Japan."

For more on this company see *Lefton China,* by Ruth McCarthy (Schiffer 1998).

GEORGE ZOLTON LEFTON CHINA COMPANY

A pair of pretty young ladies, each 7-3/4 inches high. The mark is shown. *Blumenfeld Collection.* Left - $150, Right - $175

This Lefton duck is 11 inches high. Its mark is shown. *Courtesy of Jazz'e Junque Shop, Chicago, Illinois.* $85

Mark of above Lefton head jars.

The Bluebird is 7-1/2 inches high. It has a "©Geo.Z.Lefton/289" inkstamp and Lefton paper label. *Oravitz Collection.* $300

This jar is 9 inches high and has a Lefton paper label. *Zera Collection.* $100

A partner for the duck, the cow is 12 inches high. Mark is shown. *Bosson Collection.* $85

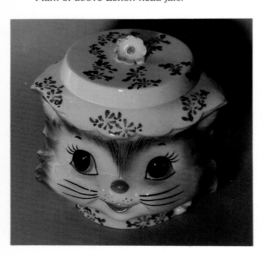

Miss Priss cat head jar, 8 inches high, with "1502" inkstamp and Lefton paper label. *Oravitz Collection.* $140

Impressed Lefton mark of the duck and the cow.

188

Canister, 9 inches high. It is marked Lefton, but details of the mark were not recorded. *Courtesy of Jazz'e Junque Shop, Chicago, Illinois.* $40

Tree stump canister, 9-1/2 inches high. The paper label reads: "©Geo.Z.Lefton/1970/6353" on three lines. *Courtesy of Jazz'e Junque Shop, Chicago, Illinois.* $25

MARSHALL FIELD & COMPANY

Marshall Burns & Company

Marshall Burns was a distributor out of Chicago that marketed dinnerware, kitchenware and ovenware made of stoneware. The company filed for a Marcrest trademark registration in July 1959, stating it had used the mark since August 1954, but how long it was active on either side of these dates has not been determined.

The Hull Pottery Company, of Crooksville, Ohio, and Western Stoneware Company, of Monmouth, Illinois, both made pieces for Marshall Burns that were marked Marcrest. It is possible that other potteries did, too.

MARSHALL BURNS & COMPANY

Marcrest stoneware crock cookie jar, 9 inches high. The mark is shown. *Courtesy of Jazz'e Junque Shop, Chicago, Illinois.* $35

Mark of stoneware crock jar.

Marshall Field & Company

The retail chain that became known as Marshall Field's was founded in 1852 when a man named Potter Palmer opened a dry goods store in downtown Chicago. Marshall Field bought into the business in 1865, became chief proprietor in 1891, and changed the name to reflect his ownership. By 1900 Marshall Field's was the largest wholesale and retail dry goods firm in the world. As of 1989, the company had 24 stores in Illinois, Wisconsin, Ohio, and Texas. In June 1990, Marshall Field's was acquired by the Dayton Hudson Corporation, of Minneapolis, Minnesota.

According to the Roerigs, the original box in which the Frango Mint Chip Cookies jar shown below was packed, indicated the jar was a product of Italy.

Marshall Field Frango Mint Chip Cookies jar, 12 inches high. No mark except the advertising. *Zera Collection.* $135

The unreadable writing on the face of the clock is "Marshall Field & Company." The jar originally held milk chocolates. It is 8-1/2 inches high. *Zera Collection.* $85

National Potteries Corporation (NAPCO)

According to a company spokesperson, this importing firm was founded by three investors in Cleveland, Ohio, in 1939. For many years it operated out of Bedford, Ohio, a Cleveland suburb. In 1984 the company was moved to Jacksonville, Florida.

NAPCO bought out International Artware Corporation (INARCO), another Cleveland area importer, in 1985, and moved the company to Jacksonville in 1986. In recent years NAPCO has severely scaled back its giftware sales, choosing instead to cater to the florist trade.

Marks of several of the jars shown below indicate they were made in the 1950s. Most that do not show dates are assumed to be from the same period. While this was a time during which many imported cookie jars were of inferior quality, the pictures show very clearly that NAPCO's jars were always a cut above those of the great majority of its competitors.

NATIONAL POTTERIES CORPORATION (NAPCO)

NAPCO "Miss Cutie-pie," 8-1/2 inches high. This jar was also made in yellow and in blue. Its mark is shown. *Blumenfeld Collection.* $200

Inkstamp mark of Miss Cutie-pie with NAPCO paper label.

Little Red Riding Hood, 9-1/2 inches high. Its mark and paper label are shown. *Oravitz Collection.* $250

Inkstamp mark and paper label of Little Red Riding Hood.

Cinderella, 9-3/4 inches high. Its mark is shown. Others in this series include Goldilocks and Little Bo Peep. *Zera Collection.* $250

Mark of Cinderella, same as Little Red Riding Hood except that the copyright symbol is missing. You would normally expect them to have different numbers.

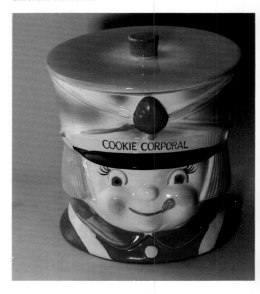

The "Cookie Corporal." He is 8 inches high with mark showing. *Blumenfeld Collection.* $250

Mark of the cookie corporal.

This spaceship is 10 inches high and was also made in yellow and maybe other colors. The mark is shown. *Bosson Collection.* $550

190

Mark of the NAPCO spaceship.

Drum, 8 inches high. The mark and paper label are shown. *Oravitz Collection.* $45

A real cookie jar. It is 10 inches high and marked with a NAPCO paper label. *Courtesy of Jazz'e Junque Shop, Chicago, Illinois.* $40

Mark and paper label of the drum. Note the different location on each label.

This is a sucker jar, a typical addition to many cookie jar collections. It is 7-1/4 inches high and has a "NAPCO" paper label plus a "K4546" inkstamp. *Oravitz Collection.* $60

NATIONAL SILVER COMPANY (NASCO)

National Silver chef and mammy. Mammy is possibly repainted. The chef is 10-1/4 inches high, the mammy 9-1/2 inches. Chef is marked "U.S.A./N.S.Co." impressed on two lines, similar to the apple on the following page. Mammy is marked, but the mark is unreadable. *Coughenour Collection.* $275 ea.

National Silver Company (NASCO)

The National Silver Company was a New York distributing firm that depended upon several potteries around the country to make the wares it marketed. Among them were the Canonsburg Pottery Company (Canonsburg, Pennsylvania), Fredericksburg Art Pottery (Fredericksburg, Ohio), French Saxon China Company (Sebring, Ohio), Gladdening, McBean and Company (Los Angeles, California), W.S. George Pottery (East Palestine, Ohio), Santa Anita Pottery (Los Angeles, California), and Southern Potteries (Erwin, Tennessee). There may have been more.

National Silver, which often used the acronym "NASCO," started in business no later than 1934, but it might have been much earlier. The head jar shown below seems to indicate it remained in business until the 1970s or 1980s. Recent attempts to locate National Silver in New York, and other places, have been unsuccessful.

The best known and most sought National Silver cookie jars are the chef and mammy. They are assumed to have been made in the 1930s or the 1940s.

National Silver chef and mammy but of a different bisque and unmarked. Molds and sizes are the same as those above. *Zera Collection.* $275 ea.

Apple, 6-1/2 inches high, mark shown. *Zera Collection.* $60

This jar is 9 inches high. Its paper label is shown. *Blumenfeld Collection.* $75

The bunny with carrot is 11-3/4 inches high. Paper label showing. *Oravitz Collection.* $50

Mark of National Silver apple.

Black and gold paper label from above NASCO jar.

Black and silver NASCO paper label on bunny with carrot.

Neiman-Marcus

Neiman-Marcus is a retailer based in Dallas, Texas, that has become well known for having one of the most expensive lines of giftware in the country. As of 1999, the company had 31 retail outlets.

NEIMAN-MARCUS

Taxi, 7-1/2 inches high. "Neiman-Marcus" on back license plate, no other identifying marks appear. *Courtesy of Jazz'e Junque Shop, Chicago, Illinois.* $200

Kitty, 7-1/2 inches high. The mark is "©Otagiri/Handpainted" impressed on two lines with a "1980" inkstamp below. *Courtesy of Jazz'e Junque Shop, Chicago, Illinois.* $45

Otagiri

James Otagiri was a Japanese immigrant who attended the Berkeley School of Commerce after graduating from the Berkeley Public Schools. This was prior to World War II. Upon the United States entering the war with Japan, Otagiri was interned by the federal government, during which time he taught Japanese at the University of Colorado Language School.

Shortly after being freed he founded Otagiri, a San Francisco importing firm. The year was 1946. James Otagiri passed away about 1976, but the company remains in business, still based in San Francisco. It wholesales house and giftware items, including cookie jars, to upscale department stores.

According to the company, 100 percent of its cookie jars are made in Japan.

OTAGIRI

The pig is 8 inches high, with "©Otagiri 1979" impressed. *Oravitz Collection.* $55

Trolley with people, 7-1/4 inches high, marked "©Otagiri 1980." Yellow banner across the front of the vehicle reads "Municipal." *Oravitz Collection.* $75

The Victorian house is 10-3/4 inches high. The mark is "©Otagiri" impressed. *Courtesy of Mercedes DiRenzo.* $95

PIPPIN

Pippin apple, 6-3/4 inches high. The mark is "USA/ Pippin" impressed. Pippin is a variety of apple. The jar was made by American Bisque. *Oravitz Collection.* $45

Over and Back, Inc.

An importer-wholesaler, Over and Back is located in Ronkonkoma, New York, a city on Long Island about 35 miles east of Kennedy International Airport. The firm, which was founded in 1976, caters to specialty shops and department stores. Over and Back describes itself as a trendy company that regularly changes its merchandise based on what's hot at any given time. As a result, it sold many different cookie jars from 1986 through 1990, but in 1991 was offering but one model to its customers.

OVER AND BACK

Original container of Country Quilt Series bear.

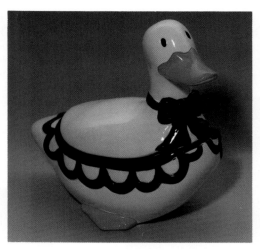

This duck is 8-1/2 inches high. Its paper label is shown. *Oravitz Collection.* $35

Over and Back "Country Quilt Series" bear. The mark is "©1987/Over & Back, Inc." on two lines, plus a "Made in Taiwan" paper label. *Courtesy of Jazz'e Junque Shop, Chicago, Illinois.* $50

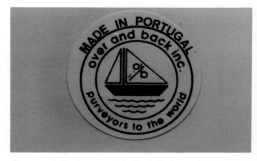

Over and Back paper label of duck cookie jar. The jar also had a "Made in Taiwan" paper label.

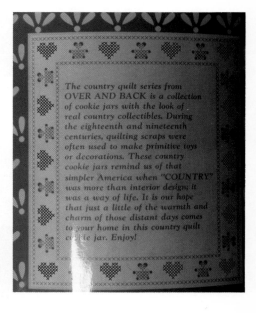

The country quilt series from OVER AND BACK is a collection of cookie jars with the look of real country collectibles. During the eighteenth and nineteenth centuries, quilting scraps were often used to make primitive toys or decorations. These country cookie jars remind us of that simpler America when "COUNTRY" was more than interior design; it was a way of life. It is our hope that just a little of the warmth and charm of those distant days comes to your home in this country quilt cookie jar. Enjoy!

Pittman-Dreitzer and Company, Inc.

A New York distributor, obviously in business as early as 1942, as shown on the mark below. Sometime prior to 1966 it became a division of Lancaster Colony Corporation, the same company that owned McCoy for a time. How long Pittman-Dreitzer remained active has not been determined. Albert Apple and Stella Strawberry are the only two cookie jars the company is known to have distributed. There were also figures made in the likeness of the cookie jars, plus other figural characters with names such as Lee Lemon and Priscilla Pineapple.

PITTMAN-DREITZER COMPANY, INC.

Albert Apple is 12-1/4 inches high. Same mark as shown except with "Albert Apple" across the bottom. *Zera Collection.* $100

Stella Strawberry, 12 inches high, marked "©FKR—PD & CO." *Courtesy of Betty and Floyd Carson.* $100

Longer mark of another Stella Strawberry that was photographed. It reads "©FKR 1942 PD & Co. Inc./Stella Strawberry" on two lines. *Zera Collection.*

Pomona

At this time no information is available on Pomona.

POMONA

Three little pigs jar, 9-1/2 inches high. "Pomona" inkstamp under the glaze. *Zera Collection.* $95

Reverse of Pomona three little pigs jar.

Pottery Guild of America

The Cronin China Company, of Minerva, Ohio, made semi-porcelain marketed by Pottery Guild of America. Pottery Guild incorporated in New York County on August 10, 1937. It was dissolved by proclamation on March 8, 1946. The founder of Pottery Guild was J. Block. After Pottery Guild went out of business, Block and other members of his family formed and ran several New York distributing firms including J & I Block Company, Rosenthal-Block China Corporation, and Block China Company.

Ivory and pink Pottery Guild Dutch girls, marked as shown, 12-1/4 inches high. *Zera Collection.* $100 ea.

POTTERY GUILD OF AMERICA

Sometimes you really have to look close to see a mark, such as this one on the Dutch girls.

As you might expect, Pottery Guild sold more than just cookie jars. Platters, pitchers, mixing bowls, casseroles, salad sets, custard cups, waffle sets and other pieces were marketed by the company. In addition to the jars shown below, it is known to have made a Dutch boy, and a jar similar to McCoy's round ball shape, but with flat handles on the sides and a recessed round knob in the lid. A 1939 Wards catalog shows the round jar in a pattern called calico fruit, in which the leaves of fruit were made to resemble cloth. The jar was on sale for $1.19.

Cronin China was located in New Cumberland, West Virginia, prior to 1934 when it moved into the Minerva plant of the defunct Owen China Company. Owen was founded by Ted Owen in 1902, went belly up in 1931. Cronin lasted until 1956 when it was taken over by the United States Ceramic Tile Company, of Canton, Ohio.

This pot shaped cookie jar is 7 inches high. Its mark is shown. *Zera Collection.* $25

Mark of pot shaped jar.

Blue Dutch girl, 12-1/4 inches high and unmarked. *Zera Collection.* $100

Unmarked Pottery Guild balloon lady, 12 inches high. *Courtesy of Jazz'e Junque Shop, Chicago, Illinois.* $160

The girl stands 11-1/4 inches high. The mark is shown. *Courtesy of Jazz'e Junque Shop, Chicago, Illinois.* $110

Peach Dutch girl, the same size as the blue and also unmarked. *Bosson Collection.* $100

Mark of the girl.

Balloon lady with a lighter skirt. Same size as the unmarked example featured above. *Zera Collection.* $160

195

Little Red Riding Hood, 12-3/4 inches high and unmarked. *Zera Collection.* $130

Reverse of Elsie.

Old King Cole, 12-3/4 inches high, *believed* to be an unmarked Pottery Guild jar. The weight, color, and feel of the bisque as well as the overall style match Pottery Guild's. The only other known Pottery Guild character is Little Red Riding Hood, which, like this one, has the name at the bottom of the base. Around the back of this jar is "Twas a merry old soul." *Bosson Collection.* Value not determined.

Borden's Elsie the Cow, 12-1/4 inches high and unmarked. *Courtesy of Jazz'e Junque Shop, Chicago, Illinois.* $325

Rooster, 12-1/2 inches high, appears to have been repainted. This jar is unmarked but many are marked "Handpainted/Pottery Guild/of America" on three lines. *Oravitz Collection.* $60

ALBERT E. PRICE, INC.

Albert E. Price

Albert E. Price founded the company that bears his name in 1929 in Philadelphia, Pennsylvania. Original focus was on jewelry. At some point the firm broadened its base to include giftware. Family problems are said to have caused a split in the company, one faction taking the jewelry business, the other retaining the giftware, along with the company name.

In 1970, Price moved across the Delaware River to Bellmawr, New Jersey, where it is still located today. The company is run by Albert E. Price's descendants. An importer, it distributes giftware nationwide to a diversified clientele that includes small specialty shops, department stores and mass-merchandisers.

Paper label of Price monkey. Covered inkstamp appears to say "Japan."

Price monkey, 10-1/2 inches high. The paper label is shown. *Oravitz Collection.* $50

Harper J. Ransburg Company

Another "pottery" that wasn't a pottery at all but a decorating and distributing firm, Ransburg was founded in Toledo, Ohio, in 1908. It moved to Indianapolis, Indiana, in 1912, where it remained in business until sometime in the 1960s, or possibly later. Cut glass was one of its early products.

In 1928 the company patented a process called "Glass of Class," which was a way of decorating plain glass with colorful raised motifs. Two years later Ransburg marketed "Glass of Class" cookie jars but with only lukewarm success, the process being too costly to sell the jars at competitive prices.

A short time later, Harper J. Ransburg and his son, Gregg, were on a business trip to Louisville, Kentucky, when the elder of the two decided to drop in on an old friend, Ed Arden, of the Louisville Pottery. At the pottery, Harper J. Ransburg spotted a vase and asked if it could be made into a cookie jar. A few minutes later the well known Ransburg no. 207 jar was born as the father and son watched one of Louisville's employees turn out a prototype on a potters wheel. Ransburg was so impressed with the crock jar that he signed for a carload - 5000 jars - in order to secure a price of about 23 cents apiece. A few years down the road the company was selling 250,000 of the no. 207 jars annually, and had to call into service another pottery, Uhl, of Huntingburg, Indiana, to keep up with the demand. The design remained popular at least through the mid-1950s, as evidenced by the Davy Crockett jars below. Ransburg no. 207 jars sold mainly in midwestern department stores.

It is said that the lids of the earliest no. 207 jars were not glazed on their undersides. Later ones were. Also, early jars bore only paper labels. The palette mark, shown below, was impressed beginning in the late 1930s.

Ransburg jars have not found a lot of respect among collectors, and apparently were not very highly thought of by the general public, either. Many of Ransburg's crock cookie jars are found in pristine condition, which is unusual for 40 to 60 year old painted jars. It probably indicates that when the jars were given as gifts, they often remained in their boxes and were stored in basements and closets without ever seeing use.

As illustrated below, Ransburg had no qualms about working with different media.

HARPER J. RANSBURG COMPANY

Ransburg no. 207 crock jar, 9-3/4 inches high and unmarked. The appearance of contouring below the rim is a reflection; it is as smooth as the others shown. This jar's lid is not glazed on the underside, a sign of the earliest no. 207 jars. The design is called the "Aster" pattern, said to be second in popularity to the "Hollyhock" pattern during the years these jars were being sold. $30

Another unmarked no. 207, its pattern name is not known. *Zera Collection.* $30

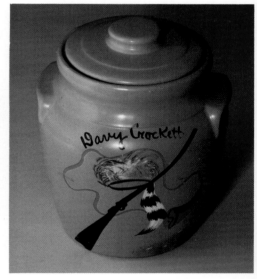

Davy Crockett no. 207 jar. Note that the lid and handles have been restyled. Its height is 10 inches. The mark is shown. *Zera Collection.* $140

Ransburg raised palette mark of aqua Davy Crockett jar.

No. 207 with "Hollyhock" pattern. This jar is also unmarked. Marks didn't appear on no. 207 jars until 1936. Earlier jars are often marked with paper labels. *Courtesy of Country Heirs Antique Shop.* $30

197

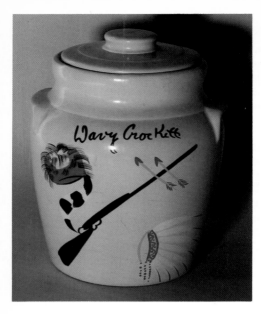

Davy in beige. The mark and size are the same as aqua jar. *Oravitz Collection.* $140

This jar has the Ransburg palette mark, but with "207" impressed below. *Oravitz Collection.* $75

Apparently modified by a previous owner. Ransburg palette mark. *Zera Collection.* $50

Humpty Dumpty is said to be a rare Ransburg cookie jar. Its mark is shown. *Zera Collection.* $75

This is not the original lid here, no doubt about that. According to an interview in *Antique Week* by authors Willard and Virginia Heiss, Gregg Ransburg said lid breakage was a major problem with the no. 207 jar, a fact to which this example attests. This repainted cookie jar has a Ransburg palette mark. *Courtesy of Jazz'e Junque Shop, Chicago, Illinois.* $15

Round ball with "Aster" pattern. The jar is 10 inches high and has a Ransburg palette mark. It is also seen in black. *Smith Collection.* $30

Impressed mark of Humpty Dumpty.

Each of these jars is 9-1/4 inches high with the impressed palette mark. It is not known for sure if the lids are replacements or whether some of the jars were made with wooden lids. *Courtesy of Dorothy Coates.* $15 ea.

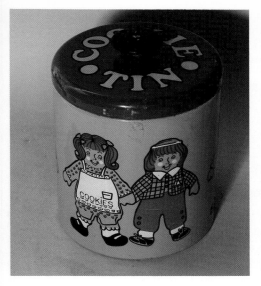

Metal cookie tin. The lid is very heavy, and the knob is wood. The height of the jar is 9-1/2 inches. The mark is shown. *Courtesy of Jazz'e Junque Shop, Chicago, Illinois.* $25

Embossed palette mark on the Ransburg cookie tin.

SEARS

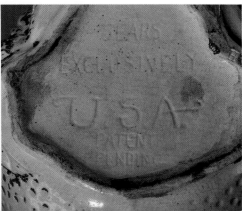

RECO International Corporation

This import company was founded in 1967. Located in Port Washington, New York, it presently has two divisions. One handles gourmet cookware, the other takes care of fine gifts and collectibles. John McClelland, designer of the jar below, is a freelance artist from Savannah, Georgia. He studied art two years at Auburn University, and another two years in New York. At the beginning of his career, McClelland worked mainly as a magazine illustrator. As that market began to dissipate, he turned to other specialties such as designing the art work for collector plates. If you are familiar with Miles Kimball Company, the mail order firm headquartered in Oshkosh, Wisconsin, you are familiar with McClelland's work. He has done the cover for the company's annual Christmas catalog since the early 1960s.

According to McClelland, the Ruffles cookie jar started out as one of a series of 24 porcelain heads, each about 3 inches high. When four of the heads proved to be especially good sellers, RECO asked him to redesign the four as cookie jars. All four jars have similar bottoms. One of the tops was a hobo, McClelland didn't remember the other two.

RECO INTERNATIONAL CORPORATION

"Ruffles" Cookie Jar Designed by award winning artist, John McClelland

RECO © 1986

Mark of "Ruffles" jar.

"Ruffles" cookie jar, 12-1/2 inches high. Mark is shown. *Coughenour Collection.* $75

Sears strawberry cookie jar, 8-1/2 inches high. The mark is shown. *Courtesy of Betty and Floyd Carson.* $50

Sears

Richard Warren Sears was railroad station agent in Redwood Falls, Minnesota, in 1886 when a local jeweler refused to accept a shipment of watches. Sears, who was 23 at the time, secured permission to dispose of the watches and sold them by mail. Having profited from the sale of the watches, he abandoned his railroad job that same year, moved to Minneapolis, and opened his own mail order firm, the R.W. Sears Watch Company. Sears hired A.C. Roebuck as the business's watch repairman. Before long the firm was moved to Chicago, where Sears sold it for $100,000 in 1889. Not content in retirement, he got hold of Roebuck, the pair returning to Minneapolis to form A.C. Roebuck & Company, a mail order jewelry and watch company. The name was later changed to Sears, Roebuck & Company, and later still to Sears.

Sears has often contracted with potteries, both domestic and foreign, to make ceramics under the Sears name.

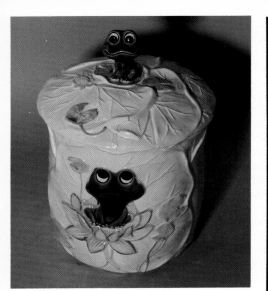

Sears canister jar, 10-1/2 inches high. The mark is shown. *Courtesy of Jazz'e Junque Shop, Chicago, Illinois.* $35

Mark of Sears frog canister.

SILVESTRI

Paper label of Father Christmas.

Sigma

According to the Roerigs, Sigma's roots go back to the late 1960s when it functioned as the giftware division of Rockville International, of Garden City, New York. At some point it was acquired by Towle International, and closed in 1985. The Roerigs classify Sigma as an importer and distributor. Today it's Klibane Cat jars and accessories are especially popular with collectors.

Star Wars, R2-D2 and C3PO. The jar is 10-1/2 inches high. Its paper label reads "©Lucas Film Ltd./Trademarks owned by Lucafilm Ltd. and used by/Sigma/the/tastesetter/Under Authorization" on six lines with small "TM" above the R in tastesetter. *Bosson Collection.* $140

These jars appear to be part of a series. The elephant on the left is 10-3/4 inches high, unmarked. The one on the right is 11 inches high, and its Sigma mark is shown. *Oravitz Collection.* $45 ea.

Reverse of Star Wars jar showing Darth Vader.

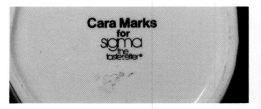

Mark of the elephant with baseball glove.

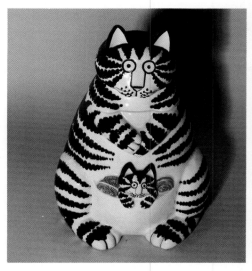

The Father Christmas jar is 12 inches high, and 11 inches in diameter at the widest point of the base. The paper label is shown. *Courtesy of Jazz'e Junque Shop, Chicago, Illinois.* $100

This cat is 10-3/4 inches high. Its mark is "©B.Kilbane" on six lines. *Courtesy of Mercedes DiRenzo.* $300

Silvestri

Silvestri is an importing company and wholesaler in Chicago. It began in 1940, but didn't switch to its present focus, Christmas, until sometime in the 1950s. It deals in ornaments, lights, and anything else that might hang on a Christmas tree. It also handles a line of giftware such as cookie jars and candle holders, all Christmas oriented. Silvestri was the first American company to offer miniature Italian white Christmas lights of the type now used by many cities and merchants to decorate for the holidays.

Taylor & Ng

Obviously located in San Francisco, this company proved elusive when searching for information about it.

TAYLOR & NG

This robot is 8-3/4 inches high. The mark and remnant of a paper label are shown. *Courtesy of Jazz'e Junque Shop, Chicago, Illinois.* $100

Mark of the robot.

Thames

Thames was apparently an importer of handpainted ceramics. If the cookie jar below is any indication, it handled some very nice wares.

THAMES

This purple cow head jar is 7 inches high. Its paper label is shown. Matching salt and pepper shakers were also made. *Saxby Collection.* $90

Paper label of purple cow.

Think Big, Inc.

Think Big is a New York City retail store that also puts out a mail order catalog. The company was founded in 1979. Today it functions as a wholly-owned subsidiary of Martin Lawrence Limited Editions. Martin Lawrence has 43 art galleries, some of which carry selected Think Big merchandise.

As mentioned in Chapter 3, Andy Warhol's infatuation with cookie jars probably did more than anything else to increase public awareness of jars and jar collectors. While Warhol is not known to have used his talents to create cookie jars, in a passive way he was partly responsible for the creation of the cookie server shown below.

According to Think Big President Robert Malcom, the company's forte is making giant models of normal size American icons such as cookies. He said the idea evolved partly from the pop art movement with which Warhol was associated, and partly from the large signs that businesses relied on back in the days when the majority of the population was illiterate. For instance, a giant size tooth hanging in front of an office was a clear indication of a dentist's office.

The piece below is no longer being made. But according to Malcom, the company intends to revive it. The new cookie server will be made of a higher quality ceramic, and is expected to retail in the $50 range.

The address to order a Think Big catalog is listed in Appendix 1.

THINK BIG, INC.

Cookie server, 2-1/4 x 10 inches. The mark is "©1985 Think Big/New York City" on two lines. *Courtesy of Jazz'e Junque Shop, Chicago, Illinois.* $40

Vandor

Vandor is an importing firm located in Salt Lake City, Utah. According to Art and Product Development Director Danne Sadler, it was started about 35 years ago by Ted Van Doorn, who sold out to a group of private investors during the late 1980s. During the thick of the 1991 recession, the staff was reduced to about 10 people, Sadler said.

VANDOR

Howdy Doody in a bumper car. The jar is 8-1/2 inches high. Its mark and paper labels are shown. *Courtesy of Jazz'e Junque Shop, Chicago, Illinois.* $400

Vandor specializes in a mixture of giftware and home decorations, which includes cookie jars and salt and pepper shakers among other things. Over the years it depended largely on freelance designers until Sadler was hired in 1990. All of its products are made overseas.

As evidenced by the jars shown, Vandor imports only the highest quality ceramics.

Marks of Howdy Doody in bumper car.

The standing Fred Flintstone is marked with an impressed "Vandor©1989" and two paper labels that read "Vandor Made in Korea" and "Pelzman Designs." *Courtesy of Jazz'e Junque Shop, Chicago, Illinois.* $150

This Howdy is 10 inches high, has a Vandor paper label. *Courtesy of Jazz'e Junque Shop, Chicago, Illinois.* $300

The Vandor Popeye is 8-1/2 inches high and unmarked. *Blumenfeld Collection.* $400

Sitting Fred Flintstone, 10 inches high, with "©1989 Vandor" impressed in bottom. *Courtesy of Jazz'e Junque Shop, Chicago, Illinois.* $250

Commonly called "cowmen Moo-Randa, "this jar is 9-3/4 inches high. Its mark is "© Vandor 1988." *Courtesy of Mercedes DiRenzo.* $150

The cookies toaster is 8 inches high. Its paper label reads "Vandor/ ©1985/Made in/Japan" on four lines. *Courtesy of Jazz'e Junque Shop, Chicago, Illinois.* $90

Whip Me...Beat Me...Don't Let Me Down, by The Egg whites, plus 19 other songs for your listening pleasure on the Vandor jukebox.

"Select-A-Cookie" jar, marked "Vandor." *Zera Collection.* $100

Dishwasher warning card packed inside every Vandor juke-box.

Section VI: Character Cookie Jars

Character cookie jars fall into two main categories, those that are copyrighted and those that are not. Woody Woodpecker and Hopalong Cassidy are examples of copyrighted characters. A company wanting to reproduce them must get permission from the copyright holder in order to do so legally. A copyright notice is generally an integral part of the mold, though sometimes it is communicated by a paper label. Humpty Dumpty and Little Boy Blue are characters in the public domain. No permission is needed to make them. There is, of course, a prohibition on copying any character cookie jar which is currently protected by a design patent, whether or not the character it is based on is copyrighted.

Sometimes character copyrights get a little cloudy. Consider Davy Crockett. No cookie jar portraying Walt Disney's 1955 movie hero carries a Disney copyright notice, the natural assumption

being that because Davy Crockett was an actual historical figure, he was free game to manufacturers. Yet Scott Bruce, in his book, *The Fifties and Sixties Lunch Box*, writes that when American Thermos began distributing a Davy Crockett lunch box, Disney lawyers came down hard, forcing the company to halt production and recall all of those already on the shelves. Perhaps the attorneys felt the Davy Crockett cookie jars were more generic in nature, none of them closely imitating the face of Crockett actor Fess Parker. Or perhaps they felt the jars were less of a threat than lunch boxes, and not worth a court battle.

Many of your favorite characters are absent from this section as it includes only those that haven't been pegged to a specific manufacturer or distributor.

Chapter 23
Santa Claus

Probably everyone's favorite character, at least when he brings all those goodies at Christmas, Santa Claus is as American in origin as the cookie jar on which he is often portrayed. Early Dutch settlers in New Amsterdam (now New York) celebrated St. Nicholas Feast Day each December 6, but referred to the 4th Century Turkish bishop as Sinter-Klass. Later, English settlers changed the name to Santa Claus, and the character gradually became associated with Christmas.

The modern image we have of Santa Claus—so aptly perpetuated by cookie jar designers—evolved in large part

from two sources, the 1822 publication of Clement C. Moore's classic poem, "A Visit from St. Nicholas," and drawings by political cartoonist, Thomas Nast, in *Harper's Illustrated Weekly* in 1863, and again in 1866. Nast, incidentally, is the illustrator who first showed Uncle Sam as a bearded figure wearing striped pants.

Most Santa Claus jars have appeared fairly recently on the cookie jar time line, and the subject has also been a popular one with hobby ceramists over the years.

This Santa Claus head cookie jar stands 9 inches high and is not marked. *Bosson Collection.* $100

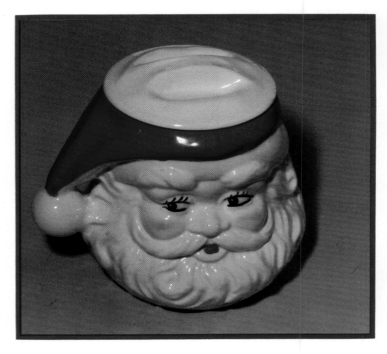

Wider and shorter than the example to the left, this unmarked jar is 8 inches high. *Zera Collection.* $90

As you can see, these jars are identical with the exception of the height. The example on the left is 8-1/4 inches high, and the example on the right is 8-3/4 inches high. Both jars are unmarked, but the one on the left has stilt marks on the bottom, while the one on the right was dry footed. The Roerigs show this jar with a Mallory mark, probably a ceramic mold company. *Blumenfeld Collection.* $60 ea.

Bottom of Santa Claus jar shown at bottom left.

This is the same as the Santas in the above picture, but the top is turned, and the glazing is different. It is probably a home ceramic jar since some of the skin is white instead of flesh color, a mistake generally not made by skilled decorators. The height of the unmarked piece is 8 inches. *Courtesy of Jazz'e Junque Shop, Chicago, Illinois.* $60

This one is 9-1/2 inches high, unmarked. *Courtesy of Jazz'e Junque Shop, Chicago, Illinois.* $35

An 8-1/2 inch high Santa, unmarked. The bottom, which is shown, is similar to McCoy, but the jar is not believed to be McCoy. *Blumenfeld Collection.* $60

Unmarked Santa holding a bell, 10 inches high. *Bosson Collection.* $75

Marked inside the lid of this 14 inch-high Santa is "Original Sculpture By Don Winton." As shown on next page, the back of this jar is just as interesting as the front. *Courtesy of Betty and Floyd Carson.* $300

205

Back of 14-inch Santa on previous page.

Standing Santa, with "Made in Taiwan" paper label, 12-1/2 inches high. *Oravitz Collection.* $35

These must be some of Santa's helpers. The jar is 8-1/4 inches high and unmarked. *Oravitz Collection.* $35

Another Santa loaded down with gifts. The height is 9 inches, the paper label reads "Made in Taiwan," and inside the lid is a light-sensitive music box. *Courtesy of Jazz'e Junque Shop, Chicago, Illinois.* $50

A teddy bear Santa, 12-1/2 inches high. Marked with "B & D©" impressed, "1986" raised, and a "Made in Taiwan" paper label. *Courtesy of Jazz'e Junque Shop, Chicago, Illinois.* $45

A 12-inch high Santa, marked "1986 George Good Corp. Calif." No information was found on this company. *Courtesy of Jazz'e Junque Shop, Chicago, Illinois.* $110

Chapter 24
Walt Disney

The 1928 release of Chicago-born Walter Elias Disney's animated film, *Steamboat Willie*, featuring Mickey Mouse and Donald Duck, began a marketing mania that eventually spread worldwide. It has kept cookie jar makers and other manufacturers busy ever since. Disney made *Steamboat Willie* as a silent film, but failed to get it released commercially until adding a sound track. Walt Disney went on to win 30 Academy Awards - still a record - before his death in 1966 at age 65.

According to Derwich and Latos, since 1972 molds for licensed Disney characters have been made by a subsidiary of Walt Disney Productions. Prior to that time manufacturers were given model sheets from which their designers worked.

Unfortunately, few of the popular Walt Disney cookie jars carry the mark of the manufacturer. Some of the potteries and distributors licensed to produce Disney characters over the years are said to be Brayton Laguna, Laguna Beach, California 1938-40; Hagen-Renaker, San Dimas, California 1955-60; Leeds China Company, Chicago, Illinois 1944-54; National Porcelain, Trenton, New Jersey 1939-42; Salem China, Salem, Ohio, 1932-34; Vernon Kilns, Los Angeles, California 1940-42; Eleanor Welborn Art Productions, Seaside, California, 1955.

This Donald Duck—Joe Carioca turnabout is 13-1/2 inches high. Its mark is simply "Walt Disney Productions," though some have a longer mark explaining the characters are from the movie *The Three Caballeros*, a 1945 animated feature film. The jar was marketed by the Leeds China Company, a Chicago distributor. *Zera Collection*. $175

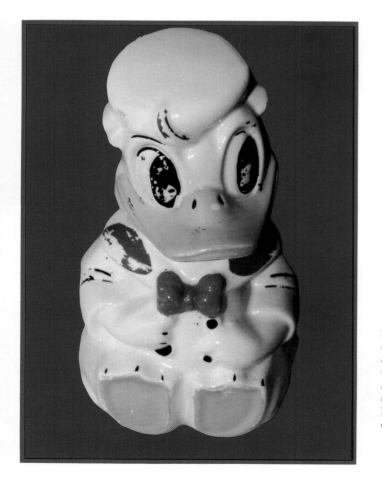

Reverse of the Donald Duck—Joe Carioca turnabout. Because Leeds commissioned several potteries to make its wares during the years it held a Disney license (1944—1954), it is uncertain as to which pottery made this jar. Based on the appearance of the bisque and the feel of the jar, however, it seems the Ludowici Celadon—American Pottery—American Bisque triumvirate is a reasonable bet. A repainted example of this cookie jar is shown in Chapter 4.

Old Donald Duck jar, 12-3/4 inches high. This cookie jar has been restored. The mark is "Donald Duck/©Walt Disney/USA" on three lines. *Coughenour Collection.* $350

Reverse of Mickey Mouse turnabout. This jar is of recent vintage and probably of Pacific-Asian origin.

Donald Duck cylinder jar, 9-3/4 inches high. The mark is shown. *Oravitz Collection.* $100

Mark of Donald Duck cylinder jar.

An unmarked turnabout, 14-1/2 inches high. *Oravitz Collection.* $95

Mickey Mouse cylinder jar. Standing 8-1/2 inches high, it has a mark identical to the Donald Duck cylinder except that it says "Mickey Mouse." *Zera Collection.* $100

This jar is 9-3/4 inches high and marked "Alice in Wonderland" in a semicircle with "©/Walt Disney/Prod." on three lines. Disney's animated version of *Alice in Wonderland* was released in 1951. *Coughenour Collection.* $100

Repaint of the Mickey Mouse cylinder jar, plus a larger unpainted companion. The heights are 9-3/4 inches and 8-1/2 inches. The mark is "Mickey Mouse/Walt Disney Productions" on two lines. *Coughenour Collection.* $100 ea.

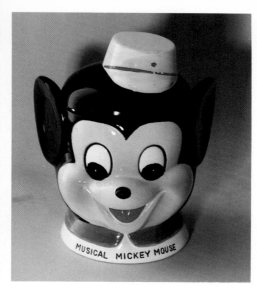

Mickey Mouse with a light-sensitive music box in the lid. The jar is 8-1/4 inches high, with a paper label that is shown. *Blumenfeld Collection.* $400

Paper label of musical Mickey Mouse.

A companion to the musical Mickey Mouse, Donald was sold by the same company. The jar is 7-1/4 inches high, and its mark is shown. *Oravitz Collection.* $350

Mark of the Donald Duck head jar.

This canister jar is 9 inches high with a "Made in Taiwan" paper label. *Oravitz Collection.* $60

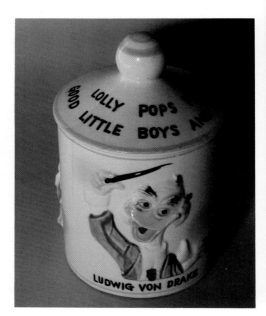

A lollipop jar, 7-1/2 inches high. The mark is "©1961 Walt Disney Productions." Besides Ludwig Von Drake, it also shows Mickey Mouse and Donald Duck. Note that the characters are in relief. *Oravitz Collection.* $150

The height here is 9 inches. The metal cylinder was made by J.Chein & Company, Burlington, New Jersey, and is so stamped. This jar has a plastic lid. *Courtesy of Jazz'e Junque Shop, Chicago, Illinois.* $35

Identical to the Chein Mickey and Minnie jar, the stamped mark reads "CHEINCO/ Housewares/J.Chein & Co/Burlington, NJ/ 03015" on five lines. *Zera Collection.* $35

Chapter 25
Other Characters

This chapter covers characters from cartoons and movies other than those of Walt Disney, and also nursery rhyme and story characters. None of the jars shown could be traced to a specific manufacturer. Also included are a few character banks, a natural outgrowth of cookie jars and cookie jar collections.

This Hopalong Cassidy cookie jar is 6-1/2 inches high. It probably dates from the late 1940s to the early 1950s, since the Hopalong Cassidy television series made its debut in 1948. The series was taken from the 66 Hopalong Cassidy films actor William Boyd made between 1935 and 1948. According to the Roerigs, this jar is sometimes found with a paper label "Peter Pan Products, Inc., Chicago, Illinois." *Courtesy of Jazz'e Junque Shop, Chicago, Illinois.* $450

Lid of above Hopalong Cassidy jar. The number signifies the Bar 20 Ranch near Crescent City, where Hoppy always fought the bad guys.

Woody Woodpecker is 14-1/2 inches high. Its mark is shown. *Blumenfeld Collection.* $750

©1967 WALTER LANTZ
ALL RIGHTS RESERVED.
A REGISTERED TRADEMARK
OF AND LICENSED BY
WALTER LANTZ PRODUCTIONS, INC.

Mark of Woody Woodpecker.

Yogi Bear, 8-1/2 inches high. The only mark is "Hanna Barbera/Productions, Inc./©1979" on three lines. *Bosson Collection.* $375

Unmarked Little Red Riding Hood, 12 inches high. Possibly the work of a home ceramist. *Oravitz Collection.* $95

Mrs. Humpty Dumpty is 8-1/2 inches high. The jar is not marked. *Courtesy of Jazz'e Junque Shop, Chicago, Illinois.* $60

Raggedy Ann is 10-1/2 inches high, has a "C-8824" inkstamp plus "©1972/By/The Bobbs-Merrill/Company,Inc." on four lines. *Courtesy of Betty and Floyd Carson.* $75

Cinderella, 11-3/4 inches high, unmarked but beautiful. This jar is from the same blank as the (who-made-it?) Cooky in Chapter 18. *Zera Collection.* $225

Little Bo Peep, 11 inches high, unmarked, but made by Enesco. *Oravitz Collection.* $250

Alf, but with no mark or copyright. Its height is 14 inches. *Bosson Collection.* $80

Ernie and Big Bird are each 11 inches high, Cookie Monster is 12 inches. Each is impressed: "©Muppets Inc." *Bosson Collection.* $75 ea.

Topo Gigo, an occasional visitor on the Ed Sullivan Show. The jar on the left is 11-1/2 inches high. Its inkstamp mark reads "45-611." The jar on the right is 9-3/4 inches high. Its mark is shown. *Oravitz Collection.* $175 ea.

Paddington Bear, a creation of children's author Michael Bond. The jar is 8 inches high. Its mark is shown. *Oravitz Collection.* $100

Although it is not prominent, the word "Nerds" appears on this guy's cap. The jar is 10 inches high, mark is shown. *Courtesy of Jazz'e Junque Shop, Chicago, Illinois.* $35

Mark of Topo Gigo.

Mark of Paddington Bear.

Decal mark of Nerds jar. Nerds is a brand of candy sold by Willy Wonka Brands, a subsidiary of Sunmark Company, in Itasca, Illinois.

Banks made in the likenesses of character cookie jars. To give you an idea of size, the American Bisque Popeye bank is 7-1/2 inches high. Little Audrey, next to Popeye, is 8-3/4 inches high. Winnie the Pooh is composition, and the rest are pottery. *Bosson Collection.* Left to right: Snoopy - $40, Donald Duck - $75, Mickey Mouse - $35, Big Al - $60, Big Al - $60, Pluto - $35, Popeye - $500, Winnie the Pooh - $70, Little Audrey - $700, Donald Duck - $125, Snoopy - $30

Section VII: Studio Artists

Studio artists are individuals who make cookie jars in their own small shops, or studios, and put a large amount of talent and hand work into each piece. During exceptionally busy periods, such as the Christmas season, they might hire a few part-time employees to perform menial tasks, but they generally work alone. They charge more for their cookie jars than large potteries do because their production costs are greater. The consumer pays the higher dollar to get the higher quality.

Some studio artists start at the beginning by designing their own cookie jars, and follow the process through to the final glaze firing. In between they model, mold, pour, clean, bisque fire, and finish their pieces. Others might join the process at any of the steps along the way.

Studio artists generally differ from hobby ceramists who sell their work at craft shows in that they have at least regional, if not national or international reputations in the field in which they have chosen to specialize.

Chapter 26
Glenn Appleman

Cookie jars don't get too much bigger than the vehicle jars of Glenn Appleman. The pictures don't show perspective, but these jars are large enough that a good size toddler could use them for kiddie cars if they had real wheels.

Appleman, a New York sculptor, made his first car in 1970, when he was only 21 years old, according to advertising. The cars and truck were made as decorative pieces, not cookie jars. But because they all have lids that lift off, cookie jar collectors are attracted to them.

Perhaps the most amazing thing about these giant jars is the low price at which they sold. In 1983 Appleman sent out a letter written in an apologetic tone that said he was going to have to raise his prices. Effective June 13, 1983, the letter said, all cars would be going up to $75 and all trucks would be raised to $100.

The business was called Appleman Auto Works. Some of the advertising showed it located at 5 Great Jones Street, New York, New York, while another sheet gave the address as 527 40th Street, Union City, New Jersey. According to the advertising, Appleman had a partner named Harry Zeller. Appleman Auto Works closed in 1987. Later Appleman made a special run of 50 Sid's Taxis which where marketed through *Cookie Jarrin', The Cookie Jar Newsletter*.

All jars displayed below are marked in a similar fashion to the humperbump police car.

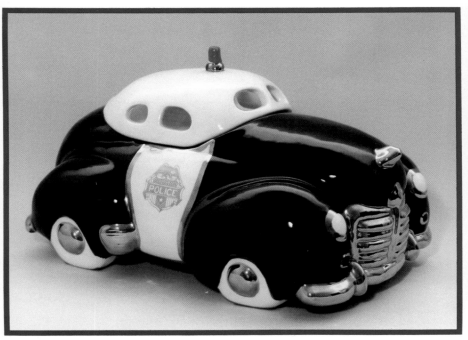

Appleman "Humperbump Police Car," 15 inches long, the first car Glenn Appleman made. Its mark is shown. *Blumenfeld Collection.* $900

Mark of "Humperbump Police Car." All Appleman jars displayed here are marked in a similar manner.

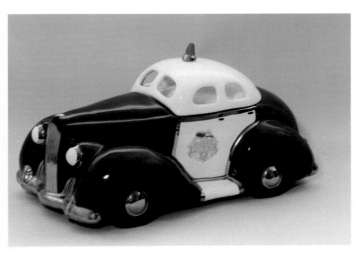

"Packard Police Car," 15-3/4 inches long. The mark indicates it was made in 1979. *Blumenfeld Collection*. $900

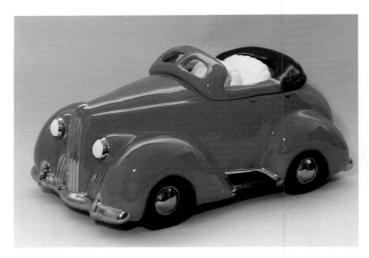

"Packard Convertible," 15-1/2 inches long, made in 1979. *Blumenfeld Collection*. $900

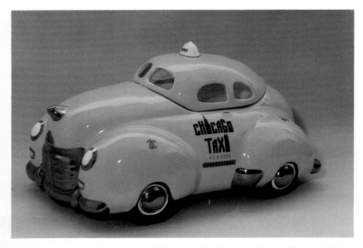

"Chicago Taxi," made in 1978. It is 14-1/2 inches long. *Blumenfeld Collection*. $700

The "Buick Roadmaster" was made in 1981. It is 15-1/2 inches long. *Blumenfeld Collection*. $750

On the back of this "Skyway Taxi" is a sign that says "Win With Wilkie," the Republican candidate for president in 1940. The jar, 15-1/2 inches long, was made in 1979. *Blumenfeld Collection*. $700

"Buick Controvertible," year of manufacture unknown, 16 inches long. *Blumenfeld Collection*. $700

Title unknown, 16-1/2 inches long. The car was made in 1984. *Blumenfeld Collection.* $1000

Tag from Appleman car.

Obviously a beer truck but official title is unknown. This is a biggie, 17 inches long. It was made in 1984. *Blumenfeld Collection.* $1000

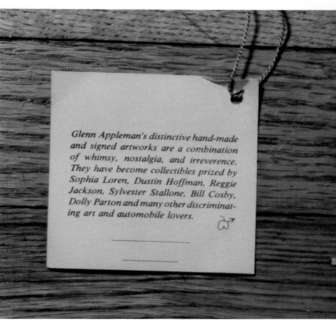

The *Who's Who* of Appleman jars.

Incised mark in beer truck lid.

Chapter 27
Carol Gifford

California-born Carol Gifford, a resident of Wanette, Oklahoma, combined two hobbies - cookie jar collecting and ceramic arts - into a business in 1986. Cookie jar collectors are still reaping the benefits.

According to Gifford, she had been working in ceramics about 15 years, and had her teaching credentials, when she decided to design the black cookie jar below called "Watermelon Mammy." Its success fostered four more black jars: "Watermelon Sammy," "Pancake Mammy," "Rocking Chair Mammy," and "Butler Servant." In the beginning, Gifford sold the five black jars separately, later only in sets. She has plans to add a sixth, a mate for the Rocking Chair Mammy. Gifford says after 250 copies of each jar have been made, she will destroy the molds.

"Watermelon Mammy," the first cookie jar Carol Gifford designed. The height is 11 inches. All jars in the five jar set are marked like "Watermelon Sammy," shown below. *Courtesy of Jazz'e Junque Shop, Chicago, Illinois.* $250; #1 Jar - $400

Mark of "Watermelon Sammy." The four jars in the series that are displayed here—Watermelon Mammy, Watermelon Sammy, Rocking Chair Mammy, Butler Servant—plus Pancake Mammy shown in Chapter 1, are from the first set poured in the molds. All are marked like this.

"Watermelon Sammy," 11 inches high. *Courtesy of Jazz'e Junque Shop, Chicago, Illinois.* $250; #1 Jar - $400

"Rocking Chair Mammy," 9-1/2 inches high. *Courtesy of Jazz'e Junque Shop, Chicago, Illinois.* $250; #1 Jar - $400

This Carol Gifford mammy, loosely based on the Mosaic Tile mammy, is 12 inches high. The mark is "Carol Gifford" incised. *Courtesy of Jazz'e Junque Shop, Chicago, Illinois.* $275

Black Santa head jar, 11 inches high. With "Carol Gifford" incised. *Blumenfeld Collection.* $200

"Butler Servant," 9-1/2 inches high. *Courtesy of Jazz'e Junque Shop, Chicago, Illinois.* $250; #1 Jar - $400

The same mammy in blue, with the same height and mark. *Courtesy of Carol Gifford Originals.* $275

Seated Santa, 11-1/2 inches high, with "Carol Gifford" incised. *Courtesy of Jazz'e Junque Shop, Chicago, Illinois.* $200

Left: Carol Gifford's interpretation of the Luzianne mammy cookie jar, which was originally used to advertise Luzianne Coffee made by Wm. B. Reily & Co., Inc. of New Orleans and Baltimore. Height is 12-1/2 inches, mark is "Carol/Gifford" incised on two lines. *Courtesy of Jazz'e Junque Shop, Chicago, Illinois.* $200

Right: Gifford's most recent creation, the "Keith Lytle" cookie jar. The mark reads "Carol Gifford Originals/made exclusively for /Cookie Jar Antiques/Don Wirfs and Associates/1990" on five lines. As you can see, Gifford's logo is impressed, and the jar shown is no. 1 in a limited edition of 250. $200

Mark of "Keith Lytle" cookie jar. Keith Lytle is a well-known cookie jar collector and dealer from Antioch, California. Over the years, Lytle's good-natured personality and massive physique, along with his cookie jar display, has become associated with Don Wirfs antique shows on the West Coast. Original plans called for the commemorative jar to be sold exclusively at Don Wirfs shows until December 31, 1991, after which Gifford would begin selling them to the general public until the limit of 250 was reached.

Mammy in different colors. The crescent shape decorations are slices of watermelon. *Courtesy of Jazz'e Junque Shop, Chicago, Illinois.* $200

Carol Gifford mammy from an Alberta's granny mold. The height is 9-1/2 inches, and the mark is "Carol/Gifford" incised on two lines. *Courtesy of Jazz'e Junque Shop, Chicago, Illinois.* $200

A jar for Christmas with holly on the apron. *Courtesy of Carol Gifford Originals.* $200

Two more Gifford color patterns from the Alberta's mold. *Courtesy of Jazz'e Junque Shop, Chicago, Illinois.* $200

Chapter 28
Rick Wisecarver

Rick Wisecarver was 20 years old when he opened his first ceramics shop in Roseville, Ohio, in 1970. He began making cookie jars 13 years later, completing 32 different models as of April, 1991.

Wisecarver lives in Roseville, his home and studio within view of Nelson McCoy Ceramics. He makes about 200 jars of each design he sculpts, but sometimes as many as 300. Never more than that, as he gets bored if he makes the same jar too many times. Wisecarver jars depict mostly blacks and country themes.

Copies of the artist's first five jars were made by another pottery for a time using Wisecarver's original molds. The jars are "Mixing Bowl Mammy," "Cookie Jar Mammy," "Churn Mammy," "Covered Bridge," and "Pig."

The copied cookie jars can be identified by lack of a signature, not to be confused with a mark. All original Wisecarvers are artist signed on the back, as shown below. The only exception is the cookstove mammy, which has Wisecarver's name on the back but not his signature. This is no problem since it wasn't one of the copied.

Rick Wisecarver "Santa," 12 inches high. Its mark is shown. *Oravitz Collection.* $200

Bottom of Wisecarver Santa.

Here's the key to whether or not any Wisecarver jar is an original. All originals, with the exception of the "Cookstove Mammy," are hand signed by the artist on the back. The signature is under the glaze. Jars that were not decorated by Wisecarver are not signed by him.

"Indian," 10-1/2 inches high. The mark is similar to others. *Courtesy of Betty and Floyd Carson.* $200

Back of the "Cookstove Mammy," the only jar not signed on the back by Wisecarver.

The jar on the left is 9-3/4 inches high, the jar on the right is 11-1/4 inches. They have the marks of original Wisecarver jars. *Blumenfeld Collection.* $110 ea.

This jar is 11-1/2 inches high. Wisecarver mark. *Courtesy of Betty and Floyd Carson.* $180

"Cookstove Mammy," 12 inches high. *Courtesy of Betty and Floyd Carson.* $150

"Mixing Bowl Mammy" and "Cookie Jar Mammy," 12 and 13-1/2 inches high, respectively. These were not made by Wisecarver. They are examples of the copied jars mentioned above. They do not present much of a problem, however, since they were made from the original Wisecarver molds and have values only slightly less than jars decorated by Rick Wisecarver himself. *Private Collection.* $200 ea.

220

"Milk Churn Mammy," also one made from an original Wisecarver mold, but not poured or decorated by Rick Wisecarver. Height is 13-1/2 inches. *Private Collection.* $200

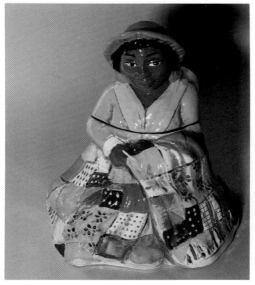

This is "Quilting Mammy." It stands 11-3/4 inches high. Mark shown below. *Courtesy of Rick Wisecarver.* $250

"Colonial Mammy." She stands 14 inches high. Mark is "Wihoa's/Cookie Classic/By Rick Wisecarver/No-44-91/RS" incised on five lines on the back. *Courtesy of Rick Wisecarver.* $150

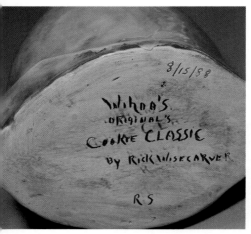

Mark of "Milk Churn Mammy." Note the difference in the Rick Wisecarver signature on this jar compared to the ones that were actually signed by the artist.

Mark of "Quilting Mammy."

"Black Miss America," 14 inches high. Standard Wisecarver mark as shown above and below. *Courtesy of Rick Wisecarver.* $200

"Morning Aggravation," 11 inches high. Wisecarver, a lover of animals, said the inspiration for this jar stemmed from his cats habitually wanting attention first thing in the morning. Typical Wisecarver mark with "#79/1991/RS" on three lines. *Courtesy of Rick Wisecarver.* $175

"Saturday Bath," 11-1/2 inches high. "Wihoa's/Cookie Classic/By Rick Wisecarver/1991/RS" incised on five lines. The "RS" mark seen on a Wisecarver cookie jar stands for Richard Sims, Wisecarver's partner, who handles the business end of the ceramic's operation. *Courtesy of Rick Wisecarver.* $200

Another of the five molds that were copied. Wisecarver said he hasn't seen a reproduction of this one, "Covered Bridge," but the mark is shown below anyway so you can compare it with your own. The jar is 7-1/2 inches high. *Courtesy of Rick Wisecarver.* $150

"Geronimo," 10-1/2 inches high. As the mark shows, this jar was made to depict the Chiricahua Apache warrior in 1905 during his later years, just four years prior to his death from pneumonia in 1909. Perhaps this is how Geronimo looked on March 4, 1905, when he attended the inauguration of President Theodore Roosevelt in Washington, D.C. *Courtesy of Rick Wisecarver.* $175

"Indian Maiden," 9-1/2 inches high. Mark on back is "Wihoa's/Cookie Classic/By Rick Wisecarver/110-80-1990" incised on four lines. Also, "®6931-0999" incised in bottom on one line. *Courtesy of Rick Wisecarver.* $175

Mark of "Covered Bridge."

Mark of "Geronimo."

This jar is called "Pickers." It measures 7-1/4 x 14-1/2 inches. *Courtesy of Rick Wisecarver.* $190

This "Witch" is 11-1/2 inches high. Mark is "Wihoa's/Cookie Classic/By Rick Wisecarver/No-34-91/RS" incised in back on five lines. *Courtesy of Rick Wisecarver.* $130

Wisecarver entitled this jar "Hill Folk." It is 12-1/2 inches high. Mark is shown. *Courtesy of Rick Wisecarver.* $150

Here is "Raccoons," standing 10 inches high. Mark on back is "Wihoa's/Cookie Classic/by Rick Wisecarver/No-71-91/RS" incised on five lines. *Courtesy of Rick Wisecarver.* $150

"Ducks in Flight," 11 inches high. Mark is shown. *Courtesy of Rick Wisecarver.* $125

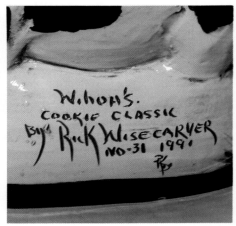

Mark of "Hill Folk." Note that the number and initials "RS" are at the top of the mark instead of the bottom.

"Three Kittens," 9-1/2 inches high. Mark is "Wihoa's/Original/Cookie Classic/By Rick Wisecarver/RS" incised in back on five lines. *Courtesy of Rick Wisecarver.* $140

"Cow and Calf" with bird finial. The jar is 9-1/2 inches high. Mark is shown. *Courtesy of Rick Wisecarver.* $125

Mark of "Cow and Calf."

While the five jars Wisecarver made in Florida—mixing bowl mammy, cookie jar mammy, churn mammy, covered bridge, and pig—are generally referred to as his first five cookie jars, this jar, "Swan," is really the original. It was made before Wisecarver went to Florida. Swan stands 8 inches high and has typical Wisecarver mark. *Courtesy of Richard Sims.* Value not determined.

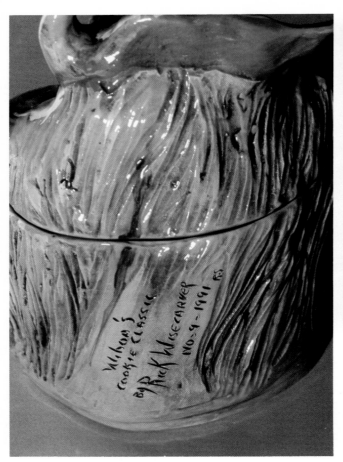

Mark of "Ducks in Flight."

Mark of one-of-a-kind "Chicken."

Copy of "Pig," 10-3/4 inches high. Mark is shown. *Private Collection.* $90

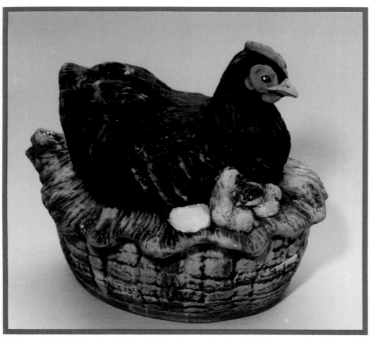

Here's something a little different, a Rick Wisecarver one-of-a-kind cookie jar. Called "Chicken," it is 10 inches high. Mark is shown. *Courtesy of Rick Wisecarver.* Value not determined.

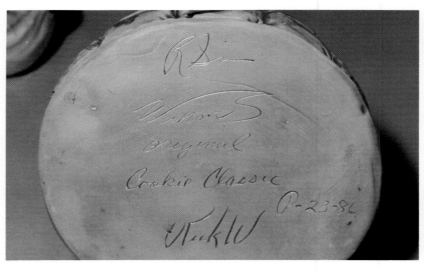

Mark of above "Pig."

Chapter 29
Others

Keith Herklotz

Keith Herkoltz is one of a several hundred stoneware potters scattered across the Untied States who makes a living the old fashioned way, by starting with raw clay and laboring over a potter's wheel to form it into useful objects.

Working as an apprentice at a New Jersey pottery while attending high school, Herklotz went on to earn a degree in art at the College of Wooster, in Wooster, Ohio, in 1979. His studio, Down to Earth Ceramics Studio, is housed in a former garage that has sprawled over the years by virtue of several additions. It is located in Wellington, Ohio, about 45 miles southwest of Cleveland.

Herklotz prepares his own clay mixture, combining clays from Ohio, Indiana, and Kentucky. He fires his cookie jars at approximately 2250 degrees F. He employs three kilns, one gas-fired of his own design and construction that has a 60-cubic foot capacity, and two smaller factory-made electric models. He uses glaze decoration, not slip decoration.

While stoneware jars don't spark the same collector interest as a McCoy cauliflower mammy or an American Bisque Fred Flintstone, they do have a simple charm about them many people find appealing. Perhaps more important, because cookie jars made their debut long after the industrial revolution, potters such as Herklotz offer cookie jar enthusiasts one of their few opportunities to include totally handmade jars in their collections. Cookie jars similar to those shown below are usually available at larger craft shows. Quality varies from artist to artist.

The address of Down to Earth Ceramics Studio, which recently moved to Franklin, Maine, is listed in Appendix I.

When pottery is hand thrown, each piece comes out slightly different. The stoneware jar on the left is 8-3/8 inches high to the rim; the one on the right is 8-1/8 inches. The mark is shown. *Courtesy of Down to Earth Ceramics Studio.* $40 ea.

Incised mark on all Herklotz cookie jars.

Herklotz cookie jar, 8⅛ inches high. *Courtesy of Down to Earth Ceramics Studio.*

This jar is 8¼ inches high. *Courtesy of Down to Earth Ceramics Studio.*

Section VIII: Foreign Cookie Jars

Identified foreign cookie jars have been divided into two categories, those from Pacific-Asian countries, which account for the majority of the imports, and those from other areas of the world.

Cookie jars made outside the United States are similar to cookie jars made within the United States in that they exhibit varying degrees of workmanship running from crude to sophisticated. At one time most collectors excluded foreign jars on general principles. While some still do, the trend today appears to be that people include foreign cookie jars in their collections based on the merits of the individual jars. As American cookie jars become less and less available, it seems almost certain that the popularity of foreign jars will continue to rise.

Chapter 30
Pacific-Asian Cookie Jars

Following their devastating defeat in World War II, the Japanese literally rebuilt their industries from the ground up, clay for the pottery industry being their most accessible material. Initial efforts produced figurines, salt and pepper shakers, and other knickknacks.

The majority of Japanese cookie jars apparently came somewhat later, from the early 1950s through the 1960s and beyond. If they had been made earlier, more would have been marked Occupied Japan, but this mark on a cookie jar is rare, if it exists at all. The Japanese were not necessarily required to use the mark during the American occupation, which lasted from 1945 until the spring of 1952. But it seems some jars, actually a great many, would have the occupied stamp had the country been producing them in quantity prior to 1952.

Japanese, and other Pacific-Asian cookie jars, are generally much lighter in weight than American jars, probably more a testament to the high cost of overseas shipping than to a lack of skills or poor workmanship.

During the 1950s American potteries complained about the Japanese pirating their designs. Ironically, as far as cookie jars are concerned, it appears this practice was more prevalent between American potteries than it was between Japanese and American potteries. There are some Japanese examples of this, such as the imitation Regal China churn boy, but as you leaf through this book, you will find much more evidence of American manufacturers imitating other American manufacturers, than you will find of Japanese manufacturers imitating the Americans.

The collecting community's feeling toward Japanese cookie jars is currently in a state of transition. At one time the jars were summarily rejected by collectors. Today they have gained acceptance to the point where they are included in the majority of collections, though most people appear to be somewhat uncomfortable about owning them. A common phrase heard when expressing interest in a collector's Japanese cookie jar is, "That's a Japanese jar," said in a tone of voice that implies "That's *just* a Japanese jar." Based on the current trend, it seems probable that in the future more and more Japanese jars will make their way into collections, and they will eventually be accepted at face value with no stigma attached.

When Japan moved on to cameras, steel, electronics, and automobiles, Taiwan served importers as the pottery road to riches. More recently, Korea and Malaysia have begun developing their ceramics industries. To the collector's advantage, when new countries jump onto the pottery bandwagon, they tend to enter the market at the current level of sophistication, instead of beginning at the bottom and working up as Japan had to do. Many Pacific-Asian countries have not yet made the inevitable change from agricultural- to industrial-based economies, so the region will probably continue to be a hotbed of cookie jar production for some time to come.

Isn't this guy great! The jar is 9 inches high, marked "Japan." On top of the hat is a windup music box. *Blumenfeld Collection.* $125

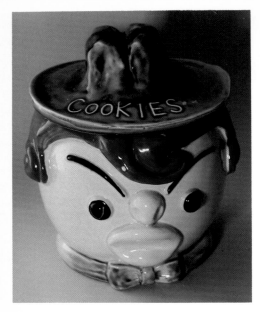

This jar is 8 inches high and marked "60/153/Japan" on two lines. *Blumenfeld Collection.* $85

This cookie jar, 11 inches high, is also seen with brown clothing. "Japan" inkstamp. *Oravitz Collection.* $75

A granny, 12 inches high, with a "Japan" inkstamp. *Oravitz Collection.* $45

Apparently a little baseball player with no bat or mitt, the jar stands 10 inches high. "Japan" impressed. *Oravitz Collection.* $75

The Japanese version of the Regal China churn boy, 10 inches high. It is marked "Made in Japan." The Roerigs show it with a reversed mold; the boy faces to his left. *Courtesy of Jazz'e Junque Shop, Chicago, Illinois.* $95

This F & F (Fiedler & Fiedler Mold and Die Works Company) look-alike is ceramic, 12-1/4 inches high, and marked "Made in Taiwan." *Courtesy of Jazz'e Junque Shop, Chicago, Illinois.* $80

No bat, but at least a mitt. The jar is 10-1/4 inches high. Although unmarked, the original box indicated it was made in Taiwan. *Oravitz Collection.* $45

An Omnibus mammy, 10 inches high. The paper label on the basket says "Omnibus/Fired Red/Non-Toxic/OC" on four lines. Omnibus is a mark used by Fitz & Floyd. *Courtesy of Jazz'e Junque Shop, Chicago, Illinois.* $200

Paper label on bottom of the Omnibus mammy.

"Gone-with-the-Wind" mammy, 10-1/2 inches high. As the paper label shows, this is a recently made jar. *Oravitz Collection.* $125

Paper label of "Gone-with-the-Wind" mammy.

The jar is 13 inches high and has a "Japan" inkstamp. *Courtesy of Jazz'e Junque Shop, Chicago, Illinois.* $60

Same as previous jar but unmarked. *Oravitz Collection.* $60

The chef is 9-1/4 inches high with "Japan" impressed. *Oravitz Collection.* $30

This 9-1/2 inch high clown head is inkstamped "Japan." *Courtesy of Jazz'e Junque Shop, Chicago, Illinois.* $60

Same as the other clown head but with no mark. *Blumenfeld Collection.* $60

Back of the clown head, quite a sight by itself.

This clown is 11 inches high, marked with a simple "Japan." *Courtesy of Sean Zera.* $40

This clown has a more complicated mark than most Pacific-Asian cookie jars: a "PY" in a circle above "Japan" with a "C" superimposed on a "N" below. The jar is 9-1/2 inches high. *Blumenfeld Collection.* $150

A somersault clown, 11-1/4 inches high, marked "Japan" in raised letters. *Oravitz Collection.* $65

Old King Cole is 12-1/2 inches high and has a "Japan" inkstamp. *Bosson Collection.* $70

The jar is 9-1/2 inches high. The paper label reads "Made in Taiwan/R.O.C." on two lines. *Courtesy of Jazz'e Junque Shop, Chicago, Illinois.* $50

Peter Pumpkin Eater, 12 inches high, with "Japan" impressed. *Oravitz Collection.* $60

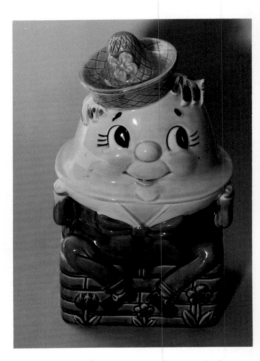

Humpty Dumpty, 13-1/4 inches high, marked "Japan." *Coughenour Collection.* $50

The jar on the left is 10-1/2 inches high, and the jar on the right is 10-1/4 inches high. The left jar is marked with an impressed "Japan," while the right jar has no mark. *Oravitz Collection.* $45 each.

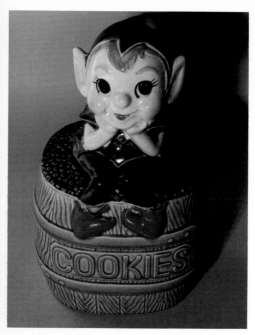

This elf is 12-1/4 inches high and has "Japan" impressed. *Oravitz Collection.* $55

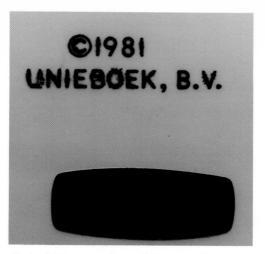

© 1981
UNIEBOEK, B.V.

Mark of "Gnome on Stump." The paper label reads "From the Gift World of/Gorham/Made in Japan" on three lines. Gorham is a giftware company based in Providence, Rhode Island. It was founded in 1831 and is known primarily for its sterling silver flatware, though it also markets kitchenware, Christmas ornaments, dolls, crystal, and collector's plates, among other things.

A real hunting dog. *Bosson Collection.* $75

More elves, 10 inches high, with "Japan" inkstamp. *Oravitz Collection.* $50

All six jars in this occupation/avocation set are 13 inches high and marked "Japan" in raised letters. *Bosson Collection.* $75 ea.

"Gnome on Stump." The mark is shown. *Oravitz Collection.* $50

The elephant is 12 inches high with "Japan" impressed. *Oravitz Collection.* $35

Bought at a discount store in 1990, this jar is 10 inches high. It has a Taiwan paper label. *Oravitz Collection.* $35

231

Although the bottoms appear to be interchangeable, they're not because of details such as the rope on the bear and suspender buttons on the cow. *Bosson Collection.* $50 ea.

A fishing hippo. *Oravitz Collection.* $50

A girl hippopotamus, 9 inches high. The paper label reads "Made in Taiwan/ROC" on two lines. A boy (minus the bow) was also made. *Oravitz Collection.* $50

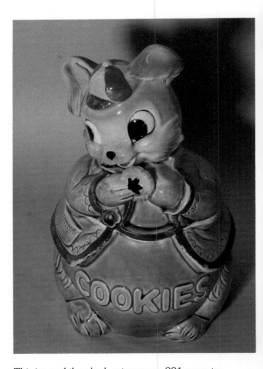

This jar and the elephant on page 231 seem to have a lot in common. Perhaps they were created by the same designer or made by the same pottery. The height is 12-1/2 inches, with "Japan" impressed. *Courtesy of Jazz'e Junque Shop, Chicago, Illinois.* $35

With the "C" on his sweater, there seems little doubt this teddy bear attends Cookie College. The jar is 10-3/4 inches high, and it has "Japan" impressed. *Oravitz Collection.* $60

This jar is 10-1/2 inches high with "Japan" impressed. *Oravitz Collection.* $55

Teddy bear, 10-1/2 inches high, with "Japan" impressed. *Oravitz Collection.* $35

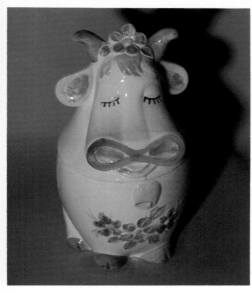

This miss is 13 inches high and has a "Japan" inkstamp. *Oravitz Collection.* $40

Paper label of the pink elephant.

Two more jars that might have come from a single pottery. *Left:* 8-1/2 inches high. *Right:* 9-1/2 inches high. "Japan" in raised letters is on both. *Oravitz Collection.* $35 ea.

The elephant is 10 inches high with a "Made in Japan" paper label. *Oravitz Collection.* $35

This jar is 10-1/2 inches high with a "Japan" inkstamp. *Courtesy of Jazz'e Junque Shop, Chicago, Illinois.* $35

Butterfly puppy, 7-1/2 inches high. Its "Japan" paper label is shown. *Oravitz Collection.* $65

Time to stop drinking. The pink elephant is 10 inches high. The paper label is shown. *Oravitz Collection.* $35

The jar on the left is 10-3/4 inches high with "Japan" impressed. The jar on the right is 11 inches high with "Japan" in raised letters. The one on the left looks very much like the jar above, but close inspection reveals it isn't. *Oravitz Collection.* $35 ea.

The mark and paper label of butterfly puppy. The bottom line of paper label reads "Crafted in Japan."

Both of these jars are 8 inches high. The one on the left has a "Made in Taiwan" paper label. The one on the right is unmarked but is assumed to be of Pacific—Asian origin, probably the same company. *Oravitz Collection.* $20 ea.

These little guys are all 7-1/2 inches high, and all have "Made in Taiwan/ROC" written on two lines on a paper label. In 1990, they sold for $5 each at discount stores. *Oravitz Collection.* $25 ea.

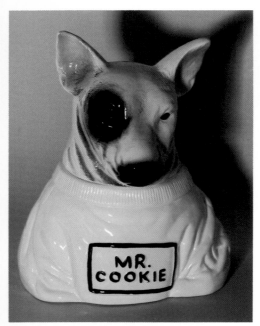

"Mr. Cookie," 10-1/4 inches high, with "Taiwan" impressed. *Oravitz Collection.* $75

Mark of the blue and white animal jar.

The owl on the left, apparently in elementary school, is 11-3/4 inches high. The owl on the right, obviously at graduation, is 12-1/4 inches high. While neither of these two jars is marked, identical jars have marks indicating Japanese origin. *Courtesy of Jazz'e Junque Shop, Chicago, Illinois.* $45 ea.

Another blue and white animal jar of questionable species. Its height is 6-1/4 inches. The paper label reads "Made in Taiwan." *Oravitz Collection.* $25

Dog or cat? It is 10-3/4 inches high. Its mark is shown. *Courtesy of Jazz'e Junque Shop, Chicago, Illinois.* $25

This owl is 10 inches high. The inkstamp is "Japan." *Bosson Collection.* $35

An Indian owl, 9 inches high, with "Japan" impressed. *Oravitz Collection.* $35

Granny duck, 12 inches high. The paper label reads "Fabrique à Taiwan." *Oravitz Collection.* $40

The height here is 10-1/4 inches. The mark is shown. *Oravitz Collection.* $35

Chicken chef, 13 inches high. It has an Omnibus paper label. *Courtesy of Jazz'e Junque Shop, Chicago, Illinois.* $35

This jar is 10-1/2 inches high and has a "Made in Japan" paper label. *Oravitz Collection.* $60

Mark of the owl clock.

The penguin on the left is 11 inches high. It has "Made in Taiwan/ROC" impressed on two lines, and a paper label that indicates the jar was copyrighted in 1985. The penguin on the right is 12-1/2 inches high and unmarked. *Oravitz Collection.* $35 ea.

Another house, 9-1/2 inches high, has "Japan" impressed. *Oravitz Collection.* $35

This house is 9-1/2 inches high, with "Japan" impressed. *Oravitz Collection.* $25

Another clock, also 10-3/4 inches high, with "Japan" impressed. *Courtesy of Jazz'e Junque Shop, Chicago, Illinois.* $30

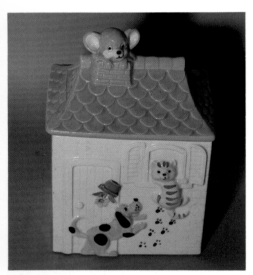

Lots of action here: a mouse being chased by a cat being chased by a dog. The jar is 10 inches high with "Japan" impressed. *Courtesy of Jazz'e Junque Shop, Chicago, Illinois.* $35

A little girl at her playhouse. Note the nice detail such as the bird on the chimney and the dog by the girl. The jar has an impressed "Japan" mark and is 10-1/2 inches high. *Oravitz Collection.* $35

This clock is 10-3/4 inches high. "Japan" is impressed along with additional letters that are unreadable. *Oravitz Collection.* $25

A stove with tea kettle, 10 inches high, with "Japan" impressed. *Courtesy of Jazz'e Junque Shop, Chicago, Illinois.* $35

A cookie house, 9-1/2 inches high. It has a "Japan" inkstamp. *Oravitz Collection.* $30

The drum is 10 inches high, and its mark is shown. *Zera Collection.* $30

Mark of the silver drum.

Just about the best subject you could get for a cookie jar. It is 9-1/2 inches high, "Japan" impressed. *Courtesy of Jazz'e Junque Shop, Chicago, Illinois.* $25

Just about the worst subject you could get for a cookie jar. This one is 9 inches high. The mark is an impressed "Japan." *Oravitz Collection.* $45

This barrel jar is 9 inches high. It is unmarked but another that was photographed has "Japan" impressed. Does anyone understand the theme? *Bosson Collection.* $35

Both jars are 10-1/2 inches high. Raggedy Ann is inkstamped "Japan," and Raggedy Andy is unmarked. *Oravitz Collection.* $45 ea.

The shoe on the left is 9-3/4 inches high, has the Brinn's paper label "Made in Japan." The shoe on the right is 13 inches high. It had felt glued to the bottom so it is unknown whether or not it is marked. *Oravitz Collection.* $30 ea.

Robot, 10-1/4 inches high, marked with "Japan" impressed. *Saxby Collection.* $75

Yellow robot, 10-1/4 inches, with "Japan" impressed. *Saxby Collection.* $75

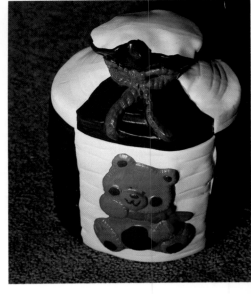

This 9-1/2 inch high cookie jar is unmarked. Original box says "JASCO, Made in Taiwan, Item no. 189." *Oravitz Collection.* $35

Robot in white, with the same size and mark as above. *Saxby Collection.* $75

This jar has a light-sensitive music box in the lid. The height is 9-1/2 inches, and the mark is "Made in Taiwan." *Courtesy of Jazz'e Junque Shop, Chicago, Illinois.* $45

Many biscuit jars were made in Japan during the postwar ear. More a fixture of the British kitchen than of the American kitchen, they were nevertheless imported to the United States. This one is 7-1/4 inches high, inkstamped "Made in Japan." On all biscuit jars the measurement is for the pottery only, which does not include the handle. *Oravitz Collection.* $40

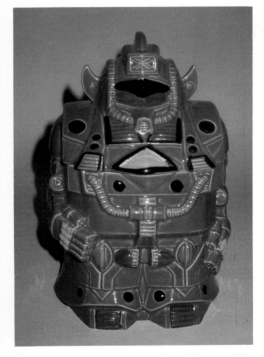

Blue robot, same as above. *Saxby Collection.* $75

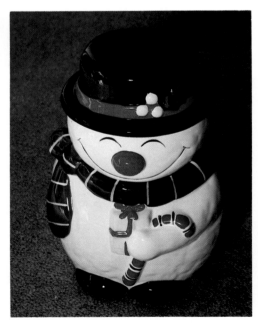

The snowman with gift is 11-1/2 inches high and has a "Made in Taiwan" paper label. *Oravitz Collection.* $35

The height of this jar is 6-1/4 inches with the inkstamp "Made in Japan." *Courtesy of Jazz'e Junque Shop, Chicago, Illinois.* $35

The jar on the left is 5-1/2 inches high and not marked. The jar on the right is 5-1/4 inches high, mark is shown. *Oravitz Collection.* $50 ea.

From *left* to *right* the sizes are: 5-3/4 inches, 6-3/4 inches, and 6-1/2 inches. The marks from *left* to *right* are: "10052" inkstamp, no mark, "Japan" paper label. *Oravitz Collection.* Right and left jars - $35 ea., Center jar - $30

Inkstamp mark of pink cat jar. The paper label "Relco/Japan" appears on two lines.

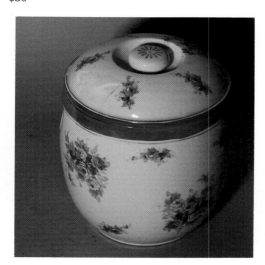

Another cat, 8 inches high, with a "Japan" inkstamp. *Courtesy of Jazz'e Junque Shop, Chicago, Illinois.* $50

A fruit fest, 6-3/4 inches high, with "Japan" inkstamp. *Courtesy of Jazz'e Junque Shop, Chicago, Illinois.* $30

Just like the pink cat above, it even has the same inkstamp mark. But the paper label is different—"Richard/Japan" on two lines. *Courtesy of Jazz'e Junque Shop, Chicago, Illinois.* $50

This canister jar, 8 inches high, is marked "Maple Ware/(likeness of a maple leaf)/Made in Japan" on three lines. *Courtesy of Jazz'e Junque Shop, Chicago, Illinois.* $25

The 6-1/4 inch high jar on the left is not marked, while the 6-3/4 inch high jar on the right is identified by the paper label "Betson's/Japan" on two lines. *Oravitz Collection.* Left - $35, Right - $60

This jar, 8 inches high, is marked "Dresden/Ware/Japan" on three lines. *Oravitz Collection.* $30

This canister jar is only 6-1/2 inches high, with a "Made in Japan" inkstamp. *Courtesy of Jazz'e Junque Shop, Chicago, Illinois.* $20

This unique jar is 9-1/2 inches high. The impressed mark reads "Shafford/Original©1979" on two lines, while the paper label is "Shafford/Japan" on two lines. *Oravitz Collection.* $75

An owl canister, 10-1/4 inches high, marked "OMC/Japan" on two lines. *Courtesy of Jazz'e Junque Shop, Chicago, Illinois.* $35

The height is 7 inches, and the inkstamp mark is "Japan." *Oravitz Collection.* $30

A rather plain cookie jar, 10 inches high, with "Made in Taiwan" impressed. *Courtesy of Jazz'e Junque Shop, Chicago, Illinois.* $20

Chapter 31
Jars From Other Countries

Mention foreign cookie jars and thoughts automatically turn to Japan. But several other countries have made cookie jars, too, some of the jars being of very high quality. Italy appears to be the most prolific. The Italians apparently were not immune to the carbon copy syndrome, as you will see if you compare the Italian clown head below to the Morton Pottery clown in Chapter 21, upon which it was obviously based.

Duck, 9-1/4 inches high. The inkstamp reads "Hand/Painted/Made in Brazil" on three lines. Paper label is shown. *Oravitz Collection.* $25

The jar on the left is 8-3/4 inches high, with "Japan" impressed. The jar on the right is 8-1/4 inches high and marked "Hand/Painted/Made in Brazil" on three lines. *Oravitz Collection.* $25 ea.

Weiss paper label of the duck cookie jar.

These two jars have the same inkstamp—"Hand-painted/Made in Brazil" on two lines. The left jar is 8 inches high; the right one is 8-1/4 inches. *Oravitz Collection.* $20 ea.

This biscuit jar, 6-3/4 inches high without the handle, was made in Czechoslovakia. Mark is shown. *Oravitz Collection*. $85

Reverse of Czechoslovakian biscuit jar.

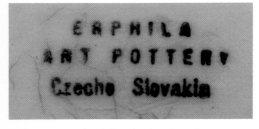

Inkstamp mark of Czechoslovakian biscuit jar. Erphila is an acronym for Ebeling & Reuss, a Philadelphia importer that started in business in 1886 and is still going today.

Paneled biscuit jar, 7-1/2 inches high without handle. The mark is "Made in England" with crown above. *Courtesy of Jazz'e Junque Shop, Chicago, Illinois*. $30

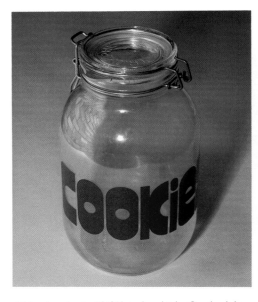

This glass jar is 10-3/4 inches high. On the lid is "Triomphe/France" on two lines. On the bottom, "France/3L" on two lines. *Zera Collection*. $20

Stoneware bean pot, 7 inches high, made in England. Mark is shown. *Courtesy of Jazz'e Junque Shop, Chicago, Illinois*. $25

Mark of the bean pot.

English pig, 11-1/4 inches high. The mark is shown. *Bosson Collection*. $125

Mark of the English pig cookie jar.

Robin Hood's friend Friar Tuck, made by Goebel, the manufacturer of world famous Hummel figurines. In addition to a Goebel "V" mark on the bottom, it has "K29" and "©1957." There is also a Friar Tuck sticker on the back. Goebel is not believed to have made very many cookie jars. A Goebel cat head jar appeared in the October 1990 issue of *Crazed Over Cookie Jars*. *Bosson Collection*. $250

West German chalet cookie jar, 6-3/4 inches high. The original price sticker inside says $1.25 with a date code that appears to indicate February of 1959. Mark is pictured. *Zera Collection.* $60

Mark of the West German chalet jar.

This 10-inch high terra cotta pig is fairly common, and more desirable than many other foreign jars as it is hand thrown with the legs and ears attached. This one is unmarked, but "Made in Italy" is clearly indicated on the yellow one. *Oravitz Collection.* $70

Inside of the red pig showing the ridges indicative of hand throwing.

Italian look-alike of the Morton clown head jar, 10-1/4 inches high. The mark is an unreadable number with "Italy" impressed. *Oravitz Collection.* $75

Hand thrown pig, signed "Italy." *Bosson Collection.* $70

Conestoga wagon, 10 inches high, with a mark that shows it was made in Italy. *Bosson Collection.* $45

This jar is 10-3/4 inches high, and marked "Italy." *Courtesy of Jazz'e Junque Shop, Chicago, Illinois.* $40

The cookie house is 8-1/2 inches high, marked "Le/324/Italy" on three lines. *Oravitz Collection.* $35

A barn that sits on its own hill. The jar is 9-1/2 inches high with "Italy" painted on bottom. *Oravitz Collection.* $65

This owl is ceramic, but at first glance you'll swear it's made of tin. The height is 14 inches, and the mark is "Italy/316" on two lines. *Oravitz Collection.* $75

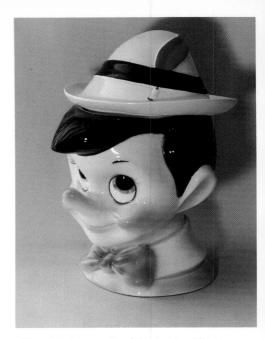

Pinocchio from south of the border, 12 inches high. This is one of the more expensive foreign jars in circulation today. Mark is shown. $800

Humpty Dumpty, 11 inches high. The mark is "B/333/Italy" on three lines, very similar to the cookie house on previous page. *Oravitz Collection.* $100

The height of this duck is 10 inches. The paper label on the lid is "Made in Mexico." *Oravitz Collection.* $25

Mark of Pinocchio.

The dog is 12-1/2 inches high. Mark is "made in Portugal." *Oravitz Collection.* $35

Apparently a canister set, the heights, left to right, are 8, 8-3/4, and 8 inches. The Italian mark is shown. *Oravitz Collection.* Left and right - $25 ea., Center - $35

Mark on the bottom of each of the canisters.

244

Section IX: The Mystery Cookie Jars

This section is made up of domestic cookie jars that for one reason or another could not be identified by manufacturer, and foreign jars that could not be positively identified by country of origin. Certainly many of these jars are not mysteries to all readers. A good number of them must have included paper labels at one time that are, presumably, still intact on jars in some collections.

It would be appreciated if readers who can identify any of these jars by marks or paper labels would contact the author in care of the publisher, so that we may have the option of updating future editions.

Chapter 32
Advertising Jars

Advertising jars appear throughout the book under the companies that made them. Chapter 35 contains several advertising jars in media other than ceramic. The ones shown here are only those for which manufacturers could not be determined.

These jars enter the world in three ways. The oldest method is that by which a company sells its product, which may or may not be cookies, in a jar bearing its name. Nearly as old is the premium offer. A consumer combines proofs of purchase with a small amount of cash to buy a jar with a company's advertising on it, at a lower price than a similar jar could be purchased without advertising. The third method, which was employed earlier but became more popular during the namedropping 1980s, is for a company to license a pottery or an importer to use its logo on jars made for the retail market.

At one time most advertising jars were made in America, but the majority of them sold today originate overseas.

The printing on this girl's apron is "Blue Bonnet Sue." The jar is 11-3/4 high, has a "Made in Taiwan" paper label, with "©1989 Nabisco" impressed. *Oravitz Collection.* $50

The Green Giant's little buddy Sprout. On the left is an unmarked musical bank, 8-1/4 inches high. On the right is the cookie jar, 12 inches high. The impressed mark on the jar is "©1988/The Pillsbury Co./Made in Taiwan." There is also a "Made in Taiwan" paper label. *Oravitz Collection.* Left - $25, Right - $50

The M & M's jar is 7-1/2 inches high. Impressed around the base of the bottom is "M & M's TM Cookie Jar/©Mars, Inc. 1982." Because this jar's bottom was covered with felt, it hasn't been determined if there were any additional marks or paper labels. *Courtesy of Betty and Floyd Carson.* $85

This jar, 11 inches high, was a 1990 mail-in premium offer from Frookie Cookies. On the bottom is a "Made in Taiwan" paper label. On the back is a "RWFrookie" decal. *Courtesy of Betty and Floyd Carson.* $35

Keebler elf, 11-3/4 inches high. Paper label reads "Made in Taiwan." *Oravitz Collection.* $50

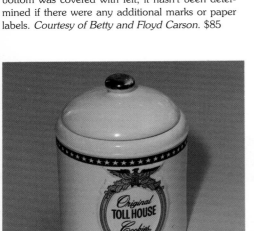

Unmarked Nestlé Toll House cookie jar, 9-3/4 inches high. Reverse is shown below. *Courtesy of Betty and Floyd Carson.* $75

An Almost Home mail in premium cookie jar, 10 inches high. According to the Roerigs, this was made by Holiday Designs. The inkstamp mark and original advertising are shown below. *Zera Collection.* $100

Say hello to Dan the Dog, lover of Alpo dog biscuits. The jar is 8 inches high, and its mark is shown. *Zera Collection.* $50

Mark of Alpo dog biscuit jar.

Reverse of Nestlé Toll House cookie jar.

Original newspaper advertisement for Almost Home cookie jar.

This mark appears inside the Almost Home jar.

This Milk-Bone jar is 7 inches high and marked "Roman/Made in Taiwan" on two lines. *Courtesy of Heidi and Nicci, the DiRenzo's Dobermans.* $100

An earlier Pillsbury jar, 10-1/2 inches high. The mark is "©The Pillsbury Co. 1973" on one line. *Courtesy of Jazz'e Junque Shop, Chicago, Illinois.* $65

The Pillsbury jar is 11-3/4 inches high, with a "Made in Taiwan" paper label. Also marked "©1988 The Pillsbury Company" in the shape of a horseshoe. *Courtesy of Jazz'e Junque Shop, Chicago, Illinois.* $30

Chapter 33
Hobby Ceramics Jars

Mushroom canister, 9-1/2 inches high. It is from an Arnel's mold, and the mark is shown. *Courtesy of Jazz'e Junque Shop, Chicago, Illinois.* $20

Look at a vase and you can normally tell in an instant whether it was made by a professional pottery or a hobby ceramist. The telltale clue is on the bottom. Professional potteries dry foot their wares for glaze firing. That means they leave protrusions on the bottom unglazed to prevent the glaze from coming in contact with the kiln, or sagger, in which case the two would be forever united. The best known examples of this would be the unglazed wedges on the bottoms of American Bisque cookie jars and the three-bar bottoms used by McCoy. Hobby ceramists glaze the bottoms of their pieces, then set them on stilts for firing. Stilts are like very small beds of nails anchored in a high-fired ceramic base. Stilts also become permanently bonded to the piece, but because they are sharply pointed, they can easily be broken free without damage after the piece has cooled. This leaves small holes in the glaze called stilt marks. They are a dead giveaway that a hobby ceramist made the piece.

But not with cookie jars. Some companies, for instance California Originals and Doranne of California, often glazed the entire bottoms of their jars and used stilts when firing them. Consequently, it is sometimes impossible to tell whether an unmarked jar has been made by a professional or a hobbyist by looking at its bottom.

There is another problem. Professional potteries sometimes use molds that are available to hobby ceramists. An example of this is the rocking horses shown below. The reddish-brown horse with the yellow mane screams of being made by a beginning hobby ceramist. The combination of colors is unattractive, and the glaze was applied too thickly and somewhat unevenly. But the white model with the brown saddle and the blue trim appears to have been done by a professional pottery. The decoration exhibits professional quality, and the sheer number of these jars that are available indicates they came from a large scale operation.

A similar situation exists with the Duncan Porky Pig. Duncan is a mold company that sells to hobby ceramists. Too many of the Porky Pigs are seen bearing quality decoration for them not to have originated in a professional pottery.

Some hobby ceramists do beautiful work. Others do terrible work. There is no reason to shy away from the better quality hobby ceramic jars as they fit well into any collection. The poorer ones fit well into any garbage can. The main thing collectors should be concerned with is recognizing the names of mold companies found on jars, because they are often confused with marks of potteries. A list of more than 60 mold companies, both past and present, is contained in Appendix II.

By becoming familiar with the names of the mold companies, you will avoid the potential pitfall of buying a low priced hobby ceramic top or bottom in hopes of someday mating it with the missing piece. Odds of making such a match would be far from favorable because each hobby ceramic jar is unique. When you consider the many different techniques, hundreds of different paints and glazes, and thousands of different transfers that are available, it is highly unlikely two jars would ever turn out the same unless made by the same hobbyist.

Arnel's mark of mushroom canister. Most of the time the mark of a mold company is a good indication the jar is homemade. But a lot of the times the mark is rubbed away when the greenware is cleaned.

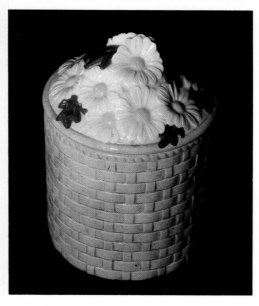

Daisy canister, 9 inches high. The mold company is unknown. *Courtesy of Sharon Isaacson.* $20

This jar is 14 inches high and marked "Arnel's." *Oravitz Collection.* $75

Sometimes you can tell a hobby ceramic cookie jar by the way it is decorated, which doesn't necessarily mean poorly. In the case of this beautifully decorated 12-1/4 inch high unmarked pixie head, no pottery could afford the time consuming hand-painting that went into the top. The artist was obviously driven by passion, not profit. *Oravitz Collection.* $90

Sleeping Beauty's castle, 12-3/4 inches high, with "Rulon/1981" scratched in the bottom on two lines. A name scratched into the bottom of a jar nearly always indicates it was made by a hobby ceramist. *Coughenour Collection.* $65

Homemade version of the Shawnee winking owl. The jar is 11 inches high. "Atlantic©Mold" is impressed around the neck of the lid, and "Betty Royal" is incised in the bottom. *Oravitz Collection.* $30

Same height as the example above. The mark is shown. Several similar jars appear in Chapter 34. Note that these two are the only ones with collars. *Blumenfeld Collection.* $90

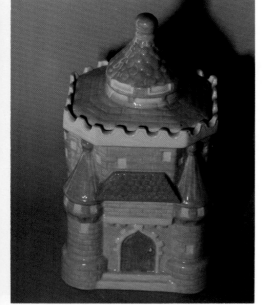

Same size as the example above, no mark. *Bosson Collection.* $55

Mark of the pixie jar with green cap.

No doubt everyone has had the experience of seeing another person who is super attractive from the back, only to have them turn around and display a face even a mother couldn't love. That's the way it is with this 12-1/2 inch high cookie jar. From the rear it is absolutely stunning. But the face is so awful it looks like it couldn't have been decorated by the same person. The signature on this jar is shown below, as is, sadly, the front. *Zera Collection.* $400

This 13-inch high unmarked jar, from an Alberta's mold, sings hobby ceramics loud and clear in several different voices. The entire jar was painted by hand, which again would have been too expensive a procedure for a professional pottery; it has that paint-by-number look that home ceramists were known for a few decades back. No one but a beginning hobbyist would have picked such an appalling color scheme. *Courtesy of Jazz'e Junque Shop, Chicago, Illinois.* $35

Same rocking horse but marked "Alberta/ ©1956" on two lines. Probably a hobby ceramist. *Oravitz Collection.* $35

Front of the cookie jar which has the beautiful back. Decoration on the front is nice, face is poorly done, hands were modeled like boxing gloves. Carl & Gari McCallum, of California, have this jar painted as a black woman, and carrying an incised mark on the bottom, "Brayton-Laguna-California-K-27." They also have a matching salt and pepper shaker of the woman and a male companion.

Different story here. Same jar, but finished by either a pottery or a decorating firm. Main clues are its professional look, the use of airbrushing where possible, and the dependence upon clear glaze to keep the cost low. Jars decorated in this same manner show up in collections throughout the nation. *Courtesy of Betty and Floyd Carson.* $85

This jar is 11 inches high. It has no mold mark but the initials "V.K" are scratched in bottom. *Courtesy of Jazz'e Junque Shop, Chicago, Illinois.* $35

Right: This cookie jar exemplifies one of the pluses and one of the minuses of homemade jars. The hobby ceramist was able to take the time to neatly paint the tiny packages in Santa's sleigh and the houses, but the jar is beginning to craze, which often happens with home ceramics. *Zera Collections.* $45

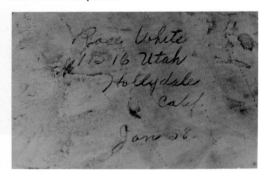

Left: Bottom of the lady with the pretty back. The fact that the bottom is not glazed is puzzling. The quality of the decoration on the dress would seem to indicate a studio artist. However, the face would seem to indicate a beginner.

The pear is 11-1/2 inches high, with "Marianne 77" scratched in the bottom. *Oravitz Collection.* $30

Little Red Riding Hood, 11-3/4 inches high. "M.D. 1969" is scratched in the bottom. *Oravitz Collection.* $40

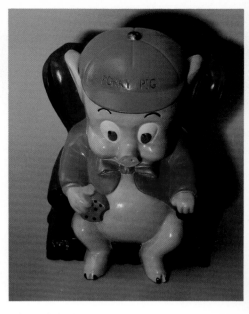

Although the Porky Pig cookie jar comes from a Duncan mold, at least three of the four jars shown—the ones with single color hats—were probably executed by a professional pottery or decorating company. This jar is 11 inches high with "Duncan/©1975 Warner Bros. Inc." impressed in the back. *Coughenour Collection.* $85

The same height as the pear, 11-1/2 inches, this jar has "©1973" impressed at the base and "E.H." scratched in the bottom. *Zera Collection.* $50

Dog biscuit jar, 8-3/4 inches high, marked "Crest Mold 1979." *Bosson Collection.* $50

Here's another guess. Both jars are made of the lightweight whiteware normally associated with hobby ceramics, both are entirely hand decorated instead of airbrushed, and the jar on the right has what appears to be an unreadable mold company mark. The jars are 11 inches high. *Courtesy of Country Heirs Antique Shop.* $35 ea.

This Porky may be a hobby ceramic product. Brush strokes seem unsteady where the yellow-orange and brown glazes meet, the cap was made unnecessarily complicated by using two colors, and the letters in Porky Pig were not executed with the same authority as the others. *Courtesy of Jazz'e Junque Shop, Chicago, Illinois.* $75

Nice work. Note the flower decals on the yellow chair. *Bosson Collection.* $90 ea.

Here's why hobby ceramics make it tough on cookie jar collectors. The cow shown in this picture and the pumpkins in the next picture were taken from a 1988 Gare catalog. The catalog showed eight different cookie jars plus a milk can canister set. Each jar has the potential to have been decorated by several hundred hobby ceramists, each free to chose his own unique design. And that is just one of the many companies. When these jars are finished by skillful hands, there is no reason to suspect they weren't done by a professional pottery. There is also no reason to exclude them from a collection.

Three ghostly pumpkins from Gare. In the future you will no doubt see them at flea markets and antique shows.

252

Chapter 34
Other Unknown Jars

The cookie jars shown below lack identifiable marks, paper labels, or attributable characteristics to indicate beyond any doubt what companies made them, and in many cases, what countries they originated from.

Obviously, many of these jars are Japanese. They would have been included in Chapter 30 Pacific-Asian Cookie Jars, except that readers deserve more than a guess when an author declares positive identification. And no matter how much a cookie jar may look or feel Japanese, calling it such would still amount to nothing but an educated guess if there wasn't a paper label or a mark to back it up. Also, as you move on through the 1970s, 1980s, and into the 1990s, the once clear differences between American and Pacific-Asian cookie jars become fuzzier and fuzzier.

Hopefully, in time, all of the jars in this chapter will be identified.

Mark of the lady in the pink dress.

This graceful lady is 10-1/2 inches high. The jar's mark is shown but gives no clue to its identity. *Oravitz Collection.* $110

Dutch woman, 11-1/2 inches high, unmarked. Quite possibly hobby ceramics. *Zera Collection.* $75

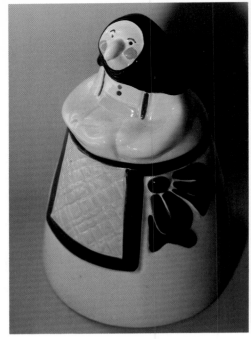

For years collectors assumed this unmarked jar was American Bisque, but when the Roerigs interviewed the late A.N. Allen, former owner of American Bisque, he claimed the company didn't make it. The height is 13 inches. *Courtesy of Mercedes DiRenzo.* Value not determined.

Unmarked peasant girl, 11 inches high. *Oravitz Collection.* $90

Some call her a "kitchen witch," others call her "Thelma." She is unmarked, 11-1/2 inches high. *Coughenour Collection.* $85

If the paint on this jar hadn't peeled, wouldn't it have made a great enlargement for the back cover? The height is 10 inches. Mark is "Circus/by/David Surell" on three lines. *Bosson Collection.* $45

Same mold as the example above, but 11-1/2 inches high, unmarked. *Zera Collection.* $90

Similar to the example above, but 1/4 of an inch taller. Note that the eyes of both jars are holes in the bisque. *Courtesy of Jazz'e Junque Shop, Chicago, Illinois.* $85

On the left is a 9-inch high granny cookie jar, on the right an 8-1/2 inch high granny bank. Neither is marked. *Bosson Collection.* Left - $50, Right - $40

This unmarked mammy is 11-1/4 inches high. Possibly put together from two jars as the top is noticeably whiter than the bottom. *Oravitz Collection.* $100

This jar is 12-1/4 inches high. It is not marked. *Bosson Collection.* $90

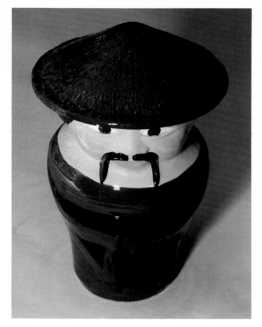

Chinese man, 10-3/4 inches high and not marked. *Zera Collection.* $45

Pirate, 10 inches high, with an unreadable remnant of paper label. *Bosson Collection.* $65

This Starnes jar is 11-3/4 inches high, unmarked. A matching boy, not shown, is dressed in bib overalls. *Oravitz Collection.* $800

This jar is 9-1/4 inches high. Mark is shown. *Bosson Collection.* $150

This fellow is made of stoneware and stands 12-3/4 inches high. Its paper label is shown. *Zera Collection.* $80

Mark of the above jar.

Unmarked Amish boy, 9-1/2 inches high. *Courtesy of Betty and Floyd Carson.* $100

Stoneware Designs West lady, 12 inches high. The paper label is below the collar and is basically the same as the example on the previous page; except the word at the top is "Porcelone" instead of "Stoneware." *Saxby Collection.* $80

Sounds like good advice to me. The unmarked jar is 9-1/2 inches high. *Courtesy of Betty and Floyd Carson.* $35

This unmarked jar is 12 inches high. It also appears in a glaze two or three shades darker than Pottery Guild's blue. *Oravitz Collection.* $125

This jar might be a mate for the Dutch girl on page 253 as the heights are the same (11-1/2 inches) and so is the blue glaze. *Courtesy of Jazz'e Junque Shop, Chicago, Illinois.* $75

This jar is 10-1/4 inches high. It is unmarked with the exception of an extremely provocative phrase "Old Shawnee Test" written on the bottom. It was photographed near Zanesville, Ohio, the home of Shawnee, so anything is possible. *Bosson Collection.* Value not determined.

A donut chef, 11 inches high and unmarked. *Coughenour Collection.* $250

Clown head, 11 inches high and unmarked. The jar is heavily poured, suggesting an American origin. In the picture of the aluminum shelves in Chapter 6, it is featured next to a duplicate that has red hair, a yellow hat with a green brim, and a yellow and green bow tie. *Blumenfeld Collection.* $450

The clown biscuit jar is 9-1/2 inches high excluding the handle. It is unmarked. *Blumenfeld Collection.* $65

Unmarked standing clown, 12-1/2 inches high. *Bosson Collection.* $45

Unmarked clown, 12 inches high. *Bosson Collection.* $95

Uncle Sam minus his top hat? Charles Dickens character? Or just a head jar that is 9-1/2 inches high and unmarked? *Zera Collection.* $95

No mark here, either. The height is 7-1/4 inches excluding the handle. *Oravitz Collection.* $40

Metlox chef head is 11-1/4 inches high and unmarked. *Oravitz Collection.* $100

Very similar to the William Hirsch monk shown in Chapter 21, but with a flat bottom. If you look closely, you'll see small differences in the mold, too. The unmarked jar is 11-1/2 inches high. *Oravitz Collection.* $50

This monk is only 10 inches high. It is not marked. *Oravitz Collection.* $50

This jar at least has an inkstamp, "E-4499," which unfortunately doesn't tell much. The monk is 9-3/4 inches high. *Oravitz Collection.* $50

The height here is 10-1/4 inches. The jar has an unreadable paper label. *Oravitz Collection.* $60

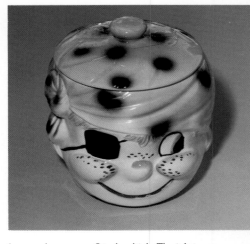

A young buccaneer, 8 inches high. The inkstamp mark is "SJ-501." *Courtesy of Betty and Floyd Carson.* $60

According to owner Mercedes DiRenzo, this jar was made in Mexico by a monk who makes cookie jars when the spirit strikes him. It is 11 inches high, unmarked. *Courtesy of Jazz'e Junque Shop, Chicago, Illinois.* $100

Like the Metlox Cookie Boy in the bottom right, but with much of the original paint intact. Its height is 9-1/4 inches, and it has the remnant of a paper label. *Oravitz Collection.* $125

This jar is 8 inches. Possibly the work of a hobby ceramist from the "M.E." that is scratched in the bottom. *Zera Collection.* $55

This jar is 11-1/4 inches high and unmarked. The hymnal is decorated with gold. The bottom, shown on the following page, has the unglazed dot in the center that's characteristic of Abingdon. *Oravitz Collection.* $400

Monk head jar, with "Thou Shalt Not Steal Cookies" barely visible on the base. The jar is 8-1/2 inches high and has an "A3438" inkstamp and the remnant of a paper label. *Oravitz Collection.* $85

The jar on the left is 8-1/2 inches high, and the jar on the right is 9-1/4 inches high. They are the Cookie Boy and Cookie Girl, made by Metlox. Neither is marked. *Blumenfeld Collection.* $125 ea.

Bottom of "Sweet Notes" jar.

Obviously a pair, but a pair of what? The scarecrow is 10-1/2 inches high, his companion 10-1/4 inches. *Bosson Collection.* $85 ea.

Candle boy, 11 inches high with no mark. *Oravitz Collection.* $50

Both were made by California Originals and are 11 inches high. Neither one is marked. *Blumenfeld Collection.* $100 ea.

Commonly called a Beatle boy after the English rock group of the 1960s, this unmarked jar is 13-1/2 inches high. *Courtesy of Jazz'e Junque Shop, Chicago, Illinois.* $150

The left pixie, by California Originals, is 11 inches high, and the right pixie is 10 inches high. Both are unmarked. *Blumenfeld Collection.* Left - $100, Right - $75

The difference in size is more noticeable in this photo than in the one above, even though it is actually less. The two outside jars are 10-3/4 inches high, the center jar 10-1/4 inches. None of the pixies are marked; the two outside jars were made by California Originals. Note that the eye treatment on the center jar is quite different than that of the other two jars. *Oravitz Collection.* Left and right jars - $100 ea., Center jar - $65

A pixie couple, she is 12 inches high, and he is 12-1/2 inches high. No marks. The eyes look similar to those above; perhaps there is a connection. *Blumenfeld Collection.* Left - $150, Right - $100

Twin Winton Leprechaun, 13 inches high, unmarked. *Zera Collection.* $75

The same unmarked jar as above, but with red trim around the neck instead of blue. *Oravitz Collection.* $100

The jar on the left is 6-1/4 inches high, and the jar on the right is 7-1/4 inches. Neither is marked. *Oravitz Collection.* Left - $60, Right - $70

This Doranne of California is 13 inches high and lacks a mark. *Oravitz Collection.* $85

A bear with a belly button, 12-1/2 inches high and unmarked. *Bosson Collection.* $45

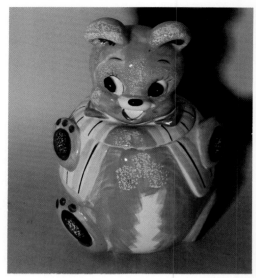

They talk about pink elephants, so why not pink bears? The jar is 10-1/2 inches high. It has a remnant of a paper label but it is unreadable. *Courtesy of Jazz'e Junque Shop, Chicago, Illinois.* $45

Both of these jars are 10 inches high. Neither is marked. The jar on the left is a little bigger around at the top, so the lids aren't interchangeable. *Bosson Collection.* $85 ea.

The big question about this cookie jar is why someone would model one of the baby's ears to look like a bear's, the other a rabbit's. The jar is 13 inches high, unmarked. *Saxby Collection.* $45

This nicely finished unmarked teddy bear is 12 inches high. *Oravitz Collection.* $60

This jar appears to be identical to one made by Maurice of California, but it is not on par with that company's work. It is 10-1/8 inches high and unmarked. *Courtesy of Jazz'e Junque Shop, Chicago, Illinois.* $35

Unmarked bear, 13-1/2 inches high. *Oravitz Collection.* $60

Except for the baby, this is very similar to a panda made by Metlox. The unmarked jar is 11-1/4 inches high. *Oravitz Collection.* $45

Another panda, this one is 10-1/4 inches high, unmarked. *Oravitz Collection.* $30

Candycane bear, 11 inches high and unmarked. *Oravitz Collection.* $55

"Cookie Panda," 12-1/4 inches high. This jar is heavily poured but unmarked. *Oravitz Collection.* $35

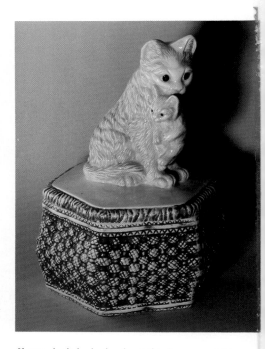

If you don't look closely at this jar you might miss the kitten. The height is 10-1/4 inches, no mark. *Oravitz Collection.* $65

Left: This unmarked jar is 9-1/4 inches high. The chain is metal. Look closely and you will see that the bear cub is beginning to push the lid off of the can. *Courtesy of Country Heirs Antique Shop.* $85

Right: What a dude! The jar is 11 inches high and is unmarked. *Oravitz Collection.* $50

Unmarked, 11-1/2 inches high. *Lilly Collection*. $30

Sailor cat, 10 inches high with no mark. *Oravitz Collection*. $30

Another unmarked cow, this one is 10 inches high. *Courtesy of Jazz'e Junque Shop, Chicago, Illinois*. $40

Mother and kitten, 11-1/2 inches high and unmarked. *Saxby Collection*. $45

This unmarked cat is 12 inches high. *Oravitz Collection*. $30

Kitty biscuit jars, both 5-1/4 inches high, both unmarked. *Oravitz Collection*. $35 ea.

Moving from the house to the farm for a moment, this cow is 9-1/4 inches high. It is not marked. *Courtesy of Jazz'e Junque Shop, Chicago, Illinois*. $50

An unmarked dog, 11 inches high. *Oravitz Collection*. $40

263

This canine, 6-1/2 inches high, is also unmarked. *Oravitz Collection.* $30

An apology is in order here. Guess I became engrossed with the color on the rear of this elephant when I photographed it. But the ear is there, and if you look closely you'll see the trunk. It is unmarked, 10-3/4 inches high. *Courtesy of Grinder's Switch Antique Shop.* $35

The Scottie biscuit jar is 6-1/2 inches high, unmarked. *Zera Collection.* $90

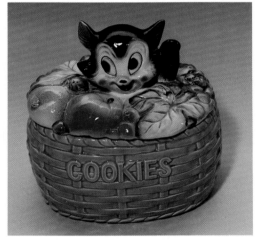

This jar is 6-3/4 inches high. It is not marked. A companion pig was made in a blue basket. *Oravitz Collection.* $35

Small monkey jar, 7 inches high, unmarked. *Oravitz Collection.* $30

The unmarked elephant with a straw hat is 12-1/2 inches high. *Oravitz Collection.* $45

Froggy went a courtin', as they say. The unmarked jar is 10-3/4 inches high. Possibly Sierra Vista. *Zera Collection.* $250

Hippo on a scooter, 10-3/4 inches high, unmarked. *Oravitz Collection.* $60

264

This mouse looks like a strong candidate for hobby ceramic status. It is 9 inches high, and not marked. *Oravitz Collection.* $45

It seems no other name but "Sneaky Pig" would be suitable here. The jar, 11-1/2 inches high, is un-marked. *Oravitz Collection.* $50

This rabbit is 12-1/4 inches high and un-marked. *Oravitz Collection.* $55

A pig chef, 11 inches high and unmarked. *Oravitz Collection.* $30

Possibly kinfolk to the standing elephant on the previous page, this jar is 6-1/2 inches high and unmarked. *Oravitz Collection.* $35

A pig head, 9 inches high, with no mark. *Oravitz Collection.* $50

Rabbit jar, 12-3/4 inches high. It is marked "Patented/USA" on two lines. A unique fea-ture is that the opening is diamond shaped instead of rounded. *Oravitz Collection.* $50

The same jar as above, although is looks a bit different because it was photographed at a different angle. The mark is different, too: "Pat.Pen." *Zera Collection.* $50

This rather simple oinker is 9-1/4 inches high. It is not marked. *Oravitz Collection.* $30

A rabbit mailing what apparently is a love letter. The jar is 11-1/2 inches high, unmarked. *Oravitz Collection.* $75

This turtle is 10-1/2 inches tall and unmarked. *Oravitz Collection.* $35

An unmarked chicken, 9-3/4 inches high, believed to be McCoy. *Lilly Collection.* $45

Unmarked, 12-1/2 inches high. *Bosson Collection.* $45

Rooster, 9-1/2 inches high and unmarked. *Oravitz Collection.* $50

This 9-3/4 inch high jar, made by Red Wing, is not marked in any way. The bottom is heavily crazed. *Courtesy of Dorothy Coates.* $70

Mother-of-pearl glaze, 11-1/2 inches high and unmarked. Possibly a hobby ceramics jar. *Courtesy of Jazz'e Junque Shop, Chicago, Illinois.* $40

This canister-type chicken cookie jar is 12-1/4 inches high. It is marked with an impressed "Made in California 1408/USA" on two lines. *Oravitz Collection.* $35

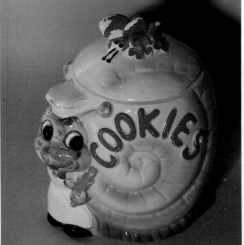

Snail, 9-3/4 inches high and unmarked. *Oravitz Collection.* $45

This jar is always referred to as a baby duck, but the pointed beak seems to indicate a chick. There is a very similar jar with a longer, rounded bill that looks more like a duckling than this one; the two more than likely are made by the same company. Both jars exhibit characteristics common to those born of the American Bisque—American Pottery—Ludowici Celadon triad. *Zera Collection.* $85

Same duck with lighter red and a different impressed mark—"USA-10." *Oravitz Collection.* $55

A 9-1/2 inch high unmarked duck. *Lilly Collection.* $45

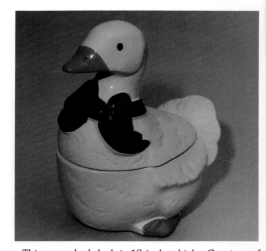

This unmarked duck is 12 inches high. *Courtesy of Virginia Sell.* $40

This duck is 12-1/2 inches high with "USA" impressed. *Zera Collection.* $55

The "Mother and Her Babies" is 10-1/2 inches high. It is not marked. *Courtesy of Jazz'e Junque Shop, Chicago, Illinois.* $35

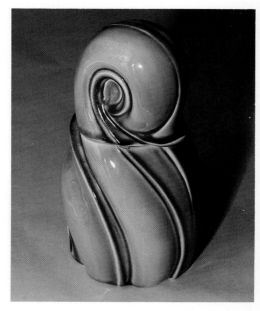

Exquisitely styled Art Deco duck, 12 inches high. It is not marked. *Zera Collection.* $125

The scarf on this duck is cloth. The jar is 7-1/2 inches high and unmarked. *Lilly Collection.* $40

The lovebirds jar is 10-3/4 inches high and ahs a "H7525" inkstamp. *Oravitz Collection.* $95

The penguin is 12-1/2 inches high. It is unmarked. *Courtesy of Jazz'e Junque Shop, Chicago, Illinois.* $35

The same apple as the one attributed to Hull, but marked with an "E" inside the lid. This jar was also made in yellow and possibly other colors. *Oravitz Collection.* $50

This owl is 10-1/4 inches high and unmarked. It is often seen without paint or repainted. *Courtesy of Jazz'e Junque Shop, Chicago, Illinois.* $45

This apple is 8-1/2 inches high and unmarked. Westfall credits this apple to Hull, but an exhaustive search yielded nothing to substantiate the jar's origin. *Zera Collection.* $65

Apple, 9 inches high. At first glance one might be inclined to think it was made by Metlox because of the blossoms. But the quality is lacking, and the jar is decorated entirely with paint that is inconsistent with Metlox's penchant for glaze. *Zera Collection.* $25

There was felt on the bottom of this owl cookie jar so whether or not it is marked is hard to determine. It is 11-3/4 inches high. *Oravitz Collection.* $35

These unmarked apples are 8-1/2 inches high. *Zera Collection.* $35 ea.

As you can see, this unmarked apple was made in several colors. It is 9-1/4 inches high. *Zera Collection.* $35

This apple is 11 inches high and has "©USA" impressed. Doranne of California. *Courtesy of Jazz'e Junque Shop, Chicago, Illinois.* $60

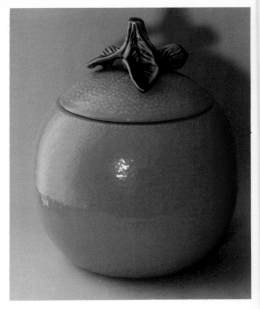

Standing 11-1/2 inches high, this jar has "8218" impressed inside the lid, "©USA 8218" impressed in the bottom, and was made by California Originals. *Taylor Collection.* $75

This apple is also unmarked and is 9-1/4 inches high. *Courtesy of Jazz'e Junque Shop, Chicago, Illinois.* $35

Barrel of apples, 7-1/2 inches high, with no mark. *Taylor Collection.* $60

Unmarked pear, 11-1/2 inches high. *Courtesy of Jazz'e Junque Shop, Chicago, Illinois.* $60

This one solves part of the mystery. Around the bottom is the impressed mark "USA." *Courtesy of Jazz'e Junque Shop, Chicago, Illinois.* $35

Orange, 7-1/2 inches high, with a "9316" inkstamp. *Taylor Collection.* $50

Pear or lemon? The shape suggests a lemon, and the stem suggests a pear. The jar is 11-1/4 inches high and marked "3732." *Courtesy of Jazz'e Junque Shop, Chicago, Illinois.* $60

269

This pear is 10-3/4 inches high and inkstamped "C-8262." Compare it to the Los Angeles Potteries' wedding pineapple shown in Chapter 21, and draw your own conclusion. *Zera Collection.* $25

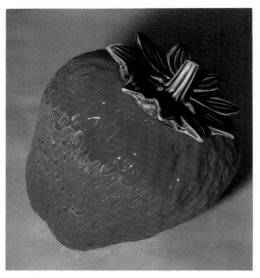

Unmarked strawberry, 9-1/2 inches high. *Lilly Collection.* $50

An unmarked cookie stack, 8-1/2 inches high. *Courtesy of Jazz'e Junque Shop, Chicago, Illinois.* $25

Heavily poured pineapple, 13-1/2 inches high, with a "1386" inkstamp. *Taylor Collection.* $95

This strawberry is 11-1/2 inches high with "8215" impressed in lid. It was made by California Originals. *Courtesy of Jazz'e Junque Shop, Chicago, Illinois.* $55

Strawberry pie, 8 inches high and unmarked. Doranne of California. *Bosson Collection.* $75

This 8-1/2 inch high pumpkin is marked "SFA 1966." *Saxby Collection.* $35

The mark here is "GK3/USA" on two lines. The strawberry is 9-1/2 inches high. *Zera Collection.* $35

Gingerbread house, 11-3/4 inches high. There is no mark. Made by CaliforniaOriginals. *Zera Collection.* $75

Gingerbread house on a smaller scale than the one above, only 8-1/2 inches high, unmarked. *Oravitz Collection.* $50

Unmarked log cabin, 11-1/2 inches high. *Zera Collection.* $40

Unknown, unmarked castle, 11-1/4 inches high. *Courtesy of Jazz'e Junque Shop, Chicago, Illinois.* $100

Unmarked house, 10 inches high. *Bosson Collection.* $50

Metlox Lighthouse, 12-3/4 inches high, unmarked. *Oravitz Collection.* $800

This windmill is 14-1/4 inches high. It is not marked. *Bosson Collection.* $45

This jar is 10-1/4 inches high and unmarked. Possibly hobby ceramics. *Bosson Collection.* $50

This unmarked jar is 13-1/2 inches high. *Courtesy of Jazz'e Junque Shop, Chicago, Illinois.* $40

Same windmill in blue. The height is 14-1/4 inches and it has no mark. *Courtesy of Jazz'e Junque Shop, Chicago, Illinois.* $45

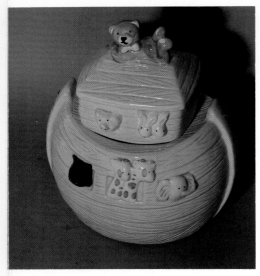

Noah's Ark, 10-1/2 inches high and unmarked. *Courtesy of Jazz'e Junque Shop, Chicago, Illinois.* $75

This locomotive is 9 inches high. It is not marked. *Courtesy of Jazz'e Junque Shop, Chicago, Illinois.* $40

Cookie car, 6-1/2 inches high and unmarked. *Bosson Collection.* $55

Another ark, 10 inches high, also unmarked. *Oravitz Collection.* $45

At the rear of this engine are the words "Cookie Cargo." The unmarked jar, 6 inches high, is made of redware. *Zera Collection.* $55

This clock is stamped "H4219." It is 11-1/2 inches high. *Courtesy of Jazz'e Junque Shop, Chicago, Illinois.* $40

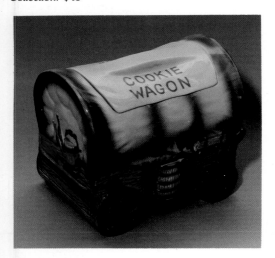

A Conestoga wagon, 6-1/2 inches high and unmarked. *Oravitz Collection.* $65

This San Francisco cable car is 6-1/2 inches high. It is not marked. *Zera Collection.* $40

This unmarked car is 6-3/4 inches high. *Courtesy of Jazz'e Junque Shop, Chicago, Illinois.* $60

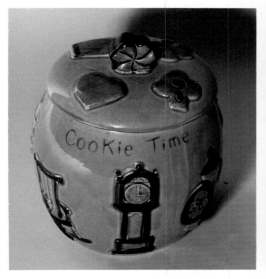

More clocks. The jar is 8 inches high. It is unmarked. *Oravitz Collection.* $35

Being separate from the rest of the jar, the propellers on this airplane actually turn. The unmarked jar is 6-1/2 inches high, 15-1/2 inches long. According to the Roerigs, it was made by North American Ceramics. *Coughenour Collection.* $700

This jar is 9-3/4 inches high, has "USA" in raised letters on the bottom. *Zera Collection.* $60

Shawnee Carousel, 9-1/2 inches high. The mark is "S4 USA." *Bosson Collection.* $150

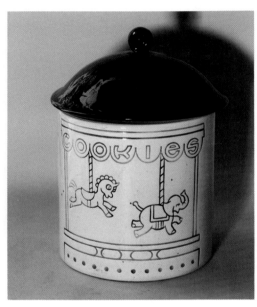

This unmarked jar is 10-1/2 inches high. *Courtesy of Jazz'e Junque Shop, Chicago, Illinois.* $40

The same jar in the same size as above, the only difference is that the "USA" is impressed instead of raised. This jar appears to be a hobby ceramic piece as it is hard to imagine a professional pottery turning out something so poorly painted. The other jar could be the product of a hobby ceramist or a professional pottery. *Oravitz Collection.* $30

The jar on the left is 6 inches high and unmarked. It has a different scene on each side. The jar on the right is 7-1/4 inches high and has a "T25" inkstamp. *Oravitz Collection.* $40 ea.

273

This cookstove is 7 inches high and unmarked. *Zera Collection.* $50

Unmarked potbelly stove. *Bosson Collection.* $35

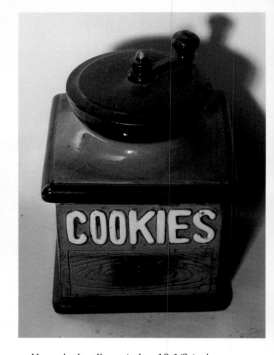

Unmarked coffee grinder, 10-1/2 inches high. *Bosson Collection.* $35

Potbelly stove, 11-1/2 inches high, with no mark. *Courtesy of Jazz'e Junque Shop, Chicago, Illinois.* $35

This milk can is 12 inches high. Though unmarked, on the front it says "Cookies/Revere Milk Co." on two lines, which might make it an advertising jar. *Oravitz Collection.* $40

A 12-inch high coffee pot, unmarked. This jar is very much like the Japanese coffee pot shown in Chapter 30, and it also may have been made by the same company. *Saxby Collection.* $45

This potbelly stove is also unmarked. It is 11-3/4 inches high. *Coughenour Collection.* $50

Cookie barrel with wicker handle, 6-1/2 inches high. Unmarked, it is made of redware. *Courtesy of Jazz'e Junque Shop, Chicago, Illinois.* $20

Shoe, 10-1/2 inches high and unmarked. *Bosson Collection.* $50

Chef head jars, 8 inches high and unmarked. *Blumenfeld Collection.* $50 ea.

The unmarked rag doll is 12 inches high. *Oravitz Collection.* $50

Same unmarked jar as above, but 7-3/4 inches high. This side is displayed when it has cookies in it. The reverse, shown below, is displayed when empty. *Oravitz Collection.* $45

Snowman, 9-1/4 inches high. Impressed in bottom is "©B.C." The Roerigs show it with "Made in USA" also impressed. *Zera Collection.* $50

Doll, 10-1/4 inches high, with no mark. *Oravitz Collection.* $75

Reverse of chef head jar.

The top half of this snowman is a teapot with the handle on the right and the spout on the left. The jar is 13-1/2 inches high, marked "Riddell/©" on two lines. *Bosson Collection.* $125

This unmarked jar is 8-1/4 inches high. It is thought to be by Holiday Designs, Inc. *Oravitz Collection.* $35

275

The flower pot is 8-1/2 inches high and unmarked. It's a California Originals jar. *Courtesy of Jazz'e Junque Shop, Chicago, Illinois.* $35

The drum is 8-3/4 inches high. It is not marked. The drumsticks look remarkably real. *Courtesy of Jazz'e Junque Shop, Chicago, Illinois.* $65

Old jar, 7-1/2 inches high, with "USA" in raised letters. *Zera Collection.* $30

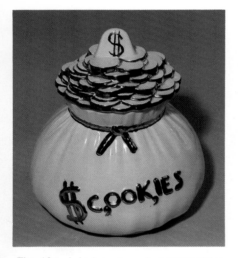

This 10-inch high jar is marked "4261/USA/J.G." impressed on three lines. The remaining bits of a nearly destroyed paper label read "...Hutchin...S, of NE...NA." The bottom appears to be from the same mold as the Abingdon money sack. *Courtesy of Betty and Floyd Carson.* $65

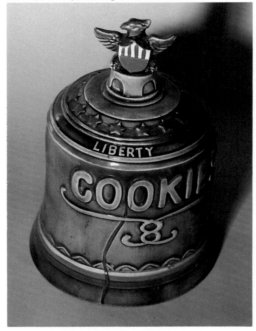

Liberty Bell, 9-1/2 inches high, no mark. *Bosson Collection.* $45

This simulated bamboo jar is assumed originally to have had a bamboo or rattan handle. It is 7 inches high, unmarked, and made of redware. *Oravitz Collection.* $20

Also missing a handle, this jar is 8 inches high and unmarked. *Zera Collection.* $25

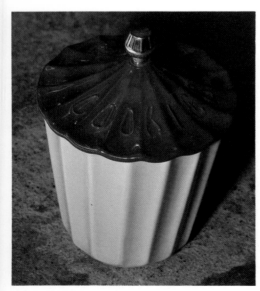

This jar has a metal finial. It is 9-3/4 inches high with "516/USA" impressed on two lines. *Courtesy of Grinder's Switch Antique Shop.* $50

An American made jack-in-the box, the mark on the bottom is "USA." The jar is 12-1/2 inches high. *Courtesy of Jazz'e Junque Shop, Chicago, Illinois.* $200

You can get cookies from both ends of this cookie jar. It is 8 inches high. The handle is missing. The mark is shown below. *Courtesy of Jazz'e Junque Shop, Chicago, Illinois.* $25

Mark of double-entry jar.

This unmarked jar is 10 inches high. Though it appears to be lacking a handle, there would be no way to securely attach one. *Courtesy of Jazz'e Junque Shop, Chicago, Illinois.* $25

Locomotive with a glaze identical to that of the rag doll on page 275. The jar is 6-3/4 inches, unmarked. *Oravitz Collection.* $25

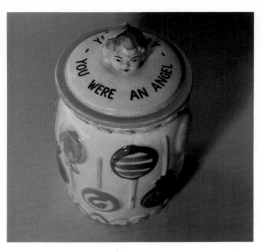

This isn't a cookie jar but a sucker jar, which like grease jars and canisters, often finds its way into cookie jar collections. This particular jar has a reversible lid. It is 7 inches high, unmarked. *Oravitz Collection.* $65

Sucker jar showing lid reversed.

Unmarked jar, 9 inches high. This is similar, but not identical, to a jar shown by Westfall that was made by Los Angeles Potteries. *Courtesy of Grinder's Switch Antique Shop.* $35

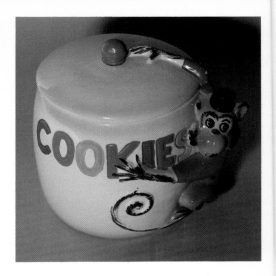

This jar is 8 inches high. It is not marked. *Oravitz Collection.* $65

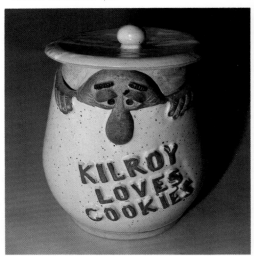

Good old Kilroy. The mark of this jar is shown, but attempts to trace it were unsuccessful. *Zera Collection.* $45

Mark of the Kilroy cookie jar.

This unmarked cookie jar is made of yellowware. It is 8-1/2 inches high. *Courtesy of Jazz'e Junque Shop, Chicago, Illinois.* $25

277

The height here is 8-3/4 inches. The jar is unmarked. *Zera Collection.* $30

A 12-1/4 inch high bull, unmarked, made by California Originals. *Oravitz Collection.* $60

This raccoon is 12-3/4 inches high. The jar is not marked. *Oravitz Collection.* $55

This jar is 11-1/2 inches high. The only mark is "©Mopsy" at the base of the bottom. *Courtesy of Betty and Floyd Carson.* $130

This appears to be the same bull as above. Though a different color, it is the same size and has no mark. California Originals, *Courtesy of Jazz'e Junque Shop, Chicago, Illinois.* $60

The turtle jar is marked "KJ20/USA" on two lines between the feet. The height is 9 inches. *Oravitz Collection.* $60

The elephant is 12 inches high and unmarked. DeForest of California. *Oravitz Collection.* $45

This bull is from a different mold than the other two. It is 11-1/2 inches high, unmarked but Twin Winton. *Oravitz Collection.* $60

A bear with his hand in the cookie jar. The height is 8-1/2 inches. There is no mark. *Bosson Collection.* $35

Game warden bear, 12 inches high with no mark but by DeForest of California. *Oravitz Collection.* $50

The little kitty is 11 inches high and has no pedigree. *Oravitz Collection.* $40

This companion puppy for the cat is 10-1/2 inches high, Made by Twin Winton. *Oravitz Collection.* $75

Pig, 11 inches high with no mark. *Oravitz Collection.* $40

Unmarked cat, 9-1/2 inches high. *Bosson Collection.* $70

Unmarked monkey, 11-1/2 inches high. *Oravitz Collection.* $50

The cat in the basket is 9-1/2 inches high and not marked. It was made by Twin Winton. *Courtesy of Betty and Floyd Carson.* $75

Lion and lamb, 14-1/4 inches high. The mark on the bottom is "928" in raised numerals. *Oravitz Collection.* $75

This walrus is 10 inches high and has "Calif." incised on the bottom. Some are unmarked. *Bosson Collection.* $60

This van is 8 inches high. *Bosson Collection.* $75

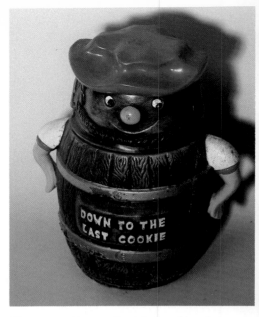

This guy must have gotten into a cookie poker game. The jar is 12-1/2 inches high and marked "R77 USA." *Bosson Collection.* $75

Unmarked shoe, 12 inches high. *Courtesy of Jazz'e Junque Shop, Chicago, Illinois.* $60

This jar is 9-3/4 inches high. It was made by California Originals. *Bosson Collection.* $60

Space cadet, 12-1/2 inches high, no mark. *Zera Collection.* $95

Nearly the same size as the other shoe, 12-1/4 inches, this jar is also unmarked. The Roerigs show it as California Originals. *Oravitz Collection.* $60

Milk can, 12 inches high, unmarked. *Oravitz Collection.* $70

This crock is 8 inches high. It appears very much like the Coors crock in Chapter 21, but is two inches shorter, with a slightly different shape, and not marked. *Courtesy of Dory and Don Jones.* $25

280

The lid is the same as the white crock, and the double ring at the shoulder is the same, but handles have been added. The height of this one is 9-1/2 inches. It is not marked. *Zera Collection*. $25

It looks like McCoy, but the handles are too big. It looks like Ransburg, but lacks the concave curve on the outside of the neck. It is 9-1/2 inches high, marked with a "CBK89" inkstamp. *Lilly Collection*. $35

Whoever modeled this jar did a nice job of making it appear to be hand thrown with attached handles; however, inside you can see by the hollow handles that the jar was poured. Its 8-1/2 inches high and unmarked. *Courtesy of Jazz'e Junque Shop, Chicago, Illinois*. $30

Very plain, this crock possibly had painted decoration at one time. Its height is 9-1/2 inches, and it has no mark. *Zera Collection*. $20

Southwestern scene, 8 inches high and unmarked. *Courtesy of Jazz'e Junque Shop, Chicago, Illinois*. $45

What kind of cookie jar leads to a collection of more than 600? This 8-inch high unmarked yellowware jar is one. It is the first cookie jar purchased by Richard and Susan Oravitz, who haven't stopped buying since. $25

This unmarked jar is 9-3/4 inches high. *Oravitz Collection*. $35

Silhouette jar, 10-1/2 inches high, marked "Made in USA." *Zera Collection*. $40

Mary and her lamb, 8-1/4 inches high. The mark is "697" impressed. *Oravitz Collection*. $45

281

Like gingerbread boy jar above, but in tan. *Courtesy of Jazz'e Junque Shop, Chicago, Illinois.* $40 each

This appears to be the same basic jar as the three blind mice above, and was probably made by the same company. The height is 8-1/4 inches, no mark. *Oravitz Collection.* $40

The bear is the same size as the rabbit and carrot, 9-3/4 inches, no mark. *Oravitz Collection.* $30

This canister-type jar is 8-3/4 inches high, and marked "4253/USA" on two lines. It seems very likely that it is a recent McCoy. *Lilly Collection.* $35

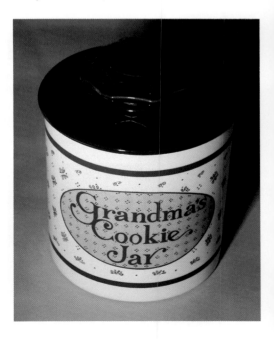

Like the gingerbread boy, this unmarked jar is 9-3/4 inches high. The condition of the paint decoration seems too good to be original. Maybe it received excellent care, perhaps a wedding present that was left in the box and never used, a fate undoubtedly common to a great many cookie jars. *Oravitz Collection.* $45

The jar on the left is 9-3/4 inches high, the jar on the right is 8-1/2 inches high. Neither is marked. *Oravitz Collection.* $30

This unmarked jar is 9-1/4 inches high. *Lilly Collection.* $40

Because it is a slightly different color, it is possible the lid on this cookie jar is not the original. The jar is 10 inches high with "USA" in raised letters on bottom. *Courtesy of Jazz'e Junque Shop, Chicago, Illinois.* $35

Nice detail in this general store mold. The jar is 9 inches high with no mark. The reverse is shown. *Courtesy of Jazz'e Junque Shop, Chicago, Illinois.* $20

Unmarked, 8-1/2 inches high. The same jar is seen in white. *Zera Collection.* $20

The height of this jar is 11 inches, and it has "USA" impressed. *Oravitz Collection.* $25

Not much to say about this plain Jane except that it is 7-1/2 inches high, marked "1528/USA" on two lines, and has a rubber gasket in the lid. Based on the mark, it is believed to be recent McCoy. *Lilly Collection.* $35

Reverse of the general store canister jar.

This obviously older jar is 7-1/2 inches high and unmarked. *Zera Collection.* $85

Nicely detailed, 9 inches high, and unmarked. The reverse is shown. If you have this jar or the green jar above and want to research them, a good place to begin might be old Hull Pottery catalogs. *Zera Collection.* $125

This canister is 13 inches high and unmarked. *Courtesy of Jazz'e Junque Shop, Chicago, Illinois.* $20

283

Reverse of canister jar on previous page.

Bean pot, 6-1/2 inches high, with its mark shown. *Courtesy of Homer and Bev Simpson.* $25

Bean pot, 7-1/2 inches high, marked "Made in USA." *Courtesy of Jazz'e Junque Shop, Chicago, Illinois.* $35

Mark of brown bean pot, possibly that of the West Bend Company, of West Bend, Wisconsin.

Cookies bean pot, 7-3/4 inches high, marked "USA." *Courtesy of Jazz'e Junque Shop, Chicago, Illinois.* $30

There are hand-painted flowers on this jar, while its mate below has a transfer decoration. The height is 7-1/4 inches, and there is no mark. *Courtesy of Jazz'e Junque Shop, Chicago, Illinois.* $30

Bean pot, 8 inches high, with no mark. *Oravitz Collection.* $30

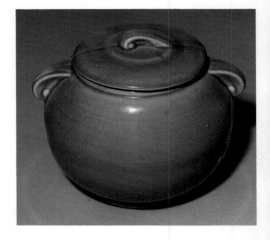

This one is 7 inches high and marked "USA." *Zera Collection.* $25

Marked "USA," this bean pot is 6-1/4 inches high. *Courtesy of Jazz'e Junque Shop, Chicago, Illinois.* $20

Like the jar above, this is 7-1/4 inches high, but it is marked "USA." *Zera Collection.* $30

Look closely and you'll see some raised fruit around the bottom of this bean pot. It is 7-1/4 inches high and marked "USA" in raised letters on the bottom. *Zera Collection.* $20

Bean pot, 6-1/4 inches high. The mark is an impressed "USA." *Courtesy of Grinder's Switch Antique Shop.* $30

Pot O' Cookies, 7 inches high, with no mark. *Courtesy of Jazz'e Junque Shop, Chicago, Illinois.* $25

The height is 6-1/4 inches, and it has "USA" impressed. This appears to be the same as the tan jar above, but with a less prominent ridge below the knob on the lid. *Courtesy of Jazz'e Junque Shop, Chicago, Illinois.* $30

Section X: Non-pottery Cookie Jars

There are probably few people outside the hobby who would ever suspect that cookie jars would be made of anything but pottery. After all, that is what everyone's mother and grandmother had, or so it seemed. Cookie jars have been made of several materials, including glass, metal, plastic and wood.

While most non-pottery cookie jars are not nearly as popular as their ceramic counterparts, some of the early plastic jars have gained a lot of momentum in recent years.

Chapter 35
From Glass to Wood

As mentioned in Chapter 1, eastern and midwestern glass-houses led the cookie jar charge in the early 1930s. American glassware from the era has been well documented through the publishing of countless books and catalog reprints. If you have an unknown early glass cookie jar, you could probably identify it by spending an afternoon deep in the stacks of a good library.

It is usually much harder, almost impossible, to determine the maker of later glass jars. Most recent glass has not been documented, and many of today's glass jars are imported from overseas.

Glass cookie jars do not capture near the interest that pottery jars do. At the time cookie jars came into being, America's glass heyday had already passed. Amberina, Burmese, brilliant cut, and other quality glass that had been produced a few decades earlier was gone, replaced for the most part by inexpensive, unimaginative lines. The better glass companies that were in business at the time, such as Fenton, Heisey, and Cambridge, for the most part tended to overlook cookie jars. Consequently, there are not a great many glass cookie jars about which to be excited.

GLASS COOKIE JARS

Early glass cookies jars were often additions to canister sets. This jar is 7-1/2 inches high. It is unmarked. *Zera Collection.* $30

Same jar as the green one but with a non-metal lid and no "cookies" sticker. The height is 7-1/2 inches, and the mark is "14" in raised numerals on the bottom. *Courtesy of Country Heirs Antique Shop.* $20

This black amethyst cookie jar is 8 inches high. It was made by the Greensburg Glass Works of Greensburg, Pennsylvania, prior to it being acquired by the L.E. Smith Glass Company. According to company literature, it was no. 675 and was also available in crystal, amber, pink, and green. *Zera Collection.* $75

Store size Dad's cookie jar minus lid. It is 11-3/4 inches high, nearly as big across, and very heavy. *Zera Collection.* Without lid - $100, with lid - $150

More recent than the previous glass jars, this one has cookies and a ginger bread boy on it. The height is 10 inches. There is no mark. *Zera Collection.* $20

Cookie jar no. 3, made by the L.E. Smith Company, of Mount Pleasant, Pennsylvania. L.E. Smith, best known for its black glass, began making green glass, along with amber, canary, amethyst, and blue, in 1926. Pink glass was added in 1927. This 8-inch high unmarked jar is known to have been made in black, but whether or not it appeared in any of the other colors has not been determined. *Zera Collection.* $125

This 8-sided jar is 8-1/2 inches high and unmarked. *Courtesy of Country Heirs Antique Shop.* $35

Another large glass jar that is missing a lid. This one is also 11-3/4 inches high. *Zera Collection.* without lid - $60, with lid - $85

Although it doesn't show up well in the picture, this jar says "Sawyer Biscuit Company" on the front. It is 11-1/2 inches high. *Courtesy of Jazz'e Junque Shop, Chicago, Illinois.* $125

Smokey glass owl, 13 inches high, unmarked. *Zera Collection.* $20

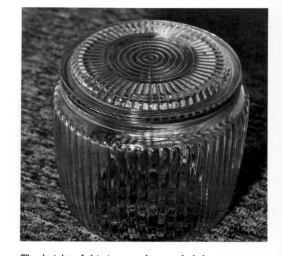

The height of this jar wasn't recorded, but it is not more than 6 or 7 inches. It is not marked. *Courtesy of Wellington Antiques.* $15

287

These two jars, 9 inches high, were made by the Jeanette Glass Company, of Jeanette, Pennsylvania, during the 1940s. The milk glass version was also made in Jeanette's shell pink color. *Zera Collection.* $50 ea.

Pear shape with applied finial, 11-1/2 inches high, no mark. *Zera Collection.* $75

Hobnail milk glass jar, 8-1/2 inches high, maker unknown. *Zera Collection.* $20

Paper label on wood base of hexagon glass cookie jar.

This 10-3/4 inch high jar is marked. On the front it says "©Carlton 1982," and on the bottom "Carlton Glass/3L/USA" on three lines. *Courtesy of Grinder's Switch Antique Shop.* $10

As the pictures show, this jar has been made in several different colors. It is 9-3/4 inches high. *Courtesy of Jazz'e Junque Shop, Chicago, Illinois.* $15

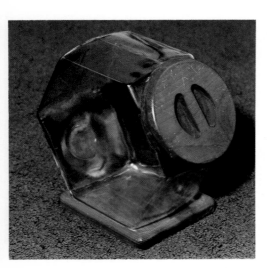

This glass jar is 8-1/2 inches high and is often seen without its wood base. The paper label on base is shown. *Courtesy of Sharon Isaacson.* $15

Slag glass cookie jar, 10-1/2 inches high, unmarked. *Zera Collection.* $75

Orange and yellow version of above jar. None of these jars are marked. *Zera Collection.* $15

Another glass jar that has been made with several different decorations. The jars are 8-1/4 inches high. They are not marked. *Oravitz Collection.* $15 ea.

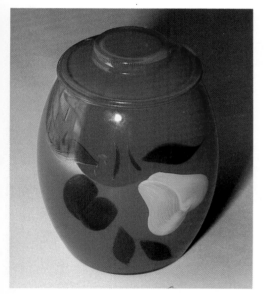

Red with petals and leaves, or pears and plums if you prefer. *Zera Collection.* $15

B.C. comic characters, 8-1/4 inches high. *Zera Collection.* $25

Glass Liberty Bell, 7-3/4 inches high. The mark is "Barlett-Collins/Sapulpa, Oklahoma" on two lines. *Zera Collection.* $25

Yellow with flowers. *Courtesy of Jazz'e Junque Shop, Chicago, Illinois.* $15

Aluminum apple and orange, each 8-1/2 inches high. The same jar was made in green. They were part of a canister set of four different sizes. Their maker is unknown. *Zera Collection.* $15 ea.

Metal Cookie Jars
The majority of metal cookie jars are made of steel. A few are made of aluminum. The current trend in metal cookie jars is for companies to pack their products (often cookies) in them to attract consumers.

METAL COOKIE JARS

289

Aluminum pear, 11-1/2 inches high, possibly by the same unknown company as the apple and orange, unmarked. *Zera Collection.* $15

Inside of Krispy Kan lid, which gives instructions on how to use its "dri-nob." Note that it mentions potato chips, popcorn, and several other foods but not cookies.

The metal clown jar is 7-1/2 inches high, unmarked. The knob on top is made of wood. *Zera Collection.* $15

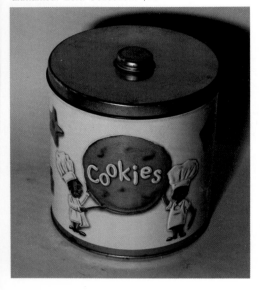

Cookie can marked "Weibro Div./J.L.Clark/Chicago/USA" on four lines. It is 8-1/2 inches high. *Courtesy of Jazz'e Junque Shop, Chicago, Illinois.* $30

Embossed mark of Krispy Kan, patent no. 2543168, indicates a patent date of 1951.

Chein Industries, of Burlington, New Jersey, made this 9-inch high cookie tin. Its mark is shown. *Courtesy of Jazz'e Junque Shop, Chicago, Illinois.* $15

Blue Magic Krispy Kans, made by the Luce Manufacturing Company, of Croton, Vermont. Cans are 8-1/2 inches high, and their mark is shown. Other designs were used, including Howdy Doody. *Courtesy of Jazz'e Junque Shop, Chicago, Illinois.* $20 ea.

Embossed mark of Chein Industries.

Chein Holly Hobbie tin, same size and mark as above. *Courtesy of Jazz'e Junque Shop, Chicago, Illinois.* $30

Barnum's Animals tin, 7 inches high. It says on the tin that it's a replica of a 1914 design and shows a copyright date of 1979. *Courtesy of Jazz'e Junque Shop, Chicago, Illinois.* $15

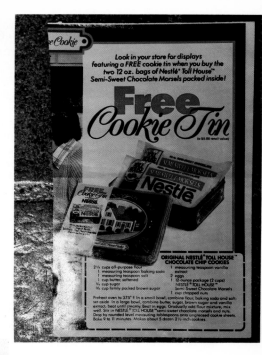

Part of advertisement for above tin from 1988.

This Chein tin is 7-1/2 inches high. Its mark reads "Sun Giant Raisins/Cheinco/Housewares/J.Chein & Co./Burlington NJ/09010" on six lines. *Zera Collection.* $15

Nestlé chocolate chip tin from 1988. *Zera Collection.* $10

This is the 1989 Nestlé Toll House chocolate chip tin. It is 6-1/4 inches high. *Zera Collection.* $15

Plastic Cookie Jars

Without a doubt the most popular non-pottery cookie jars are made of plastic. Plastic jars include both soft and hard. It's the hard plastic, and the older the better, that captures the most attention.

Fiedler and Fiedler Mold and Die Works

One of the early pioneers in hard plastic cookie jars was Fiedler and Fiedler Mold and Die Works of Dayton, Ohio, commonly called F & F because the initials appear on its logo.

PLASTIC COOKIE JARS

Aunt Jemima, made by F & F for Quaker Oats during the 1950s. It is 11-1/2 inches high, marked with standard F & F log. *Zera Collection.* $250

F & F made this dog as a premium for Ken-L-Ration dog food. It's 6-3/4 inches high, standard F & F mark. *Courtesy of Jazz'e Junque Shop, Chicago, Illinois.* $150

In the early 1950s, the Quaker Oats Company commissioned F & F to make a line of plastic Aunt Jemima-Uncle Mose premiums for its Aunt Jemima pancake mix customers. The cookie jar shown above is the largest of the pieces, which included a syrup, creamer and sugar, two sets of salt and pepper shakers, and a six-jar spice rack.

Aunt Jemima was created in the fall of 1899 when Chris Rutt, co-inventor of pre-mixed self-rising pancake flour, attended the vaudeville act of a pair of black-face comedians named Baker and Farrell, in St. Joseph, Missouri. Part of the act was a cakewalk to a song titled, "Aunt Jemima," during which Baker performed wearing an apron and red bandanna headband, a costume long associated with black southern cooks. Rutt used the title of the song, and secured the rights to the likeness of a mammy that Baker and Farrell had used on advertising posters. Rutt stamped his new trademark, along with a caricature of Aunt Jemima, on his one-pound paper sacks of pancake flour. The company changed hands several times over the years, and Quaker Oats bought it on January 15, 1926.

Production of F & F Aunt Jemima cookie jars continued into the early 1960s before Quaker halted it. By then changing attitudes brought on by the growing prominence of the Civil Rights Movement had rendered the premium campaign a liability. According to Arthur F. Marquette in *Brands, Trademarks and Good Will— The Story of The Quaker Oats Company*, 150,000 of the F & F Aunt Jemima cookie jars were made. According to the same source, 1-million syrups were marketed, 4-million salt and pepper shakers.

Quaker must have liked F & F's work because it also commissioned the plastics firm to make the yellow dog shown above as a premium for Ken-L-Ration, another of its subsidiaries. The dog also appears in salt shaker form with a white-pawed black cat for a pepper.

Reliable Toy Corporation

Brother's Alex and Saul Samuels started Reliable Toy Corporation in Toronto, Ontario, in 1920. Their parents had brought them from England to Canada when Alex, the younger of the two, was three years old. When Reliable was founded, the main product was stuffed animals, then dolls. By the early 1940s the company had begun making some metal products, but the outbreak of World War II quickly rendered metal unavailable. At that point it began experimenting with plastics, some of the first items made being bayonet scabbards and bullet heads.

According to Alex Samuels' son, Herb Samuels, who ran the company for 31 years, the Humpty Dumpty cookie jar was made in the late 1940s or early 1950s. Like all of Reliable's products, it was marketed only in Canada which would account for it being a relatively rare find in the United States.

Today Reliable makes plastic toys from jump ropes to toboggans, and is especially big on riding toys. The company's merchandise is still sold only in Canada.

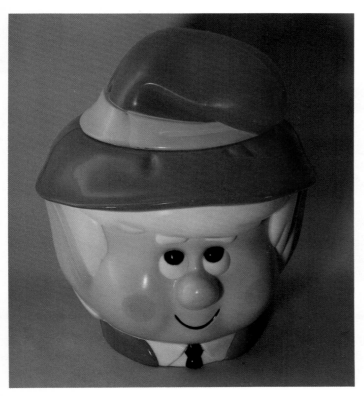

The Keebler elf, 9 inches high with F & F mark. *Blumenfeld Collection.* $100

OTHER PLASTIC COOKIE JARS

Paddy Pig was an early plastic jar by Aladdin. The jars are 9-1/4 inches high. *Zera Collection.* $45 ea.

Humpty Dumpty, 9-1/2 inches high. The mark of this hard plastic jar is "Reliable/Made in Canada" on two lines. *Zera Collection.* $150

292

Yellow and green Paddy Pig. Other colors to look for are blue with orange, and blue with red. *Oravitz Collection.* $45 ea.

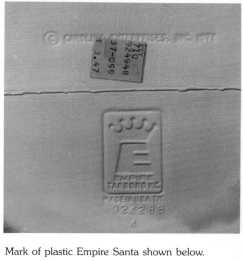

Mark of plastic Empire Santa shown below.

Maurice Lentil plastic cookie pail, with wire handle visible at upper right. The height is 6-1/4 inches. Its mark is Airlite logo ("Airlite" written across horizontal bar of a very large "A"), plus "Omaha, Neb/ 16041A" below. *Zera Collection.* $3

Mark of plastic rooster jar. Note that Burroughs called its hard plastic "Burite."

Another Aunt Jemima used as a premium by Quaker Oats during the 1950s. This one is 10 inches high, soft plastic instead of hard, and unmarked. Hard to see on the apron is "Aunt Jemima's/Cookie Jar" on two lines. *Zera Collection.* $300

On the left is the plastic Santa made by Empire, of Tarboro, North Carolina. It is 12-1/4 inches high, and its mark is shown below. On the right is a similarly styled ceramic Santa, from a mold made by Yozie Molds. The ceramic Santa is 11-3/4 inches high and marked "©Yozie." *Oravitz Collection.* $20 ea.

Burroughs jars are colored on the lower half, while the upper half is always white with a hand-painted design. Flowers are another popular motif on these jars. The mark is shown. *Zera Collection.* $35

Soft plastic Tony the Tiger, 7-3/4 inches high, unmarked except for "1968/Kelloggs Co.©" on two lines. *Zera Collection.* $135

This Teenage Mutant Ninja Turtles soft plastic jar was sold in grocery stores in 1990 and 1991. Cookies were packaged in it; paper instructions glued to the back tell how to use it for a bank. The jar is 10-3/4 inches high, unmarked except for a raised "4" on the bottom. According to the paper glued to the back, the jar was distributed by Delicious Cookie Company, Inc., of Des Plaines, Illinois. $10

The plastic Santa Claus cookie jar is 9-1/4 inches high. It is not marked. *Blumenfeld Collection.* $25

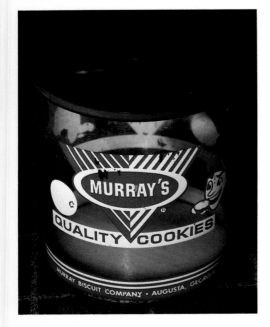

Large plastic Murray's store cookie jar. The mark is "Show Box/St. Louis, Mo." on two lines on the bottom. *Zera Collection.* $35

Wood Cookie Jars

Like glass and metal cookie jars, wood jars do not attract a large following. Many collectors consider them mundane. Wood jars do not hold up very well, which also might have something to do with why they are not in vogue.

It is too bad hardwoods are so expensive because it seems this material has a lot of potential. Crafters could use lathes to turn attractive jars of oak, walnut, cherry or other desirable woods if the cost was not prohibitive. Tole painted wood jars could probably be quite nice, too, if they were executed by a competent artist. With the price of lumber going up instead of down, it is unlikely that we will ever find out.

WOOD COOKIE JARS

Unmarked barrel cookie jar, 10-1/2 inches high, made of laminated hardwood. *Zera Collection.* $30

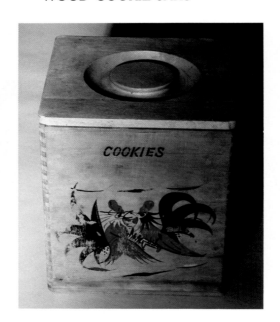

Lock joint wood cookie box, possibly part of a canister set. It is 9-1/2 inches high and unmarked. *Zera Collection.* $20

The first thought is that this could be a sewing basket, but that seems unlikely because of the girl on the front preparing to serve. The piece is 7 inches high excluding the handle. *Courtesy of Jazz'e Junque Shop, Chicago, Illinois.* $20

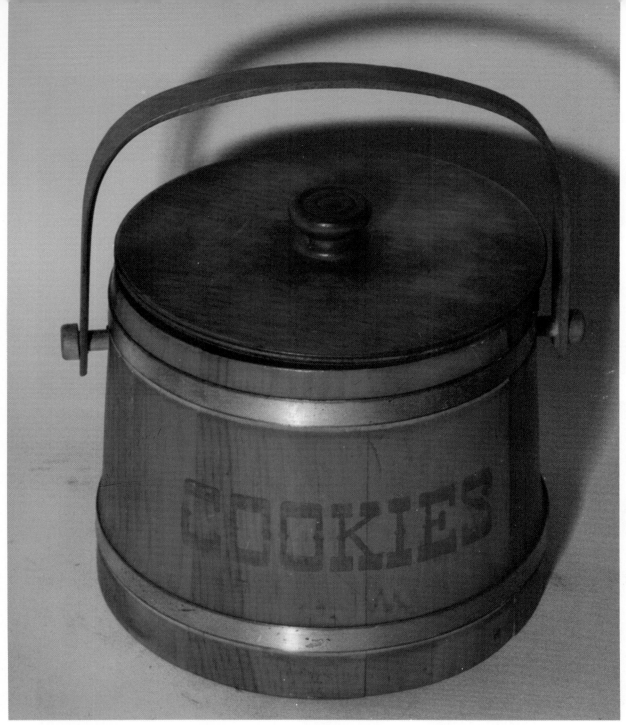

Wood bucket, 8 inches high excluding the handle. The mark is shown. *Courtesy of Jazz'e Junque Shop, Chicago, Illinois.* $20

Mark of wood bucket.

NEW ADDITIONS

This is an original American Bisque Rubbles House. It is 9-1/2 inches high, has "USA" impressed, and American Bisque wedges on the bottom. Compare it with the J.D. James reproduction shown on page 299. *Courtesy of Gary and Mimi Rhinehimer.* $1200

This jar is called "Prayer Lady," or, "Mother in the Kitchen." It is 10 inches high, and has an ENESCO paper label. A complete kitchen set with everything from a stringholder to a picture frame was made. Other colors are blue, yellow, white, and turquoise. Pink is the most common, and the most popular because people like to put together complete sets, and pink is easiest to find. Blue is second easiest. $250.

J. D. James' rendition of the Regal China Peek-a-Boo Baby. It is 10-3/4 inches high. Impressed mark reads, "Peek-a-boo / Van Tellingen / ©," on three lines. "J.D. 1993," is in ink under the glaze. Other jars reproduced by James include the following: American Bisque Casper, Sitting Horse, Popeye, and Swea' Pea; Brush Purple Cow, Formal Pig, Hillbilly Frog, Little Angel, Little Boy Blue, and Peter Pan; Gonder Pirate and Sheriff; Lane Indian; McCoy Davy Crockett and Hillbilly Bear. *Courtesy of J.D. James.* $250

Meet the lovely Metlox Little Red Riding Hood. She measures 12-1/2 inches in height, and has the standard Metlox/Poppytrail mark. *Courtesy of Gary and Mimi Rhinehimer.* $1400

This is the Metlox Mammy. Height is 13 inches. This jar was also made with blue trim, which is somewhat harder to find. The mark is shown. *Courtesy of Denise Teeters.* Yellow trim, $500; blue trim, $600

Mark of the Metlox Mammy.

This Corn Cob Frog is a fairly rare jar. It stands 9-1/8 inches high, carries a Holt-Howard paper label. *Courtesy of Gary and Mimi Rhinehimer.* $350+

This nice looking rooster has "Gilner / G-622" impressed. It is 11 inches high. *Courtesy of John Marriott.* $110

The height of this monk jar is 10-1/8 inches. Impressed in the bottom is, "8116," in the lid, "64." No other marks. Origin is probably Austria or that general area of Europe. *Courtesy of Denise Teeters.* $200

Here's a seldom seen cookie jar, an American Bisque Joe Carioca that is *not* a turnabout. It is marked on the bottom, "Joe Carioca / From / The / Three Cabelleros / © / Walt Disney / USA," on seven lines, and stands 9-1/2 inches high. *Zera Collection.* $650

Westfall refers to this as the King Card cookie jar. It's 10-3/4 inches high. Although unmarked, it was made by California Cleminsons. *Courtesy of Denise Teeters.* $1000

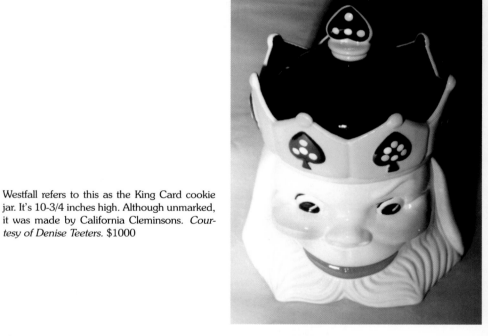

The Walt Disney Cookie bus has a Disneyland USA license plate. The jar is 6 inches high. There is no indication of the maker. *Courtesy of Gary and Mimi Rhinehimer.* $950

297

The Pearl China Watermelon
Mammy stands 11 inches high.
Unmarked, its distinctive bottom
is shown. *Courtesy of Gary and
Mimi Rhinehimer.* $5000

This is a Tat-L-Tale jar by Helen Hutula,.
It is 11-1/4 inches high, and its mark is
shown. *Courtesy of Gary and Mimi
Rhinehimer.* $1500

Bottom of Pearl China Watermelon Mammy.

Mark of the Helen
Hutula Tat-L-Tale jar.

Smokey Bear. 10 inches high, unmarked,
and maker unknown. *Courtesy of Gary
and Mimi Rhinehimer.* Undetermined
value.

Bottom of Smokey Bear.

Another Tat-L-Tale. Note that this one has suffered the
fate of many in that the left forefinger has been broken
off. A restoration specialist could fix this problem. *Courtesy of Denise Teeters.* $900, as shown; $1500, undam-
aged.

Raggedy Ann, 10-1/4 inches high, with "Pat Applied For" impressed. This jar was made by Dwight Morris, of East Palestine, Ohio. Salt and pepper shakers were made in the same design. So were banks and figurines. Some animals, too. *Courtesy of Denise Teeters.* $300

This is Olive Oyl, a reproduction of the original American Bisque jar by J.D. James of Buckeye Lake, Ohio. It is 10-1/2 inches high. Its mark is shown. While the jar itself looks about the same, the lid is somewhat different than the original. *Courtesy of J.D. James.* $200

Bottom of the J.D. James Olive Oyl jar. It shows the jar was made in 1993, and was number 43 in an issue of 250. This information is under the glaze.

Wouldn't this be great if it had the lid and didn't have the crack! A white and gold Regal China Davy Crockett. The jar is marked like the others, "Transluscent Vitrified China / © C. Miller," on two lines. *Zera Collection.* $750, in perfect condition.

The J.D. James much more recent, and much less expensive, Rubbles House. It measures 9-1/8 inches high, is signed, "J.D. 1993," in ink under the glaze. *Courtesy of J.D. James.* $200

This is the Regal China Alice in Wonderland described in Chapter 16. Unmarked, it stands 13-1/4 inches high. *Bosson Collection.* $3500

Appendix 3: McCoy Cookie Jar Designs by Year

The Number of New Cookie Jar Designs Offered Each Year by McCoy, 1939-1987

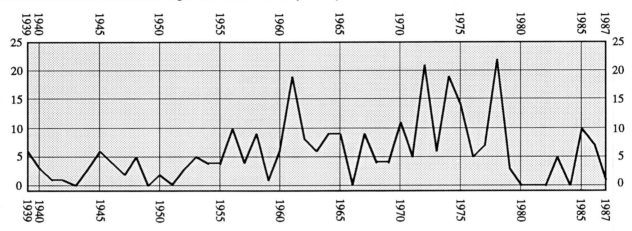

The Number of Different McCoy Cookie Jars Offered Each Year, 1939-1987

Bibliography

American Export Register: 1990, Thomas International Publishing Inc., New York, 1990.

Brands and Their Companies—9th Edition, Donna Wood, Editor, Gale Research Inc., New York, 1991.

Bruce, Scott, *Fifties and Sixties Lunch Box, The,* Chronicle Books, San Francisco, 1988.

Chappell, James, *The Potter's Complete Book of Clay and Glazes,* Watson-Guptill Publications, New York, 1977.

Companies and Their Brands—9th Edition, Donna Wood, Editor, Gale Research Inc., New York, 1991.

Cunningham, Jo, *The Collector's Encyclopedia of American Dinnerware,* Collector Books, Paducah, Kentucky, 1982.

DePasquale, Dan and Gail, and Petersen, Larry, *Red Wing Collectibles,* Collector Books, Paducah, Kentucky, 1990.

———, *Red Wing Stoneware,* Collector Books, Paducah, Kentucky, 1983.

Derwich, Jenny B., and Latos, Dr. Mary, *Dictionary Guide to United States Pottery and Porcelain (19th and 20th Century),* Jenstan, Franklin, Michigan, 1984.

Directory of Corporate Affiliations-1991, National Register Publishing Company, Wilmette, Illinois, 1990.

Drury, Elizabeth, editor, *Antiques,* Doubleday, Garden City, New York, 1986.

Florence, Gene, *Collector's Encyclopedia of Depression Glass, The,* Collector Books, Paducah, Kentucky, 1982.

———, *Kitchen Glassware of the Depression Years,* Collector Books, Paducah, Kentucky, 1981.

Hamer, Frank and Janet, *The Potter's Dictionary of Materials and Techniques,* Watson-Guptill Publications, New York, 1986.

Hastin, Bud, *Bud Hasten's Avon Bottle Collector Encyclopedia,* 11th edition, Bud Hasten, Las Vegas, Nevada, 1988.

Heide, Robert, and Gilman, John, *Cartoon Collectibles,* Doubleday, Garden City, New York, 1983.

Heiss, Willard and Virginia, "Pottery Cookie Jar Put Ransburg on Road to Success," *Antique Week,* March 21, 1988.

Henzke, Lucille, *Pennsbury Pottery,* Schiffer Publishing Ltd., West Chester, Pennsylvania, 1990.

Huxford, Sharon and Bob, *Collector's Encyclopedia of McCoy Pottery, The,* Collector Books, Paducah, Kentucky, 1982.

———, *Collectors Encyclopedia of Roseville Pottery, The* Collector Books, Paducah, Kentucky, 1976.

———, *Collectors Encyclopedia of Roseville Pottery, The, Second Series,* Collector Books, Paducah, Kentucky, 1980.

———, *The Collectors Encyclopedia of Weller Pottery,* Collector Books, Paducah, Kentucky, 1979.

Jensen, Elsa, "How Elsa Became Cat Cookie Jar Crazy," *Crazed Over Cookie Jars,* October, 1990.

Ketchum, William C. Jr., *Pottery & Porcelain,* Knopf, New York, 1983.

Kovel, Ralph and Terry, *Kovel's Advertising Collectibles Price List,* Crown, New York, 1986.

Lehner, Lois, *Lehner's Encyclopedia of U.S. Marks on Pottery, Porcelain & Clay,* Collector Books, Paducah, Kentucky, 1988.

Marquette, Arthur F., *Brands, Trademarks and Goodwill—The Story of The Quaker Oats Company,* McGraw-Hill, New York, 1967.

McDonald, Ann Gilbert, *All About Weller,* Antique Publications, Marietta, Ohio, 1989.

Meugniot, Elinor, *Old Sleepy Eye,* The Printing Press, Tulsa, Oklahoma, 1973.

Nichols, Harold, *McCoy Cookie Jars from the First to the Latest,* Nichols Publishing, Ames, Iowa, 1987.

Oravitz, Richard and Susan, handwritten notes from Mike Clum cookie jar auction, Zanesville, Ohio, July 18, 1990.

Purviance, Louise and Evan, and Schneider, Norris F., *Zanesville Art Pottery in Color,* Mid-American Book Company, Leon, Iowa, 1968.

Rinker, Harry, "How an Ohio Rubber Factory Became a Major Toy Maker," *Antique Week,* April 4, 1990.

Roberts, Brenda, *Collectors Encyclopedia of Hull Pottery, The* Collector Books, Paducah, Kentucky, 1989.

Roerig, Fred and Joyce Herndon, *The Collector's Encyclopedia of Cookie Jars,* Collector Books, Paducah, Kentucky, 1991.

Roerig, Joyce, "Jarrin' with Joyce," *Cookie Jarrin'—The Cookie Jar Newsletter,* January-February, 1991.

Saxby, Clifford and Maureen, "January Mystery Jars," *Crazed over Cookie Jars,* January, 1991.

———, "December Mystery Jars," *Crazed Over Cookie Jars,* December, 1990.

Schneider, Mike, "Hobby Ceramic Mold Companies," *Crazed Over Cookie Jars,* November, 1990.

Simon, Delores, *Red Wing Pottery with Rumrill,* Collector Books, Paducah, Kentucky, 1980.

Supnick, Mark E., *Collecting Shawnee Pottery,* L-W Book Sales, Gas City, Indiana, 1989.

Weatherman, Hazel Marie, *Colored Glassware of the Depression Era 2,* Weatherman Glassbooks, Ozark, Missouri, 1982.

Westfall, Ermagene, *An Illustrated Value Guide to Cookie Jars,* Collector Books, Paducah, Kentucky, 1989.

Williams, George III, "The Original McCoy Pontiac Indian," *Crazed Over Cookie Jars,* November, 1990.

Young, Jackie, *Black Collectables—Mammy and Her Friends,* Schiffer Publishing Ltd., West Chester, Pennsylvania, 1988.

Zera, Stan and Karen, "Cookie Jar Market is Still Influenced by Warhol Sale," *Antique Week,* April 3, 1989.

———, "Cookie Jars Don't Have to Be Pottery to Be Collectible," *Antique Week,* January, 21, 1991.

Index

A

ABC Bear (Starnes), 173
Abingdon Potteries, Inc., 84-86
Accents Unlimited, Inc., 175
After School Cookies (American Bisque), 74
Airplane (unknown), 273
Albert Apple (Pittman-Dreitzer), 194
Albert E. Price, Inc., 196
Alf (unknown), 211
Alice in Wonderland
    Regal, 127
    Unknown, 208
Alladin (McCoy), 46
Alladin, Inc., 292
Almost Home (Holiday Designs), 246
Alpo (unknown), 246
American Bisque, 3, 10-11, 15, 59-75, 82-83
American Eagle (McCoy), 57
American Pottery Company, 75-81
Amish Boy (unknown), 255
Amish Man (unknown), 83
Angel (Brush), 89
Animal Crackers (McCoy), 26
Apple
    McCoy, 37
    metal, 290
    National Silver Company, 192
    Pippin, 193
    unknown, 251, 268-269, 290
Apple House (unknown), 251
Appleman, Glenn, 213-215
Apples
    in barrel (Metlox), 117
    in barrel (unknown), 269
    in basket (McCoy), 41
Arcadia Export-Import Corporation, 176
Ark
    California Originals, 104
    Twin Winton, 150
    unknown, 272
Asparagus (McCoy), 39
Astronauts (McCoy), 43
Apollo (McCoy), 43
Aunt Jemima
    F& F, 291
    plastic, 291, 293
Avon Bear (California Originals), 100
Avon Products, 176

B

Baa Baa Black Sheep (McCoy), 54
Baby (Abingdon), 86
Bakery, Elf, (Twin Winton), 150
Bake Shop (Judy of California), 162
Ball Shape (McCoy), 50-51
Balloon Boy (Brush), 89
Balloon Lady (Pottery Guild), 195
Bananas
    McCoy, 39
    Red Wing, 121
Banjo Player (Wisecarver), 220
Bank (Cookie Bank) (McCoy), 44
Banks, 212
Barefoot Boy

Arnel's, 249
Hull, 113
Barn
    Italy, 244
    McCoy, 44
    Treasure Craft, 145
Barnum's Animals
    McCoy, 42
    metal, 291
Barrel
    American Bisque, 70
    Frankoma, 153
    Japanese, 237
    McCoy, 50
    Metlox, 117
    unknown, 269, 274, 294
    with apples, 117, 269
    wood, 294
Bartlett-Collins Company, 289
Basketweave (wide weave), (McCoy), 56
Bartender (San Jose Potteries), 154
Baseball Boy
    California Originals, 103
    (Japan), 228
    Taiwan, 228
Bauer Pottery, 151
B.C. (glass), 289
B & D, 206
Bean Pot
    Doranne of California, 110
    England, 242
    McCoy, 47, 51
    Pottery Guild, 195
    Western Stoneware, 174
    unknown, 282, 284-285
Bear
    American Bisque, 63, 67, 77-78
    American Pottery Company, 78
    Avon, 176
    Brush, 93
    California Originals, 98, 100
    Dayton-Hudson, 179
    Doranne of California, 107-108
    FAPCO, 154
    Japanese, 232
    Marcia Ceramics of California, 163
    McCoy, 28-30
    Metlox, 115
    Over and Back, 193
    Regal, 126
    Royalware, 80-81
    Starnes, 173
    Toscany, 212
    Treasure Craft, 141, 144
    turnabout, 79
    Twin Winton, 146
    unknown, 250, 261-262, 278-279
Bearded Man (unknown), 257
Bee Hive (Ethan Allen), 182
Bell
    Amercan Bisque, 74
    McCoy, 50
Betsy Baker (McCoy), 26
Betsy Ross (ENESCO), 182
Big Al
    bank, 212
    Treasure Craft, 144
Big Bird

California Originals, 101
Demand Marketing, 180
unknown, 211
Biscuit jar
    Czechoslovakia, 242
    England, 242
    Japan, 238-239
Black Man (bust), (Wisecarver), 220
Black Miss America (Wisecarver), 221
Black Woman (bust), (Wisecarver), 220
Blue Bonnet Sue (Taiwan), 245
Bobbs-Merrill, 211
Bobby the Baker (McCoy), 26
Book (California Cleminsons), 151
Books (Shafford), 240
Bo Peep
    American Bisque, 85
    unknown, 211
Bottle (Chianti) (Doranne of California), 110
Boy
    Arnel's, 249
    Cardinal, 178
    Japan, 227
    unknown, 255, 258
Boy Buccaneer (unknown), 258
Boy on Baseball (McCoy), 26
Boy on Football (McCoy), 26
Broccoli (Metlox), 117
Brown Bag (Doranne of California), 109
Brownie (American Bisque), 82
Brush Pottery Company, 7, 13, 87-96
Brush Art, 177
Bucket
    Basketville, 295
    Twin Winton, 150
    wood, 293-295
Bud (Robinson-Ransbottom), 128
Bugs Bunny (McCoy), 54
Buick Convertible (Appleman), 214
Buick Roadmaster (Appleman), 214
Bull (unknown), 278
Bum (in barrel) (Imperial Porcelain), 161
Burlap Bag (McCoy), 49
Burroughs, 293
Butler Servant (Gifford), 217
B.W. Bear (Dayton-Hudson), 179

C

Cable Car (unknown), 272
Caboose (McCoy), 42
Cactus (Treasure Craft), 145
California Cleminsons, 151
California Originals, 6, 17, 97-104
Camel (Doranne of California), 107
Candle Boy (unknown), 259
Candy Babies (American Bisque), 71
Candy Cane Bear (unknown), 262
Canister
    American Bisque, 11, 69-70
    Arcadia, 176
    Arnel's, 248
    Autumn Leaf, 156
    Flare Ware, 157-158
    Franciscan, 155
    Gladdening, McBean, 155
    Haeger, 156
    Hall, 156-157

Hocking Glass, 9
Holiday Designs, 160
Japanese, 240
Jewel Tea pattern, 156
L.E. Smith Glass, 9, 287
Lefton, 189
Metlox, 118
McCoy, 51
National Potteries Corporation
        (NAPCCO), 191
Pennsbury, 166
Pippin, 193
Pottery Guild, 195
Purinton, 167-168
Robinson-Ransbottom, 131
Roseville, 169
Sears, 200
unknown, 11, 249, 266, 277, 282-283,
        286
Weller, 173
wood, 294
Canning Jar (Doranne of California), 109
Captain (American Bisque), 82
Cara Creations, 235
Car
Appleman, 213-215
Neiman-Marcus, 192
McCoy, 41
unknown, 272
Carbone, Inc., 177
Cardinal China Company, 177-178
Carousel
American Bisque, 70
unknown, 273
Casper (American Bisque), 65
Castle
Cardinal, 178
unknown, 249
Cat
American Bisque, 65-66, 75, 81
Doranne of California, 106
ENESCO, 181
Grantcrest, 184
Hi Mark, 185
Maurice of California, 164
Holiday Designs, 159
Kilbane, 200
Lefton, 188
Ludowici Celadon, 75
Marcia Ceramics of California, 163
McCoy, 31-32
N.S. Gustin, 185
Metlox, 116
Otagiri, 192
Pacific Stoneware, 166
Relco, 239
Richard, 239
Robinson-Ransbottom, 131
Sigma, 200
Taiwan, 231
Treasure Craft, 9, 141
unknown, 262-264, 279
Cat in Basket (American Bisque), 81
Cat with Indented Spots (American
Bisque), 75
Cats in Shoe (Maurice of California), 164
Cauliflower Mammy (McCoy), 27
Chairman of the Board (McCoy), 28

Chalet (West Germany), 243
Cheerleaders (American Bisque), 63
Chef
American Bisque, 60
Cardinal, 178
Dept. 56, 180
Green Products, 184
McCoy, 25
National Silver, 191
Omnibus, 235
Pearl China, 166
Red Wing, 120
Regal China, 124-125
Robinson-Ransbottom, 129
Shawnee, 140
Treasure Craft, 142$Stl
unknown, 256-257, 265, 275
Chef (Bust) (McCoy), 25
Chef (Chicken) (Omnibus), 235
Chef (Donut) (unknown), 256
Chef (French) (Cardinal), 178
Chef (Pig) (unknown), 265
Chein Industries, 290-291
Cherries (Brush), 96
Chest (Early American) (McCoy), 47
Chest (Pirate's) (McCoy), 48
Chest (Treasure Chest) (Brush), 96
Chianti Bottle (Doranne of California), 110
Chicago Taxi (Appleman), 214
Chick
American Bisque, 78
Brazil, 241
Brush, 94
Lefton, 188
unknown, 266-267
Chick with Indented Spots (American
Bisque), 78
Chicken (also see Chick, Hen, and Rooster)
Burroughs, 293
Omnibus, 235
Plastic 293
unknown, 251, 266
Wisecarver, 224
China and Glass Distributors, 179
Chinese Lantern (McCoy), 50
Chinese Man
Japan, 229
unknown, 255
Chipmunk (McCoy), 32
Chipmunk/Squirrel (Maddux), 163
Choir Boys (unknown), 258
Christmas Tree (McCoy), 25
Chocolate Dollop (Brush), 95
Chuck Wagon (coffee pot) (McCoy), 46
Churn
American Bisque, 72
McCoy, 45
Churn Boy
American Bisque, 60
Japan, 228
Regal China
Church (House of Webster), 160
Cinderella
NAPCO, 190
unknown, 211
Cinderella's Pumpkin (Brush), 90
Circus Horse (Brush), 92
Circus Wagon (California Originals), 104

Clock
American Bisque, 72, 84-85
Brush, 95
California Originals, 104
Cara Creations, 235
ENESCO, 181
Japanese, 236
Marshall Field, 189
McCoy, 48
Pfaltzgraff, 167
Twin Winton, 147
unknown, 272
Clown
American Bisque, 60-61, 64, 79
American Pottery Company, 78
Brush, 87-88
Cardinal, 178
California Originals, 98
Doranne of California, 105-106
Italy, 243
Japan, 229-230
Maurice of California, 164
McCoy, 14, 24, 26
metal, 290
Metlox, 118
Morton, 165
Pan American Art, 170
Ransburg, 198
Reco, 199
San Jose Potteries, 170
Shawnee, 139
Sierra Vista, 170
Treasure Craft, 142
Taiwan, 230
Unknown, 256-257
Clover Leaf (Brush), 95
Clyde (Dog) (McCoy), 31
Coalby Cat (McCoy), 31
Coca-Cola (McCoy), 48
Coffee Grinder
House of Webster, 160
Japan, 8
McCoy, 46
unknown, 274
Coffee House (Judy of California), 161
Coffee Mug (McCoy), 47
Coffee Pot
American Bisque, 71-72
Japan, 8
McCoy, 46
Morton, 164
unknown, 274
Colonial Kitchen, 288
Conestoga Wagon
Italy, 243
McCoy, 42
unknown, 272
Cookie (Doranne of California), 109
Cookie Bag
American Bisque, 73
Cardinal, 178
Cookie Bakery (California Originals), 103
Cookie Balloon (Treasure Craft), 145
Cookie Bank (McCoy), 42
Cookie Barrel (American Bisque), 70
Cookie Basket (American Bisque), 73
Cookie Book (California Cleminsons), 151
Cookie Boy (McCoy), 25

Cookie Box (McCoy), 47
Cookie Cabin (McCoy), 43
Cookie/Candy Jar (McCoy), 56
Cookie Cargo (unknown), 272
Cookie Chef (Treasure Craft), 142
Cookie Churn (McCoy), 45
Cookie Counter (Twin Winton), 147
Cookie Corporal (NAPCO), 190
Cookie House
    Brush, 95
    Italy, 243
    Japan, 236, 238
    McCoy, 43
    Sierra Vista, 171
Cookie Jug
    McCoy, 48-49
    Western Stonware, ll
Cookie Kettle (McCoy), 47
Cookie Monster
    California Originals, 17, l0l
    unknown, 17, 211
Cookie Nut (Twin Winton), 147
Cookie Poke (Bauer), 151
Cookie Pot (McCoy), 46
Cookie Round Up (unknown), 282
Cookie Safe
    California Originals, 97
    Cardinal, 178
Cookie Server (Think Big), 201
Cookie Stack
    Japan, 237
    unknown, 270
Cookie Time Clock
    American Bisque, 84-85
    California Originals, 104
Cookie Tray (American Bisque), 74
Cookie Truck (American Bisque), 73
Cookie Wagon (unknown), 272
Cookies and Milk (American Bisque), 73
Cookies of the World (American Bisque), 73
Cookies out of This World (NAPCO), 190
Cookies Panda (unknown), 262
Cookies Railroad (American Bisque), 70
Cookstove
    McCoy, 45
    unknown, 274
Cookstove Mammy (Wisecarver), 220
Cooky
    Pearl China, 166
    Shawnee, 137-138
Coors Ceramics, 152
Cop
    American Bisque, 83
    Twin Winton, 149
Corn
    McCoy, 40
    Stanford, 172
    Treasure Craft, 141
Count, The (California Originals), 102
Country Quilt Series (Over and Back), 193
Covered Bridge (Wisecarver), 222
Covered Wagon
    Brush, 90
    Italy, 243
    McCoy, 42
    unknown, 272

Cow
    American Pottery Company, 76
    Brush, 13, 92
    Gare, 252
    Japan, 232-233
    Lefton, 188
    McCoy, 36
    Metlox, 115-116
    Pottery Guild, 196
    Thames, 201
    Twin Winton, 147
    unknown, 263
Cow and Calf (Wisecarver), 223
Cowboy Boots (American Bisque), 74
Cowmen Moo-Randa (Vandor), 202
Cow Jumped over the Moon
    American Bisque
    Doranne of California, 106
    Robinson-Ransbottom, 12, 130
Crock
    Brush, 95
    Brush Art, 177
    Coors, 152
    Herklotz, Keith, 225-226
    Marcrest, 189
    McCoy, 52
    Ransburg, 197-198
    Red Wing, 122
    Robinson-Ransbottom, 131
    unknown, 280-283
    Western Stoneware, 174
    Cronin China, 194-96
Cupcake (Doranne of California), 109

D

Dad's Cookies, 287
Daisy Mae (Imperial Porcelain), 161
Dalmations (McCoy), 30
Dan the Dog (unknown), 246
Darth Vader (Sigma), 200
Davy Crockett
    American Bisque, 61
    Brush, 88
    McCoy, 24
    Ransburg, 197-198
    Regal, 124
Davy Crockett Accessories (American Bisque), 61
Davy Crockett Mug (Brush), 88
Dayton-Hudson Corporation, 179
Deer (American Bisque), 67
DeForest of California, 152
Demand Marketing, 180
Dept. 56, 180
Derby Dan (Pfaltzgraff), 167
Dino (American Bisque), 64
Dinosaur
    Marcia Ceramics of California, 163
    Metlox, 116
Displays of cookie jars, 21-22
Dog
    Alpo, 246
    American Bisque, 66, 81
    California Originals, 100
    Crest, 251
    Dayton-Hudson, 179
    F & F, 291
    Grantcrest, 184

    Holiday Designs, 159
    Japan, 231
    McCoy, 31, 36
    Plastic, 291
    Portugal, 244
    Shawnee, 8, 135
    Taiwan, 234
    Treasure Craft, 141, 144
    unknown, 263-264
Dog House
    McCoy, 30
    Milk-Bone, 247
Doll (black) (Treasure Craft), 145
Donald Duck
    bank, 212
    California Originals, l0l
    Holt Howard, 186
    Leeds, 16
    unknown, 207-209
Donkey with Cart (Brush), 94
Donut Chef (unknown), 256
Doranne of California, 105-110
Double Entry Jar, 277
Dove/Duck (FAPCO), 153
Drum
    Japan, 236
    McCoy, 49
    NAPCO, 191
    unknown, 276
Drummer Boy (Shawnee), 139
Duck
    Art Deco, 267
    Brazil, 241
    Hull, 113
    Japan, 241
    Lefton, 188
    McCoy, 34, 37
    Metlox, 117
    Mexico, 244
    Over and Back, 193
    Taiwan
    unknown, 267
    Wisecarver, 223
Duck/Dove (FAPCO), 153
Ducks in Flight (Wisecarver), 223
Dumbo/Pluto Turnabout (unknown), 80
Dumbo Turnabout
    Leeds
    unknown, 79-80
Dutch Boy
    American Bisque, 60
    McCoy, 52
    Red Wing, 129
    Robinson-Ransbottom, 129
    Shawnee, 138
    unknown, 80, 256
Dutch Girl
    American Bisque, 60
    McCoy, 52
    Metlox, 118
    Pottery Guild, 194-195
    Red Wing, 119-120
    Regal, 124
    Robinson-Ransbottom, 129
    Shawnee, 137-38
    Twin Winton, 149
    unknown, 80, 253
    wood, 294

Dutch Treat (McCoy), 44

E

Eeyore (California Originals), 102
Eggs in Basket (McCoy), 41
Elephant
    American Bisque, 3, 69
    Brush, 94
    California Originals, 98
    Doranne of California, 107-108
    Fitz and Floyd, 183
    Japan, 231, 233
    Kenwood, 136
    McCoy, 30
    Shawnee, 136
    Sigma, 200
    Twin Winton, 149-150
    unknown, 264, 278
Elephant with Baseball Cap (American Bisque), 69
Elephant with Clown (California Originals), 98
Elephant with Paws in Pockets (American Bisque), 3
Elephant with Ice Cream Cone (Brush), 94
Elephant with Split Trunk (McCoy), 30
Elf
    Japan, 231
    Keebler, 246
    Twin Winton, 149
Elf Bakery (Twin Winton), 150
Elf on Bee Hive (unknown), 261
Elf School House (California Originals), 103-104
Elsie (Pottery Guild), 196
Empire, 293
ENESCO, 181-182
Ernie
    California Originals, 101
    unknown
Erphila, 242
Ethan Allen, 182

F

FAPCO (Fredericksburg Art Pottery)
Farmer John (Regal), 126
Farmer Pig (American Bisque), 68
Fat Boy (Abingdon), 86
Fat Lady (Surrell), 254
Father Christmas (Silvestri), 200
Feed Sack (American Bisque), 74
F & F, 291-292
Fiedler and Fiedler Mold and Die Works, 291-292
Fire Chief (American Bisque), 83
Fire Hydrant (Doranne of California), 109
Fireman (American Bisque), 15
Fireplace, Colonial (McCoy), 45
Fish (Doranne of California), 108
Fitz & Floyd, 182-83
Flower Pot (unknown), 276
Fluffy (Ludowici Celadon), 75
Forbidden Fruit (McCoy), 40
Formal Pig (Brush), 93-94
For Smart Cookies (Cardinal), 177
Fortune Cookie (McCoy), 50
Franciscan (Gladdening, McBean & Company), 155

Frango Mint Chip Cookies (Marshall Field), 189
Fred Flintstone
    American Bisque, 64
    Vandor, 202
Fredericksburg Art Pottery (FAPCO), 153-154
Frankoma, 152-153
French Chef
    Cardinal, 178
    Dept. 56, 180
Friar Tuck (Goebel), 242
Friendship 7 (McCoy), 43
Frog
    California Originals, 98-99
    Doranne of California, 108
    Maurice of California, 164
    unknown, 264
    Sears, 200
Frontier Family (McCoy), 43
Frookie Cookies (Taiwan), 246
Fruit in Basket
    McCoy, 40
    Shawnee, 139

G

Game Warden Bear (unknown), 279
Garage (Cardinal), 178
Garbage Can (McCoy), 50
Garbage Can Bear (unknown), 262
Garfield (ENESCO), 181
General Store (unknown), 283
George Borgfeldt Corporation, 176
George Good Corporation, 206
George Zolton Lefton China Company, 188-189
German Gentleman (West Germany), 9
Geronimo (Wisecarver), 222
Gifford, Carol, 9, 20, 216-218
Gilner, 154-155
Gingerbread Boy
    glass, 287, 289
    Hull, 113
    McCoy, 54
    unknown, 282
Gingerbread House
    Treasure Craft, 145
    unknown, 270-271
Girl in Play House (Japan), 236
Girl with Cookie (unknown), 255
Gladdening, McBean & Company (Fransican), 155
Globe (McCoy), 42
Gnome on Stump (Gorham), 231
Goat (Marcia Ceramics of California), 163
Gob (Shawnee), 139
Goebel, 242
Goldilocks (Regal), 125
Gone-with-the-Wind Mammy, 229
Good Fortune Cookies (Japan), 229
Goose
    McCoy, 35
    Metlox, 116
    Treasure Craft, 145
    Twin Winton, 149
Gorham, 231
Graduate (Cardinal), 177
Grandfather Clock (McCoy), 48
Grandma's Cookie Jar (unknown), 282

Grandpa (unknown), 256
Granny
    Alberta's, 20
    American Bisque, 59-60, 86
    bank, 254
    Brush, 88
    Carol Gifford, 20, 218
    Fitz & Floyd, 183
    McCoy, 27
    unknown, 254
Granny Goose (Metlox), 116
Grantcrest, 183-184
Grapes
    Metlox, 117
    Red Wing, 121-122
Great American Housewares, 184
Green Products, 184-185
Gumball Machine (California Originals), 104
Gypsy Pot (McCoy), 47

H

Haeger Potteries, 156
Hall China Company, 156-158
Hamburger (Japan), 237
Hamm's Bear (McCoy), 28
Happy (Shawnee), 138
Happy Bunny (Brush), 92
Harper J. Ransburg Company, 197-199
Harpo (Regal), 123
Hat, Uncle Sam's (McCoy), 57
Have a Happy Day (McCoy), 2
Heating Stove (Japan), 236
Hen
    American Bisque, 65
    Brush, 95
    Doranne of California, 108
    FAPCO, 153
    Italy, 243
    McCoy, 33
    Morton, 164
Herklotz, Keith, 225-226
Hill Folk (Wisecarver), 9, 222
Himark, 185
Hippotamus
    American Bisque, 85
    Brush, 91
    Doranne of California, 91
    Japan, 232
    Taiwan
    unknown, 264
Hobby Horse (Brush), 92
Hoan Ltd., 185
Hobnail Pattern (McCoy), 51
Hocking Glass Company, 9
Hoenig of California, 158
Holiday Designs, 15, 158-160, 246
Holt Howard, 186
Honeycomb (McCoy), 56
Holly Hobby (Chein), 291
Hopalong Cassidy
    Peter Pan Products, 210
    unknown, 1
Horse
    American Bisque, 67
    Brush, 92
    Japan, 232
    McCoy, 32
    Twin Winton, 147

Hot Air Balloon
    McCoy, 42
    Treasure Craft, 145
Hot Chocolate Mug (American Bisque), 72
House
    Almost Home, 246
    Avon, 176
    ENESCO, 181
    Holiday Designs, 246
    Italy, 244
    Japan, 236, 238
    Judy of California, 161
    McCoy, 43-44
    Otagiri, 193
    Shawnee, 139
    Sierra Vista, 172
    Treasure Craft, 144-145
    Twin Winton, 150
    unknown, 270-271
House of Webster, 160-161
Howdy Doody
    Purinton, 167
    Vandor, 201-202
Hull Pottery, 111-113
Humperbump Police Car (Appleman), 213
Humpty Dumpty
    Abingdon, 126
    American Bisque, 86
    California Originals, 102
    Italy, 244
    Japan, 230
    Maddux, 163
    McCoy, 54
    plastic, 292
    Purinton, 167
    Ransburg, 198
    Regal, 126
    Reliable, 292
    Sierra Vista, 171
Humpty Dumpty, Mrs. (unknown), 211
Humpty Dumpty with Beanie (Brush), 90
Humpty Dumpty with Cowboy Hat (Brush), 90

I

Ice Cream Cone
    Doranne of California, 109
    McCoy, 41
If Grandma Says No, Ask Grandpa (unknown), 256
Imperial Porcelain Corporation, 161
INARCO (International Artware Corporation), 186
Indian
    McCoy, 23
    Southeast Minnesota Pottery, 172
    Williams, 18
    Wisecarver, 220
Indian Maiden (Wisecarver), 220
International Artware Corporation (INARCO), 186

J

Jack (Robinson-Ransbottom), 128
Jack-in-the-Box (American Bisque), 70-71
JASCO, 238
J. Chein & Company, 209
Jeanette Glass Company, 288
Jewel Tea Pattern (Hall), 156

J.L. Clark, 290
Jocko (Robinson-Ransbottom), 129
Joe Carioca/Donald Duck turnabout, 208
Jolly Pirate (American Bisque), 10, 82
Judy of California, 161-162
Jug
    McCoy, 48-49
    Shawnee, 140
Juggler (California Originals), 103
    Treasure Craft, 145
    Vandor, 203

K

Kangaroo (McCoy), 27-28
Keebler Cookie Jar (McCoy), 48
Keebler Elf
    F & F, 292
    Taiwan, 246
Keebler Tree House
    McCoy, 25, 156
    Haeger, 156
Keith Lytle (Gifford), 217-218
Kilroy Loves Cookies (unknown), 277
King of Tarts (Red Wing), 121
Kilbane Cat (Sigma), 200
Kitchen Witch (unknown), 254
Kitten (also see cat)
    American Bisque, 65-66
    McCoy, 32, 37
    Wisecarver, 223
Kitten on Basketweave (McCoy), 37
Kitten on Bee Hive (American Bisque), 65
Kittens with Ball of Yarn
    American Bisque, 66
    McCoy, 32
Kitten on Coal Bucket (McCoy), 32
Koala (Metlox), 115
Kookie Kettle (McCoy), 46
Kooky-K-Egg (Green Products), 185
Kooky-Kook (Green Products), 184
Kraft Marshmallow Bear (Regal), 126
Krispy Kan, 290

L

Lamb
    American Bisque, 67-68, 75
    McCoy, 36
    Metlox, 116
    Treasure Craft, 143
    Twin Winton, 148
Lamb on Basketweave (McCoy), 36
Lamb with Paws in Pockets (American Bisque), 67
Lamb with Red Suspenders (American Bisque), 75
Lantern
    American Bisque, 72
    Brush, 96
Laurel Sales, 187
Leeds China Company, 16, 187
Lefton China Company, 188-189
Lemon (McCoy), 38
Lemon/Pear (unknown), 269
Leprechaun
    McCoy, 25
    unknown, 260
L.E. Smith Glass Company, 9, 287
Liberty Bell
    Barlett-Collins, 289

Glass, 289
House of Webster, 161
McCoy, 50
unknown, 276
Light (unknown), 276
Light Bulb (M. Kamerstein), 187
Light House (unknown), 271
Lion
    Belmont, 5
    Brazil, 241
    Doranne of California, 198
    Holiday Designs, 159
    Ludowici Celadon, 5
    Twin Winton, 148
Lion with Lamb (unknown), 279
Little Audrey bank, 212
Little Boy Blue (Brush), 89
Little Miss Muffet
    Abingdon, 86
    McCoy, 54
Little Red Bean Pot (McCoy), 47
Little Red Riding Hood
    Brush, 89
    California Originals, 102
    Hull, 111-112
    NAPCO, 190
    Pottery Guild, 196
    unknown, 211, 215
Little Red School House (Holiday Designs), 159
Locomotive
    American Bisque, 70, 73, 85
    California Originals, 104
    McCoy, 42
    Pfaltzgraff, 167
    Sierra Vista, 170-171
    Treasure Craft, 143
    unknown, 272, 277
Log Cabin (unknown), 271
Lollipops (McCoy), 56
Los Angeles Potteries, 162
Love Birds
    McCoy, 35
    unknown, 268
Luce Manufacturing Company, 290
Lucky (Shawnee), 136
Ludowici Celadon, 4, 75-81
Lunch Bucket (McCoy), 50
Luzianne Mammy by Carol Gifford (Gifford), 217

M

Maddux of California, 162-163
Magic Bunny (American Bisque), 68
Mailbox
    Doranne of California, 110
    unknown, 266
Majorette
    American Bisque, 63
    Regal, 123
Mammy
    Abingdon (repaint), 86
    Carol Gifford, 20, 216-218
    Giacomini, Mary Jane, 18
    Gilner, 155
    Gone-with-the-Wind, 229
    Mary Jane Giacomini, 18
    McCoy, 26-27
    MJ's, 18

National Silver, 191
Omnibus, 228
Mosaic Tile, 165
Pearl China, 166
Taiwan, 228
unknown, 254
Weller, 174
Wisecarver, 220-221
Mammy with Cauliflowers (McCoy), 27
Maple Ware, 239
Marcia Ceramics of California, 163
Married Mammy (MJ's), 18
Marshall Burns & Company, 189
Marshall Field & Company, 189
Mary Had a Little Lamb
    Ransburg, 198
    unknown, 281
Mary, Mary Quite Contrary (McCoy), 54
Maurice Ceramics of California, 164
Maurice Lentil, 293
McCoy, 2, 9, 11, 14, 23-58, 266
Metlox, 114-118
Mickey Mouse
    California Originals, 101
    ENESCO, 181
    Hoan, 185
    turnabout, 79
    unknown, 208-9
Mickey Mouse/Donald Duck (Chein), 209
Mickey Mouse/Minnie Mouse
    Chein, 209
    turnabout (unknown), 208
Milk-Bone Dog House (Taiwan), 247
Milk Can
    McCoy, 54-55
    unknown, 274, 280
Milk Churn Mammy (Wisecarver), 221
Milk Glass, 288
Milk Wagon (American Bisque), 73
Mill (Judy of California), 162
Minnie Mouse/Mickey Mouse (unknown turnabout), 208
Minnie Mouse bank, 212
Miss America, Black (Wisecarver), 221
Miss Cutie-Pie (NAPCO), 190
Mixing Bowl Mammy (Wisecarver), 220
M. Kamenstein, 187
M & M's, 246
Money Bag
    Abingdon, 85
    Treasure Craft, 141
    unknown, 276
Monk
    Hirsch, 158
    McCoy, 27
    Mexico, 258
    Red Wing, 120-121
    Treasure Craft, 143
    Twin Winton, 150
    unknown, 257-258
Monkey
    Doranne of California, 107
    Price, 196
    Robinson-Ransbottom, 129
    Treasure Craft, 144
    unknown, 264, 279
Mopsy (unknown), 278
Morning Aggravation (Wisecarver), 221

Morton Pottery Company, 164-165
Mosaic Tile Company, 165
Mother Goose
    American Bisque, 85
    McCoy, 34
    Twin Winton, 149
Mouse
    California Originals, 6
    Doranne of California, 109
    McCoy, 33
    Metlox, 115
    Treasure Craft, 143
    Twin Winton, 149
    unknown
Mouse Chef
    Doranne of California, 109
    Metlox, 115
Mr. Cookie (Taiwan), 234
Mrs. Humpty Dumpty (unknown), 211
Mugsey (Shawnee), 8, 135
Municipal Railway (unknown), 272
Murray's Quality Cookies, 294

N

Nabisco (McCoy), 57
NAPCO (National Potteries Corporation), 190-190
NASCO (National Silver Company), 191-192
National Potteries Corporation (NAPCO), 190-191
National Silver Company (NASCO), 191-192
Neiman-Marcus, 192
Nerds (unknown), 212
Nestle Toll House Cookies (unknown), 246, 291
Nibble Kettle (McCoy), 47
N.S. Gustin, 185
Nun (DeForest of California), 152
Nuts (INARCO), 186

O

Old King Cole
    Japan, 230
    Pottery Guild, 196
    Robinson-Ransbottom, 130
Old MacDonald (Regal), 126
Old Shoe (Brush), 91
Olive Oyl (American Bisque), 21
OMC, 240
Omnibus, 228
1001 Cookie Delights (Chein), 290
Open Bucket (McCoy), 57
Orange
    Holiday Designs, 160
    McCoy, 38
    Metlox, 117
    unknown, 269
Original Toll House Cookies, 246
Oscar (Robinson-Ransbottom), 19-20
Oscar the Grouch
    California Originals, 101
    Demand Marketing, 180
Otagiri, 192-193
Owl
    Accents Unlimited, 175
    American Bisque, 65
    Atlantic, 249

    Brush, 94
    California Originals, 99
    Cara Creations, 235
    Carbone, 177
    glass, 287
    Hall, 156
    Holiday Designs, 158
    Italy, 244
    Japan, 234-235, 240
    McCoy, 34
    Metlox, 115
    Robinson-Ransbottom, 129
    Shawnee, 136-137
    Shawnee look-alike, 249
    Sierra Vista, 171
    Treasure Craft, 144
    Twin Winton, 148
    unknown, 268
Owl on Stump (California Originals), 99
Ozark Hillbilly (Morton), 165

P

Pacific Stoneware, 165-166
Packard Convertible (Appleman), 214
Packard Police Car (Appleman), 214
Paddington Bear (Toscany), 212
Paddy Pig (Alladin), 292-293
Pail, Plastic (unknown), 293
Pancake Mammy (Gifford), 9
Panda
    Brush, 93
    Holiday Designs, 159
    McCoy, 29
    unknown, 262
Panel (McCoy), 56
Pantry Parade, 179
Peach Cobbler (McCoy), 53
Peanut (McCoy), 57
Pear
    glass, 288
    Holiday Designs, 160
    McCoy, 37
    metal, 290
    Red Wing, 122
    unknown, 251, 269, 270
Pearl China Company, 166
Pears on Basketweave (McCoy), 37
Peasant Design (Red Wing), 120
Peasant Girl (unknown), 254
Peasant Woman
    Dept. 56, 180
    Rose White (Brayton Laguna), 250
Peek-a-Boo Baby (Regal), 124
Pelican (Metlox), 117
Pencil (M. Kamenstein), 187
Penguin
    ENESCO, 182
    McCoy, 35
    Metlox, 116
    Taiwan, 235
    unknown, 235, 268
Pennsbury Pottery, 166
Pepper
    Doranne of California
    McCoy, 40
Peter Pan (Brush), 89
Peter Pumpkin Eater
    Brush, 89
    Gilner, 155

Japan, 230
Robinson-Ransbottom
Vallona Starr
Pfaltzgraff Pottery, 167
Phonograph (California Originals), 104
Pickers (Wisecarver), 222
Picnic Basket (McCoy), 40
Pie, Strawberry (unknown), 270
Pig
    Alladin, 292-293
    American Bisque, 3, 67-68, 76-78
    Brush, 93-94
    California Originals, 100
    Cardinal, 178
    ENESCO, 182
    England, 242
    Italy, 243
    Japan, 231
    Los Angeles Potteries, 162
    McCoy, 36
    Otagiri, 192
    Pacific Stoneware, 165
    Pfaltzgraff, 167
    plastic, 292-293
    Regal, 124
    Robinson-Ransbottom, 130
    Shawnee, 132-135
    Terrace Ceramics, 140-141
    turnabout, 67
    unknown, 265
    Wisecarver, 224
Pig, Farmer (American Bisque), 68
Pig, Formal (Brush), 93-94
Pig with Indented Clover (American Bisque), 77-78
Pig with Indented Spots (American Bisque), 77
Pig with Paws in Pockets (American Bisque), 3
Pig with Red Suspenders (American Bisque), 76
Pilgrim
    American Bisque, 83
    Stoneware Designs West, 255
Pillsbury Baker (Taiwan), 247
Pineapple
    Los Angeles Potteries, 162
    McCoy, 38-39
    Red Wing, 122
    unknown, 270
Pinecones on Basketweave (McCoy), 37
Pink Elephant (Japan), 233
Pinky Lee (American Bisque), 63
Pinocchio
    Doranne of California, 105
    Metlox, 114
    Mexico, 244
Pippin, 193
Pirate
    Twin Winton, 147
    unknown, 255
Pirate Chest
    American Bisque, 71
    McCoy, 48
Pitcher (McCoy), 49
Pittman-Dreitzer Company, 194
Pixie (unknown), 249, 259-260
Pluto/Dumbo turnabout (unknown), 80

Poke (Bauer), 151
Police Chief Bear (Twin Winton), 146
Pomeroy the Pig (ENESCO), 182
Pomona, 194
Pontiac Indian Reporduction (Williams), 18
Poodle
    American Bisque, 66
    Twin Winton, 147
Poodle Cookie Counter (Twin Winton), 147
Popeye
    American Bisque, 64
    McCoy, 54
    Vandor, 202
Porky Pig (Duncan), 251-252
Potatoes in Basket (McCoy), 41
Potbelly Stove
    American Bisque, 72
    McCoy, 45
    unknown, 274
Pottery Guild of America, 194-196
Powell & Mason (unknown), 272
Preacher (American Bisque), 82
Pretzel Jar
    Hocking Glass, 9
    Hull, 113
Prunella the Pig (ENESCO), 182
Pumpkin
    Brush, 90
    Gare, 252
    Hoenig of California, 158
    Holiday Designs, 15
    McCoy, 40
    SFA, 270
Puppy
    American Bisque, 66
    Brazil, 241
    Brush, 92
    California Originals, 97
    Doranne of California, 105
    Japan, 233
    Treasure Craft, 143
    unknown, 279
Puppy in Basket (unknown), 279
Puppy on Quilted Base (American Bisque), 66
Puppy Police (Brush), 92
Purinton Pottery Company, 167-68
Purple Cow
    Brush, 13
    Thames, 201
Puss-n-Boots
    Regal, 124
    Shawnee, 135

Q

Quaker Oats
    McCoy, 48, 125
    Regal, 125
Quilting Mammy (Wisecarver), 221

R

R2-D2 (Roman), 168
R2-D2/C3PO (Sigma), 200
Rabbit
    American Bisque, 3, 68, 81
    Brush, 92
    Borgfeldt, 176

    California Originals, 100
    Doranne of California, 107
    Japan, 235-236
    McCoy, 32
    Metlox, 115
    National Silver, 192
    Treasure Craft, 141
    Twin Winton, 148
    unknown, 265-266, 282
Racoon
    Doranne of California, 106
    Fitz and Floyd, 183
    Wisecarver, 223
Radio (Vandor), 8
Rag Doll
    Starnes, 173
    unknown, 275, 278
Raggedy Andy
    Japan, 237
    Maddux, 162
    Metlox, 118
Raggedy Ann
    Bobbs-Merrill, 211
    Brush, 89
    California Originals, 102
    Japan, 237
    McCoy, 27
    Metlox, 118
Ransburg, 197-199
Raspberry (House of Webster), 160
Recipe Jar (American Bisque), 70
Reco International Corporation, 199
Red Wing, 119-122
Regal China Company, 123-127
Reindeer (Marcia Ceramics of California), 163
Reliable Toy Corporation, 292
Religious Figure (unknown), 255-256
Riddell, 275
Ring Jar (American Bisque), 69
Rio Rita (Fitz and Floyd), 182
Robinson-Ransbottom, 12, 19-20, 128-131
Robot (Taylor & Ng), 201
Rocking Chair Mammy (Gifford), 217
Rocking Horse
    Alberta, 250
    McCoy, 32
    Treasure Craft, 143
    unknown, 250
Roman Cermanics, 168
Romper Room (Laurel Sales), 187
Rooster
    American Bisque, 65
    McCoy, 33
    Pottery Guild, 196
    Sierra Vista, 171
    unknown, 266
    Rose (Metlox), 117
Roseville Pottery, Inc., 169
Round Plain (McCoy), 57
Royal Ware, 80-81

S

Saddle (American Bisque), 74
Sad Iron (American Bisque), 71
Sailor
    Robinson-Ransbottom, 128
    Shawnee, 139
Sailor Cat (unknown), 263

Sandman Cookies (American Bisque), 63
Sandwich Board Clown (American Bisque), 62
Sandwich Board Girl (American Bisque), 62
Sandwich Board Hobo (American Bisque),62
San Jose Potteries, 154, 170
Santa
    B & D, 206
    Brush, 96
    Empire, 293
    Fitz and Floyd, 183
    Gifford, 217
    Good, 206
    Holt Howard, 186
    Mallory, 205
    McCoy, 25
    plastic, 293-294
    Taiwan, 206
    unknown, 204-206, 250
    Winton, Don, 295
    Wisecarver, 219
Sawyer Biscuit Company, 287
Scarecrow
    California Originals, 103
    unknown, 259
School
    American Bisque, 74
    California Originals, 103
    Holiday Designs, 159
School Bus (McCoy), 41
Scottie Dog (unknown), 264
Sea Bag (American Bisque), 71
Sears, 199-200
Serving Tray (American Bisque), 74
SFA, 270
Shafford, 240
Shawnee, 8, 132-140
Sheriff
    California Originals, 102
    Robinson-Ransbottom, 130
Shoe
    Japan, 237
    Twin Winton, 150
    unknown 237, 274, 280
Sierra Vista Ceramics, 170-172
Sigma, 200
Silvestri, 200
Skyway Taxi (Appleman), 214
Slag Glass (unknown), 288
Sleeping Beauty's Castle (unknown), 249
Smokey Bear (Roman), 168
Smiley (Shawnee), 132-134
Snail
    California Originals, 98
    unknown, 266
Sneaky Pig (unknown), 265
Snowman
    B.C., 275
    Fitz and Floyd, 183
    Riddell, 275
    Robinson-Ransbottom, 129
    Taiwan, 238
    unknown, 275

Snoopy
    bank, 212
    Holiday Designs, 159
    McCoy, 31
Soldier (Robinson-Ransbottom, 128
Somersault Clown (Japan), 230
Southern Belle
    Pan American Art), 170
    San Jose Potteries, 170
Southeast Minnesota Potteries, 172
Space Cadet (unknown), 280
Space Ship
    American Bisque, 73
    McCoy, 43
    NAPCO, 190
Sprout (Taiwan), 245
Spuds (Taiwan), 234
Square Jar (McCoy), 55
Squirrel
    Brush, 92
    California Originals, 99
    Maddux, 163
    Metlox, 116
    Sierra Vista, 171
    Triangles Studios, 173
    Twin Winton, 147
    Vallona Starr, 173
Squirrel on Log (Brush), 91
Squirrel on Nut (Twin Winton), 147
Squirrel on Pine Cone (Metlox), 116
Squirrel on Stump
    California Originals, 99
    Triangle Studios, 173
    Vallona Starr, 173
Stanford Pottery, 172
Starnes, 173
Stella Strawberry (Pittman-Dreitzer), 194
Sternwheeler (American Bisque), 73
Stoneware Designs West, 255-256
Strawberry
    McCoy, 38
    Metlox, 117
    Sears, 199
    unknown, 270
Strawberry Basket
    House of Webster, 161
    McCoy, 40-41
Strawberry Pie (unknown), 270
Stroh's Truck (Appleman), 215
Stump with Frog Finial (McCoy), 35
Stump with Monkey Finial (McCoy), 36
Stump with Owl (California Originals), 99
Stump with Squirrel (California Originals), 98
Stump with Squirrel Finial (McCoy), 35
Sucker Jar
    NAPCO, 191
    unknown, 277
Sundae (Doranne of California), 109
Sunday Bath (Wisecarver), 221
Sun Giant Raisins (Chein), 291
Superman (California Originals), 101
Surrell, David, 254
Swan (Wisecarver), 223
Swee Pea (American Bisque), 64

Sweet Notes (unknown), 258
Sweet Tooth (Taiwan), 234

T

Taxi (Appleman), 214
Taxi Cab? (McCoy), 41
Taylor & Ng, 201
Tea Kettle (McCoy), 46
Teapot
    McCoy, 46
    unknown, 280
Teddy Bear
    B & D, 206
    Brush, 93
    Japan, 232
    Treasure Craft, 141
    unknown, 261
Teddy Roosevelt? (American Bisque?), 83
Teenage Mutant Ninja Turtles (plastic), 294
Teepee (McCoy), 44
Telephone
    Cardinal, 178
    House of Webster
    Sierra Vista, 172
Terrace Ceramics, 140-141
Thames, 201
Thelma (unknown), 254
Think Big, Inc., 201
Thread Spool (American Bisque), 71
Three Bears
    Abingdon, 86
    Brush, 95
Three Blind Mice (unknown), 282
Three Kittens (Wisecarver), 223
Three Little Kittens (McCoy), 32
Three Little Pigs (Pomona), 194
Tiger
    California Originals, 100
    plastic, 294
Tigger (California Originals), 100
Toaster (Vandor), 203
Toby Cookies (Regal), 124
Tomato
    China and Glass Distributors, 179
    McCoy, 38
    Metlox, 118
    Pantry Parade, 179
Tomatoes in Basket (McCoy), 41
Tony the Tiger (plastic), 294
Topo Gigo (unknown), 212
Tortise and Hare
    American Bisque, 64
    California Originals, 98
Toscany, 212
Toucan (HiMark), 185
Touring Car (Brush), 90
Toy Soldier
    Cardinal, 177
    Metlox, 114
Traffic Light (McCoy), 41
Transformer
    Great American Housewares, 184
    Japan, 238
Treasure Chest
    American Bisque, 71

Brush, 96
Treasure Craft, 9, 142-145
Trolley (Otagiri), 193
Trolley Car (Treasure Craft), 143
Tug Boat
  McCoy, 42
  Sierra Vista, 171
Tuggle (Sierra Vista), 171
Turkey (McCoy), 33-34
Turnabouts
  Donald Duck/Joe Carioca, 16, 207
  Dumbo, 79-80, 187
  Dumbo/Pluto, 80
  Mickey Mouse/Minnie Mouse, 79, 208
  Pig with paws in pockets, 67
Turtle
  California Originals, 98
  Doranne of California, 108
  unknown, 266, 278
Twin Winton, 146-150

U

Umbrella Kids (American Bisque), 60
Uncle Mistletoe look-a-like (unknown), 127
Uncle Sam's Hat (McCoy), 57
U.S. Mail (Doranne of California), 110

V

Van (unknown), 280
Vandor, 8, 201-203

Victorian House
  Otagiri, 193
  Treasure Craft, 144

W

Waiter (American Bisque?), 83
Walt Disney, 16, 79, 80,100, 101, 127, 176, 181, 186, 187, 207, 208, 209, 212, 244, 185
Walrus (unknown), 279
Water Bucket (American Bisque), 72
Watermelon Mammy
  Gifford, 216
  Weller, 174
Watermelon Sammy (Gifford), 216
W.C. Fields (McCoy), 24
Wedding Jar (McCoy), 57
Wedding Pineapple (Los Angeles Potteries), 162
Weller Pottery, 173-174
Western Stoneware Company, 11, 174
Whale (Robinson-Ransbottom), 130
Williams, George, 18
William H. Hirsch Manufacturing Company, 158
Windmill
  American Bisque, 85
  FAPCO, 154
  Fredericksburg Art Pottery, 154
  McCoy, 44
  unknown, 271

Wind-up Phonograph (California Originals), 104
Winking Pig (McCoy), 36
Winnie Pig
  Shawnee, 132, 133, 135
  Terrace Ceramics, 141
Winnie the Pooh (California Originals), 100
Winnie the Pooh bank, 212
Wishing Well
  House of Webster), 161
  McCoy, 45
Wisecarver, Rick, 9, 219-224
Witch (Wisecarver), 222
Woman
  Stoneware Designs West, 256
  unknown, 253-254
Woodsey Owl (McCoy), 34
Woody Woodpecker (unknown), 210
Wren House (McCoy), 33
World War I Soldier (American Bisque), 83

Y

Yarn Doll (American Bisque), 62
Yogi Bear
  American Bisque, 64
Yosemite Sam (McCoy), 11
You Name It (Haeger), 156
You're an Angel, Have a Cookie (unknown) 258

More Titles from Schiffer Publishing

1002 Salt and Pepper Shakers Larry Carey and Sylvia Tompkins. This new volume focuses on nodder salt and pepper shakers with over 300 nodders as well as hundreds of early/discontinued Fitz and Floyd sets and Parkcraft sets, many of which have never before been shown in a book. All are shown in clear color photographs. This comprehensive guide includes for each set its identification, color, size, and design variations.

Size: 8 1/2" x 11"	Price Guide	112 pp.
ISBN: 0-88740-789-7	soft cover	$19.95

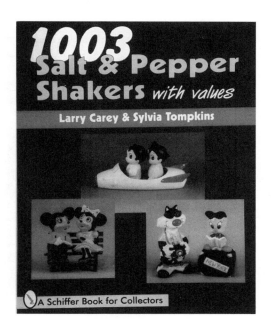

1003 Salt & Pepper Shakers Larry Carey & Sylvia Tompkins. This third volume by Larry Carey and Sylvia Tompkins focuses on character salt and pepper shakers. Featured in this book are popular television, movie, and cartoon characters. Also included are well-known mascots or symbols, such as the Loch Ness Monster and Smokey Bear. A large part of 1003 Salt & Pepper Shakers focuses on characters created by Walt Disney. The color, size, manufacturer, design variations, and value range for over 700 examples of character salt and pepper shakers is provided.

Size: 8 1/2" x 11"	300 color photos	176 pp.
Value Guide		
ISBN: 0-7643-0112-8	soft cover	$29.95

1004 Salt & Pepper Shakers Lary Carey & Sylvia Tompkins. The increasingly collectible categories of nursery rhymes and literary characters, including children's stories and fables, provide the focus for this fourth book of salt and pepper shakers by experts Larry Carey and Sylvia Tompkins. This very popular area of salt and pepper shakers appeals to a wide range of collectors—it's the book for collectors who love classic literary characters such as those from Dickens, fairy tales, and Aesop's fables, to modern day characters such the Cat in the Hat and Curious George. Wonderful sets, from Aladdin and His Lamp to Wizards with Dragons, and everything in between (including series) are depicted in over 700 color photographs. A comprehensive guide, this book details each set's color, size, manufacturer, design variations, and value ranges along with licensing information as marked on the sets.

Size: 8 1/2" x 11"	700 color photos	160 pp.
Price Guide		Index
ISBN: 0-7643-0553-0	soft cover	$29.95

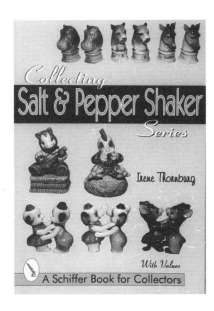

Collecting Salt & Pepper Shaker Series Irene Thornburg. This is the most comprehensive guide to salt and pepper shaker series ever published. Never before have so many shaker series been pictured in one book. Shown in full color are more than 850 sets, making up more than 125 series. Included are well-known names such as Rosemeade, Ceramic Arts, Lefton, Enesco, and more. This will be an indispensable reference book for both beginning and longtime collectors who have always wondered which sets "belong" together. Measurements, manufacturers, countries, and current values are provided. If you have never had an interest in salt and pepper shakers before, this book will open your eyes to a wonderful collectible!

Size: 6" x 9"	361 color photos	144 pp.
Price Guide		
ISBN: 0-7643-0493-3	soft cover	$19.95

Art Pottery of America (Revised) Lucile Henzke. This is a completely new study of American art pottery by the author of the leading, pioneer book published twelve years ago. Arranged alphabetically by the potteries, the text includes important historical data, photographs of each pottery's representative forms, and a complete series of the identifying marks. Here the novice as well as advanced collector will gain knowledge to help identify and interpret the art pottery produced in America from the late nineteenth and early twentieth centuries.

Size: 8 1/2" x 11"	549 color & b/w photos	368 pp.
Price Guide	Index	
ISBN: 0-7643-0159-4	hard cover	$45.00

Spongeware and Spatterware (Revised & Expanded) Kevin McConnell. Spongeware and spatterware, colorful country pottery which was traditionally a favorite of the American public, remains enormously popular with today's many collectors of antique ceramics. This revised and expanded identification and price guide provides those collectors with an expansive pictorial cross-section of eighteenth, nineteenth, and twentieth century spongeware and spatterware. Additionally, the detailed text offers clear insight into the history and development of these attractive, desirable wares. Over two hundred examples of spongeware and spatterware are illustrated in this book with full color photographs and complete information, including a price guide.

Size: 6" x 9"	200 color photos	128 pp.
Price Guide		
ISBN: 0-7643-0768-1	soft cover	$16.95

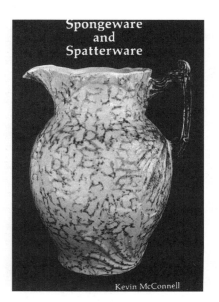

California Potteries: The Complete Book Mike Schneider. From the 1930s to the 1960s numerous potteries in Southern California turned out some of the finest figural pottery ever made in America. For decades these beautiful wares lingered in obscurity, but now they have rocketed to the forefront of collectibility.

They are illustrated here with over 800 color photographs covering more than 75 companies. Among them are companies such as Brayton Laguna, Kay Finch and Hedi Scoop. Lesser known companies like DeLee Art, Robert Simmons, and Walker-Renaker are represented too. Information about the potteries, tips for collectors, and a realistic price guide make this an indispensable book for collectors.

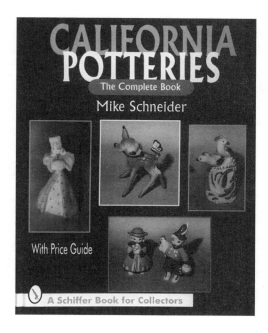

Size: 8 1/2" x 11"	800 color photos	256 pp.
Price Guide		
ISBN: 0-88740-877-X	hard cover	$49.95

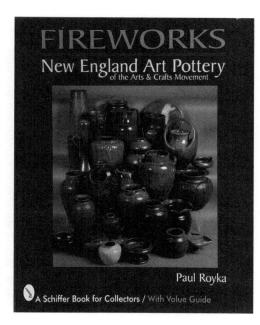

Fireworks: New England Art Pottery of the Arts and Crafts Movement Paul A. Royka. American art pottery is one of the most dynamic collecting fields, with prices soaring up to $200,000 for one piece. Paul A. Royka examines New England art pottery made from 1872 to 1928. Sold through auctions and galleries and found in attics and homes throughout the United States, the pieces illustrated here have a combined value of over one million dollars.

The most comprehensive work of its kind, Fireworks examines the origins of the Arts and Crafts Movement and the influences manufacturing companies had on it. It provides help in identifying marks, evaluating, and pricing the works of Chelsea Keramic Art Works, Dedham, Low, Grueby, Hampshire, Crook, Merrimac, Walley, Marblehead, Saturday Evening Girls, and Dorchester Pottery. A beautiful book with more than 450 color photographs, it is a must for the pottery collector and a wonderful gift for any art lover.

Size: 8 1/2" x 11"	450 color photos	192 pp.
Price Guide		
ISBN: 0-88740-988-1	hard cover	$69.95

Rookwood Pottery: The Glaze Lines Anita J. Ellis. The Rookwood pottery, founded in Cincinnati, Ohio, produced experimental decorated and commercial pottery from 1880 until 1967. This new book stands ahead of all other references by offering the most complete understanding of Rookwood products, and it places Rookwood's glaze lines in the context of the pottery's history.

Author Anita Ellis conclusively explains the Decorated Wares, especially those made after 1915 which have always been problematic, and categorizes and defines the Commercial Ware for the first time. The book is unique in offering the most complete set of Rookwood pottery, potter and decorator marks; a thorough glossary of terms; and all the glaze lines. Over 200 beautiful color photographs of the elegant Rookwood pottery shapes illustrate the glaze lines. A values reference and charts of the talented decorators are included.

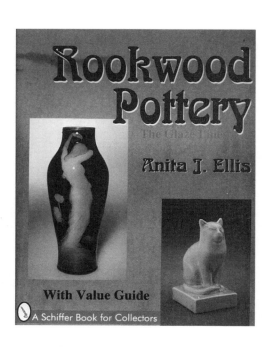

Size: 8 1/2" x 11"	288 photographs	240 pp.
Value Reference		
ISBN: 0-88740-838-9	hard cover	$69.95

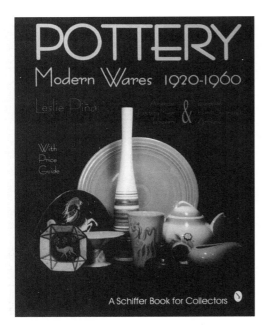

Pottery, Modern Wares 1920-1960 Leslie Piña. This handsome new book explores production pottery, the factory-made and hand-decorated wares produced by selected American and European companies that are of special interest to collectors. Familiar firms such as Cowan, Susie Cooper, Clarice Cliff and Roseville Futura made this modern pottery, as did old favorites such as Homer Laughlin's Fiesta, Russel Wright's American Modern, and firms with lesser-known names. Museums are already exhibiting these attractive, useful wares yet they can still be found at sales.

582 color photographs of the wares, details and maker's marks together with essays on the companies and designers, plus a bibliography, index and price guide make this book a necessary new reference for pottery collectors, historians and dealers.

8 1/2" x 11"	582 color photos	240 pp.
Price Guide		Index
ISBN: 0-88740-692-0	hard cover	$49.95

The Book of Buffalo Pottery Violet and Seymour Altman. Buffalo pottery is constantly growing in popularity as a collectible. This documentary volume preserves all available background information and lists and pictures many of the firm's products.

Here, in eleven concise, information-packed chapters, with well over 400 pieces illustrated, are all the facts, statistics, and details. Every kind of ware the firm is known to have made is discussed or pictured. Here, too, is the fascinating background story of the John D. Larkin mail-order company which founded the pottery that made Deldare, Albino, blue Willow, advertising and commemorative pieces, game sets, pitchers and jugs and other articles dating from its early days that are cherished and highly valued today.

Size: 8 1/2" x 11"	378 illus & photos	192 pp.
Price Guide		Index
ISBN: 0-88740-088-4	hard cover	$27.50

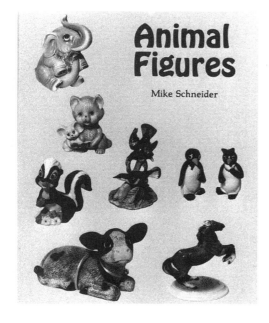

Animal Figures Mike Schneider. While collecting small animal figures has been a popular hobby for some years, information about them has been scanty. Mike Schneider explores this popular collectibles field in depth. Included are figures produced by such well know firms as Frankoma and Royal Doulton, plus the works of lesser know but important artisans such as Chester Nicodemus and Howard Pierce.

There are also generic chapters that cover animals by species: bears, cats, dogs, donkeys, deer, elephants, and many more. Included, too, is carnival chalkware, characters such as Mickey Mouse, and useful animal figures such as bottle openers and banks. Animals appear in all mediums from porcelain to peach pits, from brass to glass. Animal Figures is amply illustrated with more than 800 color photographs. A price guide is included.

Size: 8 1/2" x 11"	1029 photos	256 pp.
Price Guide		
ISBN: 0-88740-275-5	soft cover	$29.95

Josef Originals: Charming Figurines Dee Harris, Jim and Kaye Whitaker. Ceramic figurines of beautiful and romantic young women were made in hundreds of different poses and costumes by Josef Originals. This all-color illustrated new book follows the art of California ceramicist, Mauriel Josef George, from 1945 through the 1980s. Packed with hundreds of cheerful images, this book will be an invaluable aid in the dating and identification of these abundant figurines.

Size: 8 1/2" x 11"	574 photographs	128 pp.
ISBN: 0-88740-647-5	soft cover	$24.95

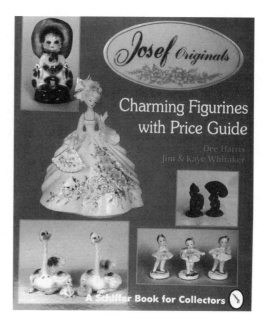

Josef Originals: A Second Look Jim & Kaye Whitaker. Enchanting ceramic figurines made by Muriel Joseph George have captivated collectors since World War II. Originally made to fill the empty hours while her husband was away at war, they soon became a means for Murial to express her love of children, families, animals, and all things bright and beautiful. For more than 40 years--until 1985--new "Josef Originals" models were produced by the company she started, most designed by Murial herself.

This new book contains full-color photographs of almost 700 Josef Originals never before published, including many that collectors never knew existed. No collector of miniature figurines should be without this valuable reference, which identifies model and series names, sizes, and color variations, along with a current price guide.

Size: 8 1/2" x 11"	700 color photos	160 pp.
ISBN: 0-7643-0161-6	soft cover	$29.95

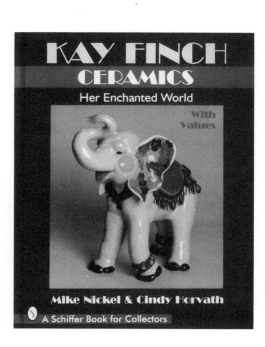

Kay Finch: Ceramics Mike Nickel and Cindy Horvath. The art pottery figurines, vases, banks, and planters made by Kay Finch in Corona del Mar, California, between 1939 and 1963, are adorable! Dogs and cats, farm and wild animals, fish, cute children and stylized adults and birds occupy her creative world. Nearly 400 color and 36 vintage photographs display her very collectible pottery and Kay Finch making them.

Size: 8 1/2" x 11"	431 photographs	176 pp.
Price Guide		
ISBN: 0-7643-0008-3	hard cover	$29.95

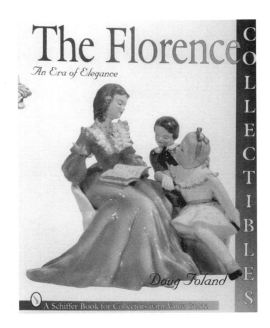

Florence Collectibles: An Era of Elegance Doug Foland. The lovely Florence figures, made in Pasadena, California, by Florence Ward and the Florence Ceramics Company from 1939 into the 1960s are featured in this first book on the subject. With over 400 color photographs, readers are introduced to the lovely ladies in elegant, lace-trimmed gowns, perfectly behaved children standing or sitting quietly as angels, and gentlemen dressed like dandies in their short pants and fancy coats.

This history of the Florence collection includes complete details about the early factory and the step-by-step process used in the creation of figurines as related by Florence's son, Clifford Ward, Jr. Some of largest Florence collections in the country are represented along with a price guide of yesteryear, Florence artware, Florence pairs, and children figurines.

Size: 8 1/2" x 11"	400 color photos	144 pp.
Price Guide		
ISBN: 0-88740-870-2	soft cover	$29.95

Grindley Pottery: A Menagerie Mike Schneider. The Grindley Artware Manufacturing Company made figural pottery in Sebring, Ohio, from 1933 until 1952. With 160 color photographs Mike Schneider guides the reader along the exciting paths of the Grindley menagerie of dogs, cats, horses and many other animals. An Art Deco donkey here, a natural looking dog there. Even a few of the rare Grindley people figurines appear, as do banks, pitchers, and salt and pepper shakers. Marks and measurements are given plus a price guide.

Size: 6" x 9"	160 color photos	128 pp.
Price Guide		
ISBN: 0-7643-0085-7	soft cover	$16.95

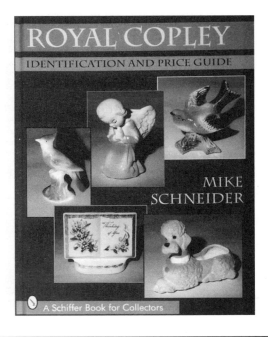

Royal Copley, Identification and Price Guide. Mike Schneider. Originally sold in five-and-ten-cent stores during the 1940s and 1950s, expertly modeled and colorfully decorated Royal Copley figurines, banks, planters, and other items have become one of today's hottest ceramic collectibles.

Mike Schneider uses more than 500 color photos to present 875 pieces of Royal Copley, including many previously unknown examples that have never appeared in a book before. Estimated values, based on the current market, are included in the captions, along with measurements and information about marks. Also included is a brief history of the Spaulding China Company, the Sebring, Ohio, pottery that manufactured Royal Copley.

Whether you are a collector, historian, or simply someone who would like to take a nostalgic stroll through the decorative accessories of your parents' or grandparents' homes, you will find this latest volume in Schneider's repertoire of books on mid-twentieth century pottery a pleasing and important addition to your library.

Size: 8 1/2" x 11"	508 color photos	144 pp.
Price Guide		
ISBN: 0-88740-739-0	hard cover	$29.95

American Bisque: A Collector's Guide with Prices Mary Jane Giacomini. This lively, photo-filled reference book is a delight for all interested in figural pottery. The American Bisque Pottery, operating in Williamstown, West Virginia from 1919 to 1982, and the American Pottery Company produced popular cookie jars, ashtrays, doorstops, sprinkle bottles, banks, planters, lamps and much more. Many of these items have never been pictured in any book before.

With American Bisque in hand, you will be able to identify little-known pieces including airbrushed planters of yarn dolls as well as the most sought-after cookie jars.

Size: 8 1/2" x 11	645 color photos	160pp.
Price Guide		
ISBN: 0-88740-623-8	soft cover	$29.95

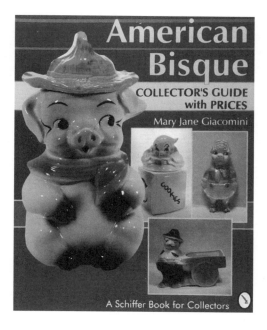

Stangl and Pennsbury Birds: Identification and Price Guide Mike Schneider. Brightly colored Stangl Pottery earthenware bird figurines were made in New Jersey from the 1940s into the 1970s. The very similar Pennsbury birds were hatched in Pennsylvania during the 1950s by former Stangl employees. Today both companies' wares are eagerly sought by collectors in all parts of the country.

Mike Schneider shows the entire Stangle Birds of America series plus 60 examples of Pennsbury birds in beautiful individual color photos. There is also a chapter on the little known but highly desirable Stangl animal figures. This user-friendly book, in which the Stangl birds are listed by the model number, also includes an alphabetically arranged name index for complete and easy cross referencing and close up photos of marks. A price guide based on the current market makes this beautiful volume an invaluable tool for collectors and dealers.

Size: 6" x 9"	209 color photos	160 pp.
Price Guide		Index
ISBN: 0-88740-612-2	hard cover	$19.95

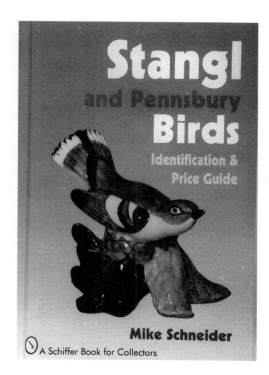

Staffordshire Spaniels Adele Kenny. No Victorian parlor was complete without a Staffordshire Spaniel on the mantel. This fascinating text focuses exclusively on these popular Victorian era antiques produced in Staffordshire, England from circa 1840 through the turn of the century. A detailed look at all of the Spaniel variations, along with the history of this "breed" of Staffordshire figure, and the more recent reproductions is provided and beautifully illustrated with over 285 color photographs and illustrations.

Also included are the historical context into which these Spaniels fit, background on the Staffordshire potteries and canine statuary, molding processes, decorating techniques, Spaniel types and sizes, tips for collectors, and a helpful glossary. Informative captions offer descriptions, sizes, dates of manufacture, and current market values.

Size: 8 1/2" x 11"	292 photos & illus.	144 pp.
Value Guide		
ISBN: 0-7643-0216-7	hard cover	$39.95

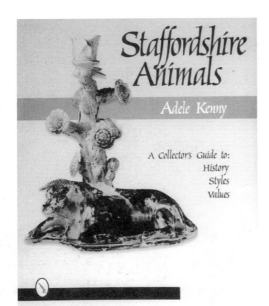

Staffordshire Animals: A Collector's Guide to History, Styles, and Values Adele Kenny. This comprehensive new reference focuses on the variety of animal figures produced in Staffordshire during the eighteenth and nineteenth centuries. Characterized by a cottage industry quaintness, Staffordshire figures were known as "image toys" and "chimney ornaments" in their day. Countless subjects were produced but the animal models comprise a Noah's Ark of some of the most charming and endearing figures. Today, Staffordshire animals are among the bestselling and most widely collected antique ceramics.

Beautifully illustrated with over 400 color photographs, this book traces animal figure evolution through chapters on animals in art, British ceramics, Staffordshire potters and potteries, and production techniques and styles. Informative captions provide descriptions, dates of manufacture, and current values.

Size: 8 1/2" x 11"	415 photos & illus	192 pp.
Price Guide		Index
ISBN: 0-7643-0422-4	hard cover	$49.95

Victorian Staffordshire Figures 1835-1875, Book One: Portraits, Naval & Military, Theatrical & Literary Characters A. & N. Harding. The collecting of Staffordshire figures, a particularly English folk art, has expanded from its origins to include much of the English speaking world. This work, in two books, details and illustrates the range and depth of figures made by the potters. Over 2,900 figures are illustrated in Book One and Book Two, virtually all in the brilliant color which was imperative for the beauty and simplicity of the figures to be fully appreciated. Many of these figures have never before been recorded. A history of the figures, together with many sources and relevant bibliographical details, are included, along with a guide to current prices. *Victorian Staffordshire Figures 1835-1875, Book One* is the definitive work on Portrait figures, and also includes Naval and Military, and Theatrical and Literary Characters (including Opera, Ballet, and Circus).

Size: 9" x 12"	1,184 color photos	416 pp.
Price Guide		Index
ISBN: 0-7643-0464-X	hard cover	$95.00

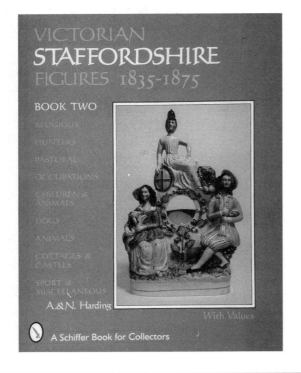

Victorian Staffordshire Figures 1835-1875, Book Two: Religous, Hunters, Pastoral, Occupations, Children & Animals, Dogs, Animals, Cottages & Castles, Sport & Miscellaneous A. & N. Harding. Collecting Staffordshire ceramic figures, a particularly English folk art, has expanded from its origins to include much of the English speaking world. This work, in two books, details and illustrates the range and depth of figures made by the potters. Over 2,900 figures are illustrated in the two books, virtually all in the brilliant color which was imperative for the beauty and simplicity of the figures to be fully appreciated. Many of these figures have never before been recorded. A history of the figures, together with sources and relevant bibliographical details, are included, along with a guide to current prices.

Victorian Staffordshire Figures 1835-1875, Book Two details Religous and Temperance Figures; Hunters and Huntsmen; Shepherds, Gardeners, Harvesters, and Pastoral Scenes; Other Pursuits, Pastimes, and Occupations; Children with Animals; Dogs; Animals; Houses, Cottages, and Castles; and Sport and Miscellaneous.

Size: 9" x 12"	939 color photos	320 pp.
Price Guide		Index
ISBN: 0-7643-0418-6	hard cover	$79.95